Paternalism Beyond Borders

We live in a world in which the international community aspires to protect and promote the quality of human life. To do so often requires the exercise of control over the very individuals, societies, states, and peoples that are the objects of concern. In other words, power is a prominent feature of a global ethics of care. This book examines paternalism beyond borders from the nineteenth century to the present, and in everyday practices of humanitarianism, human rights, development, and other projects designed to improve the lives of others. It offers a provocative look at the subtle and variable ways that power works its way in and through global ethics, and considers whether and when paternalism might be justified.

MICHAEL N. BARNETT is University Professor of International Affairs and Political Science at the George Washington University. Among his many books are *Eyewitness to a Genocide: The United Nations and Rwanda* (Cornell University Press, 2002), *The Empire of Humanity* (Cornell University Press, 2011) and, most recently, *The Star and the Stripes: A History of the Foreign Policies of American Jews* (Princeton University Press, 2016).

Paternalism Beyond Borders

Edited by
MICHAEL N. BARNETT

The George Washington University

CAMBRIDGE
UNIVERSITY PRESS

CAMBRIDGE
UNIVERSITY PRESS

University Printing House, Cambridge CB2 8BS, United Kingdom

Cambridge University Press is part of the University of Cambridge.

It furthers the University's mission by disseminating knowledge in the pursuit of education, learning and research at the highest international levels of excellence.

www.cambridge.org
Information on this title: www.cambridge.org/9781107176904

© Cambridge University Press 2017

First published 2017

Printed in the United Kingdom by Clays, St Ives plc

A catalog record for this publication is available from the British Library

Library of Congress Cataloging in Publication data
Names: Barnett, Michael N., 1960– editor.
Title: Paternalism beyond borders / edited by Michael N. Barnett.
Description: Cambridge; New York: Cambridge University Press, 2016. |
Includes bibliographical references and index.
Identifiers: LCCN 2016028348 | ISBN 9781107176904 (hardback) |
ISBN 9781316625712 (paperback)
Subjects: LCSH: Paternalism. | Individualism. | Liberty.
Classification: LCC JC571 .P314 2016 | DDC 327.1–dc23
LC record available at https://lccn.loc.gov/2016028348

ISBN 978-1-107-17690-4 Hardback
ISBN 978-1-316-62571-2 Paperback

Contents

Contributors

Séverine Autesserre is an Associate Professor of Political Science, specializing in international relations and African studies, at Barnard College, Columbia University (USA). She works on civil wars, peacebuilding, peacekeeping, humanitarian aid, and African politics. She has written many articles and two award-winning books *Peaceland: Conflict Resolution and the Everyday Politics of International Intervention*, and *The Trouble with the Congo: Local Violence and the Failure of International Peacebuilding*. Before becoming an academic, she worked for humanitarian and development agencies in Afghanistan, Kosovo, the Democratic Republic of Congo, Nicaragua, and India.

Michael N. Barnett is University Professor of International Affairs and Political Science at The George Washington University. Among his books are *Eyewitness to a Genocide: The United Nations and Rwanda*, *Empire of Humanity: A History of Humanitarianism*, and, most recently, *The Star and the Stripes: A History of the Foreign Policies of American Jews*.

David Chandler is Professor of International Relations, Department of Politics and International Relations, University of Westminster, London and editor of the journal *Resilience: International Policies, Practices and Discourses*. His most recent books are *The Neoliberal Subject: Resilience, Adaptation and Vulnerability* (2016) and *Resilience: The Governance of Complexity* (2014).

Didier Fassin is Professor of Social Science at the Institute for Advanced Study in Princeton and Director of Studies at the École des Hautes Études en Sciences Sociales in Paris. A former vice-president of Médecins Sans Frontières, he is currently President of the French Medical Committee for Exiles. His recent publications include: *Contemporary States of Emergency: The Politics of Military and Humanitarian Interventions* (with M. Pandolfi, 2010), *Moral Anthropology: A Companion* (2012), *Moral Anthropology: A Critical Reader* (2014), as editor; *The Empire of Trauma: An Inquiry into the Condition of Victimhood* (with R. Rechtman, 2009), *Humanitarian Reason: A Moral History of the Present* (2011), *Enforcing Order: An Ethnography of Urban Policing* (2013), and *Prison Worlds: An Ethnography of the Carceral Condition* (2016).

Ilana Feldman is Professor of Anthropology, History, and International Affairs at The George Washington University. She is the author of *Governing Gaza: Bureaucracy, Authority, and the Work of Rule, 1917–67* (2008) and *Police Encounters: Security and Surveillance in Gaza under Egyptian Rule* (2015); and co-editor (with Miriam Ticktin) of *In the Name of Humanity: The Government of Threat and Care* (2010). Her current project traces the Palestinian experience with humanitarianism in the years since 1948, exploring both how this aid apparatus has shaped Palestinian social and political life and how the Palestinian experience has influenced the broader post-war humanitarian regime.

John M. Hobson is Professor of Politics and International Relations at the University of Sheffield and is a Fellow of the British Academy. His theoretical and empirical work is situated in the vortex of global historical sociology, international relations/IPE and post-colonialism. He has published eight books, the latest of which is *The Eurocentric Conception of World Politics: Western International Theory, 1760–2010* (Cambridge University Press, 2012). His current research, which picks up from his earlier non-Eurocentric book, *The Eastern Origins of Western Civilisation* (Cambridge University Press, 2004), seeks to chart the formation and development of the world economy in the last millennium in an IPE context.

Stephen Hopgood is Professor of International Relations and co-Director of the Centre for the International Politics of Conflict, Rights and Justice at SOAS, University of London. He is the author of *The Endtimes of Human Rights* (2013), *Keepers of the Flame: Understanding Amnesty International* (2006), "The Last Rites of Humanitarian Intervention: Darfur, Sri Lanka and R2P," *Global Responsibility to Protect* 6, 2 (2014) and is co-editor (with Jack

Snyder and Leslie Vinjamuri) of *Human Rights Futures* (Cambridge University Press, forthcoming).

Sally Engle Merry is Silver Professor of Anthropology at New York University. She is also a Faculty Director of the Center for Human Rights and Global Justice at the New York University School of Law, and past president of the American Ethnological Society. She is the author or editor of fifteen books, including *Colonizing Hawai'i* (2000), *Human Rights and Gender Violence* (2006), *Gender Violence: A Cultural Perspective* (2009), *The Practice of Human Rights* (co-edited with Mark Goodale, Cambridge University Press, 2007), and, most recently, *The Seductions of Quantification: Measuring Human Rights, Gender Violence, and Sex Trafficking* (2016). She received the Hurst Prize for *Colonizing Hawai'i* in 2002, the Kalven Prize for scholarly contributions to sociolegal scholarship in 2007, and the J.I. Staley Prize for *Human Rights and Gender Violence* in 2010. In 2013 she received an honorary degree from McGill School of Law and was the focus of an Author Colloquium at the Center for Interdisciplinary Research (ZIF) at the University of Bielefeld, Germany. She is an adjunct professor at Australian National University.

Vibhuti Ramachandran is a Ph.D. candidate in Anthropology at New York University. Her research interests span prostitution in legal and activist frameworks; anthropological perspectives on law and the state; NGOs; and governmentality. She is currently writing her doctoral dissertation, *"Immoral Traffic": Law, Prostitution and the Politics of Truth Production in India*, which examines how courts, shelters, and NGOs in India respond to prostitution.

Henry S. Richardson is Professor of Philosophy at Georgetown University. He is the author of three books: *Practical Reasoning about Final Ends* (Cambridge University Press, 1994), *Democratic Autonomy: Public Reasoning about the Ends of Policy* (2002), and *Moral Entanglements: Medical Researchers' Ancillary-Care Obligations* (2012). He was a member of the World Commission on the Ethics of Science and Technology (a UNESCO body) 2010–2013 and its rapporteur from 2011 to 2013 and president of the Human Development and Capability Association from 2014 to 2016. He is currently the editor of *Ethics*.

Aisling Swaine is Associate Professor of Practice of International Affairs at the Elliott School of International Affairs, The George Washington University. She received her Ph.D. in law from the Transitional Justice Institute, Ulster University (2012) and her MSc. in Humanitarian Assistance (2000) and B.A. (1999) from University College Dublin, Ireland. She teaches and researches on issues of violence against women related to armed conflict, global gender equality policy; the women, peace, and security agenda; feminist legal theory and transitional justice. Prior to her current post, Swaine worked extensively with the United Nations and international non-governmental aid organizations in humanitarian settings, as well as at international policy levels. She has worked as an independent consultant to a number of international organizations including UN Women, the Trust Fund for Victims of the International Criminal Court, and Irish Aid.

Acknowledgments

This volume has been many years in the making, which means that there are many people and institutions that require thanks. The project began to come together at a conference at The George Washington University in October 2014. It was made possible by funding from The George Washington University and the Elliott School of International Affairs' Program on Humanitarian Governance, and the extraordinary organizational skills of Jessica Anderson. In addition to the contributors, several others participated in the lively discussion: Jens Meierhenrich, Steve Krasner, Kathryn Sikkink, Martha Finnemore, Jennifer Brinkerhoff, Ron Waldman, Biju Rao, and James Foster.

I have been wrestling with the question of international paternalism for many years, and my thinking has evolved as a consequence of presentations at various conferences and institutions, and conversations with many individuals. I have given talks at the Graduate Institute of International and Development Studies, Simon Fraser University, the University of Minnesota, Northwestern University, Yale University, Georgetown University, McGill University, the World Health Organization, MSF-Geneva, University of Texas-Austin, Cambridge University, University of London-SOAS. Special thanks to the following people: Peter Trubowitz, Antje Weiner, Joe Soss, Ron Krebs, Bud Duvall, Joan Tronto, Leslie Vinjamuri, Keith Krause, Eric Grynaviski, Shannon Powers, Allan Dafoe, David Kennedy, Ian Hurd, and Karen Alter. A special thanks to Shannon Powers for helping get the manuscript into shape, and Danielle Gilbert for putting it through its final paces.

A much earlier article, "International Paternalism and Humanitarian Governance," *Global Constitutionalism*, 1, 3, November, 2012, 485–521, informed both the Introduction and the Conclusion.

Introduction: International Paternalism: Framing the Debate

MICHAEL N. BARNETT

We live in a world in which the international community vigorously protects and promotes the quality of human life. Within twenty-four hours of a natural disaster, emergency relief organizations deploy armies of aid workers to provide medical care to the survivors. The International Committee for the Red Cross visits prisoners of war and political prisoners to ensure that their basic rights, as listed in the Geneva Conventions, are honored. The international community now has a "responsibility to protect" populations who are victims of geno-cide, war crimes, and crimes against humanity. Peacebuilders in post-conflict countries aspire to help societies remove the root causes of conflict and to create the conditions for a full, just, and lasting peace. Organizations, such as the United Nations Commission for Refugees and Refugees International, provide direct assistance to refugees and other displaced peoples. Thousands of rights-based organizations, including Fédération Internationale des Ligues des Droits de l'Homme and Amnesty International, struggle to protect children, women, gays, and other vulnerable populations. Labor and rights-oriented monitoring agencies organize to improve the conditions of workers. Often operating in the shadow of major global initiatives, such as the Millennium Development Goals, development organizations provide all manner of aid, including job training, micro-financing, and techni-cal assistance. The World Health Organization, the Gates Foundation, and other global health organizations cover all dimensions of physical and mental health, from reproductive health, to trauma counseling, to the containment and eradication of disease. Educators in the West collect textbooks for internationally funded schools in sub-Saharan Africa. Health and human rights organizations monitor and report on organ trafficking, including trying to stop the world's rich from treat-ing the world's poor as a supermarket for body parts. Everywhere we look the international community is committed to the protection of people from unfavorable conditions, from others, and from themselves.

These practices of care are inspired by, and are the realization of, a growing sense of humanity. Historically speaking, it was not too long ago that compassion was largely circumscribed by boundaries of family, residence, and religion. Certainly there were real material limitations placed on the lengths that individuals and communities could go to help distant strangers. Until there were advances in communication technologies, it was impossible to know about the hardships experienced by others in faraway lands when it was happening. Until there were advances in transportation technologies, it was nearly impossible to do something about it. Yet the limits also were set by the moral imagination – whether individuals and communities felt a sense of obligation to these suffering strangers. Connections are not just physical; they also are emotional. And it was only when those experiencing hardship were near and dear to them that communities became sufficiently moved to act.

Beginning in the late eighteenth century, both material technologies and moral imaginations began to expand, propelled by independent forces but combining to create what Didier Fassin calls a "humanitarian reason," the belief that we can and should do something when others are in danger, in need, and experiencing deprivation.[1] By the nineteenth century, the notion that all humans were of equal worth and concern became increasingly voiced, reflecting and feeding into a new discourse of humanity. It became a mark of our humanity that we cared about distant strangers, and a mark of our own inhumanity if we did not. Not only humans were expected to demonstrate humanity, so too was the "international community." How the world treated the most marginalized and vulnerable populations now became a sign of its moral progress, or lack thereof. By the beginning of the twentieth

---

[1] Didier Fassin, *Humanitarian Reason: A Moral History of the Present* (Berkeley: University of California Press, 2012); Thomas Haskell, "Capitalism and the Origins of the Humanitarian Sensibility, Part 1," *American Historical Review* 90 (1985): 339–61; Steven Pinker, *The Better Angels of Our Nature: Why Violence has Declined* (New York: Penguin Books, 2012); Lynn Hunt, *Inventing Human Rights* (New York: Norton, 2008); Michael N. Barnett, *Empire of Humanity* (Ithaca: Cornell University Press, 2011); Andrew Linklater, *The Problem of Harm in International Relations* (New York: Cambridge University Press, 2011); Thomas Laqueur, "Mourning, Pity, and the Work of Narrative in the Making of 'Humanity'," in *Humanitarianism and Suffering: The Mobilization of Empathy*, eds. R.A. Wilson and R. Brown (New York: Cambridge University Press, 2009), 31–57.

century, this widening of the moral imagination became institutionalized in a growing global architecture of care, as the world began to first add categories of people that deserved special protection – such as fallen and captured soldiers, refugees, children, women, religious minorities – and second, tackle the causes of suffering – such as war, poverty, and disease. These practices and sentiments have accumulated into a "humanitarian government ... [T]he administration of human collectivities in the name of a higher moral principle that sees the preservation of life and the alleviation of suffering as the highest value of action."[2] In the present moment in much of the world, the state's welfare net for its citizens is being moth-eaten, but the international community still maintains an aspiration to create and distribute all kinds of nets.

This realm of care is venerated in part because it represents a sacred space for ethics in a world that is overwhelmed by the profanity of interests and power. And thanks to the tireless struggles by moral entrepreneurs, transnational activists, and all types and stripes of crusaders, ethics has won enough battles with state power over the decades to create a greater expanse for humanitarian governance. Humanitarian governance, in short, provides something of a sanctuary and staging ground for ethics. Consequently, it has a reputation of being a "power free" zone. Yet no form of governance is without power, and this includes humanitarian governance. And this form of power goes beyond the "power to" use ethics in the service of humanity. It also includes "power over" – power over the very individuals, societies, and states that are the objects of concern.

The examples of global care in the opening paragraph neglected the existence of power, but power is often a major, but hidden, part of the story. If peacebuilders want to help states move from war to peace, then they usually must be prepared to take matters into their own hands and to act according to their own instincts; to listen to the "wishes" of the (most powerful segments of) society would simply reproduce the status quo and its war-inducing properties. From the perspective of the local populations, their presence can become

[2] Didier Fassin, "Humanitarianism: a Nongovernmental Government," in *Nongovernmental Politics*, ed. Michael Feher (New York: Zone Books, 2007), 151. Also see Michael Agier, *Managing the Undesirables: Refugee Camps and Humanitarian Government* (Maden, MA: Polity Press, 2012).

oppressive. In nearly every post-conflict operation the local population is heard to wonder when they are going to be liberated from the rule of the NGOs. Refugee organizations do not just try to take care of the needs of refugees, they also often decide for them what those needs are and what solutions would be in the refugees' interests.[3] It is not just refugee organizations that deliver first and ask questions later, if ever – the same can be written about the entire humanitarian sector.[4] Human rights activists often descend on countries to try and fight for those rights that they believe are most pressing; yet, quite often, these are not the rights that local populations feel would potentially make the greatest impact on their lives. Voting rights are desirable, but from the perspective of many local groups, they pale in comparison to land tenure rights. International development experts are widely purported to be dismissive of local knowledge.[5] Western-based health organizations frequently run mandatory immunization programs and drugs trials in the Third World that violate the rights possessed by patients in the West.[6] The world of care might present itself as an antidote to the world of power and interest, but it is not as innocent as it pretends to be.

There is a concept that captures this mixture of care and control that runs throughout much of humanitarian governance – paternalism. Precisely what counts as paternalism is a matter of debate, both in this volume and in the broader academic and policy community. The continuing existence of this intense debate, though, speaks to the significance of the issue at hand: how is power intertwined with practices of compassion? Those of us who study humanitarian governance have been keenly aware that even the most basic "gift" and heart-felt

---

[3] Barbara Harrell-Bond, *Imposing Aid: Emergency Assistance to Refugees* (New York: Oxford University Press, 1986).

[4] Richard Garfield *et al.*, "Common Needs Assessments and Humanitarian Action," Network Paper no. 69 (Overseas Development Initiative: Humanitarian Practice Network, 2011), www.odihpn.org/documents/ networkpaper069.pdf (accessed July 23, 2014).

[5] See David Mosse, *Adventures in Aidland: The Anthropology of Professionals in International Development* (New York: Berghahn Books, 2013); William Easterly, *The White Man's Burden: Why the West's Efforts to Aid the Rest Have Done So Much Ill and So Little Good* (New York: Penguin Books, 2007); and William Easterly, *The Tyranny of Experts: Economists, Dictators, and the Forgotten Rights of the Poor* (New York: Basic Books, 2013).

[6] Jessica Ho, "The Quest for an HIV Vaccine," www.vaccineethics.org/issue_ briefs/HIV_clinical_trials.php.

expression of care can also be entangled with forms of domination. Certainly not all acts of humanitarianism are laden with paternalism; there are plenty of instances in which forms of assistance are given freely, with no expectations, and no reciprocal obligations. But a fair amount is. Different contributors pick up the trail in different places. For some, paternalism can be an attitude of arrogance and high-mindedness, best detected by the recipients whose dignity has been injured. For others, paternalism exists when outsiders presume that they know what is best for others. And others want to reserve paternalism for when some form of coercion is used to impose one's views on another on the grounds that it is in her best interests. Paternalism, just like care and power, comes in many different forms.

This volume explores paternalism beyond borders, the mixture of emancipation and domination that inhabit everyday practices of humanitarian governance. We have several goals. The most fundamental is to convince readers that paternalism is alive and well in global affairs and that the concept can illuminate critical and enduring features of global order. Because of its toxicity, there are few sober analyses of paternalism in global affairs and, more often than not, it is hurled as an accusation and allegation.[7] Accordingly, a first step toward resurrecting the analytical utility of the concept is to distinguish between paternalism's diagnostic and normative dimensions. This exercise, we hope to show, delivers conceptual, historical, and ethical payoffs.

Second, because paternalism is a composite of care and control, it forces a consideration of how power is implicated in relations of care.[8] It is impossible to understand fully the power that exists in relations of

---

[7] For three important and recent exceptions, see David Long, "Paternalism and the Internationalization of Imperialism: J.A. Hobson on the International Government of the 'Lower Races'," in *Imperialism and Internationalism in the Discipline of International Relations*, eds. David Long and Brian Schmidt (Albany: SUNY Press, 2005), 71–93; John Hobson, *The Eurocentric Conception of World Politics: Western International Theory, 1760–2010* (New York: Cambridge University Press, 2012); and Thomas McCarthy, *Race, Empire, and the Idea of Human Development* (New York: Cambridge University Press, 2009).

[8] For statements on an ethics of care as it relates to global relations, see Fiona Robinson, *Globalizing Care: Ethics, Feminist Theory, And International Relations* (Boulder: Westview Press, 1999); Fiona Robinson, *The Ethics of Care: A Feminist Approach to Human Security* (Philadelphia: Temple University Press, 2011); Joan Tronto, "Care as a Basis for Radical Political Judgments," *Hypatia* 10, 2 (1995): 141–9; Virginia Held, *The Ethics of Care: Personal, Political and Global* (New York: Oxford University Press, 2005).

care without a consideration of power in all its dimensions. At times
paternalism occurs from direct imposition and coercion. Nineteenth-
century civilizing missions routinely threatened, and often deployed,
violence to force native populations to abandon those cultural practices the colonizers and missionaries found to be sinful and detrimental to the moral development of the local population. At times
paternalism works through institutional arrangements. For instance,
UNHCR has manipulated food rations to encourage refugees to leave
their camps and return home to situations of continuing danger on the
grounds that their return will only become more dangerous over time.
There are more hidden forms of power, as well. Global discourses of
gender, race, and primitive/modern, uncivilized/civilized, and back-
ward/advanced often produce self-identified "rational" actors who
believe that they have a responsibility for the welfare of actors who
are unable to act in their own best interests. Scholars influenced by
the critical thought of Michel Foucault often twin his concepts of governmentality and pastoral power to consider how those with moral,
legal, and political authority enact new rationalities and mechanisms
of self-control that dispose the multitudes to develop the responsibility to exercise their freedom on their own.[9] Like power, paternalism is
perhaps at its most potent when it is least visible.

Third, this conceptual work points to paternalism's historical dimensions. It is widely accepted that paternalism was a defining characteristic of the age of empire and colonialism, yet paternalism did not begin
or end with Western imperialism. Indeed, because practices of care
are widely understood to have expanded over the last century, and
because practices of care are often accompanied by forms of power,
paternalism might be as healthy as ever – even if it has a "light footprint." If paternalism's practices changed with the times, then the obvious follow-on question is: why and how? Because of the spread of values such as liberty, consent, equality, and self-determination? Because

[9] Michel Foucault, *Security, Territory, Population: Lectures at the College de
France, 1977–1978* (New York: Palgrave, 2007), 127–9; Michael Merlingen,
"Governmentality: Towards a Foucauldian Framework for the Study of IGOs,"
Cooperation and Conflict 38, 4 (2003): 361–84; Ole Jacob Sending and
Iver Neumann, "Governance to Governmentality: Analyzing NGOs, States,
and Power," *International Studies Quarterly* 50, 3 (2006): 651–72; Stephen
Campbell, "Construing Top-Down as Bottom-Up: The Governmental Co-
option of Peacebuilding 'From Below'," *Explorations in Anthropology* 11, 1
(2011): 39–56.

it is no longer politically correct to assume that others are inferior and incapable of making their own decisions? Because it is less acceptable to use force? Because of a change in the nature of the "international community" and its felt obligations to distant strangers? Because of a change in what paternalism is supposed to accomplish? Because of the growing presence of experts and technocratic action? The process of looking for historical variation requires a consideration of the difference between a change in paternalism and a change of paternalism.

In the conclusion I will suggest that we are now living in an era of "paternalism lite" that owes, first and foremost, to the institutionalization of the liberal international order. Values such as autonomy, liberty, choice, consent, and freedom have obtained a hegemonic acceptance, and while these values are not owned and operated by liberalism, they are closely identified with it. These values not only provide a normative benchmark to judge the legitimacy and desirability of global practices, but they have become embedded in the very institutions of global governance. The age of empires was proceeded by the globalization of sovereignty, self-determination, and the principle of non-interference. The modern history of human rights can be read as a modern history of revolts against paternalism. As William Talbott emphatically states:

[T]he entire history of human rights is a history of rebellion against paternalistic rationales for oppression; the belief the that [*sic*] the commoners needed a monarch to look after their interests; that colonials needed colonialists to look after that their interests; that slaves needed a master to look after their interests; that women needed a father and then a husband to look after their interests; that people with disabilities needed custodians rather than the removal of the barriers that prevent them from living independently.[10]

The liberal international order, so it seems, is also an anti-paternalist order.

Yet alongside the call for self-restraint and respect of another's choices, the contemporary liberal order exhibits impulses of interference.[11] Many (but by no means all) of the great campaigns of human

[10] William Talbott, *Human Rights and Human Well-Being* (Oxford: Oxford University Press, 2010), 308–9.
[11] George Sorenson, *A Liberal World Order in Crisis* (Ithaca: Cornell University Press, 2011); James L. Richardson, *Contending Liberalisms in World Politics: Ideology and Power* (Boulder: Lynne Rienner, 2001); Martin Hall and

emancipation over the last century have been conducted to the themes of liberalism. Beginning with the political thought of John Stuart Mill, liberals who otherwise railed against paternalism found room to maneuver if the goal was to help the backward peoples achieve a level of maturity that would allow them to deserve liberty and practice it responsibly. Although such thinking is rumored to have died with colonialism, strikingly similar sentiments exist in contemporary projects to promote human security and to give individuals the capabilities that they need for human flourishing. Human rights might have a strong streak of anti-paternalism, but it also has its paternalist inclinations; as captured by several of the contributions, it exhibits a willingness to limit the choices of others if those choices are seen as ill-informed, as the consequence of cultural oppression, or as an obstacle to human development. Such impulses to intervene to better humanity, a hallmark of the "international community," have grown in intensity and scale in recent decades. In general, this liberal world order, defined by impulses of restraint and interference, has constituted a modern structure of global governance that is driven by the contradictory impulses to "live and let live" and to nurture moral progress.[12]

Fourth, paternalism is something of a "fun-house" mirror for reflecting on the history of global ethics. It reveals the practices of control in relations of care. It reminds us that all good things do not necessarily go together and that any sort of interventions for the good of others pits deeply held values against one another. Discussions of paternalism almost always refer to first-order values such as autonomy, power, freedom, dignity, consent, liberty, obligation, and interference. Paternalism seems to violate another's autonomy and dignity. But what do we mean by these terms? What is the practical meaning of liberty? Are there areas in which liberty can be justifiably suspended? Are we concerned with all areas of life, including the most trivial? Paternalism frequently implies that some action is taken without the consent of the

John M. Hobson, "Liberal International Theory: Eurocentric but not Always Imperialist?," *International Theory* 2, 2 (2010): 210–45.

[12] Although most of the chapters operate with the backdrop of global liberalism, paternalism exists in many other political ideologies. Marxism has its paternalism. How else to interpret the dictatorship of the proletariat? Chinese Marxism and the Great Leap Forward contained a deadly paternalism. Most cultural and religious systems have paternalistic practices. Universalizing ideologies and modernist thought also have strong hues of paternalism.

person who is affected by it. What counts as consent, and can consent ever be overridden? Are values such as autonomy, liberty, and dignity so sacrosanct that they should be allowed to trump the possible positive welfare effects that result from unwarranted interference? How much are these values worth? Fights over paternalism and its justification are, indeed, fights over fundamental values and commitments.

When, if ever, can paternalism be justified? This question makes many deeply uncomfortable, especially those whose vocation and avocation is dedicated to improving the lives of the world's most vulnerable populations. For many, paternalism is a sin, pure and simple, because it violates another person's autonomy and/or insults her dignity. Yet much of humanitarian and global governance is replete with practices of control that many practitioners and scholars are prepared to defend. There are rights-based organizations that want to ban, or strictly regulate, the ability of individuals in the Third World to sell their organs to the highest bidder in the West. There are international women's organizations that want to outlaw crossing a border to engage in sex work. There are campaigns to ban the practice of female genital cutting, even for women over the age of eighteen who have given consent. In these examples, human rights organizations are often implicitly and explicitly claiming that individuals need to be protected not only from others but also from themselves. There are cases where communities that have survived a natural disaster request immediate assistance to bury their dead, but aid agencies believe that shelter and clean water should get priority in order to keep fewer people from having to be buried. These and comparable practices are justified according to a consequentialist logic – assaulted principles or bruised feelings are more than compensated by the improvement of the target's welfare. Autonomy is a wonderful thing, but autonomy that leads to deprivation or death seems wildly overrated.

This debate about when paternalism can be justified implicates liberal and critical theory in surprisingly similar ways. Both are concerned with the ability of actors to control the conditions of their existence and shape their futures as they see fit. Liberalism has a long history of fighting with paternalism. For die-hard anti-paternalists, the only justification for interfering in another person's rightful space is harm to self or others. As Mill famously declared in his defense of liberty, "the only purpose for which power can be rightfully exercised over any member of a civilized community, against his will, is to prevent harm to others."[13] In the same way that Mill was worried that moral busybodies might undermine individual liberty, critical theory has a long history of concern that self-anointed projects designed for human improvement might nevertheless be a stealth mechanism of control. Karl Marx famously condemned the philanthropists and humanitarians that had delusions of doing good when in fact they were only helping to maintain the system of exploitation; this line of thought has influenced students of the welfare state and humanitarianism. For both liberal and critical theorists, practices of care can be sources of domination.

Yet liberal and critical theorists appear to defend paternalism, in practice if not in name, under certain circumstances. For many liberal political theorists, there are probably times when the state (and others) can, and should, restrict another person's liberty for his own good. For theorists of international liberalism, these normative concerns have fueled heated debates about the principle of non-interference and the conditions under which state sovereignty can be trammeled or disregarded. Critical theory also welcomes interference for human emancipation. Marxists have justified the establishment of one kind of vanguard or another on the grounds that it was necessary to remove the chains of bondage that oppress people in body and spirit. Various empowerment movements are designed to rid people of their artificial identities and to allow them to embrace their "objective" interests. However, precisely when and how critical theorists are prepared to defend a top-down emancipation is a conversation that they are reluctant to hold.[14] There is an interesting dialogue to be had between liberal and critical theory on the justifications for paternalism.

Paternalism is no trivial matter – not conceptually, theoretically, historically, or ethically. The goal of this volume is to use the concept to catalyze a conversation regarding the intersection of care and control in world affairs. The contributors to this volume are well positioned to do so for three reasons. First, each has wrestled with the fundamental question of the entanglement of control and care in humanitarian governance in their scholarship. Second, they bring to the discussion an interdisciplinary perspective – representing and crossing

---

[13] John Stuart Mill, *On Liberty* (Oxford: Oxford University Press, 1859), 21–2.
[14] However, see James Ferguson, *Give a Man to Fish: Reflections on the New Politics of Distribution* (Durham, NC: Duke University Press, 2015).

different disciplines. Third, they are attentive to the overlapping and layered networks that exist in world affairs, and how some of these networks can be distinguished by different expressions and practices of paternalism. This volume examines states, transnational activists, aid workers, expert communities, international civil servants, and on and on. Sometimes these networks operate relatively independently of each other, and at other times they are enmeshed in complicated and complex ways.[15] Fourth, most of the contributors have one eye on the world of scholarship and the other on the world of practice. Some are drawing from their own experiences as practitioners to reflect on how they have navigated the issues raised by paternalism. Others have interacted with practitioners as a way to better inform their understanding of how practices of care are wrapped up with power. And still others have dug deeper into the power in care in the hopes of helping practitioners unravel some of their toughest ethical knots. In general, moving across borders, disciplines, and knowledge communities helps to illuminate paternalism in all its significance, richness, and complexity.

The remainder of this Introduction proceeds as follows. The next section provides a brief introduction to the debate over the definition: it begins by reviewing some of the more popular definitions; argues that different understandings of power underlie some of the important differences between them; proposes that paternalism can be defined as the attempted or accomplished substitution of one person's judgment for another's on the grounds that it is in the latter's best interests, for their welfare or happiness; and closes by alerting the reader to some of the baggage this definition carries. The following section discusses the social relations of paternalism. Paternalism is often analyzed at the level of individual judgment – one individual judging herself to be able and obligated to interfere in the actions of another who is lacking in judgment. However, I want to draw attention to the underlying structures that produce the social capacities to make such judgments. Two concepts – roles and authority – frequent discussions of paternalism because they provide the connection between underlying

---

[15] For an excellent example see Alan Lester and Fae Dussart, *Colonization and the Origins of Humanitarian Governance: Protecting Aborigines across the Nineteenth-Century British Empire* (New York: Cambridge University Press, 2014).

structures and relations of superiority and inferiority. Having identified the boundaries of paternalism, the next section darkens those lines
by distinguishing it from solidarity, persuasion, voluntarily designed
institutions of self-restraint, and self-interested domination. I conclude
by summarizing the contributions to this volume.

Paternalism: What's In a Name?

How do we know paternalism when we see it? The *Merriam Webster*
dictionary defines it as "the attitude or actions of a person, organization, etc., that protects people and gives them what they need but does
not give them any responsibility or freedom of choice."[16] According
to the *Oxford Dictionary*, paternalism is "The policy or practice on
the part of people in positions of authority of restricting the freedom
and responsibilities of those subordinate to them in the subordinates'
supposed best interest."[17] Other definitions highlight not the attempt
by one person to improve the circumstances of another, but instead the
intent to "prevent him from harming himself, either when he would
harm himself voluntarily or when he would do so involuntarily."[18]
According to another, frequently cited definition by Gerald Dworkin,
it is "the interference with a person's liberty of action justified by
reasons referring exclusively to the welfare, good, happiness, needs,
interests or values of the person being coerced."[19] In a recent review
of the contending definitions, Dworkin marches through seven candidates, including Seana Shiffrin's influential take, which emphasizes not
the interference with another actor's interests but rather the interference in another actor's proper sphere of autonomy and judgment.[20]
Scholars of paternalism have given us a healthy range of choices to

---

[16] *Merriam Webster*, s.v. "Paternalism," www.merriam-webster.com/dictionary/
paternalism (accessed July 22, 2014).
[17] *Oxford Dictionaries*, s.v. "Paternalism," www.oxforddictionaries.com/us/
definition/american_english/paternalism (accessed July 22, 2014).
[18] Rutger Claassen, "Capability Paternalism," *Economics and Philosophy* 30, 1
(2014): 61.
[19] Gerald Dworkin, "Paternalism," *The Monist* 56, 1 (1972): 64–84,
especially 70–6.
[20] Gerald Dworkin, "Defining Paternalism," in *Paternalism: Theory and Practice*,
eds. Christian Coons and Michael Weber (New York: Cambridge University
Press, 2013), 25–38; Seana Shiffrin, "Paternalism, Unconscionability Doctrine,
and Accommodation," *Philosophy and Public Affairs* 29 (2000): 205–50.

pick from – varying in what first-order principles have been assaulted, and even whether an assault has occurred.[21]

Following the work of Shiffrin and other critical theorists, I favor the following definition: paternalism is the attempt by one actor to substitute his judgment for another's on the grounds that it is in the latter's best interests or welfare.[22] It shares with these and other definitions three core elements – care, an ethic of consequences, and power. It is its handling of power, I want to suggest, that distinguishes it from some prevailing alternatives, including Dworkin's.

First, there is the presence of care, compassion, and benevolence. Why do some actors feel as if they have short- and long-term responsibilities to others? Perhaps there is a compassion gene that has strengthened because of socio-biological processes. Perhaps it is because of anxiety and a sense of guilt. Thomas Hobbes is reported to

[21] For a sampling of the definitional debate, see Dennis Thompson, *Political Ethics and Public Office* (New York: Harvard University Press, 1990), 148–77; David Archard, "Paternalism Defined," *Analysis* 50, 1 (1990): 36–42; David Garren, "Paternalism, Part I," *Philosophical Books* 47, 4 (2006): 334–41; David Garren, "Paternalism, Part II," *Philosophical Books* 48, 1 (2007): 50–9; Dworkin, "Paternalism"; Rolf Sartorius, ed., *Paternalism* (Minneapolis: University of Minnesota Press, 1983); Bernard Gert and Charles Culver, "Paternalistic Behavior," *Philosophy and Public Affairs* 6 (1976): 45–58; Donald VanDeVeer, *Paternalistic Intervention: The Moral Bounds of Benevolence* (Princeton: Princeton University Press, 1986); Lawrence Mead, "The Rise of Paternalism," in *The New Paternalism: Supervisory Approaches to Poverty*, ed. L. Mead (Washington, DC: Brookings Institution, 1997), 1–38; Douglas N. Husak, "Legal Paternalism," in *The Oxford Handbook of Practical Ethics*, ed. Hugh LaFollette (New York: Oxford University Press, 2003), 387–412; Robert Young, "John Stuart Mill, Ronald Dworkin and Paternalism," in *Mill's 'On Liberty': A Critical Guide*, ed. C.L. Ten (New York: Cambridge University Press, 2008); Ronald Dworkin, *Sovereign Virtue: The Theory and Practice of Equality* (Cambridge, MA: Harvard University Press, 2000); Steven Kelman, "Regulation and Paternalism," *Public Policy* 29, 2 (1981): 219–54; Kalle Grill, "The Normative Core of Paternalism," *Res Publica* 13 (2007): 441–58; Russ Shafer-Landau, "Liberalism and Paternalism," *Legal Theory* 11 (2005): 169–91; Robin Hanson, "Making Sense of Medical Paternalism," *Medical Hypotheses* 70 (2008): 910–13; William Talbott, *Human Rights and Human Well-Being* (Oxford: Oxford University Press, 2010); and Thomas Schramme, ed., *New Perspectives on Paternalism and Health Care* (Cham, Switzerland: Springer, 2015).

[22] See Seana Shiffrin, "Paternalism, Unconscionability Doctrine, and Accommodation," *Philosophy and Public Affairs* 29, 3 (2000): 205–50; Julian Le Grand and Bill New, *Government Paternalism: Nanny State or Helpful Friend* (Princeton: Princeton University Press, 2015), 7–24.

have defended giving to a beggar on the street on the grounds that he was trying to relieve not the distress of the beggar but rather his own. Perhaps it is because of blood and belonging, which is particularly pronounced when considering a sense of obligation one family member feels for another. It can be because of a sense of humanity. It might be that those events that shock the human conscience are tests of our own morality; the failure to respond represents a failure of our own humanity. Religion also might play a role. Many religious doctrines have codes of charity and compassion, and to be a good Hindu, Jew, Christian, or Muslim requires caring for the less fortunate. Perhaps it owes to diffuse reciprocity, though this seems more plausible when considering small-scale societies rather than the global community.

The second element is an ethic of consequences. Caring is not enough – the presumption is that the act of care will leave the target actor better off than if he was able to decide for himself what to do. There are two important background presumptions that should be foregrounded. One is that allowing some actors to determine their own fate will lead to an inferior outcome or quality of life. The other is that there are more important things in life than having one's autonomy respected. Those who oppose paternalism under any and all circumstances are essentially arguing that autonomous choice trumps everything else. Those who accept some form of paternalism believe that welfare concerns can sometimes justify hurt feelings. Paternalists are not necessarily out to win popularity contests but rather to reduce the suffering and improve the welfare of others. Of course they would rather be liked than resented, and their popularity rating is often an important factor in the success of their initiated programs.[23] But there often are more important things at stake than feeling empowered.

And last, but most important, is power. Precisely what counts as power is a matter of dispute, of course, and different definitions of paternalism implicitly incorporate different ways of conceptualizing power in social relations. Dworkin's definition, for instance, restricts paternalism to those instances of liberty-constraining actions when it is possible to empirically trace the connections between the commands of one actor and the forced action of another. In many ways, then, his definition of paternalism is dependent on a standard, Weberian model of power – the ability of A to get B to do what B would otherwise not do.

---

[23] Séverine Autesserre, *Peaceland* (New York: Cambridge University Press, 2013).

Other definitions of paternalism, though, see the possibility of paternalism when circumstances, institutions, and structures preclude the ability of an actor to make decisions that affect their welfare. Importantly, and in contrast to Dworkin's definition of paternalism that relies on making a visible connection between the actions of one actor and another, the substitution of judgment can occur in various ways. It occurs when institutions set an agenda that removes some possibilities from the menu of choice and from discussion. It occurs when actors occupy roles that give them the authority and duty to act in someone else's best interests. Parents often rely on their judgment when making decisions that they believe is in the best interest of their children. Dissertation advisers often do the same vis-à-vis their graduate students. Some of the examples of paternalism in this volume rely on a more standard definition of power and look for visible moments when one person forces another to do something that she would rather not do, but many others allow for the possibility that the very failure to consult with another, whether intentional or not, also can qualify.

Parenthetically, my preferred definition of paternalism does not refer to the concept of consent. In part because of the influence of liberal political theory on this literature, often the lack of consent is seen as a necessary feature of the presence of paternalism. But what counts as consent? Does consent have to be explicit? The medical field has had a revolution in patients' rights, which often means that no medical procedure or intervention can occur without the explicit, written, and informed consent of the patient. Consent, however, could be implied. It also could be inferred. It is because implied consent can camouflage subtle and not-so-subtle mechanisms of control, though, that many ethicists prefer to err on the side of caution, insisting that consent must either be explicit or "obvious" from what "most" people would want under the circumstances.[24] Consent does not mean the absence of constraints, but at what point do constraints become so severe that choice becomes, for all intents and purposes, no choice. What does consent mean in conditions of gross power asymmetries? Aid agencies arrive with considerable resources. Sometimes they make

---

[24] Govert den Hartogh, "Can Consent be Presumed?" *Journal of Applied Philosophy* 28, 3 (2011): 294–307.

suggestions, but suggestions coming from the powerful with easy exit options can sound like commands, and recipients might prefer to keep quiet than bite the hands that feed them.[25] Structural theories of power raise an additional problem with the language of consent: preferences are formed in a social context, and these preferences might not represent the "true" and "objective" interests of the powerless but rather the interests of the powerful. Can individuals make informed decisions if they are, for instance, so thoroughly indoctrinated into their culture that they cannot imagine alternative ways to live that might enhance their development?

The difficulty of settling on a definition of paternalism extends beyond the obvious to include several other noteworthy aspects. One is that paternalism has analytical and normative dimensions, which complicates the attempt to build a concept for empirical analysis. The normative can easily overpower the analytical; many approaches to paternalism build the stigma directly into the definition. For instance, some definitions allude to the feelings and personality characteristics of those on the giving and receiving ends. Arrogant, high-minded, and moralizing are common descriptions of a paternalist. Yet, not always. Paternalists are not always on a power trip; often they would rather be spared the burden of having to be responsible for another person, play that part reluctantly, and look forward to the moment that they can be released from their obligations. The paternalized often describe feeling demeaned, infantilized, disrespected, and stripped of their dignity. Yet, not always. When Liesl sang "I am Sixteen Going on Seventeen," she is telling Rolf that she could not be trusted to make good decisions, needs someone to protect her from herself, and wants him to play that role. As a teenage Nazi in love, Rolf happily accepted the invitation. Although deeply aware of the largely pejorative association with paternalism, in theory and practice, the contributors do not presume that paternalism is necessarily good or bad. The concluding chapter, though, takes up the normative challenge to consider whether paternalism should be banned outright or whether it might have its time and place.

A related concern is that the concept of paternalism might contain various unhidden biases – the root of paternalism after all is pater or

---

[25] Barbara Harrell-Bond, *Imposing Aid: Emergency Assistance to Refugees* (New York: Oxford University Press, 1986).

father. In this regard, an obvious worry is that the concept is gendered, and should be substituted with a more gender-neutral concept, or perhaps even maternalism. This volume uses paternalism rather than maternalism for the following reasons. It has a level of familiarity that, for many, requires little explanation. It is the concept most closely associated with the central theme of this volume – the intersection of control and care. Maternalism does not have as clear an association. For some, maternalism represents an ethic of care in contrast to a masculine will to power; if so, it doesn't capture the dynamics that concern us. In contrast to the essentialized notion of the maternal, there are discussions of maternalism that do try and recover the power that is present in an ethics of care. Some of these discussions, in fact, come quite close to the prevailing definitions of paternalism. The decision to go with paternalism rather than maternalism, though does not mean an inattention to gender. A considerable amount of paternalism in world affairs takes place in the area of gender and sexuality; this volume features several chapters on these topics. This regularity probably owes to gender in general and the presumption that women are less able to make rational decisions and are in greater need of protection from themselves and others. Justifications for paternalism also often have a gendered dimension. As Swaine forcefully argues in this volume, gender is intertwined in paternalism in various ways.

A final concern is epistemological and concerns the process of concept formation. Stylistically speaking, there are two camps – essentialist or analytic, and nominalist or interpretivist. Essentialism, in this context, refers to the attempt to identify what elements are necessary features of the kind under observation or discussion. This introduction is an example of such an effort, many of the contributors follow in this spirit as they attempt to understand when a pattern of relations qualifies as paternalism, and Henry Richardson provides the most detailed defense of this position. A clear advantage of this analytic move is that it makes possible conversations about what is and is not paternalism, whether paternalism takes different forms, and how patterns of paternalism might alter across time and place. In other words, it facilitates empirical and comparative analysis. The obvious disadvantage is that a group of scholars might agree amongst themselves on a definition of paternalism, but which has no relationship to how the concept is understood, practiced, and made meaningful by the participants themselves. It is equally possible that by starting with how paternalism is understood by the participants, or even by attempting to isolate the functions it plays in society, we might uncover features of paternalism that would otherwise go undetected.

Interpretivism is the other camp, and it is distinguished by the claim that concepts should be related to the understandings, meanings, and practices of the actors themselves. In this volume Didier Fassin makes a strong argument for this approach. Among the advantages of an interpretivist approach are its offer of the promise of a historically sensitive definition, its recognition that to understand practices requires the recovery of meanings, and its increased ability to ensure that no definitional possibility goes overlooked. It has several disadvantages. It provides no clear way to determine when we have crossed from one kind to another; for instance, it makes it difficult to determine the boundaries between paternalism, solidarity, and hegemony. It also complicates the goal of comparative analysis. If everyone constructs an idiosyncratic meaning, then it becomes nearly impossible to compare within and across populations and historical periods. Although I have suggested that analytical and interpretivist approaches are opposed, in fact most scholars, including those in this volume, draw from both to understand paternalism. The definition of paternalism that I proposed, for instance, is intended to be flexible enough to accommodate as many possible variations without being so elastic that there are no limits to the concept.[26]

The Social Relations of Paternalism

This section decomposes the social relations of paternalism into two elements: the belief by the would-be paternalizer that an actor's rationality and reasoning processes are deficient and could lead to self-harm (inferiority); and the sense by the would-be paternalizer that it has the authority and obligation to intervene in the lives of another (superiority). And almost by definition, elements of superiority or inferiority are relational and hierarchical. Although many approaches to paternalism focus on the judgments by individuals regarding their and others' capacities and competencies, my emphasis on social relations suggests

[26] Christian Coons and Michael Weber, "Introduction," in *Manipulation: Theory and Practice*, eds. Christian Coons and Michael Weber (New York: Oxford University Press, 2014), 2; Le Grand and New, *Government Paternalism*, 7.

that a structural approach is more appropriate. Structural approaches "begin with political relations rather than unencumbered individuals, emphasizing that paternalism is an authority relationship based on unequal status and power."[27] In this spirit, I want to discuss the underlying roles and authority relations that often underlie the acts of paternalism before turning to the elements of superiority and inferiority.

Social roles figure prominently in many discussions of paternalism. Paternalism is often enacted by those who occupy the role of parent, teacher, government official, expert, aid worker, human rights activist, and on and on. Roles have several distinguishing characteristics that are intrinsic to paternalism. They have normative expectations attached to them; to perform a role successfully means to behave in conformity with its societal expectations. At times these expectations include obligations and duties. The Latin origins of paternalism, *pater*, refers to the father, which includes the duties a father has for his children. States are expected to have an obligation to the public. Experts, and especially those who serve in an official capacity, are supposed to use their knowledge for the betterment the public. Teachers have a duty to help their students. These roles are relational to the extent that the existence of one role is often dependent on the existence of another role: parents and children, teachers and students, husbands and wives, masters and slaves, doctors and patients, state officials and citizens, aid workers and victims. Moreover, there are different social capacities attached to these roles. Furthermore, these roles are not just relational, but they also are often hierarchical, distributing differential social capacities. In a traditional marriage, the husband and wife not only occupy differential roles but also have uneven voice, rights, and entitlements. Those that occupy the role of father and husband are expected to provide for their family, and those who occupy the role of mother and wife are expected to take care of the home but defer to the "head of the house." Parents have obligations to provide for the welfare and upbringing of their children, and children are told to respect their parents who only have their best interests at heart.

The concept of authority looms over this discussion. Authority can be understood as the discursive and institutional resources that enable

---

[27] Joe Soss, Richard Fording, and Sanford Schram, *Disciplining the Poor: Neoliberal Paternalism and the Persistent Power of Race* (Chicago: University of Chicago Press, 2011), 24–5.

one actor to be conferred the right to speak by another actor.[28] There
are several features of authority relations that are necessary supple-
ments to any discussion of roles and the social relations of paternalism. Authority is about control, and control is associated with power,
but authority and power are not the same thing. Power gives the ability but not necessarily the right. The hacker has the power, but not
the authority, to steal my identity.[29] Authority, therefore, operates
with some degree of consent. Authority relations figure prominently
in discussions of paternalism because often: the intervening actor
believes that s/he has the right to try and improve another's welfare;
and the paternalized believes that those in authority both know better and have the right to make decisions that affect their lives.

Also pertinent to this discussion is the distinction between being
"in authority" and "of authority."[30] Actors whose authority derives
from the institutional roles they occupy can be said to be "in authority"; these roles grant them the right to speak and perhaps even enjoy
enforcement mechanisms to make sure that the audience does what
they say. Those who hold public office have authority that comes from
the institution, and when they leave office those rights and powers
disappear. In contrast, to be "an authority" is to be conferred the right
to speak because of credentials, education, training, and experience.
In other words, authority of this kind adheres to the individual who
has it, regardless of changes in the institutional role. Those who have
this kind of authority often feel entitled to offer an opinion on subjects
they claim to have mastered (and sometimes even subjects they know
nothing about).

Lastly, there are different kinds of authority. Four kinds of authority
satisfactorily cover the possibilities in international paternalism. There
is delegated authority, whereby the authority possessed by one actor

---

[28] Bruce Lincoln, *Authority: Construction and Corrosion* (Chicago: University
of Chicago Press, 1994); Joseph Raz, ed., *Authority* (New York: Cambridge
University Press, 1990); Barry Barnes, "On Authority and Its Relationship to
Power," in *Power: Action and Belief*, ed. J. Law (New York: Routledge, 1987);
Richard Friedman, "On the Concept of Authority in Political Philosophy,"
in *Concepts in Social and Political Philosophy*, ed. Richard Flathman
(New York: Macmillan, 1973); and Richard Flathman, *The Practice of
Political Authority* (Chicago: University of Chicago Press, 1980).
[29] This example is a desperate attempt to update the standard mugger–victim
example.
[30] Friedman, "On the Concept of Authority."

is transferred or delegated to another agent. There is rational-legal authority, whereby authority is derived from seemingly impersonal and objective laws, procedures, standards, and rules that are applied evenly and without discrimination. Third is moral authority, whereby authority is derived from various kinds of transcendental appeals and discourses; actors who link themselves to theological and humanist claims are generally based on this form of authority. And, finally, there is expert authority, whereby authority is claimed and conferred on the basis of specialized knowledge.[31] The distinction between in and of authority, and the different kinds of authority, is useful for understanding the theory and practice of international paternalism.

Inferiority

Paternalism is motivated by a desire to help – not just anyone, but those who are deemed unable to act in their own best interests. Consequently, implicit in an act of paternalism is a judgment about the competence and capacity of the subordinate actor. These judgments can be made on a case-by-case basis, according to categorical analysis, or assumed to be part of the human condition. If we begin with the assumption that all individuals are autonomous creatures that are entitled to live their lives as they see fit, then are there times when this presumed autonomy should be suspended? One reason might be because they are proposing to undertake actions that are clearly self-injurious. There are laws that prohibit individuals from committing suicide or electively amputating a healthy limb on the grounds that anyone who wanted to do so was, by definition, not of "sound mind and body."[32] As discussed by Merry and Ramachandran, and Hopgood, in this volume, many activists that advocate the abolition of sex work and female genital mutilation/cutting assume that anyone, regardless of age, who submits to these practices must have been either tricked, coerced, or otherwise unable to make a proper judgment – and therefore needs protection from herself.[33]

In contrast to the scenario where individuals are presumed to be worthy of autonomy unless otherwise indicated, there are categories

---

[31] Michael N. Barnett and Martha Finnemore, *Rules for the World: International Organizations in Global Politics* (Ithaca: Cornell University Press, 2004).
[32] Shafer-Landau, "Liberalism and Paternalism."
[33] Talbott, *Human Rights and Human Well-Being,* 277.

or classes of individuals who are presumed to be unable to make decisions in their own best interests. Famously, John Stuart Mill took a strong anti-paternalist line, though making exceptions in the case of children and barbarians.[34] Why? Neither was able to act in their own best interest because they lacked moral and cognitive intelligence. Sexism and racism assumes that members of a gender or race have lesser abilities; women are emotional and irrational, and non-Caucasians lack basic cognitive skills. The United States, Australia, and other countries with large indigenous populations had a policy of removing children from their homes and placing them in residences that were presumably a better, civilizing influence. Some of the best known binaries in international affairs, including civilized/uncivilized, modern/pre-modern, advanced/traditional, well-governed/failed, presume that those in the inferior role are not just inferior but unable to make rational decisions. Implicit in the designation of "victims" in the aid world is that they are in their situation not only because of circumstance but also because they lack the ability to make good decisions.[35] The chapters in this volume highlight the discourses of gender, civilization, and victim that inform the view that categories of populations, such as women, impoverished, and the needy, are unable to serve their own best interests.

Although the case-by-case and categorical analysis suggests that lower level reasoning abilities might be temporary and circumstantial, another emerging line of thinking is that all of us are lacking in judgment. It begins with a simple question: what if individuals do not have stable preferences or there are factors that interfere with a rational decision-making process? Psychology, experimental economics, and behavioral economics offer considerable empirical evidence

[34] Don Habibi, "The Moral Dimensions of J.S. Mill's Colonialism," *Journal of Social Philosophy* 30, 1 (1999): 125–46. Mehta Sankar Muthu, *Enlightenment Against Empire* (Princeton: Princeton University Press, 2003); Jennifer Pitts, *A Turn to Empire: The Rise of Imperial Liberalism in Britain and France* (Princeton: Princeton University Press, 2005); Uday Singh Mehta, *Liberalism and Empire: A Study in Nineteenth-Century British Liberal Thought* (Chicago: University of Chicago Press, 1999); and Hobson, *The Eurocentric Conception of World Politics*.

[35] Barnett, *Empire of Humanity*; Didier Fassin and Richard Rechtman, *The Empire of Trauma: An Inquiry into the Condition of Victimhood* (Princeton: Princeton University Press, 2009).

that individuals do not make choices as economic textbooks portray. There are various factors that might lead to impaired choice: preferences over options can be shaped by framing, preferences can be affected by individuals' psychological state at the moment preferences are expressed, preferences might be affected by irrelevant information, and preferences might be different if experts had a chance to present the information.[36] The 2015 World Bank Development Report acknowledges that everyone exhibits biases in the processing of information, but those individuals that suffer from constant deprivation, a lack of education, and hardship will be particularly hard hit and least able to afford the costs of a poor decision because they have no margin for error.[37] Development experts, including the World Bank, should take such matters into consideration as they provide their advice and design their programs (and should also become more attentive to their own biases in reasoning).

Superiority

If some are inferior, then others must be superior. Although a sense of superiority can exist for various reasons, pre-existing authority relations are a common element. Being in or an authority not only suggests the occupation of a superordinate role, it also often includes a sense of duty or responsibility to those who are deemed less capable. The parent has authority and a responsibility for the welfare of the child, which includes looking after its immediate and long-term welfare; when parents fail or neglect their responsibilities, then the child might become a ward of the state, which has the authority and a responsibility to protect.

---

[36] See Amos Tversky and Daniel Kahneman, "The Framing of Decisions and the Psychology of Choice," *Science* 211, 4481 (1981): 453–8; Amos Tversky and Daniel Kahneman, "Judgment under Uncertainty: Heuristics and Biases," *Science* 185, 4157 (1974): 1124–31.

[37] World Bank, *World Development Report: Mind, Society, and Behavior* (Washington, DC: World Bank Press, 2015); Esther Duflo, "Paternalism versus Freedom?" Tanner Lectures, May 2012, www.google.com/url?sa=t&rc t=j&q=&esrc=s&source=web&cd=1&ved=0CCAQFjAA&url=http%3A%2F %2Feconomics.mit.edu%2Ffiles%2F7904&ei=WnwpVLv9LsHGsQTGooKI DA&usg=AFQjCNGnfYLrtP53-y11-o47jDUEeqBFZQ&sig2=NTrIfEmbtYY ZcBZUL8ZfCw (accessed November 7, 2015).

The sense of superiority that inheres in authority can derive from two different kinds of epistemes. The first is based on preternatural commitments whose core principles cannot be challenged by empirical evidence. Assertions that refer to God or humanity have these qualities.[38]

Alternatively, confidence can be founded on claims to superior knowledge. Such knowledge can come from experience. It is simply a matter of living long enough and having enough experiences. Sometimes it is because of learning through doing, that is, "experiential" or "practical" knowledge. In modern society, though, the presumption is that evidence-based knowledge, obtained through scientific methods, and stamped by certifications of advanced and superior training, trumps lived knowledge.[39] Those who possess such superior knowledge have expert authority and are known as experts.[40] The discourse of expertise generates authority, relations of superiority and inferiority, and a license to intervene in the following ways. Experts claim to know more and expect to be treated with deference, especially

[38] Stephen Hopgood, "Moral Authority, Modernity and the Politics of the Sacred," *European Journal of International Relations* 15, 2 (2009): 229–55; and Ilana Feldman and Miriam Ticktin, "Government and Humanity," in *In the Name of Humanity: The Government of Threat and Care*, eds. Ilana Feldman and Miriam Ticktin (Durham, NC: Duke University Press, 2011), 1–27.

[39] Christina Boswell, *The Political Uses of Expert Knowledge: Immigration Policy and Social Research* (New York: Cambridge University Press, 2009), 23–24, cited in Lorna Schrefler, "Reflections on the Different Roles of Expertise in Regulatory Policy Making," in *The Role of "Experts" in International and European Decision-Making Processes*, eds. Monika Ambrus *et al.* (New York: Cambridge University Press, 2014), 63 n. 1; and Harry Collins and Robert Evans, *Rethinking Expertise* (Chicago: University of Chicago Press, 2007).

[40] For various statements on these issues, see Cass Sunstein, *Free Markets and Social Justice* (New York: Oxford University Press, 1997), 128–50; Stephen Brint, *In an Age of Experts: The Changing Role of Professionals in Politics and Public Life* (Princeton: Princeton University Press, 1996); Thomas L. Haskell, ed., *The Authority of Experts: Studies in History and Theory* (Bloomington: Indiana University Press, 1984); Michael Goldman, "The Birth of a Discipline: Producing Authoritative Green Knowledge, World Bank-Style," *Ethnography* 2, 2 (2001): 191–217; Ambrus *et al.*, *The Role of "Experts" in International and European Decision-Making Processes*; David Kennedy, "Challenging Expert Rule: The Politics of Global Governance," *Sydney Law Review* 27 (2004): 1–24; Barnett and Finnemore, *Rules for the World*; Jan Klabbers, "The Virtues of Expertise," in Ambrus *et al.*, *The Role of "Experts" in International and European Decision-Making Processes*, 82–101; and Jacqueline Best, *Governing Failure: Provisional Expertise and*

in relationship to non-experts.[41] Global governance institutions are increasingly staffed by experts who, by virtue of their superior knowledge, feel as if they know best and that others should listen and do as they say. Such mentalities, according to many in the humanitarian sector, are particularly prevalent when those with advanced knowledge are asked to help "victims," who, almost by definition, are victims because they were, and continue to be, unable to act in their own best interests. Those in global and humanitarian governance often believe that they have a license to interfere – indeed, they would not be doing their jobs if they were not constantly intervening to improve the lives of others.

Such expert authority, therefore, generates a sphere of autonomy. Because of the presumptively objective character of this knowledge, experts are seen as better able to work for the public interest, overcome private interests, and keep politics at bay. Expertise, in this way, contains depoliticizing effects that render rule by experts, that is, technocracy, superior to the rule of the people, that is, democracy. As Larson aptly states, "because such crucial decisions are both assisted by expert advice and esoteric technologies, and increasingly involved with matters of great scientific and technological complexity, the average person is ... disenfranchised by his lack of expert knowledge."[42] These qualities – reliance on objective knowledge and acting in the public interest – provide the space for experts to intervene in the world. Indeed, not only do they have the authority to intervene in the world, they have an obligation to do so. Simply put, they would not be

<hr/>

the *Transformation of Global Development Finance* (New York: Cambridge University Press, 2014).

[41] Julie Anne White, *Democracy, Justice, and the Welfare State: Reconstructing Public Care* (University Park, PA: Pennsylvania State University Press, 2000), 5; Joe Soss, Richard C. Fording, and Sanford F. Schram, *Disciplining the Poor: Neoliberal Paternalism and the Persistent Power of Race* (Chicago: University of Chicago Press, 2011).

[42] Magali Sarfatti Larson, "The Production of Expertise and Constitution of Expert Power," in Haskell, *The Authority of Experts*, 39; also see Steve Rayner, "Democracy in the Age of Assessment: Reflections on the Roles of Expertise and Democracy in Public Sector Decision-Making," *Science and Public Policy* 30, 3 (2003): 161–70; Helga Nowotny, "Democratising Expertise and Socially Robust Knowledge," *Science and Public Policy* 30, 3 (2003): 151–6; and Angela Liberatore and Silvio Funtowicz, "'Democratising' Expertise, 'Expertising' Democracy: What Does this Mean, and Why Bother?" *Science and Public Policy* 30, 3 (2003): 146–50.

doing their job, or enacting their identity, if they were not constantly attempting to intervene to improve the world.[43]

The sense of authority and superiority that leads to paternalism also can be produced by the very discourse of compassion and an ethic of care. Hannah Arendt's observation that modernity has made possible a "passion of compassion" represents one such approach.[44] It begins with what she calls the "social question," that is, the existence of poverty and deprivation. Although compassion has a long pedigree, it was not until the eighteenth century that compassion became part of politics. At this moment, she argues, the repugnance of suffering became a mark of one's humanity and moral character, and, importantly, became part of a revolutionary zeal and a reformist politics. "Necessity" becomes the rallying cry, and liberty becomes a necessary casualty. As a "social" revolution is carried out in the name of the "people" and a "general will," in other words, an anti-democratic spirit takes hold. Elites operating in the name of compassion and for the "people" now see themselves as having the authority to act in their name without actually having to solicit their views. The general will, Arendt argues, replaces the notion of consent and stands superior to the aggregation of private interests. Furthermore, this passion of compassion both corresponds to the sentiment of pity and is bound up with a politics of domination. It is, in her words, a perversion of genuine compassion. What is pity's apposite? Solidarity. But solidarity requires more than one person taking pity on another. It also requires that the "other" be granted authority and voice, and that the fortunate and powerful also be aware that they might be implicated in the conditions of the poor. Revolutionaries, those who are in the vanguard of the social question, can become insensitive to the very people who they want to assist.

Her analysis can be extended to humanitarian governance.[45] The world is now replete with organizations whose purpose is to address the "social question." Although not all humanitarians count themselves

[43] Mosse, *Adventures in Aidland*, 4; Magnus Boström and Christina Garsten, *Organizing Transnational Accountability* (Northampton, MA: Edward Elgar Publishing, 2008); Adam Branch, "Against Humanitarian Impunity: Rethinking Responsibility for Displacement and Disaster in Northern Uganda," *Journal of Intervention and Statebuilding* 2 (2008): 152–73.

[44] Hannah Arendt, *On Revolution* (Harmondsworth: Penguin Press, 1965).

[45] Barnett, *Empire of Humanity*; Juha Käpylä and Denis Kennedy, "Cruel to Care? Investigating the Governance of Compassion in the Humanitarian

as part of a revolutionary class (indeed, many aid workers are highly suspicious of utopian politics, which is why they stick to saving lives), they are motivated by the discourse of necessity. And while humanitarians claim to operate in the name of the "people" and to be in solidarity with the oppressed, the language of needs also arguably comes at the expense of "liberty." Humanitarians rush at the sight of suffering to attend to the needs of the victims; at such a moment, they can easily treat the act of consultation and consent as disposable. Much like Arendt's revolutionaries, humanitarians speak vaguely in the name of the people and the dispossessed, but are frequently accused of allowing their "passion of compassion" to generate a politics of pity that creates structures of domination.

Paternalism is a relationship defined by elements of care and control, and as an enduring relationship, it contains both structure and process. For several of the chapters, paternalism is part of a set of ongoing, structured interactions. For others, relations of inequality are not set in stone but rather are a result of the quality of the encounter. Importantly, then, relations that begin on a basis of equality can become unequal. Conversely, relations that begin as unequal can become equalized. Consequently, although actors might actively decide to be paternalistic – that is, they might self-consciously decide that they should substitute their judgment for another's on the grounds that it is in her best interests – often no decision is deliberately made. Instead, paternalism is an emergent property, as the chapters by Feldman and Autesserre detail. Paternalism results from structures, practices, and decisions.

Is It Paternalism, Or Something Else?

Paternalism is the substitution of one person's judgment for another's on the grounds that it is in the latter's best interest. However, if we tweak the motives from concern for others to self-interest, then we quickly move from paternalism to domination; if we accept that those in a position of inferiority might have voluntarily chosen their

Imaginary," *International Theory* 6, 02 (2014): 255–92; Ian Wilkinson, "Social Suffering and Critical Humanitarianism," *World Suffering and Quality of Life* 56 (2015): 45–54; Didier Fassin, *Humanitarian Reason* (Berkeley: University of California Press, 2011).

position, then we quickly move from paternalism to persuasion and
voluntarily formed institutions designed to further individual and collective interests; and if we allow for the possibility that the person
providing assistance is simply following the wishes of the recipient,
then we can migrate from paternalism into forms of solidarity. In other
words, whether or not a social relationship qualifies as paternalism
depends on the assessment of the (e)quality of the relationship. Each
of the chapters touches on these issues.

Those involved in humanitarian governance often characterize
themselves as acting in solidarity with those in need and the victims of
the world. Solidarity is premised on a feeling of unity between people
who have the same interests, goals, and objectives. If a labor union in
France helps workers in Bangladesh, it represents an act of solidarity,
not paternalism. When believers in one country help co-religionists
in another country by providing aid for rituals, they are not engaging in proselytization but rather in fellowship and religious solidarity.
When Amnesty International and other human rights agencies engage
in letter-writing campaigns on behalf of political prisoners, they are
typically acting in solidarity with the imprisoned. When aid workers
scramble to help the victims of a natural or man-made disaster, they
are acting in solidarity with those in need and in accordance with their
belief in the unity of humanity. Solidarity, rather than paternalism, is
the more accurate description of these acts because the benefactor is
responding to the wishes and interests of the beneficiary.

Yet it is common for those who profess to be acting in solidarity
with others to be accused of sliding into paternalism, because they
have failed to properly listen to the views of those they want to help
and unilaterally substituted their judgment for theirs. Those in solidarity might assume that they know the interests of those they want
to help without ever asking. Those in the West spend a lot of time
attempting to save those in the Third World, but it is not always clear
that those in the Third World feel as if they need to be saved, at least
not in the way perceived by Westerners. Those living under oppressive conditions are quite likely to want to better their human rights
but might have a very different idea about what those rights are and
which rights should be prioritized. Additionally, outsiders might be
attempting to further the interests of those in need in ways that the
latter defines them but be interfering in a manner that the recipient
finds inefficient or even harmful. Western-based NGOs that attempt to

defend the interests of underage workers being subjected to slave-like factory conditions have pursued policies that have left the children jobless, homeless, and forced into an even more dangerous situation on the streets. Sometimes those suffering under oppression welcome economic sanctions as a way to pressure their governments to enact serious political reforms, but at other times they have asserted that such sanctions do more harm than good and that other kinds of interventions are preferable. In these situations, acts of "solidarity" can feel demeaning and disrespectful.

Paternalism is also not synonymous with persuasion. Paternalism is the substitution of one person's judgment for another. Persuasion suggests that there has not been the forced substitution but rather the attempt to offer reasons, evidence, and arguments to convince another person to decide for herself, based on the merits of the case, to alter her direction.[46] Persuasion typically includes most, if not all, of the following elements: a belief that another is thinking or acting in a wrong-headed manner; the attempt to steer them in a different direction because of a concern for their welfare; an approach that communicates respect for the other's autonomy and capacity for making an informed decision; the avoidance of coercion; and the right of refusal by the person being persuaded. Our emotions often sensitize us to the difference between persuasion and paternalism. When someone engages in genuine acts of persuasion, I feel as if they have convinced me to change my mind for my own good, they have recognized my dignity, autonomy, and ability to judge for myself what is in my best interest.

A critical way in which solidarity and persuasion differ from paternalism is that the former two are presumably reflective of relations of (relative) equality and not relations of hierarchy. However, there are relations of hierarchy that generate superordinate and subordinate positions which nevertheless might not qualify as paternalism. Specifically, there are instances when an actor has voluntarily delegated the authority to another to act in ways that the authority

---

[46] George Tsai, "Rational Persuasion as Paternalism," *Philosophy & Public Affairs* 42, 1 (2014): 79. Tsai's assertion is not that all forms of persuasion count as paternalism, but rather that "not all instances of rational persuasion are morally on a par," and that some acts of persuasion exhibit paternalism because they are guided by a distrust of someone's ability to make a reasonable judgment and might, in the process, intrude on someone's agency.

believes is in the best interest of the actor in the subordinate position. Why would anyone do such a thing? Presumably because she
believes that it is in her best interest to enter into an arrangement
where another actor has the authority to restrict or guide her choices
in the future. We might do so when experiencing collective action
problems, a self-awareness that we are sacrificing long-term gains
for immediate gratification, or to improve our welfare by seeking
out another's assistance. For instance, William Talbott distinguishes
between legal paternalism, which "overrules the target population's
judgment about what is good for them," and a legal solution to a collective action problem, which "gives effect to the target population's
judgments about what is good for them by bringing about an overall
outcome they generally regard as better for them than the outcome
that would eventuate if there was no law."[47] To perform this welfare-
enhancing role, the agent must be relatively autonomous from the
(most powerful) members. Critical to this arrangement working out
the way the principals imagined, of course, is that the decision to
yield some authority is truly a result of consent and not coercion,
the agent or institution is truly interested in acting in the best interests of the principals, and the transfer of authority is temporary or
can be retrieved if the principal decides that the agent or institution
is pursuing an alternative agenda that is not in her best interests.
Institutionalist and principal-agent approaches capture this logic
and have been used to understand why states might voluntarily sur-
render some part of their sovereignty to a third party. For instance,
David Lake's influential writings on international governance adopt
a rationalist, voluntary framework to argue that many relations of
hierarchy are, in fact, the result of a consensual agreement between
the inferior and superior party.[48]

An emerging – and controversial – argument both labels these
sorts of institutional arrangements as paternalistic and applauds
their presence. The argument runs as follows. It begins with a simple
question: what if individuals do not have stable preferences, or there
are factors that interfere with a rational decision-making process?

---

[47] Talbott, *Human Rights and Human Well-Being*, 277 (italics in original).
[48] David A. Lake, *Hierarchy in International Relations* (Ithaca: Cornell University
Press, 2011). Also see Alexander Cooley, *The Logics of Hierarchy: The
Organization of Empires, States, and Military Occupations* (Ithaca: Cornell
University Press, 2008).

Psychology, experimental economics, and behavioral economics offer considerable empirical evidence that individuals do not make choices as economic textbooks portray. There are various factors that might lead to impaired choice: preferences over options can be shaped by framing, preferences can be affected by individuals' psychological state at the moment preferences are expressed, preferences might be affected by irrelevant information, and preferences might be different if experts had a chance to present the information.[49]

If so, then the question is not whether there are factors that interfere in an actor's choice, but whether those factors can and should be influenced by a third party to produce an outcome that is prospectively closer to the interests of the actor and Pareto-improving. This role can be played by institutions.[50] In this spirit, Robert Thaler and Cass Sunstein advocate for "libertarian paternalism."[51] Institutions are

---

[49] See Tversky and Kahneman, "The Framing of Decisions and the Psychology of Choice"; Tversky and Kahneman, "Judgment under Uncertainty." The demand side of paternalism, though, might be generated more by those who believe that they already demonstrate some discipline and that those who are lacking such discipline need the extra help. Sofie Kragh Pederson, Alexander Koch, and Julia Nafziger, "Who Wants Paternalism?" *Bulletin of Economic Research* 66, 1 (2014): S147–S166.

[50] Cass R. Sunstein, "Behavioral Economics and Paternalism," *The Yale Law Journal* 122, 7 (2013): 1826–99; Neil Levy, "Forced to be Free? Increasing Patient Autonomy by Constraining it," *Journal of Medical Ethics* 40, 5 (2014): 293–300.

[51] See Cass R. Sunstein and Robert H. Thaler, "Libertarian Paternalism Is Not an Oxymoron," *The University of Chicago Law Review* 70, 4 (2003): 1159–202; Robert H. Thaler and Cass R. Sunstein, *Nudge: Improving Decisions About Health, Wealth, and Happiness* (New Haven: Yale University Press, 2008); Richard H. Thaler and Cass R. Sunstein, "Libertarian Paternalism," *American Economic Review* 93, 2 (2003): 175–9; Cass Sunstein, "Preferences, Paternalism, and Liberty," *Royal Institute of Philosophy Supplement* 59 (2006): 233–64; Shlomo Cohen, "Nudging and Informed Consent," *American Journal of Bioethics* 13, 6 (2013): 3–11; Mark Sagoff, "Trust versus Paternalism," *American Journal of Bioethics* 13, 6 (2013): 20–1; Mozaffar Qizilbash, "Sudgen's Critique of Sen's Capability Approach and the Dangers of Libertarian Paternalism," *International Review of Economics* 58, 1 (2011): 21–42; Sigal Ben-Porath, *Tough Choices: Structured Paternalism and the Landscape of Choice* (Princeton: Princeton University Press, 2010); Adam Oliver, "Nudging, Shoving, and Budging: Behavioral Economic Informed Policy," *Public Administration* 93, 3 (2015): 700–14; Riccardo Rebonato, "A Critical Assessment of Libertarian Paternalism," *Journal of Consumer Policy* 37 (2014): 357–96; Martin Binder and Leonhard Lades, "Autonomy-Enhancing Paternalism," *Kyklos* 68 (2015): 3–27.

supposed to help "nudge" people to make choices that are good for themselves and good for society. As they forthrightly state:

> The paternalistic aspect consists in the claim that it is legitimate for private and public institutions to attempt to influence people's choices and preferences, even when third-party effects are absent. In other words, we argue for self-conscious efforts, by private and public institutions, to steer people's choices in directions that will improve their own welfare. In our understanding, a policy therefore counts as "paternalistic" if it attempts to influence the choices of affected parties in a way that will make choosers better off.[52]

They call their approach "libertarian paternalism" because it "preserves the freedom of choice but ... encourages both private and public institutions to steer people in directions that will promote their own welfare."[53] A critical part of their defense of preserving freedom of choice is the assumption that these arrangements are being made in a liberal, democratic context, in which the political institutions have significant legitimacy and the "planners" called to guide decisions are accountable to its citizens. However, these conditions do not exist in international governance, thereby undermining its easy application to global affairs.

What solidarity, persuasion, and voluntary self-binding all share is an interest in the needs of the target and the use of non-coercive tools to change its behavior. However, the moment we suspect that one's motives are not as benign or altruistic as they are presented to be, then we have moved away from paternalism and into domination. Many scholars object to the very possibility of paternalism on the grounds that actors care about no one but themselves. This is a powerful critique. Actors are constantly presenting their private interests as beneficial to others and in the public interest.[54] And, even if actors sincerely believe that they are intervening for the benefit of others, they might be ignorant of either their true motives or how their actions serve the

---

[52] Cass R. Sunstein and Robert H. Thaler, "Libertarian Paternalism Is Not an Oxymoron," *The University of Chicago Law Review* 70, 4 (2003): 1162.

[53] *Ibid.*, 1201. Also see Ben-Porath, *Tough Choices*; Sarah Conly, *Against Autonomy: Justifying Coercive Paternalism* (Cambridge: Cambridge University Press, 2013).

[54] Yet the central issue is not whether individuals understand their "true" motives, or even whether acts of caring might advance the interests of others; instead, it is whether actors are motivated by the sincere desire to aid another.

interests of the powerful. The powerful typically delude themselves into believing that they know what is best for everyone. We should be worried whenever actors become convinced of their benevolence. In this view, the liberal empires of the nineteenth century were not paternalists but pure imperialists. To call them paternalists is to give them too much credit.

Overview

Paternalism in humanitarian governance and world affairs does not have a single persona but rather has multiple personalities. As I noted earlier, we do not adopt a common definition of paternalism. Indeed, many of the contributors distinguish their approach from mine or those adopted by others in the volume. What might be a problem I prefer to see as a virtue. We are all interested in the relationship between care and control. Although what counts as care is largely left unexplored, what truly distinguishes the chapters is how they understand the workings of power, both conceptually and historically. The variation is evident throughout the chapters, though the contrast is starkest and most explicit between Richardson and Fassin. Whether one is preferable to another is dependent not only on epistemological commitments but also on the puzzle that demands solving and the ethical principle that has been transgressed. This volume does not intend to settle this conceptual debate, only to make it apparent.

The contributors are interested in different formulations and dimensions of the social relations of paternalism. Without belaboring the earlier discussion, these social relations of paternalism have several defining elements that are the bones for all the chapters. At base, they recognize paternalism as primarily relational and hierarchical. This relational and hierarchical feature is often constituted by pre-existing structures and authority relations that distribute different roles with differential social capacities. In turn, these structures generate positions of superiority and inferiority. The chapters identify various structures and relations of superiority and inferiority – civilizational, class, gender, epistemic, and discourses of humanity. In many cases there is not one defining structure but several that overlap and are layered, sometimes congruent but at other times discordant. Relatedly, these authority structures can help identify the reasons why those in the superordinate position believe that they are superior to those who are deemed inferior, and that the former have a duty to help the latter. How the superior come to "know" that the inferior are truly unable to act in their own best interest comes from one of three origins: specific acts, categories of kinds, and generalized circumstances. The recognition of these deficits and capacity for self-harm by another both provides the impulse to intervene *and* helps to reinforce these relations of superiority and inferiority. One effect of the practices of care is to reproduce these pre-existing relations of inequality. However, many of the chapters also note that such intrusions can stir the paternalized to resist not just the practice of care but the very presumption that they are incapable of making choices for themselves. The chapters offer a variety of perspectives on these aspects of paternalism beyond borders.

Chapters 1 and 2 are paired because they make explicit appeals to alternative analytical and interpretive approaches to paternalism. Neither chapter makes the case that one approach is right and the other is wrong based on evidence, convention, common usage, or consensus opinion among scholars; instead, each refers to how different epistemological commitments open and close the door to different features of the intersection of care and control that should or should not be a matter of concern. In Chapter 1, Henry Richardson calls for a narrow definition. In his view, paternalism is thrown around casually and carelessly, resulting in category errors and unfair accusations. Drawing from Anglo-American moral philosophy and Dworkin's classic definition, he argues that true paternalism "combines two distinct morally problematic features: that of intervening illegitimately with the liberty of others and the arrogance or highhandedness of assuming that the others need help pursuing their own good." Such cases of paternalism, Richardson claims, are relatively rare, especially when compared to cases of "aggravated paternalism," which fails or refuses to consult with others about what they believe is good for them. If we distinguish true from aggravated paternalism, according to him, then we will discover that humanitarian assistance has various other vices that are either in or outside the ballpark of paternalism.

Analytical distinctions and precision, Richardson insists, are absolutely necessary to normative assessment. If everything is called paternalistic, then it loses its meaning and ability to capture what we find offensive about various kinds of well-meaning interventions. In this spirit, Richardson advocates liberal political theory's emphasis on liberty limitation. Interventions can be offensive, wrong, and misguided for lots of reasons, but we should reserve paternalism for well-meaning interventions that are intended to limit the liberty of another for their own good. Using this liberty-constraining property as a defining feature of paternalism, Richardson proceeds to run through various acts of well-meaning interventions that are often labelled paternalistic, from individual attempts to monitor another's diet for their own good to medical ethics at home and abroad, to the US foreign assistance program to reduce HIV/AIDS, to humanitarian assistance more generally.

In Chapter 2, Didier Fassin uses Western states' asylum policies to demonstrate the utility of an interpretivist approach and its ability to expose features of paternalism that might otherwise go undetected. In contrast to Richardson's method of stipulating a definition a priori and then using that definition to distinguish what does and does not count as paternalism, Fassin argues for a more inductive approach that is grounded in actual practices. The advantage of this method, according to Fassin, is that it might unearth aspects of the relationship between care and control that might otherwise remain hidden. He demonstrates the insights of interpretivist approaches in the curious case of asylum law. It is "curious" for various reasons, though mainly because it does not fit in the "ballpark of paternalism" because this is a case of a convergence of interests – asylum requests are exactly that, requests by the nominally weaker party for assistance from the nominally stronger party. It is an odd case in this volume for the additional reason that the other chapters concern the physical crossing of a border in order to provide care and protection for those who reside in another country. Yet asylum law concerns protection for those who have crossed borders to seek protection.

So precisely how is asylum law an instance of paternalism? In contrast to Richardson who argues that paternalism is dependent on liberty-limiting action, Fassin counters that it is best seen as an instance of domination because asylum policy is "historically inscribed in asymmetrical international relations – between colonizers and colonized, the North and the South, the West and the rest." In other words, there is a prior existence of hierarchical relations in which this form of domination (as protection) occurs. In turn, practices of paternalism help to reproduce these existing hierarchies. Fassin makes these observations in the case of the shift in asylum policy from "traditional political grounds to cultural differences constructed as civilizational clashes." Specifically, whereas once asylum was granted to those who

faced persecution by the state because of political beliefs, in France
(and elsewhere) it has become based on gender and sexuality and the
desire to protect women from female circumcision, forced marriage,
and trafficking, and gays from state and community-based violence.
Among the effects of this form of generosity, Fassin argues that it "radicalizes the representation of un-civilized and non-democratic others,"
and it valorizes the superiority of the West. In other words, asylum
policy is both an effect and a cause of enduring hierarchies that instantiate a moral superiority by the West.

The following two chapters can be read as dueling perspectives on
the question of whether or not there has been a change in the kind
of paternalism that prevails in the international liberal order. In
Chapter 3 John Hobson argues that paternalism is a constant feature
of an international liberal order, beginning in the early nineteenth century and continuing through today's post-Cold War order. By emphasizing continuity rather than change, Hobson makes several critical
observations. First, he identifies eight elements of paternalism that he
asserts have been enduring features of the international liberal order,
though perhaps the most fundamental is a civilizational discourse.
Nineteenth-century liberal interventions explicitly referred to civilizational categories, sometimes based on scientific racism but always
on "institutional/cultural" factors that use institutional categories to
distinguish the rational and civilized from the irrational and uncivilized societies. In general, there is a common "paternalist-Eurocentric
monism rather than a 'tolerant' cultural pluralism" in the liberal
international order.

Second, in contrast to the belief that liberalism breeds tolerance and
a live-and-let-live attitude, the Eurocentric and civilizational properties of the liberal order generate a desire to intervene in, and transform, the uncivilized South. In other words, discourses of civilization
can generate both the authority and duty to intervene. Much of liberal international relations theory, much like the practices of liberal
empires in the nineteenth century, treats the non-Western world as
not yet possessing the reason and rationality necessary for deserving
long-term autonomy, and Western peoples as having a duty to create
what does not exist. In the process, liberal internationalism necessarily
discards the principle of consent and only a liberal West can properly
see into the future of non-Western societies, and only it can deliver
such societies to the future promised land of liberal freedom. Third,
these interventions, often justified on the basis of generosity, help to

reproduce discourses of superiority and inferiority, a point also made by Fassin. Consequently, Hobson suggests that the growing "duty to care" that accompanies the West's sense of goodness, in fact, generates a lack of humility and a continued sense of its own status as a standard bearer of universal values.

In contrast to John Hobson's claim that the core features of global paternalism are basically the same as they always have been, David Chandler argues in Chapter 4 that global paternalism has shifted from an old to a new school. Traditionally, paternalistically influenced international policies were based on hierarchical assumptions of capacities or competences and the direct interference by one country in the affairs of another. According to Chandler, in this century there has been the rise of a "new" paternalism, which is less about direct intervention in another country's affairs and more about the desire to reform the international institutional context (both formal and informal) – essentially to work on Western responsibility for causing problems. This paternalism does not take the form of Western superiority or of imposing knowing guidelines or rules in order to transform the subjects of other societies but seeks instead to work on Western/international interactions with non-Western states and societies to facilitate or enable local "bottom-up" solutions to problems.

Moreover, this paternalism blames the Western-constructed international regimes of regulation for indirectly institutionalizing inequalities and a lack of rights and seeks to overcome these international institutional barriers to development, democracy, and peace. In the absence of international reforms, it is held that power relations – the needs of Western big business elites, for example – reinforce inequalities institutionally, preventing alternative, more sustainable, or organic solutions. The new international paternalism can be seen in the field of international law, in critiques of the sovereignty regime, in the work of new institutionalist economists, and in moral philosophy. In these approaches, traditional paternalist understandings are seemingly rejected. However, liberation or moral improvement is still the task of Western agents and consumers.

The remaining four chapters look at specific contemporary instances of humanitarian governance, bringing into relief the myriad structures and discourses of inequality that create relations of superiority and inferiority, how different kinds of categories of actors, actions, and circumstances trigger an imperative or duty to intervene for the good of others, and whether and how it is possible for the paternalized to resist or change the terms of the benevolence. In Chapter 5, Séverine Autesserre draws on many years of fieldwork in conflict zones to dissect the paternalism in international peacebuilding. The politics of need and the politics of knowledge, she argues, are the root causes. Indeed, as she describes it, paternalism seems to be an occupational hazard of all peacebuilding. It begins with the observation that populations are in need because they are unable to help themselves, and a major reason why they cannot help themselves is because they lack the necessary skills, resources, expertise, and capacities. Enter the peacebuilders who possess what local populations lack. Consequently, peacebuilders occupy a position of superiority and local populations a position of inferiority, and peacebuilders often radiate the arrogance of superiority. In short, the discourse of peacebuilding first necessitates and legitimates interference, and second, produces a discourse of care that generates hierarchies between outsiders and locals.

Local populations, Autesserre continues, do not enjoy either being in this position of inferiority or suffering the quasi-colonialist attitude of the peacebuilders. In response, they regularly resist, challenge, or reject the international programs that are meant to help them. Importantly, then, local populations are not resisting the "liberal" values of peacebuilders per se, because many are quite accepting of their various programs and assistance activities. Instead, they are resisting because they refuse the implicit indignity that comes with them. At times, peacebuilders do, in fact, break the cycle of paternalism, often under the rubric of participation and partnership. However, three main obstacles – the role of accountability structures, the dilemma that international interveners face, and the detrimental byproducts of the politics of knowledge at work in the peacebuilding field – make it particularly difficult to change and end these widespread practices.

In Chapter 6 Aisling Swaine provides a fascinating reflection on her life as part of the "gender police" in UN peacekeeping and peacebuilding operations in Darfur and other hot spots around the world. One of the book's arguments is that the concept of paternalism forces us to acknowledge the nearly inherent contradictions that are contained in practices of care, and Swaine's chapter provocatively provides an insider's account of such tensions as she attempts to wrestle with her involvement in the protection of women in peace operations. She opens with an account of why UN officials neglected the basic security concerns of women in the Darfur refugee camps, and how the women were able to stage a protest that successfully forced UN officials to take into account their concerns.

Before the reader gets too comfortable, though, Swaine quickly acknowledges this was a rare event in her experience, indicting not just the paternalism of peacebuilding but also her own. Based on her experiences and autocritiques, Swaine points to two dominant discourses that generate relations of superiority and inferiority – gender and knowledge. There is little question that a male-dominated peacebuilding profession assumes that women are incapable of knowing how to best protect themselves. In this respect, she adds an important gender dimension to the paternalism in peacebuilding observed by Autesserre. Yet, Swaine confesses to the uncomfortable realization that her paternalism owes less to gender than it does to the belief in her superior knowledge, training, and expertise. In general, Swaine highlights how the presence of overlapping discourses of race, nationality, knowledge, and gender produce the view that refugee women are unable to know or act in their best interests. But beliefs of superiority and inferiority do not necessarily translate into demands to do something. She argues that aid workers such as herself are animated not just by discourses of inequality that operate behind their backs but also by the painful reality that there are vulnerable populations that *do* need help. As she puts it, "I am compelled to emphasize that, in the context of many humanitarian settings, the concept of 'care' often falls short of fully capturing the magnitude of the feelings experienced by an aid worker faced with what typically features in crises today ... These contexts are acute. They are intense. The events and harms experienced by fellow human beings are often beyond many of our imaginations." These are circumstances that demand a response.

By recognizing the presence of pre-existing hierarchies that generate feelings of superiority *and* the very real desire to help those in desperate circumstances, Swaine must confront the very difficult question: Can paternalism be excused or perhaps even condoned? As a former aid worker and UN official, she acknowledges that, under certain conditions, outsiders must use their judgment when deciding to help others. Assuming that paternalism is a sometimes-desirable trait in professions of care, what sorts of constraints should be put on them? As she states, there is no stable compromise but rather a set of mental and institutional checks that should be in place to give outsiders some discretion without risking a runaway paternalism. But, her experiences

and the case of women's security suggest that there are strong tendencies to presume that women simply lack the capacity to know what is
in their best interests, which justifies not simply overriding their views
but not even bothering to solicit them.

In Chapter 7, Sally Engle Merry and Vibhuti Ramachandran explore
a central issue in contemporary paternalism – the meaning and sali-
ence of consent. Consent is a critical issue for a wide range of human
rights violations, which are generally understood as abuses to which
the person has not consented. Yet, in practice, determining when a person consents is hardly straightforward, which means that it is equally
unclear when human rights policies step over the line into paternalism. This conundrum is central to the current campaign against sex
trafficking, and this chapter demonstrates the construction of institutional and legal categories that are more or less open to the necessity
of consent.

Sex trafficking is generally defined as recruitment to exploitative
labor without consent, yet advocates differ about whether sex work
is always akin to slavery or whether it is possible to consent to it. All
choices are made under constraints, especially for those who have
few choices. Determining consent is central to defining a human
rights violation, but deciding whether a person has consented is difficult since consent ranges along a continuum from explicit choice to
habitual obedience, duty, or moral obligation. Moreover, the activists that define human rights violations differ in their willingness
to accept consent as vitiating the violation. In other words, some
activists are more willing to cross the line into paternalism than are
others.

In Chapter 8, Stephen Hopgood examines the case of female genital mutilation/cutting (FGM/C). On the face of it, there is no cultural practice more demanding of international paternalism than
FGM/C. Much international advocacy makes the story a simple one
of barbarism versus enlightenment. Certain acts are just wrong and
cannot be justified or consented to. Yet, as Hopgood notes, there are
two competing authorities with two competing beliefs about what is
in the best interests of the child and insist that they are motivated by
an ethics of care. Drawing from discourses of natural law and civilization, international activists claim to be attempting to eradicate
a practice that they deem inhumane and violating the fundamental

rights of a child who is unable to give consent. Drawing from their parental authority, parents, and mainly mothers and grandmothers, defend a practice that they believe will best enable the girl to become part of society and make her eligible for marriage. For international activists who are convinced of the rightness of their position, there is no debate to be had over the possible morality of the practice. Instead, the only debate is over strategy to end the practice: between a "hard" paternalism that is willing to use coercion and the law versus a "soft" paternalism that attempts to persuade parents and communities.

Through an historical analysis that compares colonial and post-colonial interventions, Hopgood traces the continuities in, and changes that have occurred over, the forms of interventions adopted by international activists. He observes that the underlying discourses used to motivate and justify intervention have remained largely the same; missionaries of the nineteenth century drew from religious and civilizational discourses while modern human rights activists draw from religious, secular, and civilizational discourses. The principal change in practices of paternalism revolves around the strategies for cultural change. Whereas during colonialism missionaries and reformers often relied on coercion, contemporary activists have shifted toward tools of persuasion that are intended to change the attitudes of parents and communities. Although the shift from hard to soft paternalism might suggest a less ambitious set of goals, Hopgood argues that this soft paternalism is embedded in a broader movement that is productive of a liberal subject. In other words, the goal is not just to banish a practice viewed as barbaric, but also to inculcate a broader acceptance of the principle that individuals should be freed from tradition and have a *right* to make claims against the state, society, and parents.

In Chapter 9 Ilana Feldman uses the Palestinian refugee experience of living as an object of humanitarian governance for nearly seventy years to explore the complexities of "actually-existing" paternalism. The Palestinian experience reveals the existence of a network of relations that are productive of, and produced by, a set of paternalistic practices. Similar to other chapters, Feldman notes the presence of multiple, nested, and overlapping hierarchies, including geopolitics, patriarchy, and, primarily, humanitarian assistance. And just like those

who are on the giving end of paternalism, those on the receiving end
have very mixed feelings about humanitarian assistance. On the one
hand, such assistance is both needed and signifies that the international community has an obligation to the Palestinians. On the other
hand, the international community sees such assistance as a symbol of
its generosity and this assistance often reinforces the Palestinian position
of powerlessness.

But Palestinians are not just effects of practices, their experiences
and awareness of the disempowerment that accompanies these forms
of paternalism lead them to try to resist. Similar to Autesserre's chapter on peacebuilding, Feldman shifts our attention from the practices
of paternalism to their reception. Specifically, Palestinian refugees
perceive these hierarchical relationships as deeply paternalistic, and
importantly, the acceptance of aid is seen as buying into the aid-giver's
existing perceptions that they are weak, dependent, and lacking in
agency. In protest and resistance, Palestinians often seek to change
humanitarianism itself and alter the terms of the relationship between
the "giver" and the "recipient." In some cases Palestinians simply
refuse aid. In others they attempt to skirt the rules of such acceptance and proactively attempt to produce a qualitatively different kind
of engagement in situations of need. How successful are these practices of resistance? "None of them are able to undo the hierarchies
of humanitarian intervention or remove the paternalism from this
enterprise," Feldman writes. "But they also confirm that is possible
to have an effect on the operations of humanitarianism, to introduce
limits to its paternalism, and to redirect certain practices." Regardless
of whether they are successful or not, the very act of refusal exposes
the paternalism in humanitarianism.

The Conclusion offers a retrospective of some of the general findings of the contributions and prospective thoughts on how this
conversation might evolve. It proceeds in two parts. The first part
examines the historical-institutional variation of global paternalism,
suggests that paternalism comes in different flavors, proposes that
trends in global paternalism are migrating from a strong to a weak
variety, and that global structures of liberalism and rationalism are
responsible for this evolution. The second part moves from the analytical and historical to the normative, putting front and center the
question of whether paternalism can be defended. Although most
of the contributors are uniformly critical of paternalism, few will

go so far as to suggest that paternalism is a categorical sin. Indeed, they acknowledge that there are times when paternalism might be defensible. What might be some of those conditions, and what kinds of mechanisms can be developed to ensure that paternalism does not degenerate into despotism?

PART I

The Boundaries of Paternalism

1 | Only in the Ballpark of Paternalism: Arrogance and Liberty-Limitation in International Humanitarian Aid

HENRY S. RICHARDSON

I propose to concentrate on international humanitarian assistance that really lives up to its name. Accordingly, I will be confining my attention to well-meaning international interventions. To be sure, some interventions carried out under the banner of alleged humanitarian assistance are really attempts to grab power or to pursue national or institutional interests. Such interventions are not worthy of the name "humanitarian assistance." I will limit my attention to the well-meaning cases. To be sure, as we will see, those who mean well may operate with blinkered or parochial or condescending ideas about what would assist others; but they do mean well, unlike those who use the appearance of humanitarianism to further their narrow self-interest. I will also limit my attention to interventions. Some well-meaning attempts to influence international affairs should not be counted as interventions. For example, offering asylum to people overseas because they seem to need exit from where they are, though intended to influence their situation, does not seem to interfere with them or with the nation in which they live.[1] Again, I propose to focus my attention on well-meaning international interventions, of which international humanitarian assistance, properly so-called, is a special case.

Although the kind of example just given would complicate any analysis, an intervention is an action intended to alter another's life or activities. Since I will be focusing on interventions, I will not be directly concerning myself with attitudes such as arrogance or structural

[1] I owe this point to Didier Fassin and, in this relatively strong formulation, to Ilana Feldman.

I am grateful to the late Alan Wertheimer for helpful comments on an early draft and to my co-participants in the workshop on International Paternalism organized at George Washington University, October 4–5, 2013, by Michael N. Barnett, for stimulating and useful discussion.

problems such as an absence of consultation mechanisms, except insofar as these give rise to problematic actions. Nonetheless, since I will
analyze paternalism as a kind of action that is taken from a certain
attitude, my account will help pinpoint relevant attitudes; and since
structural problems can often be seen to tend to give rise to objec-
tionable actions, my account could also indirectly help indicate what
structural problems exacerbate or give rise to paternalist interventions.

Those engaged in international humanitarian assistance have become
used to being called paternalistic – not only by those they are intend-
ing to aid but also by various third-party commentators. This is hardly
a neutral description. As Michael N. Barnett observes, "[W]hereas in
the nineteenth century being called a paternalist was not necessarily
an insult, today it is."[2] No doubt this is in part because nowadays it is
frowned upon to set oneself up *in loco parentis* in relation to people elsewhere in the world.[3] For this sort of reason, it is not uncommon to find
the charge of paternalism bundled with charges of neocolonialism and
neoimperialism.[4]

In cases where the banner of humanitarian assistance is a mask for
the narrow interests of the superpowers, the latter two of these charges
will be apt. Perhaps paradoxically, however, the charge of paternalism
will not be. The paternalism charge, understood as a morally important and distinctive one, well fits only cases of well-meaning interventions. Or so I will argue. It will be my main thesis that in the context of
international humanitarian assistance truly paternalistic interventions
are quite rare. Yet I cannot leave things there, for I must explain why,
despite this fact, the charge of paternalism is so common in this arena.
Accordingly, I will explain that there are other vices in the ballpark
of paternalism – vices that are much more common in international

[2] Michael N. Barnett, *Empire of Humanity: A History of Humanitarianism*
(Ithaca: Cornell University Press, 2013), 233.
[3] Distinguishing the two stereotypical parents, one might reasonably pursue an
account of paternalism that took its cue from the difference between standing
as a father to someone, inscribed in the term's etymology, and standing as a
mother to someone. That might lead one to see the former in terms of bullying
and the latter in terms of care. On the approach I take here, by contrast,
I suggest understanding paternalism as a case of morally fraught care – care
that, because it limits someone's liberty for his or her own good, requires a
special justification.
[4] See, for example, Séverine Autesserre, *The Trouble with the Congo: Local
Violence and the Failure of International Peacebuilding* (Cambridge: Cambridge
University Press, 2010), 97.

humanitarian assistance than true paternalism – that do properly call for criticism: high-handedness, arrogance, condescension, and parochial understandings. If I am right, the critics are using the term "paternalism" too loosely. To be sure, I do not ultimately care about how this word ought to be used; what matters, as I will argue, is that the common use of this word fails to mark morally important distinctions, lumping together phenomena of quite different moral significance. Not all criticizable wrongdoings are equally bad or bad in the same way. I take it that paternalism is a wrong-making feature, but one that, given an adequate and sound justification, can be overridden. To be frank, however, sometimes when humanitarian interventions are criticized as "paternalist," I struggle to find any even potentially wrong-making feature in them, despite having benefited on this score from the insights of my fellow contributors to this volume. The reason for caring about the use of the term "paternalism" in this context, then, is twofold. First, it is important to mark out a category that is intelligibly morally criticizable in a way that is worthy of this distinctive label. Second, it is important to recognize that there are principled distinctions to be drawn between core cases of paternalism and peripheral ones. As I proceed, addressing the first of these tasks will put us in a position to carry out the second.

Here is a preview: What I will call *true paternalism* combines two distinct morally problematic features: illegitimately intervening with the liberty of others and arrogantly or high-handedly assuming that the others need help in pursuing their own good. Beyond this, what we might call *aggravated paternalism* involves an additional vice: that of condescendingly failing or refusing to consult with the others about how they understand what is good for them. Because it identifies a distinctively difficult to justify combination of morally troubling features, "paternalism" is thus a valuable label. Other, less confounding labels are readily available for true paternalism's cousins.

It is not only in context of international humanitarian assistance that "paternalism" has lately come to be used quite loosely. In the United States, the word has been used more and more broadly as domestic politics tilts ever more strongly against the dreaded, so-called "nanny state." For example, even a columnist as intelligent as David Brooks was recently found writing about nudges that encourage organ donation as if they were paternalistic.[5] I fear that his reasoning may have been

[5] David Brooks, "The Nudge Debate," *New York Times*, August 8, 2013, op-ed page.

as follows: Thaler and Sunstein talk about paternalism in connection
with nudges; an organ-donation opt-out default is a nudge; therefore,
it is paternalistic.[6] But paternalism, as had been agreed, involves limiting someone's liberty for that person's own good. Even if setting up
drivers' licenses with opt-out provisions for organ donation is liberty-
limiting – which I doubt – it is patently not done for the benefit of the
drivers in question, who will be dead by the time they donate their
organs. It is instead done for the benefit of the many other people
in need of organs. Thus, the term "paternalism" is adrift in popular
discourse. So that I can be clear about where I'm coming from, let me
bring the term back to a proper mooring.

In selecting this point of anchor, I take my bearings from discussions of paternalism in Anglo-American moral philosophy. I believe
that I hear elements of this understanding of "paternalism" in discussions of paternalism in the context of international humanitarian aid,
including in many of the contributions to this volume: To repeat, however, I do not mean to legislate how the meaning of "paternalism" is to
be understood, whether on the basis of some supposed abstract grasp
of Platonic ideas or in any other way. Again, what moves me here is the
importance of marking moral distinctions, for the relevance of which
I will argue, in part by appeal to cases. In getting started, however, it
seems useful to start out with how the term "paternalism" has been
rigorously understood in at least one tradition of discourse.

Consider Gerald Dworkin's influential gloss of what paternalism is:

> By paternalism I shall understand roughly the interference with a person's
> liberty of action justified by reasons referring exclusively to the welfare,
> good, happiness, needs, interests or values of the person being coerced.[7]

An "interference," here, is an intervention that violates, nullifies,
or attempts to remove a right. As Dworkin immediately goes on to
note, "it is not easy to find 'pure' examples of paternalistic interferences." A hackneyed purported example is that of a law mandating the

---

[6] Cf. Richard H. Thaler and Cass R. Sunstein, *Nudge: Improving Decisions
about Health, Wealth, and Happiness* (New York: Penguin, 2009). I come to
another possibility, below, which involves broadening the standard definition
of "paternalism" to extend it to include measures that are justified solely by
getting people to fulfill their imperfect duty of helping others.
[7] Gerald Dworkin, "Paternalism," *Monist* (1972): 64–84, 65.

wearing of seatbelts. This law definitely interferes with people's liberty of action, in a sense that I shall explore; and it is surely to be justified by reasons appealing to the welfare and interests of the drivers whose liberty it limits. But is the justification of the policy one that refers *exclusively* to the welfare and interests of the drivers? This is doubtful, for as is well known, part of the justification has to do with the costs imposed on the health-care system – and so on other people besides drivers – by emergency rooms' having to deal with beltless drivers who end up in accidents. If other people's interests in fact enter into the justification of the policy, even alongside considerations referring to the good of the person whose liberty is interfered with, then – according to Dworkin's gloss – that policy is not paternalistic.

Some distinguish sharply between characterizing policies or authoritative determinations as paternalistic, on the one hand, and characterizing actions as paternalistic solely on the basis of their motive, on the other. In line with Dworkin's gloss and the example just discussed, I suggest that these two elements need to be combined. Paternalistic action is a liberty-limiting action – so, often a policy or authoritative determination – that is motivated in a certain way. The characterization of an interference as "justified" in a certain way is not best interpreted as referring to some objective catalogue of the reasons that might be cited by some third party to rationalize the interfering action; rather, it is a reference to the reasons that the interfering agent, reasonably and without self-deception, actually acted upon, taking those reasons as his or her basis for interfering.[8] What matters, for these purposes, is what these reasons actually are, not what the interfering agent says they are.

The philosophical inspiration for much contemporary writing about paternalism is John Stuart Mill's harm principle. Abbreviating it so as to emphasize the continuity with Dworkin's gloss of paternalism, and interpolating an explanatory gloss, what the harm principle says is that "The sole end for which mankind are warranted, individually or

---

[8] I will come back to the non-self-deception condition below. With regard to reasonableness, consider the cases of forced conversions in the Spanish Inquisition. While some of these may have been instances of torture in which the perpetrators thought they were acting for the sake of the victims' good, this belief may not have been reasonable. Assuming that it was not, we should not classify such cases as cases of mere paternalism. Rather, they were (on this assumption) cases of gross human rights violations.

collectively, in interfering with the liberty of action of any of their number ... is to prevent harm to others." Others, that is, besides the person whose liberty of action is interfered with. Mill continues, writing that the interferee's "own good, either physical or moral, is not a sufficient warrant."[9] We can see that Dworkin's gloss of paternalism picks up both on the type of reason Mill accepts as justifying an interference with liberty and on Mill's insistence that benefiting the person interfered with is an insufficient reason. We can also see that Dworkin echoes the important language about "liberty of action."

Like seatbelt laws, even quite coercive measures taken in international settings partly for the benefit of those coerced will generally fail to count as paternalistic on this standard because they, too, will have what Mill would count as an acceptable kind of justification, namely an appeal to the interests or well-being of others. For instance, the UN High Commission on Refugees (UNHCR) might forcibly resettle a group of displaced people in a camp.[10] This will largely be for the benefit of these refugees, no doubt; but the UNHCR's action will also typically take into account the effect on the nations that had been and would be hosting the refugees. Having a large group of refugees assembled at one's border is likely to destabilize the surrounding communities of permanent residents. In cases where forcible relocation is justified also on grounds pertaining to the effects on the hosting territory and on international relations in the relevant area, the forcible relocation is not paternalistic, on Dworkin's gloss. Another possible example is the action of peacekeepers. Peacekeepers sometimes have to take relatively draconian measures to keep order. For instance, they might set up checkpoints around the center of a town, requiring all those who drive into town to show their papers. This limitation on the liberty of the local drivers might be justified in part by protecting the welfare of those very drivers; but it is also justified by protecting the welfare of everyone in the town – presumably by deterring drivers intent on harming the residents.

[9] John Stuart Mill, *Collected Works of John Stuart Mill*, 33 vols., ed. John M. Robson (London and Toronto: Routledge and University of Toronto Press, 1963–1991), Vol. XVIII, 223. The *Collected Works* are available online at the *Online Library of Liberty*.

[10] I take this example, and the one about peacekeepers, from Michael N. Barnett's Introduction to this volume.

A better case of a paternalistic action by peacekeepers might seem to be a nighttime curfew. This forbids everyone from going out at certain times, and so leaves hardly anyone left over as an "other" who might be harmed. But it is only Mill's harm principle that talks about "others." Dworkin's gloss of paternalism does not, instead talking about "reasons referring exclusively to the welfare, good, happiness, needs, interests, or values of the person being coerced." How this applies to the curfew case, in which each of us have our liberty curtailed in order to prevent some of us from harming others of us, may initially seem to be unclear, until we remember that the criminal law has an analogous form. The criminal law forbids *each* of us from engaging in murder and fraud. It does so in part to prevent some of us from murdering or defrauding others of us. From this parallel we should conclude, I suggest, that Mill's wording is defective insofar as it may suggest that the criminal law is unjustified. Such provisions are justified, and can be seen to be justified on the basis of the kind of reason Mill respects: that of preventing some people from harming others. We should respect those kinds of reasons, too, and should not be apologetic about them.

A more serious issue, in connection with international humanitarian aid, is whether it is paternalistic to force people to fulfill their imperfect duties to help others. Perhaps David Brooks had something like this in mind in writing that setting up organ-donation opt-out forms was paternalistic. How could this go? One person's failure to help another implicates reasons grounded in another's interests and well-being. The relevant other person, presumably, would be benefited by the help. It would completely lose touch with the settled meaning of "paternalism" to refuse to recognize that this appeal to a third party's well-being is a non-paternalistic basis for interfering. Furthermore, Mill's harm principle arguably interprets "harm" broadly enough to imply that it is not unjustified to limit people's liberty in order to ensure that they do not fail to help other people. Whether a proper interpretation of Mill implies this has recently been interestingly contested by Piers Turner, who argues that a broad reading of "harm," one that includes failure to benefit, better fits Mill's texts.[11] If, however, contra Turner, Mill's harm principle does rule out liberty-limiting interferences that are justified solely by preventing failure to help others, then, I submit,

---

[11] Piers Norris Turner, "'Harm' and Mill's Harm Principle," *Ethics* 124 (2014): 299–326.

its prohibitions are broader than a ban on paternalism would be. And
in any case, the main point, here, is that if the justification of a policy,
such as instituting organ-donation opt-out defaults, is the benefit for
third parties, then its justification is not based solely in the "welfare,
good, happiness, needs, interests or values" of the person being nudged
or interfered with.

To remain at all close to the core meaning of "paternalism" as
captured by Dworkin's gloss, one might try expanding this list of
interference-centered grounds by adding "dutifulness." Thus, one
might propose, a limitation on someone's liberty of action is paternalistic if its sole justification is to see to it that the person limited does
his duty. So to limit people's liberties certainly does seem moralistic
and perhaps also to be marked by a failure to mind one's own business and a failure to respect others as autonomous beings. Surveying
the world of international humanitarian assistance, however, one has
to conclude that this oddly narrow and moralistic justification is never
the only one offered – if indeed it is offered at all. Instead, the justification is that if you can get people to help others (which they perhaps
ought anyway to do), that will enhance the well-being of those others, or otherwise serve their interests. In other words, the justification offered for seeing to it that people help others is generally one
that refers to the interests of third parties who need help, not just the
moral interests of those whose liberty is being impinged upon. Thus,
the justification offered for humanitarian assistance is generally not a
paternalistic one of this moralistic kind. Not, at any rate, if we stick
with the understanding of "paternalism" provided by Dworkin's gloss
and bolstered by Mill's harm principle.

Shiffrin's Ill-Motivated Broadening

Philosophical probing of a concept such as "paternalism" involves a
delicate back and forth between abstract reasoning and an inductive
sensitivity to cases. Overemphasizing the former pole, and losing touch
with the complexities of the moral phenomena that are revealed by
considering specific cases, Seana Shiffrin has defended a much broader
reading of "paternalism." Unlike Dworkin's reading, Shiffrin's would
classify almost all international humanitarian assistance as paternalistic. Examining why Shiffrin's account goes wrong will at the same
time provide some of the grounds for my own, which is much closer

to Dworkin's. In my view, her broader reading is ill-motivated in itself, and its implications for humanitarian assistance are both misleading and counter-intuitive. Shiffrin has argued for an understanding of paternalism that drops any mention of liberty-limitation. She attempts to support this view by adducing the following hypothetical case:[12]

Suppose B has no valid claim to A's assistance but asks A, an acquaintance, for help building a set of shelves. A refuses, but not because A is too busy or disinclined to help. In fact, A is eager to deploy her carpentry skills. She declines on the ground that B too often asks for assistance to his own detriment: he is failing to learn for himself the skills that he needs, or perhaps he displays unwarranted insecurity in his own skills. If A voices these reasons and persuades B to do it himself, her persuasive efforts and her subsequent abstention would not be paternalist. But were A just to refuse baldly to help for those reasons, then it seems to me that A's omission would be paternalist – even though it is a legitimate exercise of A's autonomy right, violates no distinct right of B's, and does not, in any meaningful way, diminish B's freedom.

Largely on the strength of this case, Shiffrin builds an account of paternalism that drops the liberty-interference condition. She explains that this account

aim[s], in part, to show that there is more to respect for autonomy than merely filling autonomy rights. A paternalist action may not involve any particular action that violates a distinct autonomy right. Nonetheless, a paternalist motive can make an otherwise permissible action wrong because this motive is inconsistent with respect for autonomy.[13]

Now, respect for autonomy is, itself, a protean and disputed notion. In the sentence just quoted, Shiffrin uses the idea of respect for autonomy in a sense that implies that failure to respect autonomy is, absent some special justification, wrong. Once we understand that this is how she is using respect for autonomy, we should expect this concern, which is far broader than concerns about paternalism, not to line up with it.

---

[12] Seana Shiffrin, "Paternalism, Unconscionability Doctrine, and Accommodation," *Philosophy and Public Affairs* 29 (2000): 205–50, 213.

[13] Shiffrin, "Paternalism," 237.

In any case, I do not share Shiffrin's core intuition about the case. I see nothing wrong with the carpenter refusing to help with the shelves on the grounds that (as she thinks) B's request for help is misguided. Shiffrin stipulates that B has no claim to A's assistance, but that A is an acquaintance. What work is that idea of acquaintanceship doing in the example? I think that it is misdirecting us. I suggest that the mention of acquaintanceship begins to insinuate a basis for thinking of A as being required to take the time and trouble to try to persuade B that his request is misguided. Among acquaintances – say, two people who regularly run into one another in the woodworking shop and exchange pleasantries – this degree of consideration might be required. Note that Shiffrin says that it would not be paternalistic to engage in this kind of effort to engage in dialogue or discourse with the other in an attempt to improve the other's understanding, even though this effort would, just like the refusal to help she does find paternalistic, be grounded in one's confidence that one has a superior understanding on this matter. This makes clear that what is moving Shiffrin, in the case of this example, is the existence of a possible or purported *positive* obligation, resting in this specific case in part on the acquaintanceship, to try by giving reasons to set the acquaintance straight, or to try to encourage the acquaintance to develop more independence in his woodworking. (I will come back to the importance of dialogue at the end of the chapter.) It seems that Shiffrin has confused this positive obligation for a negative obligation not to act on the basis of one's judgment that the other is doing something misguided. Again, though, the sign that she cannot consistently mean the latter is that she holds that attempting to persuade the other that he was planning to do something stupid is not paternalistic.

To be sure, if the carpenter, in refusing to help, simply says "I'm not going to help with such a stupid project" or "Why should I waste my time trying to help you achieve a decent level of work?" that would be gratuitously hurtful, arrogant, and condescending. One does not need advanced moral theory, however, to grasp that making such statements would be disrespectful and wrong.

Another way to explain what is going wrong in Shiffrin's view is to focus on the key phrase in her official gloss of paternalism. One of its clauses says that paternalism "involves the substitution of A's judgment or agency for B's."[14] She does offer some cases involving substituted

[14] Shiffrin, "Paternalism."

agency. I will offer another at the end of the chapter. In one of her cases of substituted agency, the allegedly paternalistic agent cuts off a colleague who is stumbling over himself in trying to make a point, and says, "Look, what he is trying to say is ...," thus launching into a long speech. This is a clear substitution of agency: if the introduction is truthful, the one who butts in is attempting to take over the effort that the other had initiated. The carpenter who decides not to help the other, however, is doing no such thing.[15] Quite the opposite: he leaves the other in more complete control of his own shelving project than he would have been if the carpenter had decided to help. One might think, then, that Shiffrin's official gloss of paternalism could not classify such a refusal to help as paternalistic, but it is not so. To the contrary, she suggests very broad and metaphorical ways of reading the idea of substituted agency. These misleading and tendentious readings make it come out that the carpenter who has refused to get involved has substituted his agency for the other's.

A similar tendentiousness seems to have crept into many discussions of paternalism in the context of international humanitarian aid. As I have indicated, I think that there is a great danger that would-be international helpers will exhibit high-handedness, arrogance, condescension, and parochial understandings. It is very important to respect others – and especially the vulnerable – by avoiding arrogance and condescension toward them. This basic obligation of respect is more general and fundamental than an obligation not to engage in paternalistic action. One also has, as I have just mentioned, positive obligations to promote the autonomy of others.[16] Everyone's autonomy is vulnerable. Everyone's autonomy needs to be fostered when they are children, or they will never attain it. I do think that those engaged in humanitarian assistance are typically sufficiently involved with those they are helping that they come to have positive duties to promote the autonomous decision-making capacity of those they are

[15] Shiffrin also appeals to a cluster of cases involving a park ranger who, for various reasons that would count as fulfilling the motivational condition of paternalism, refuses to issue someone a climbing permit. Since such a refusal to issue an official permission is a clear interference with liberty, I have no objection to those cases and agree with Shiffrin that the motivational condition of paternalism should be broadly construed. It is the liberty-limiting condition that should not be dropped.

[16] I offer some defense of this claim in my book *Moral Entanglements: The Ancillary-Care Obligations of Medical Researchers* (Oxford: Oxford University Press, 2012).

helping – stronger such duties, even, than those that exist between acquaintances in a woodworking shop. But, of course, part of the reason that these positive duties are so strong is that those in need of humanitarian assistance are typically in situations that challenge their abilities to exercise, and even to maintain, their capacities for autonomous decision. Hence, efforts to discharge this positive duty will satisfy the motivational condition for paternalism. If these positive obligations exist, then Shiffrin's view would commit her to counting these efforts as paternalistic. But the moral implications of such a stance are unpalatable and potentially self-defeating.

Consider a case of an NGO engaged in famine assistance. In the course of providing famine assistance, they ought to do what they can to promote the autonomy of those they are helping. They might do this, for instance, by beginning to train some of those who have received adequate nutrition to help provide food to others. It makes no sense, though, to sit them all down in a room beforehand and attempt to engage in dialogue with them, the way Shiffrin imagines the carpenter doing, to try to persuade them that, out of consideration for the fragile autonomy of each, they should go along with a policy of seeking volunteers within the group to help feed the others. No. First the famine workers need to provide food to everyone. Then, to help build back the recipients' confidence in their autonomy, the famine workers may unilaterally institute the policy of seeking volunteers to help feed the others. In fact, if they explained that "we are seeking to get you members of the threatened community to help feed your comrades, not because we need your help or because we think you'll be particularly effective at providing it, but because we want to rebuild your fragile autonomy," *that* would be condescending and self-defeating.

What's Involved in Interfering with Another's Liberty

Against Shiffrin, I have argued that we should stick with Dworkin's gloss of "paternalism." In particular, we should understand paternalistic action not only as action taken on grounds having to do with someone's welfare or their acting as they should but also as action that interferes with that person's liberty. What, then, to say about a well-meaning international organization or NGO that sweeps into a country struggling from poverty, disease, or disaster, and starts performing functions that are normally considered core government functions?

Suppose that what they are doing, in interfering with everyone in the locality, is justified by the aim of preventing some of those people from harming others – the kind of justification often offered in defense of the restrictions embodied in the criminal law. Is it likely that their actions will be paternalistic, in the sense captured by Dworkin's gloss?

I think not, because I think that these actions are highly unlikely to interfere with their liberty; but to establish this will require a careful examination of the idea of the liberty of action, and of what it takes to interfere with the liberty of action. To begin this examination, I will explore a case from another context – an example from Richard Arneson, which he rather callously calls *Pouting Young Adult*. Here is the example:

> Tom is unreasonably distressed at some disappointment he has suffered. Perhaps he has been bested in competition for a job he coveted ... Whatever the cause of his distress, he is unhappy, and feels vaguely cheated by the world at large, and wants at the moment nothing more than to express his disappointment by committing suicide. He is not deceived, is aware that if he lives, he will come to forget his disappointment and to go on with his life, but he right now has no interest in doing that. He wants above all to die. He is not mentally ill or incompetent; he just has unusual and unusually self-indulgent and immature preferences.[17]

Alan Wertheimer, mentioning this case, writes that "Arneson thinks Tom is acting autonomously and that any interference would be the case of (perhaps justifiable) hard paternalism" – that is, paternalism that interferes with an individual's autonomous action.[18] Understanding "paternalism" along the lines suggested by Dworkin, as I have suggested we do, is that a sensible thing to think? Whether it is depends upon what one means by "interference."

Suppose that Max, the parent of one of Tom's old schoolmates, hears Tom talking to someone else at a school reunion, and rightly infers that Tom's state of mind is as described. As the reunion is breaking up, Max goes over and says, "Hey, Tom, you may not remember me. I'm Bill's Dad. Listen, you sound like you could use a little break to cheer

---

[17] Richard Arneson, "Joel Feinberg and the Justification of Hard Paternalism," *Legal Theory* 11 (2005): 259–84, at 278–9.

[18] Alan Wertheimer, *Rethinking the Ethics of Clinical Research: Widening the Lens* (Oxford: Oxford University Press, 2011), 24.

you up. Would you like to come sailing with us this weekend?" Since
Tom's plight might be thought not to be Max's "business," this might
be thought to be an interference.[19] It is certainly an intervention, in
the sense glossed at the outset. It is not a liberty-limiting one, though.
A sufficient reason why not is that it adds to Tom's real options, rather
than subtracting from them. This will still be true even if Max knew,
before he said this, that Tom loved nothing better than sailing, but
couldn't afford to sail on his own. After all, since Tom is seriously considering ending his life, surely there is a clear sense in which he could
refuse even this offer. The offer might count as manipulative if Max
chose to mention this activity because Max knew that Tom loved it,
but it is hardly coercive.

What would clearly count as a paternalistic interference in Tom's
case would be involuntarily committing him to a mental institution
for his own protection. That would be a very serious limitation of his
liberty, indeed.[20]

But what if, instead of doing that – which would, as the father of
one his classmates, be a move that was anyway out of his reach – Max
offered to give Tom a ride home, having gathered that he planned
to do himself in at home. Then suppose that, once Max had him in
the car, he kept taking him to other places that were roughly on the
way to Tom's home, and stopping at them on some pretext or other,
hoping thereby to distract Tom from his suicidal purpose. "Hey, they
are having a clambake at the local beach – we'll just stop by there to
get some of those delicious steamers before heading to your place."
Predictably, pouting Tom will be quite put out by this; but he doesn't
have other transport. This version of the case is, I think, closer to what
is going on in many cases of humanitarian assistance, ones in which
well-funded international organizations and NGOs barge in and start
doing things their way. But would Max be limiting Tom's liberty by
driving him around in this way? It is a nice question. I am inclined to
answer "no."[21] Let me explain why.

---

[19] For a well-taken critique of the idea of "minding your own business," see
Sarah Buss, "Appearing Respectful: The Moral Importance of Manners,"
Ethics 109 (1999): 795–826.

[20] Sometimes, of course, seriously limiting someone's liberty is justified, all things
considered.

[21] I am also inclined to think that Max would be acting well in such a case,
all things considered, and certainly not acting wrongly. The whole point of
talking about paternalism, however, is not to talk about all-things-considered

In explaining my answer to this question, I finally come back around to the crucial phrase that Dworkin picked up from Mill: "liberty of action." Paternalism, on Dworkin's gloss, involves limitations on someone's liberty of action that are justified in a certain way. What is liberty of action? It is not freedom of the will: the policies and interferences discussed under the heading of paternalism do not touch freedom of the will. You can interfere with someone's freedom of the will by administering heavy-duty sleeping pills; but that is not what we are discussing. Liberty of action is also importantly different from the possibility of action (that is, of having the real option to do something). Liberty of action is a normative concept, one that contains the idea of a right. The domain of one's liberty of action is the domain of what one has a right to do, in the sense of not having a duty not to do it.[22] Seatbelt laws, even if not paternalistic, interfere with the liberty of action, in this sense, by putting people under a duty to wear seatbelts.

Perhaps you are not convinced by this reading of liberty of action – or, if you are, you may think that Mill has sent us down a blind alley by using the phrase. If you think either of these things, I would like to convince you that you are mistaken. I will do so by means of another non-international case. Cafeterias are a common setting, now, of examples of paternalism. The common example is that of arranging the food in a cafeteria so that the healthy food is front and center and the high-fat and junk food is off in a far corner.[23] Passing over, as fairly obvious, why this way of designing cafeterias does not limit people's liberty, I would like to offer a different cafeteria example. Suppose you are in line at a normally arranged cafeteria. Behind you in line is your co-worker Jack, whose doctor has told him he needs to lose weight, or else he is at high risk of a heart attack. You know that Jack has been having trouble with this, due to his weakness for chocolate cake. You notice that there is only one piece of chocolate cake, and you snag it – not because you plan to eat it, but solely "to save Jack from himself."

---

rightness or wrongness, but to single out a distinctive wrong-making feature, paternalism. One of the essential conditions of paternalism as a wrong-making feature, as I have argued, is that it involves liberty-limitation. It is that feature we are now examining.

[22] Alan Wertheimer has rightly pointed out to me that this statement in the text is overly simple, as it does not take account of the different registers (moral, legal) in which one can speak of duty and liberty.

[23] E.g., Wertheimer, *Rethinking the Ethics of Clinical Research*, 23.

Your motivation, here, fits well enough with paternalism; but have
you done anything deserving of the least moral criticism or suspicion?
Again, as with Shiffrin's case of the carpenter who is asked for help,
I submit that you have not. Had you wanted to eat the cake yourself,
it would have been perfectly within your rights to take it. That's the
way cafeteria lines work: first come, first served. This established practice shapes the customers' liberties in a morally relevant way.[24] Your
reason for taking it is immaterial to that. Is your reason disrespectful
of Jack? Hardly. You are acting out of concern for Jack, knowing of
his weakness; and you have done so tactfully, without mentioning why
you are taking the cake. Yes, you have limited Jack's options; but you
have done so in the same innocent way that is pervasive in our society – so, for example, just in the same way as if, still ahead of him, you
take the last empty seat in the cafeteria. Doing that, too, is perfectly
within your rights and morally unproblematic. But the paternalistic
interference with liberty of action that Mill and Dworkin are talking
about is supposed to be morally problematic, and in need of a special
justification. From this we can infer that they must be talking about
something else.

I believe that, by the same token, when Max stops by the clambake
on the way to dropping suicidal Tom at home, Max is perfectly within
his rights. The details may matter here. Certainly if the ride to his
home is a forty-five-minute drive, it would be permissible for Max unilaterally to decide to stop by the clambake and get a few clams on the
way. Max is permitted to do this because it is his car and he is driving.
Unlike a paid taxi driver, he is doing Tom a favor by giving him a ride
home. Accordingly, while politeness would require him to announce
that he is just stopping by the clambake for a short while, there is
nothing wrong with his stopping. As in the cafeteria case, I cannot see
how this otherwise morally unproblematic action can be converted
into a problematic one by Max's having an altruistic purpose, that of
rekindling a young man's love of life.

As these examples remind us, because these actions are perfectly
well within their agents' rights, it does not matter why you take the

---

[24] How exactly to work this out is another nice question. Roughly, it seems that
everyone has the liberty to go for whatever food he or she chooses, as long as
he or she acts in accordance with the well-established and publicly accessible
rules of the establishment – one of which, in the normal cafeteria case, is first
come, first served.

last piece of cake or why Max stops by the clambake. Similarly, I suggest, when PEPFAR spends millions of dollars to purchase and staff a fleet of HIV testing and counseling vehicles in Cameroon, it is perfectly within its rights. It will have obtained the necessary government permits. Perhaps, temporarily, PEPFAR's big purchase of trucks will use up the local supply, making it hard for others to buy trucks. This is the way that economies work: first come, first served. Taking actions that marginally limit others' possibility of action does not by itself even begin to raise the issue of paternalism.[25]

What raises the issue of paternalism, as I say, is action that limits another's liberty of action where that is understood partly in terms of that person's absence of duties not to act in certain ways. To illustrate this point in a way not wholly unrelated to international humanitarian aid, let me briefly take up the interesting case of the regulation of human-subjects research by the US government and, more informally, by such bodies as the Council of International Organizations of Medical Societies (CIOMS). The concept of paternalism has recently come to the fore in the discussion of these "ethics" regulations. Because such regulations effectively limit when funding is available for medical research, even by private entities, their impingement upon the liberty of action of sponsors of medical research has serious consequences. Further, as Alan Wertheimer has pointed out, because medical research on human subjects essentially involves bilateral relations between researchers and their individual subjects, these regulations indirectly limit the liberty of action of actual and potential subjects of medical research, as well.[26] In many areas of life, including high-risk activities such as white-water rafting and unprotected sex, most societies are content to leave things to the discretion of consenting adults. In medical research, because of some horrific scandals in the past, such as the Tuskegee syphilis study, things are not so. Instead, interactions between researcher and subject are burdened with a special set of requirements.

[25] See the next section for a brief discussion of gross interference with another's range of options.
[26] Alan Wertheimer, "Facing up to Paternalism in Research Ethics," in Alan Wertheimer, *Rethinking the Ethics of Clinical Research: Widening the Lens* (New York: Oxford University Press, 2011), 19–44. The notion of "indirect paternalism" is introduced on p. 23. This chapter is a revised version of Franklin Miller and Alan Wertheimer, "Facing up to Paternalism in Research Ethics," *Hastings Center Report*, 37, 3 (2007): 24–34.

Not least among these requirements is a special, heavy-duty form of consent called "informed consent." (Whatever "consent" means, in general, it is clear that the kind of "informed consent" that medical researchers are supposed to obtain from their research subjects goes beyond it.) Since most matters of medical research are quite complicated, obtaining what is considered by the regulators to be adequately informed consent is quite difficult in most developing country settings, where literacy rates tend to be relatively low. Researchers accordingly do things like hiring local troupes of actors who will try to convey the essential information in a series of skits. Yet all the world over, so far as I know, people are allowed to buy and consume fatty foods without having first to sit through special information sessions about the risks of consuming them, significant though these risks are and complicated though the underlying biochemistry is.

The prevailing regulations on medical research with human subjects take away from those who would like to participate as research subjects the right to proceed with an ordinary, low-key consenting transaction between adults. Many communities in developing countries would be very glad to host more medical research – in part because, given the huge (and presumably unjust) disparities in access to health-care around the world, they rightly believe that having medical researchers at work in their communities will enhance their access to care. The regulations I have mentioned limit these communities' liberty of action by ruling out research studies undertaken using a more ordinary, everyday standard of consent. Because of the non-trivial costs of obtaining the special, informed consent in some places and concern about the cultural possibility of obtaining it in others, sponsors of medical research will take their projects elsewhere.

Some of the regulation of medical research is non-paternalistic in the same way that my hypothetical curfew is. It limits the liberties of each in order to prevent some from harming others – that is, from severely violating their rights, as occurred in the Tuskegee experiments. But a lot of the regulation of medical research is indeed paternalistic – limiting the liberties of potential and actual subjects of medical research solely in order to protect them from harm. To be sure, just because it is a case of paternalism does not mean that it is unjustified. Because my main message is that most international humanitarian aid is not paternalistic, I have left to one side the question of the conditions under which paternalistic interventions are justified. In any case, medical research, though often international, is not a form of humanitarian aid.

Liberty, Constitutively Constrained by the Idea of a Like Liberty for Each

A long tradition of thought about liberty, which reached a high point of explicitness in the political philosophy of Immanuel Kant, has recognized that the liberties of each need to be regarded as being modulated so as to be made compatible with a like liberty for all.[27] In accordance with that idea, not every limiting effect on one's options that results from the actions of another counts as a limitation on liberty. Instead, it may be acceptable as part of the mutual accommodation that the system allows. In my narration of the case of Max giving troubled Tom a ride home, I was, in effect, taking it that our system of the mutual accommodation of liberties allows the vehicle owner, in such case of taking on a voluntary passenger, some leeway in the route.

To be sure, some actions so sharply limit options that they grossly interfere with another's liberty. Kidnapping, for instance, grossly interferes with another's freedom of movement. Mugging, by contrast, seems to me to have a different problem. Mugging involves a blatant and coercive violation of rights, but generally not a violation of liberty. Whether or not I am right about this, I think we may safely assume that the humanitarian organizations we are talking about are generally not involved in kidnappings or muggings or in such gross violations of people's liberty.[28]

For the purposes of the present discussion, then, let us set aside cases of interference with liberty that are at the same time gross and coercive violations of rights. In effect, they were already largely put aside by my restriction of our attention, from the outset, to cases of well-meaning interventions.[29] The important remaining way to interfere with

[27] "*Freedom* (independence from being constrained by another's choice), insofar as it can coexist with the freedom of every other in accordance with universal law, is the only original right belonging to every man because of his humanity." Immanuel Kant, *The Metaphysics of Morals*, trans. Mary Gregor (Cambridge: Cambridge University Press, 1996), Ak. 6:237, 30.

[28] Forcible quarantine would be an interesting exception. Is forcible quarantine ever carried out by a non-governmental organization?

[29] Only "largely": unfortunately, of course, well-meaning interventions can also result in gross violations of rights.

someone's liberty of action, I suggest, thus requires being an authority, or at least purporting to be an authority, by which I mean, someone purporting to have the power to alter another's duties.[30] This thought, by the way, is built into the definition of paternalism in Webster's *Seventh New Collegiate Dictionary*, which reads as follows: "**paternalism:** a system under which an authority treats those under its control in a fatherly way esp. in regulating their conduct and supplying their needs." This link to purported authority makes sense. For one thing, it connects well with the root of the word "paternalism." The paternalist effectively sets himself up as another's parent. Like parents, those who are thought of as acting paternalistically at least *think* they are acting justifiably. To be a purported authority in the relevant sense means to be a person or entity that can credibly purport to put someone under a new duty. States do this by enacting new laws. The suggestion, then, is that only an authority or a purported authority can act paternalistically, because only someone whose directives are responded to as if they were authoritative can limit someone's liberty. Peacekeepers often assume this kind of at least purported authority, albeit in a fragile form. The UN High Commission on Refugees has this kind of authority. What prevented my earlier examples involving these two entities from counting as paternalistic is not that authority was not exercised, shifting people's duties – it was – but that their justifications for their actions were not solely grounded on the well-being of the people whose liberties of action they were limiting.

Such authority or purported authority is not limited to governments or to NGOs stepping in to take the place of governments. Suppose you are the manager of the company cafeteria, where you run a tight ship, and suppose, as in the previous version of the example, you are concerned about Jack's risk of heart attack. Out of this concern, and this concern only, you issue a policy or rule, which you firmly

[30] This understanding of "authority" is influentially elaborated in Joseph Raz, *The Morality of Freedom* (Oxford: Oxford University Press, 1986). It is also central to my *Articulating the Moral Community: Toward a Constructive Ethical Pragmatism* (Oxford University Press, forthcoming). This understanding of authority is relational, but abstractly so, leaving unspecified what can put someone in a position to alter the duties of another. Raz develops one account of that for the political case. I develop another account of that for the moral case. Those who merely purport to have authority of this type, of course, are only loosely constrained by the conditions for their actually having it.

impress upon all of your employees: *no chocolate cake for Jack*. That would be a paternalistic intervention, and a morally criticizable one. It limits Jack's liberty of action in the relevant sense – indirectly, as in the medical-research case – for it limits what he effectively has a right to do.

True paternalism, then, involves limiting another's liberty in a way justified solely by that other's good. Marginal reductions in another's set of options, like taking the last piece of chocolate cake, do not limit another's liberty. In the context of well-meaning interventions, only purportedly authoritative interventions are likely to do that. Paternalistic interventions are especially problematic because they interfere with another's autonomy – with another's control of his or her own pursuit of the good. This characterization of true paternalism, however, leaves open how, in justifying the action, the interfering agent determines what is good for the person being interfered with. It would be possible to start with a fully participative and open-ended dialogue that seeks to determine how the others understand their good, and then to proceed on that basis with a truly paternalistic intervention. That is bad enough. Things are even worse, however, when the interfering agent simply presumes to know what is good for the other. Interfering with the liberty of another solely on that kind of basis is what I propose to call "aggravated paternalism."

Paternalism, Not the Culprit in International Humanitarian Aid

I now have sufficiently unpacked the concept of paternalism to explain, succinctly, why I think there is very little true paternalism in international humanitarian aid. Sometimes – as in peacekeeping, refugee work, disaster assistance, and fighting epidemics and famines – the exigencies of the situation call for the assisting entities to assume temporary authority in the situation. Those very exigencies, however, which speak loudly of the possibility of catastrophe in every direction, will also make it very unlikely that the humanitarian aid is justified solely by reference to the well-being of the people whose liberties they limit in the course of getting a handle on the situation. It is of the nature of catastrophes that their consequences are hard to cabin. Thus, the justification of the liberty-limitation that has to go on will almost always – as in the refugee and peacekeeping cases I have discussed – include justifications that refer to the well-being of people besides those whose liberties of action are limited by a given regulation. They therefore will not count as paternalistic.

In most other contexts of international humanitarian aid, the issue of paternalism does not even properly come up, because the agencies and NGOs in question are neither acting coercively nor assuming authority, and are instead simply acting in a way that is perfectly within their rights. This is true, for instance, of the actions of one Waseem Saeed, a foreign doctor helping out in Haiti in the aftermath of the recent earthquake. Dr. Saeed had to make difficult triage decisions between doing leg amputations on many and doing a series of more complex operations on a smaller number. There was no suggestion of removing someone's limb against his or her will; rather, Dr. Saeed was offering free medical services, which he was perfectly within his rights to do, and was going beyond that, in this emergency situation, to try to optimize his efforts by saving as many lives and as many limbs as possible. Hence, in addition to acting within his rights and not exercising any duty-generating authority, he was justifying not offering complex surgeries to some, not on the basis of benefits to that person, but on the basis of benefits to the broader group of people in need of limb surgery.[31] Accordingly, he was not acting paternalistically.

In the Ballpark of Paternalism

Why, then, is the charge of paternalism so pervasive in the context of international humanitarian assistance when actual paternalism in that context is so rare? The answer, I think, is ready to hand. As I said at the outset, I have been strict about the meaning of "paternalism" because it is the label for a combination of morally problematic features that is distinctively troubling. Interfering with another's liberty for his own good is harder to justify than interfering with some so as to protect others and harder to justify than promoting someone's good without interfering with them. Even so, some of these

[31] The case of Dr. Saeed, a plastic surgeon from England, is presented in David Brown, "Surgeon Seeks to Prevent 'Unnecessary Amputations' in Haiti," *Washington Post*, January 20, 2010, www.washingtonpost.com/wp-dyn/content/article/2010/01/20/AR2010012004646.html (accessed November 7, 2015). I owe this reference to Michael N. Barnett.

Table 1.1 *Paternalism and Its Cousins*

Well-meaning interventions		Limiting liberty of action	Not limiting liberty of action
Justified solely on the basis of the intervenees' good	as the intervener sees it	Aggravated paternalism	Arrogant & condescending intervention
	as the intervenees see it	True paternalism	Arrogant intervention
Justified not solely on the basis of the intervenees' good		Liberty-limiting intervention	Mere well-meaning intervention

Key: Paternalism: in dark gray; paternalism's cousins: in light grey

components of paternalism, taken on their own, mark out important vices. These other vices that lie in the ballpark of paternalism are laid out in Table 1.1.

Although true paternalism thus does not appear to me to be a serious or widespread concern in the context of international humanitarian aid, there remain, as I've said, a series of related worries that are very powerful: worries about high-handedness, arrogance, condescension, and proceeding on the basis of parochial assumption.[32] Recall that, as I said at the outset, I am confining my attention to the context of humanitarian assistance worthy of the name, and so to well-meaning interventions. Within that context, the account that I have given enables us to see how these vices participate in one aspect or another of true paternalism.

To begin to illustrate these, I will return to the case of the UNHCR forcibly resettling people in a camp. As we saw, this is not truly paternalistic action because it is justified – I was imagining – in part by reference to broader goods of order and peaceable relations between the state from which they have fled and the one in which they have taken refuge. Since, however, the UNHCR is in such a case at least purporting to act as an authority, this is a liberty-limiting intervention. If

[32] I am grateful to my fellow participants in the workshop at George Washington University, from whom I learned a lot about these matters.

there would have been an alternative, whereby the refugees might have collectively decided to move without having been forced to do so, that would have been preferable. In general, any limitation of another's liberty needs to be justified. Because this kind of action shares the liberty-limiting feature with true paternalism, it is in the ballpark of paternalism. Accordingly, we can understand how some of the special opprobrium that rightly attaches to true paternalism rubs off on simple cases of (possibly justified) liberty limitation.

The other way to depart from true paternalism while remaining within its ballpark is to intervene with others' affairs in a way that, while not liberty-limiting, is justified solely on the basis of the others' good. Especially when this is done by the powerful, it tends to be high-handed in a criticizable way. Return to my case of PEPFAR buying up trucks in Cameroon. As I have said, I think that PEPFAR is perfectly within its rights to go into Cameroon and, as long as it takes pains to secure the required permits, to spend millions of dollars on a fleet of HIV testing and counseling trucks. Accordingly, as I argued, this intervention is not a liberty-limiting one. It accordingly does not raise a worry about true paternalism. It does, however, raise a problem about arrogance or high-handedness because it at least threatens to ride roughshod over the autonomy of the people of Cameroon. Even though it does not interfere with their liberty, that specially protected sphere of autonomous action, it does interfere with their control over local affairs, substituting PEPFAR's agency for that of locals. PEPFAR might reply that this was the point: that in order to see to it that their important mission was carried out right, they wanted to do it themselves. Especially, however, if this effort could be done well with more involvement of local actors, that would be preferable, and less high-handed. While my argument against Shiffrin showed that this kind of substitution of one's own agency for that of another is not enough to constitute true paternalism, it is one of the elements of true paternalism. Accordingly, again, it is understandable that such actions should come under the umbrella of "paternalism," as that term has come loosely to be used.

There is also the question of how the mission, which is to promote an aspect of the good of those in whose lives PEPFAR is intervening, is defined and determined. To address this topic, I leave historical fact behind and speak instead about hypotheticals. Suppose that, although the mission is rightly described as promoting an aspect of the good of (some) people in Cameroon, the process of defining the mission failed to take account of local priorities. Suppose the health officials in Cameroon see the control of child diarrhea as being a higher priority than HIV prevention, in part because so many more lives may be saved per dollar spent. For PEPFAR, a US government agency, simply to forge ahead with a mission defined in Washington, without extensive conversation and consultation with people in Cameroon, would be not merely arrogant but also condescending ("why should we listen to them?") and probably also parochial ("surely our own understandings of what is good for people are the best"). Again, we are not here dealing with true paternalism, because no limitation of liberty would be involved. Even so, it is especially understandable that those who exhibit these vices are often charged with being paternalists – and neocolonialists and neoimperialists – for they share an essential feature with aggravated paternalism. Subtract only the limitation of liberty from aggravated paternalism, and these vices remain.

Although Table 1.1 classes all cases of well-meaning intervention that do not limit liberty but are justified solely on the basis of the good of those intervened with as arrogant interventions, there is obviously a spectrum here. The details matter. Suppose that, instead of PEPFAR, we are instead talking about the Bill and Melinda Gates Foundation and its activities in Cameroon; and suppose that the Cameroonian health officials respectfully request the Foundation to shift some of their funds away from HIV vaccine research there in order to beef up their efforts in fighting child diarrhea, Guinea worm, and the like. But suppose the answer comes back: "This is Bill's foundation, and Bill really cares a lot about HIV so, with due respect, we will keep up our HIV-prevention activities in Cameroon." Contrary to what some have argued about the duties of philanthropic organizations – Thomas Pogge, for instance – I believe that such private foundations, and their founders, have considerable moral discretion to choose what they want to focus on.[33] Arguably, the US government, which is – contrary to what some may think – not properly thought of as steered by the preferences of one or a few multi-billionaires, has a stronger obligation to

---

[33] Thomas Pogge, "How International Nongovernmental Organizations Should Act," in *Giving Well: The Ethics of Philanthropy*, eds. Patricia Illingworth, Thomas Pogge, and Leif Wenar (Oxford: Oxford University Press, 2011), 46–66.

defer to the Cameroonians' priorities than does the Gates Foundation. If that is so, though, it is a difference only of degree.

Of course, problems of high-handedness, arrogance, condescension, and failure to understand other cultures can plague any kind of humanitarian effort at the level of implementation. Whatever an agency or NGO is doing, it will do well to form local partnerships that involve really listening to the intended beneficiaries, giving them a real voice in large projects, and learning from them about what is important. When a foreign agency or NGO sends a team, typically backed by ample resources, into a place where humanitarian assistance is needed, it will do well to remember that the people it is trying to help are not only needy but also, very likely, unempowered and yet endowed with considerable local knowledge. Extra efforts to empower them as partners in a joint effort are called for, not as a matter of avoiding stepping on their liberty of action, but as a matter of righting both economic and epistemic injustice.[34]

As I have tried to show, it is not simply that there is a constellation of vices, common in international humanitarian assistance, that are cousins of paternalism. More to the point, they reflect one or another of the components that come together to characterize true paternalism. As such, we can understand how people, speaking loosely, might come to refer to all of these vices as versions of paternalism. By the same token, because true paternalism consists in an especially problematic combination of two troubling features, we can also see why it might be important to reserve the term "paternalism" for what I have called "true paternalism," and to use the labels of "liberty-limiting interference" and "arrogant intervention" for the vices and offences that only partially partake of true paternalism.

From the outset, I have limited my focus to interventions, and so to actions of a certain sort. In closing, let me relax this restriction and consider what are sometimes called "paternalistic attitudes." Séverine Autesserre's chapter in this volume eloquently catalogues a diverse series of cases in which humanitarian agencies and NGOs exhibited paternalistic attitudes, such as condescension, arrogance, bossiness,

---

[34] For the concept of epistemic injustice, see Miranda Fricker, *Epistemic Injustice: Power and the Ethics of Knowing* (New York: Oxford University Press, 2007).

and a belittling attitude.[35] To this catalogue, Aisling Swaine adds the vivid idea of those moved by "the tyranny of the urgent."[36] On my account, these sorts of attitude are one of two main constituents of paternalistic intervention – the other being liberty-limiting action. Arrogance is a constituent of what I have called "true paternalism"; condescension, a belittling attitude, and bossiness, which can be motivated by the inflated sense of self-importance to which those pursuing urgent tasks are sometimes prey, belong among the constituents of "aggravated paternalism." For this reason, my account allows us to see that these attitudes do not merely lead people to undertake paternalistic – and even aggravatedly paternalistic – interventions, but are also constituent elements thereof. Structural problems such as hegemonic power and a lack of established consultatory mechanisms can also conduce to paternalistic action. The attitudes my colleagues have catalogued do that, but they also count as *elements* of paternalistic action. My account thus gives us good reason to refer to these attitudes as "paternalistic."

What should we say, though, about cases in which these attitudes do not generate liberty-limiting interventions? In that case, it seems to me that the simplest thing to do is just to criticize the attitudes as arrogant, condescending, belittling, or bossy. Relatedly, clarity will be served by limiting "paternalism" to cases where liberty-limiting action is also present. For this reason, I have stuck to speaking of "true paternalism" rather than saying, more cautiously, "truly paternalistic action."[37]

Finally, what should we say about the important kind of case in which people are self-deceived about the grounds of their action? Perhaps they think they are intervening in a liberty-limiting way (say, by making a group of refugees move from one camp to another) simply to help the people of a given place, when really what they are doing is acting to secure their country's oil supply. In that case, I think we should say that we do not have a case of paternalism

---

[35] Séverine Autesserre, Chapter 5, this volume.

[36] Aisling Swaine, Chapter 6, this volume.

[37] For those with an appetite for complex philosophical analyses, I note that it would be possible to characterize a complex psychological attitude such as an intention or general disposition to undertake liberty-limiting actions that is motivated by an arrogant or condescending attitude. In my view, this complex psychological state would well deserve the label "paternalistic."

because what we have is *morally worse* than paternalism. While not intentionally evil, it is not really well-meaning, either. It is a self-serving interference in the liberty of others – and so, an unjustified violation of their rights – that is merely masquerading as a paternalistic action.

2 | Rethinking Paternalism: The Meaning of Gender and Sex in the Politics of Asylum

DIDIER FASSIN

The use of the concept of paternalism by the social sciences poses two epistemological problems. First, it is a polemical term: its connotation is generally negative. One does not like to have one's action being called paternalistic and would rather have it qualified as, for instance, benevolent or humanitarian. Conversely, describing someone else's action as paternalistic implies a pejorative undertone and indicates a sort of disapproval. Like populism or fascism, paternalism is not a word that social scientists can use as if it were neutral. Second, it is an equivocal notion: its definition depends on the user. Political theorists regard it as a doctrine implying an interference with individuals against their will but for their own good. Common sense views it as an attitude of protection having to do with a fatherly behavior but not necessarily with an imposition or prohibition. Social scientists have therefore to decide whether to adopt Durkheim's nominalism, and start with a definition, or Weber's comprehension, and rely on people's understanding. To claim that we should address these two issues before any discussion on paternalism means on the one hand that we should be aware of the values attached to the word and on the other hand that we have to choose between two approaches which are both legitimate and analytically orthogonal. This awareness and this choice have important consequences for our approach to paternalism.

Let us consider first the polemical dimension. As reminded by Gérard Noiriel, the term "paternalisme" was initially used in the nineteenth century by the French labor movement to criticize the way employers

The research on which this text is based has been funded by an Advanced Grant of the European Research Council. I am grateful to the rapporteurs and magistrates who have facilitated the fieldwork I conducted with Carolina Kobelinsky at the National Court of Asylum. I am also indebted to Patrick Brown for his attentive copyediting and especially to Michael N. Barnett for his incisive comments.

reproduced traditional forms of domination typical of the rural world in their relationship with their workers;[1] by contrast, those defending this mode of production pointed to the sociologist Frédéric Le Play who pleaded in favor of a voluntary relationship of interest and affection between the employer and his workers, which he named "patronage."[2] Rather than dismissing it, we can consequently turn the polemical connotation into a political meaning. Taking the debates about the term and their implications seriously we are led to assume that, for those who use it, paternalism entails domination, that is, a structurally unequal relationship between agents. This is what most interpretations of paternalism seem to elude. The examples provided by Ronald Dworkin are telling in that regard: "The government requires people to contribute to a pension system. It requires motorcyclists to wear helmets. It forbids people from swimming at a public beach when lifeguards are not present. It forbids the sale of various drugs deemed to be ineffective." And also: "Doctors do not tell their patients the truth about their medical condition. A husband may hide the sleeping pills from a depressed wife. A philosophy department may require a student to take logic courses."[3] What such situations have in common is that, in the view of those who make the decision, "they are justified solely on the grounds that the person affected would be better off, or would be less harmed." All these illustrations imply imposition, prohibition or concealment, but they ignore domination. In his legitimate effort to de-polemicize paternalism, the author depoliticizes it, thus losing the critical edge of the concept.

But are imposition, prohibition or concealment even necessary to the description of paternalism? Indeed, if we move to the second problem, the classic definition of the concept, according to Ronald Dworkin, is the following: "the interference with a person's liberty of action justified by reasons referring exclusively to the welfare, good, happiness, needs, interests or values of the person being coerced."[4] It is from this clear delineation that the examples previously mentioned

[1] Gérard Noiriel, "Du 'Patronage' au 'Paternalisme': La Restructuration des Formes de Domination de la Main D'oeuvre Ouvrière dans L'industrie Métallurgique Française," *Le Mouvement Social* 144 (1988): 17–35.

[2] Michael Brooke, *Le Play: Engineer and Social Scientist* (London: Longman, 1970).

[3] Ronald Dworkin, "Paternalism", in *The Stanford Encyclopedia of Philosophy*, (summer 2016 edition, Edward N. Zalta), http://plato.stanford.edu/archives/sum2016/entries/paternalism/.

[4] Ronald Dworkin, "Paternalism," *The Monist* 56 (1972): 64–84.

are derived. We can therefore call it an a priori definition, since it is provided before being developed through concrete cases, which merely illustrate it. What if we do the opposite, that is, if we build a definition a posteriori, from empirical evidence? Here again, history is helpful. In his study of Victorian social philosophy during the early period of industrialization in England, David Roberts shows that paternalism, which was initially "authoritarian, hierarchic, organic, and pluralistic," changed due to the increasing pressure of individualism and entrepreneurialism as well as to the development of values of "philanthropy and voluntarism,"[5] paternalism henceforth being "thought of as a form of education into self-help and self-reliance."[6] This paternalism does not match with the criterion of "interference with a person's liberty of action": on the contrary, it is intended to develop the individual's autonomy. Should we dismiss what social agents mean when they use the word because it does not fit our postulate? The historian would rather accept the facts and question the definition.

There are thus two reasons for my challenging the dominant understanding of paternalism in political science and philosophy. The first reason is general: this critique offers an opportunity to differentiate two radically different epistemological paradigms. One, typical of political theorists, establishes a definition, examines situations corresponding to it, and excludes those not consistent with it. The other, more common among social scientists, analyzes the characteristics of the phenomenon as it is experienced by agents or interpretable within a larger context and eventually formulates a definition in accordance with them. To put it more simply, we can call the former deductive and the latter inductive. Both approaches have their merits, but I defend the inductive perspective because it is grounded in the analysis of actual practices and their meaning, either explicitly formulated or not, rather than a delineation decided upon in advance. The second reason is specific: my case study on asylum does not suit the classic definition. It does not involve interference, and the action is not undertaken against the will of those who will benefit from it. There is interaction but not imposition, prohibition, or even concealment: instead, both the paternalist and the paternalized, so to speak, share the same objective. What

[5] David Roberts, *The Social Conscience of the Early Victorians* (Stanford: Stanford University Press, 2002).
[6] George Revill, "Liberalism and Paternalism: Politics and Corporate Culture in 'Railway Derby', 1865–75," *Social History* 24, 2 (2008): 196–214.

differs is the signification they attach to the action undertaken or at least the interpretation of it. This leaves me with the alternative of either renouncing my case or abandoning the definition. Not surprisingly, I will opt for the latter, less because of the case itself than because I think it can help rethink the definition of paternalism.

More precisely, using this empirical study, I hope to show that paternalism can be better understood as a relation rather than a doctrine, that it is not an interference with others but a form of domination, that it does not necessarily imply imposition, prohibition, or concealment, but works better when based on an apparent convergence of interests, that it cannot be merely analyzed through a series of timeless propositions but only makes sense in a historical context. Thus, to take the ideal-typical example of international paternalism, if humanitarianism can rightly be viewed as such, it is neither because it represents an "interference justified explicitly with reference to another's interests," nor because it "violates the principle of consent"[7] – although the first element is constant and the second one may exist. Rather, it is because it involves a symbolic and practical domination. It entails moral obligation rather than coercion, that is, a relation between the obliging and the obliged, epitomized through the general principle of an exchange in which the gift has no counter-gift.[8] This domination, which we can call soft paternalism because it is benevolent and accepted, is historically inscribed in asymmetrical international relations – between colonizers and colonized, the North and the South, the West and the rest. To limit paternalism to the violation of the principle of consent would analytically restrict the concept and critically diminish its political meaning.

The case I will study does not concern, however, humanitarianism, but rather human rights, and more specifically the right of asylum. I contend that although asylum implies protection without domination – it is a right and not an obligation – and should therefore not be seen as paternalism, recent developments in its extension and implementation, particularly regarding the introduction of issues of gender and sex in its jurisprudence, indicate a paternalist turn. Or perhaps,

[7] Michael N. Barnett, "International Paternalism and Humanitarian Governance," *Global Constitutionalism* 1, 3 (2012): 485–521.
[8] Didier Fassin, *Humanitarian Reason. A Moral History of the Present* (Berkeley: University of California Press, 2012).

this extension and implementation merely uncover a profound feature that had remained unseen or unnoticed: that contemporary asylum is a form of paternalism, as the increasing reference to humanitarian rationale suggests.

The Discredit of Asylum Seekers

Asylum is an institution dating back to antiquity when Greek temples were considered *asulon*, or inviolable sanctuaries, for priests in times of war and when later a site outside of Rome, called *asylum*, served as a safe haven for banned persons, criminals, and even sometimes enemies. The institution has been substantially consolidated during the first half of the twentieth century under the auspices of the League of Nations and was formally instituted through the 1951 Geneva Convention on Refugees.[9] At the time, it was "limited in scope to persons fleeing events occurring before 1 January 1951 and within Europe," that is, the victims of World War II, one million of whom remained displaced. It was only in 1967 that the New York Protocol permitted "expanding the definition of a refugee" beyond the initial geographical and temporal scope.[10] The fact that a UN convention "relating to the status of refugees" could have initially been restricted to Europeans, in spite of the universal character of the category one would have imagined and in the context of a global and conflictive process of decolonization, is certainly revealing of the great divide underlying the very conception of the right of asylum. It is all the more significant that, whereas the text primarily concerned the Jews persecuted by the Nazi regime, who could obtain refugee status to become integrated in their host country, it excluded the Palestinians displaced by the creation of the state of Israel, who had a distinct organization to protect them in the camps where they had found refuge.

This initial scene thus inaugurates what will become the two major contemporary paradigms of asylum: on the one hand, the recognition of refugees on an individual basis in Western countries, with administrative and juridical processes for evaluating the merits of the

---

[9] Michael Marrus, *The Unwanted: European Refugees in the Twentieth Century* (Oxford: Oxford University Press, 1985).

[10] United Nations High Commissioner for Refugees, *Convention and Protocol Relating to the Status of Refugees*, 2010 ed., www.unhcr.org/3b66c2aa10.html (accessed November 7, 2015).

claimants' petitions, leading to a possible integration for those granted
the status; on the other hand, the massive internment of refugees in
the global South, with little prospect of integrating into the local communities and limited possibility of normalizing their situation, particularly in terms of rights.[11] In the first case, the national administration of the host country as represented by bureaucratic and/or judicial
authorities examines the applications and decides on the appeals. In
the second one, international organizations in the host countries guarantee the protection almost indiscriminately except when selecting the
happy few proposed for resettlement in richer countries. If we consider
the consequences of the civil war in Syria where one-fifth of the population had fled violence by mid-2015, the contrast between the two
paradigms translates into millions of refugees in Middle Eastern countries compared to thousands of asylum seekers in Western Europe.
This asymmetrical situation, in which protection remains a national
prerogative in the North while it is often delegated to international
entities in the South, is little debated.

At the same time, from a demographic perspective, the contrast
between the two worlds is immense: 80 percent of the twenty-six million refugees worldwide are located in developing countries, while only
one Western nation, Germany, ranks among the ten most hospitable.[12]
Created for Europeans, the politics of asylum in rich countries became,
indeed, more restrictive when the Third World began to invite itself
into the process. More precisely, it took two different paths: Western
governments granted social rights, including access to benefits, schooling, and employment, to small numbers of claimants they recognized as refugees, while providing financial support to international
organizations in charge of the refugee camps in countries neighboring
war zones. In other words, their generosity was differentially distributed: protection in the North under restrictive conditions, funding for
the South with relative largesse. The objective was explicitly formulated: Western benevolence toward developing countries was officially
meant to limit the flow of asylum seekers – or, perhaps more cynically,
to legitimize the increasing restrictions brought to the system.

[11] Didier Fassin, "The Precarious Truth of Asylum," *Public Culture* 25, 1 (2013):
39–63.
[12] United Nations High Commissioner for Refugees, *A Year of Crises: Global
Trends 2011*, 2011, www.unhcr.org/4fd6f87f9.html (accessed November 7,
2015).

Indeed, the most remarkable phenomenon in the past four decades has been the sharp decline in the recognition rates of refugee status in the global North. The French case, on which I have conducted my research, is telling. In the mid-1970s, the French Office for the Protection of Refugees and Stateless People (OFPRA) granted asylum to more than nine out of ten claimants (up to 95 percent in 1976). Thirty years later, the proportion had plummeted to fewer than one out of ten (as low as 8 percent in 2005). Contrary to the explanation generally provided, this evolution is not mainly due to a defrauding of the system by migrants attempting to take advantage of it. Although the number of claimants has definitely grown during this period, the decrease in recognition rates does not statistically correlate with the increase in applicants' flow.[13] The decline of asylum is mostly due to the reversal of immigration policies, which had until then facilitated the arrival of workers for the reconstruction of the country after World War II but took a restrictive turn in 1974 with the so-called closing of the borders. As the new orientation was progressively implemented, asylum increasingly fell under the logic of immigration control. Although the two policies were supposed to be entirely distinct, since asylum is a right sanctioned by an international convention whereas immigration is a process submitted to national sovereignty, they increasingly converged over the course of a series of summits meant to harmonize European policies.

To account for the drop in rates of recognition, one has therefore to complicate the explanation. Two symmetrical facts seem to have coincided to discredit asylum seekers beginning in the 1980s.[14] First, more immigrants started to claim refugee status. This was a direct consequence of the new immigration policies, but in an unexpected way. Until the mid-1970s, the employment contract served as an official document authorizing and proving legal residence. Because this contract was relatively easy to obtain due to an important demand for labor, people fleeing their country due to the dangers to which they were exposed were content with it, thus avoiding the assessment of

[13] Office Français de Protection des Réfugiés et Apatrides, Rapport D'activité 2005, www.ofpra.gouv.fr/sites/default/files/atoms/files/rapport_dactivite_2005. pdf (accessed November 7, 2015).
[14] Didier Fassin and Carolina Kobelinsky, "How Asylum Claims are Adjudicated: The Institution as a Moral Agent," *Revue Française de Sociologie* 53, 4 (2012): 444–72.

their case by the asylum bureaucracy. When it became more difficult to secure an employment contract, they began to seek refugee status instead.

Second, official discourses began to depict asylum seekers as economic migrants trying to exploit the generosity of their host country. Several cases of fraud served to legitimize the stigmatization of claimants and justify the strictness of the authorities. Through a tautological reasoning easily disseminated in the public, low rates of recognition were often used as evidence of the applicants' duplicity. In a period when xenophobia was fueled by a rising far right, the disqualification of asylum seekers combined the advantages, for the government, of showing its inflexibility with regard to controlling the immigration influx while appearing to maintain its defense of the protection of refugees: the Minister of the Interior, who is significantly the one in charge of this domain, could ensure that asylum was granted so long as the applicants were genuine victims of persecutions.

Rather than the asylum seekers themselves, it is the representation of them that has changed over the past decades in France. In the mid-1970s, political opponents to Augusto Pinochet fleeing Chile were regarded as combatants of freedom fighting right-wing dictatorship while boat people trying to escape Vietcong repression by leaving Vietnam on makeshift rafts were viewed as absolute victims of the Communist regime. Admiration for the former and compassion for the latter were the dominant sentiments, which translated into rates of recognition beyond 90 percent. Three decades later, Chechens invoking the repression of the Russians in the name of counter-terrorism or Darfuris asserting the massacres of their families by government-supported Janjaweed militias did not inspire these positive affects but instead elicited suspicion. By 2010, the proportion of those granted asylum fell to 14 percent and 17 percent, respectively.

The French situation was by no means different from that of most Western countries, where suspicion toward claimants similarly led to a sharp decrease in the rate of recognition of refugees. In this context of generalized discredit with respect to asylum seekers, it is all the more noteworthy that two new categories of persons eligible for Geneva Convention protection have emerged: the first based on gender, the second on sexual orientation.

The Rise of Social Groups

In 2010, approximately 30,000 asylum seekers were rejected in France, whereas 10,000 individuals were granted refugee status, half of them as the result of an administrative decision, the other half after a judicial process of appeal.[15] Indeed, as is the case in most Western countries, the procedure comprises two main moments. The application is first examined by the administrative authority, OFPRA, where an officer peruses the documents and generally interviews the claimant: on the basis of these elements, a recommendation is made, later verified, and ratified by a superior. In case of rejection, the applicant then has the option, which has become almost systematic, to appeal the decision before the National Court of Asylum (CNDA), previously named the Commission of Appeal for Refugees (CRR), where a public hearing, introduced by a report on the case, is held by three magistrates in the presence of the claimant and his or her lawyer. With a little over one-fourth of the applicants being granted asylum by the OFPRA or the CNDA, 2010 was a good year for refugees, especially when compared with previous ones, when the rates were approximately two times lower.

One remarkable element had significantly contributed to this evolution: the high rate of asylum granted to Malians either under the Geneva Convention or under the less beneficial "subsidiary protection." Three-fourths of asylum seekers from Mali had obtained refugee status. By contrast, the rate of recognition was 20 percent for Sri Lankans, afflicted by a long civil war, 12 percent for Congolese, confronted with a conflict deemed to have caused more than two million casualties, 6 percent for Turks, chiefly Kurds whose country was barred from entering the European Union precisely due to lack of respect for their rights, and 1 percent for the Bangladeshis, in spite of the repression by the Awami League against political opponents and religious minorities well documented by international organizations. The proportion of Malians being granted asylum was therefore between four and seventy-five times higher than nationals from these countries where extreme violence had occurred and where human rights were violated. Yet, at the time, Mali was considered one of the

---

[15] Office Français de Protection des Réfugiés et Apatrides, *Rapport D'activité 2010*, www.ladocumentationfrancaise.fr/var/storage/rapports-publics/114000200.pdf (accessed November 7, 2015).

safest, most peaceful, and most democratic nations on the African continent. As a consequence of this favorable context, claimants from the former French colony would almost never be granted asylum. In 2001, for instance, the rate of recognition for Malians was less than one in 1,000. What could then account for its 750-fold increase in less than a decade? Such a dramatic evolution was unprecedented in the history of asylum in France, even for nationals from countries under dictatorships or where genocides had taken place.

The reason for the extraordinary success of Malian applications is the recognition of female circumcision as a form of persecution. Under relatively recent jurisprudence, girls who have not been submitted to this traditional practice and are able to prove that it would be undertaken against their will were they to return to their country are granted asylum as well as their parents if they can establish that they want to shield their daughter from the operation.[16] The first case goes back to 1991, when Aminata Diop, a young woman "belonging to the Senufo ethnic group," sought the protection of France, alleging that she had fled her country to escape the ritual circumcision after her best friend died as a result of it and that her parents were forcing her to undergo the procedure before her wedding. Although her application was rejected by both OFPRA and the CRR, the latter recognized that this operation "constitutes a mutilation of women's body [*sic*]" and "would represent persecution against women wishing to avoid it" but only "on condition those concerned were personally exposed to it against their will."[17] Evidence of this personal risk and of specific resistance was not found in the case of this young woman, which created, however, a precedent in the French jurisprudence since it was argued that "women can be considered to be a member of a certain social group when they struggle against serious discrimination hindering the enjoyment of their fundamental human rights or threaten their life, liberty, or physical integrity." Indeed, under the Geneva Convention, a refugee is a person who "owing to a well-founded fear

[16] Guillaume Cholet, "Droit D'asile: le Conseil d'État aux Prises avec les Mutilations Génitales Féminines," Revue des Droits de l'Homme, Lettre Actualités-Droits-Libertés, February 18, 2013, https://revdh.files.wordpress.com/2013/02/lettre-adl-du-credof-18-fevrier-2013.pdf (accessed November 7, 2015).

[17] Commission des Recours des Réfugiés, *Mlle Diop Aminata*, 164078, July 17, 1991, www.refworld.org/docid/3ae6b7294.html (accessed November 7, 2015).

of being persecuted for reasons of race, religion, nationality, membership of a particular social group or political opinion, is outside the
country of his nationality, and is unable to, or owing to such fear, is
unwilling to avail himself of the protection of that country." Prior to
the Aminata Diop precedent, the notion of "particular social group"
had sometimes been used, notably for asylum seekers from Southeast
Asia, based on objective situations such as their specific social origins.
The novelty of the case was, however, that for the first time it served
to describe a group on the basis of the sex of its members, to recognize the existence of gender-specific persecutions and to acknowledge
a subjective dimension through the explicit refusal of the practice.
Under certain circumstances, women could be regarded as a "particular social group" protected by the Geneva Convention.

Not all persecuted women could assert their "membership" to such
a protected group, though. Chinese women subjected to the threat of
forced abortion or sterilization or to repression for having given birth
to several children were not considered as belonging to a particular
social group under the specious argument that the one-child legislation indiscriminately applied to everyone in the country.[18] Algerian
women contesting the gendered oppression exerted upon them in
the name of tradition or religion were also not deemed to constitute
a particular social group for the same ambiguous reason of universal application of the law in their country.[19] Although political rape,
forced marriage, and sexual exploitation through trafficking were
occasionally regarded as legitimate grounds for asylum, the conditions
to establish evidence in these cases being rarely met, at least under the
suspicious scrutiny of the officers and magistrates deciding the cases,
ritual circumcision was by far the most frequent cause of gender-based
granting of the refugee status: the notion of "particular social group"
could be used on the presumption that within certain African cultures
such practice was both generalized and coercive.

The first positive decision explicitly referring to "female genital
mutilation" was rendered in 2001, involving the Sissokos from Mali,

---

[18] Commission des Recours des Réfugiés, *Sections réunies, Zhang,* 228044, June
8, 1993, www.refworld.org/docid/3ae6b67914.html (accessed November
7, 2015).
[19] Commission des Recours des Réfugiés, *Sections réunies, Mlle Elkebir Nauta,*
237939, July 22, 1994, www.refworld.org/docid/3ae6b64514.html (accessed
November 7, 2015).

who allegedly opposed the ritual operation for their daughters. Both the girls and their parents were qualified as members of a "particular social group," thus benefiting from the Geneva Convention.[20] This jurisprudence, expanding the perimeter of asylum to include the parents of daughters at risk of ritual circumcision, became increasingly used during the 2000s by Malians, as well as nationals from Senegal, Ivory Coast, Somalia, etc., the former being by far the most numerous for historical reasons of their migration to France. In reaction to this trend, which raised doubts within the asylum administration and generated anxieties among public authorities, both OFPRA and the CRR adopted more restrictive criteria and granted a less advantageous status: claimants had to prove that they "had expressed their opposition to this practice for themselves or refused it for their children" and the "subsidiary protection" they were granted was accompanied with serious constraints, in particular the need for the girls to have a medical examination each year to ensure that they had not undergone the operation. Denounced by non-governmental organizations as "discriminatory and stigmatizing,"[21] this anatomical verification questioned the parents' protective role toward their children since it clearly indicated that their sincerity was contested.

Girls and women at risk of traditional circumcision are not the only so-called social group to have entered the definition of refugees in recent years. Another category of asylum seekers has benefited from the same qualification in the quest for protection in France: LGBT persons. The first case concerned an Algerian transsexual, Ourbih, which was initially rejected by both OFPRA and the CRR, but after an appeal to the Conseil d'État[22] was heard a second time by the CRR, which acknowledged in its decision of 1998 that "considering the reprobation they face, the discrimination they endure and the abuses to which several of them have been subjected with impunity, transsexuals are exposed in Algeria, due to the very characteristics they have in common, to persecution from large fractions of the population that are

[20] European Institute for Gender Equality, *Case Law: Commission de Recours des Réfugiés, SR, M & Mme Sissoko*, 369776 (Vilnius: Eige, 2001).

[21] Coordination Française pour le Droit d'Asile, *De la Protection à la Suspicion: L'exigence Annuelle du Certificat de Non-excision* (Paris: CFDA, 2012).

[22] Conseil d'État, *SSR, Ourbih*, 171858, June 23, 1997, www.refworld.org/docid/ 3ae6b67c14.html (accessed November 7, 2015).

deliberately tolerated by the authorities, and constitute under these circumstances a social group in the sense of the article 1 of the Geneva Convention."[23] The following year, a gay man, Djellal, also from Algeria, became the first homosexual to be granted asylum as a member of a "particular social group," described in very similar terms.[24] This was the occasion to define more precisely the criteria of membership to the group, that is, to have claimed one's homosexuality and manifested it through one's behavior, this dual characterization being adapted from another category of the Geneva Convention: "political opinion."[25] After this case, many homosexuals from Tunisia, Morocco, Mali, or Iran were granted asylum as members of a social group – in the latter country the second criterion did not even have to be established since it was considered that under the mullah regime mere suspicion of being a homosexual could lead to persecution. By contrast, cases from Bosnia and Cameroon, not deemed members of a social group but admittedly threatened in their country and not protected by their authorities, obtained subsidiary protection, while others from Gabon and Ukraine were merely rejected.

The evolution of French jurisprudence exemplifies a broader phenomenon. Indeed, the category of particular social group based on gender or sexual orientation has definitely been an essential instrument to expand the realm of asylum in many countries. This expansion is grounded in a 1985 case by the United States Bureau of Immigration Appeals called *Matter of Acosta*. According to this decision, a particular social group refers to "a group of persons all of whom share a common, immutable characteristic," which "might be an innate one such as sex, color or kinship ties, or in some circumstances it might be a shared past experience such as former military leadership or land ownership."[26] Although this definition has a possibly wide scope of

---

[23] Xavier Créac'h, "Les Évolutions dans L'interprétation du Terme Réfugié," *Hommes & Migrations* 1238 (2002): 65–74.

[24] Christine Pauti, "L'homosexualité Devant le Juge Adminnistratif et les Autorités Administratives Indépendantes," in *Le Traitement Juridique du Sexe*, eds. Guillaume Delmas, Sarah-Marie Maffesoli, and Sébastien Robbe (Paris: L'Harmattan, 2010), 169–85.

[25] Carolina Kobelinsky, "L'asile Gay: Jurisprudence de L'intime à la Cour Nationale du Droit D'asile," *Droit et Société* 82 (2012): 583–601.

[26] United States Department of Justice, *Matter of Acosta In Deportation Proceedings A-24159781*, 1985, www.justice.gov/eoir/vll/intdec/vol19/2986.pdf (accessed November 7, 2015).

application, "of particular significance are cases in a number of states recognizing homosexuals and women as groups eligible for protection."[27] After the 1991 Aminata Diop case in France, a series of similar arguments considering the risk of "female genital mutilation" to be a legitimate ground for the status of refugee have been used in court in many countries: Canada in 1994, the United States in 1996, Australia in 1997, the United Kingdom in 2000, Austria in 2002, Belgium in 2007, etc.[28] Similarly, since the 1981 recognition of sexual orientation as a cause of persecution in the Netherlands, numerous countries have deemed LGBT claimants as members of particular social groups: although statistics are not always available, it is estimated that more than 8,000 decisions might concern them in Europe each year.[29] Persecutions based on gender and sexual orientation have thus been two major additions to the definition of legitimate grounds for asylum in recent decades, even though restrictions in the implementation of the new criteria are frequently observed in actual cases, as certain officers or magistrates use all sorts of subterfuge to discredit applicants who allege to be the victims of such persecutions.

Liberal Paternalism

A normative and somewhat optimistic perspective regarding the trends just described would go as follows. Asylum is an ancient institution protecting the victims of persecutions that has often been adapted to the changing realities of the world. When the Geneva Convention was ratified in 1951, gender-based and sexual orientation-related persecutions, unlike those due to race, religion, nationality, or political opinion, were absent from the seminal text as they were absent from public debates at the time. In the past two decades, however, they have

---

[27] Alexander Aleinikoff, "Protected Characteristics and Social Perceptions: An Analysis of the Meaning of 'Membership of a Particular Social Group'," in *Refugee Protection in International Law*, eds. Erika Feller, Volker Türk, and Frances Nicholson (Cambridge: Cambridge University Press, 2003), 263–310, 286.

[28] United Nations High Commissioner for Refugees, *Guidance Note on Refugee Claims Relating to Female Genital Mutilation*, 2009, www.refworld.org/pdfid/4a0c28492.pdf (accessed November 7, 2015).

[29] Sabine Jansen and Thomas Spijkerboer, *Fleeing Homophobia: Asylum Claims Related to Sexual Orientation and Gender Identity in Europe* (Amsterdam: COC Netherlands and VU University Amsterdam, 2011).

finally been recognized for what they are, with the consequence that refugee status can now be granted on the grounds of various forms of violence which had previously been ignored, such as "female genital mutilation," "forced marriage," "political rape," "sex trafficking," and "homophobia." The intimate realm has entered the political domain, and as a result, gender and sexuality have been acknowledged as potential objects of persecution. This expansion of the scope of asylum is a moral progress reflecting the evolution of contemporary societies, especially in the Western world, where issues of gender and sexual orientation, including domination, discrimination, stigmatization, and marginalization, are increasingly debated publicly and taken into consideration in policies. By recognizing oppressed women and sexual minorities as particular social groups, enlightened nations offer them protection against evils persisting in various parts of the world where moral backwardness still prevails. This positive evolution represents a significant victory for human rights. Being the product of the convergence between activist organizations and national agencies, it attests to the vitality of contemporary pluralist democracies.

In contrast, a critical and perhaps more realistic stance would, however, suggest the following alternative account. The institutionalization of asylum in the mid-twentieth century has been facilitated by economic factors (the need for a cheap labor force for the reconstruction of Europe and the growth of North America) as well as ideological reasons (the contribution of refugees to the demonization of Communist regimes). Generosity was that much easier since it brought material and symbolic benefits to the benevolent nations eager to protect victims of persecution. With the restructuring of Western economies in the 1970s and the fall of the Iron Curtain in the 1980s, asylum seekers began to be assimilated with immigrants and therefore disqualified as candidates for refugee status. Rates of recognition plummeted, the official explanation being not that more restrictive interpretations of the Geneva Convention were implemented, but that more claims were illegitimate. Even for those alleging they had fled countries where civil war, ethnic cleansing, racial discrimination, political oppression, or religious violence was occurring, it became increasingly difficult to be granted asylum on these traditional grounds. However, under the pressure of feminist and gay rights movements, a new type of persecution, based on gender or sexual orientation, was acknowledged under the flexible category of particular social group. This flexibility allowed for some type of violence to be recognized but not others: genital cutting but not forced abortion under constraining reproductive laws, forced marriage but not repression against feminist activists, transgender and homosexual individuals from North African and Middle Eastern countries more easily than those from sub-Saharan and East European ones. Due to this redefinition of the boundaries of asylum, a person currently has a significantly higher probability of being granted refugee status if he or she claims to have one's daughter at risk of being ritually circumcised than if one asserts to be at risk of being murdered as a political opponent, if one alleges to be persecuted for being gay than for being a member of an oppressed minority. In the hearings I attended in the National Court of Asylum in France, whereas applicants alleging that they had been harassed or tortured because of their belonging to a trade union or a human rights organization had to go through long inquisitorial questioning often ending in the denial of their petition, others affirming they had been reviled and threatened because of their homosexuality were sometimes not even requested to give more detail before being granted asylum, since they were believed on their word and appearance.

According to this critical account, gender and sexual abuse has thus become more legitimate than ethnic or religious mistreatment – which does not mean that these criteria always suffice to obtain refugee status. The shift in the evaluation of applications can be analyzed as a shift from traditional political grounds to cultural differences constructed as civilizational clashes. The case of female circumcision, significantly renamed genital mutilation, is telling in that regard. As Janice Boddy has shown in her historical study, the attempt to eradicate this practice, or at least the most damaging forms of it, was part of the "civilizing" mission British colonizers assigned to themselves in Sudan and elsewhere in Africa during the early twentieth century. To do so, they employed a soft type of paternalism based on legislation and education. "When they tie your hands, they tie you with silk, not with iron chains," an Arab Sudani commented, echoed by the US historian Robert Collins: "The Sudanese frequently misinterpreted actions motivated by paternal concern and devotion as only another device to maintain imperial rule."[30] The practice was described by the

---

[30] Janice Boddy, *Civilizing Women: British Crusades in Colonial Sudan* (Princeton: Princeton University Press, 2007).

British as "barbarous" and "cruel," "repulsive" and "harmful," attesting to the "moral and economic backwardness" of the region and its inhabitants.

Remarkably, this representation has lasted until today: it is expressed in the writings accompanying the international crusade against "FGM," female genital mutilation. In the United States, the first case of asylum granted to a woman claiming she was fleeing her country, Togo, to avoid the operation, concerned Fauziya Kasinga.[31] After having been rejected by an immigration judge, she appealed the decision and her story was widely publicized in a national newspaper, an element that probably helped her obtain the status of refugee.[32] Hyperbolic statements concerning "tribal ritual" and mere lies about the "devoutly Muslim family" made the story seem more truthful for the public as well as more effective in court. Her case became emblematic for feminists defending the right of asylum on the basis of gender, but was also an opportunity to present a caricatured and, as far as the story of the young woman goes, factually untruthful vision of Togolese society, as demonstrated by Charles Piot who led an ethnographic investigation in her village of origin.[33] While opening a new avenue for asylum seekers, the case also reinforced prejudices regarding Africa.

"Do Muslim women need saving?" asks Lila Abu-Lughod as she examines the increasing focus of Western governmental agencies and non-governmental organizations on gendered practices associated with Islam, whether they concern female circumcision, honor killing, veil-wearing, or polygamy.[34] Considering the inflation and success of a literary genre she names "pulp non-fiction," such as the books published by Ayaan Hirsi Ali, a strong critic of Islam who admitted to falsifying her story in order to obtain asylum in the Netherlands on the basis of an alleged forced marriage, she links this fascination for,

---

[31] United States Department of Justice, *In Re: Fauziya Kasinga Applicant File AZ73 476 695*, 1996, www.justice.gov/eoir/efoia/kasinga.htm (accessed November 7, 2015).

[32] Celia Dugger, "Women's Plea for Asylum Puts Tribal Ritual on Trial," *New York Times*, April 15, 1996, www.nytimes.com/1996/04/15/nyregion/ woman-s-plea-for-asylum-puts-tribal-ritual-on-trial.html?pagewanted=all (accessed November 7, 2015).

[33] Charles Piot, "Representing Africa in the Kasinga Asylum Case, and Beyond," unpublished paper.

[34] Lila Abu-Lughod, *Do Muslim Women Need Saving?* (Cambridge, MA: Harvard University Press, 2013).

and denunciation of, women's suffering in Muslim societies with the
current state of international relations where Islam is increasingly represented as the major danger for the global order. It is indeed necessary to contextualize the Western discourse on women's rights and its
translation into gender-based asylum in relation to Islamic countries.
Actually, in Europe, Muslims have become the embodiment of a cultural and often racial form of radical otherness.

In France, the public and legislative debates about the "veil" have
revealed the depth of this otherization of Islam. Indeed, the official call
for "Republican values," first and foremost a rigorous version of "sec-
ularism," to justify the passing of a law banning the wearing of "conspicuous signs" of religious affiliation cannot be taken at face value
since it is contradicted by the fact that such signs only became a problem when Muslim women exhibited them. The secular claim never
concerned Christians or Jews before. But the promoters of the legislation across the political spectrum not only invoked abstract universal
principles regarding the relationships between the state, civil society,
and religious beliefs. To legitimize their public action they also declared
that it was meant to protect women and liberate them from patriarchal domination. The explicit message suggested the "superiority of
French gender relations" and their association "with higher forms of
civilization," thus contributing, in Joan Scott's terms, to "a consolida-
tion of sides in a clash between 'Islam' and 'the West'" that was in fact
a continuation of a colonial relationship between the French and the
"Muslims" – the term used to designate North Africans in the first half
of the twentieth century.[35] During the 1990s and 2000s, the increasing anxiety about the "national identity," defined as white, Christian,
and attached to the values of the Enlightenment, led to the obsessive
construction of a supposed anomaly epitomized by immigrants and
their children, who are Arabs and blacks, generally Muslims, presumably rejecting human rights and more specifically women's rights. Such
prejudice is conspicuous in the naturalization ceremonies I attended.
At the end of this grandiloquent ritual, which concludes the several-
year process of testing the applicants' knowledge and respect of
so-called Republican values before they may be granted French citizenship, the representative of the state insists in his or her speech on

---

[35] Joan Wallach Scott, *The Politics of the Veil* (Princeton: Princeton University
Press, 2007), 16 and 19.

the need for the newly naturalized to implement the principle of gender equality, described – somewhat presumptuously – as a defining character of French culture which they will have to assimilate.[36] In this context where the granting of citizenship is regarded as a "favor" as in many others where the recognition of the refugee status is described as a "humanitarian" gesture rather the application of a right, the disqualification of "them" implies a valuation of "us" – their benefactors in the case of naturalization, their protectors in the case of asylum.

It is in this light that the introduction of gender-based and sexual orientation-related grounds for asylum must be understood. The generosity of the protection offered to women and gays accomplishes two things. First, it radicalizes the representation of uncivilized and non-democratic others. Genital cutting is barbarous, homophobia nefarious. Africans who practice the former exhibit their backwardness. Muslims who display the latter show their intolerance. "The tragedy of Africa is that the African has not fully entered into history," the French president Nicolas Sarkozy declared in his 2007 Dakar speech. The expansion of asylum through particular social groups thus contributes to the production of a moral geography of the world. Second, it values the liberality of the West as promoter of women's rights and sexual democracy at the same time as it detracts attention from the dramatic decrease in the rate of recognition of asylum seekers on racial, ethnic, national, religious, or political grounds, and more broadly from the increasingly dismissive and hostile attitude of governments toward immigrants. France becomes again the land of human rights. "Not all civilizations are of equal value," as the French Minister of the Interior Claude Guéant stated at a 2012 political meeting in Paris, referring to the superiority of Western values over Islamic ones.

This ambiguous combination of the discrediting of "their traditions" and the celebration of "our values" corresponds to what Éric Fassin analyzes as "the sexual politics of Frenchness."[37] But although it has a national component, such ambiguity entails a broader signification, producing a global human rights divide. Thus, in the case

---

[36] Didier Fassin and Sarah Mazouz, "What Is it to Become French? Naturalization as a Republican Rite of Institution," *Revue Française de Sociologie*, 50 Suppl. (2009): 37–64.

[37] Éric Fassin, "National Identities and Transnational Intimacies: Sexual Democracy and the Politics of Democracy in Europe," *Public Culture* 22, 3 (2010): 507–29, 511.

of "human trafficking" and "sex trade," Elizabeth Bernstein shows
the ideological convergence between evangelical groups and feminist movements in what they see as a global form of "social justice
activism," which opposes victims being rescued and oppressors being
punished in a striking amalgamation of humanitarianism and retrib-
utivism.[38] Responding to this aggressive benevolence, an Indian sex
workers' collective took for a slogan: "Save us from our saviors. We're
tired of being saved." Indeed, the supposed victims may sometimes
see their benefactors as oppressors. But this is certainly not the case
for those seeking asylum, who can definitely bear with this aggressive
benevolence as long as it allows them to be granted the precious refugee status for which they applied.

Undoubtedly those who have to decide on the fate of refugee applicants genuinely believe in the noble character of their mission. After
the hearings, CNDA magistrates would communicate in our private
conversations their satisfaction at being able to offer protection to
women or gays from all sorts of violence and their conviction of having made fair decisions regarding the rejection of so many others who
claimed to be persecuted on political, religious, or ethnic grounds.
Sometimes they would openly express the sense of superiority and
goodness their activity afforded them, but more often it remained
largely implicit.

Yet, rather than in their individual attitudes, it is in the project of
the state that paternalism manifests itself: a paternalism that involves
benevolence but not coercion. On the contrary it implies a form of convergence of interests between the asylum seekers and those who assess
their case: when they grant refugee status to these women and men who
claim to have been victims of gender-based or sexual orientation-related
persecution, CNDA magistrates meet their expectation. It is certainly
what renders this form of paternalism not only well accepted but also
difficult to recognize. It is nevertheless important to acknowledge this
soft domination. Officers and magistrates have more than the power to
grant asylum and therefore to decide on the life of the claimants; they
have the power to choose which criteria they will privilege, to give more
credit to persecutions related to gender and sexual orientation than to

[38] Elizabeth Bernstein, "Militarized Humanitarianism Meets Carceral Feminism:
The Politics of Sex, Rights and Freedom in Antitrafficking Campaigns," *Signs:
Journal of Women in Culture and Society*, 36, 1 (2010): 45–71, 65.

persecutions related to political, religious, or ethnic oppression, and by doing so to establish moral hierarchies not only among asylum seekers but also between their own society and that of the claimants.

Conclusion

Political theorists generally define paternalism as an interference with a person's liberty of action for his or her own good; according to them, it is a combination of coercion and benevolence. I have argued in the present text that this is too restrictive an interpretation and that it is probably even wrong. Paternalism implies benevolence and domination rather than coercion. It is better exerted through the convergence of interests, the display of the dominant's generosity, and the expression of the dominated's gratefulness. This is what inductively emerges from empirical work. In the case of asylum, the selective protection of victims satisfies both those who grant and those who are granted the refugee status: magistrates provide what the claimants are eager to obtain – although the process can be regarded as being conducted at the expense of other applicants who can be more easily delegitimized. No coercion, here, but domination, which resides in the relation thus created between the granter and the grantee, this troubling way to debase an oppressive "them" and exalt a magnanimous "us," to affirm cultural superiority and display political largesse.

This is not to say that paternalism cannot be tough and impose or prohibit certain types of action for the supposed good of the beneficiaries. But such features are not consubstantial to paternalism. Authoritarian paternalism uses coercion. Liberal paternalism values cooperation. However, what characterizes paternalism in its broader sense is the combination of benevolence and domination in the relationships between individuals, groups, organizations, or states. Thus, re-establishing the foundational role of domination in paternalism is much more than reaching a better definition of the concept. As the contextualization of the recent evolution of asylum demonstrates, it implies historicizing and politicizing a relation that is simultaneously one of protection and obligation. And ultimately, though we should certainly applaud the inclusion of persecution related to gender or sexual orientation in the criteria for invoking the Geneva Convention, we should not ignore its historical background and political meaning. Even moral consensus must be subjected to critical thinking.

PART II

Paternalism, Old and New

3 Eurocentric Pitfalls and Paradoxes of International Paternalism: Decolonizing Liberal Humanitarianism 2.0

JOHN M. HOBSON

Paternalism is a key property of life in the modern Western world. Even at its best, it is a two-headed creature, with a benign face looking one way and a controlling face looking the other. Accordingly, paternalism can have a sweet-and-sour taste for those on its receiving end in that while it can provide various benefits, it comes at an inevitable cost – specifically, a sense of loss of ownership or agency by those on the receiving end. And this can evoke a range of negative feelings running from quiet irritation to outright anger, and from passive complacency to alienation. But there is another dimension of paternalism that reflects its two-faced nature. Paternalism faces both inwards to the domestic sphere and outwards into the international arena. Its dual-faced property is ultimately significant because its nature differs depending on which spatial arena we focus upon.

In the domestic arena "at home," paternalism is often attached to the "progressive" provision of services based on *specialist expertise*, found particularly in the education system and health services as well as the welfare state. For example, while university undergraduates might dream of telling the lecturer what exactly it is that they should study, the reality is that teaching at the undergraduate level is inherently paternalist precisely because students cannot know exactly what it is that they might want to learn until they have learnt that which they need to know. Only once they have been "properly equipped" with the "requisite portfolio" of educational skills and knowledge can they "be allowed" in the fullness of time to progress to a position where they can be in full control of their own learning destiny – specifically at the Ph.D. level.

Paternalism, and, I would add, maternalism, are yet more prevalent within the welfare state – especially in the caring professions and the

99

health-service industry. Doctors, with their specialist expertise, will make decisions on behalf of their patients often without fully explaining why they are doing so and often not bothering to gain explicit consent. The welfare state is highly paternalist, not to mention maternalist, in that social workers, for example, make decisions "on behalf of" children to which their parents, not to mention their children, might have little or no recourse. Or, again, those receiving welfare benefits will be subjected to all manner of regulations which they otherwise might prefer to avoid, and they will need to passively accept the largesse that they receive in whatever fashion the welfare authorities, in all their paternalist wisdom, deem appropriate.

Equally, the political system of representative democracy exhibits various forms of paternalism. Governments impose laws often on the basis that these are "best" for the citizenry even when the majority reject them (the case of abolishing the death penalty in most Western countries being a poignant example). However, it goes much further than this. For many academics of the left-of-center variety, the idea of a working-class Conservative/Republican voter (or what in Britain is euphemistically called the "working class Tory") often appears as a confounding contradiction in terms. But for those members of this particular group, it is usually the perceived paternalism of the left-of-center party elite that they find most irksome, especially given that many members of this elite are middle- or upper-class "privileged" people. "How dare these elites, most of whom know nothing personally about poverty, push us into welfare dependency rather than provide the means by which we could better ourselves through our own hard work and enterprise?" you will hear them say. The case of the British Labour Party's preference for "comprehensive schooling" (free state schools for all) and its rejection of "grammar schools" (free schools where selection is based on merit) hinges on this very issue. And it is precisely the paternalism of left-of-center politics that many right-wing parties ultimately stand against. Even so, though, the very act of government, whether it be conducted by right- or left-wing parties, is inherently paternalist given that the citizenry prefers to hand over political decision-making powers to bodies that can work "on their behalf." Paternalism in this instance results not so much through a defection to other peoples' expertise – in this case political parties – but more as a function of the fact that citizens prefer to spend their time engaged in other activities, specifically a full-time job, and therefore do not have the time to spend making political decisions.

All of which suggests that while domestic forms of paternalism might not constitute an ideal modus operandi, they clearly have benefits and that if one were to call for the rejection of domestic paternalism, this would have to be done in the full recognition that it would entail a vast skilling up of the people that is simply not possible to do, coupled with an extension of the working day from twenty-four to forty-eight hours that is, of course, equally implausible. Given this, one might conclude that domestic paternalism has its negatives but that, at the very least, it would be unfair to write it off altogether and, at most, it remains a necessary, if not the only, means by which progressive ends can be met.

But when we turn to the international sphere we encounter a very different set of factors in play that, I will argue, render international paternalism highly problematic. There are two key interrelated problems here. First, while there is basic consent at the domestic level for paternalism in its various guises, in the international sphere there is little to none vis-à-vis those who are on the receiving end. Of course, in the domestic sphere, it is clearly the case that doctors, teachers, social workers, and politicians/political parties rarely ask for consent in an explicit manner. But this is because such consent is implicit, for otherwise the patient would not repeatedly ask for medical treatment when needed, the student would not continue with her course, welfare "dependents" would get a job, and the electorate would voluntarily disband as it would no longer be willing to vote in representative political parties. However, when a state intervenes in another state, no such consent on the part of the target society is explicitly asked for, nor can it be effectively marshalled, nor is it implicit. Instead it is simply *presumed* on the grounds that the interventionist Western state takes on the self-appointed role of "our brother's keeper." Acting in such a way means that the sovereign self-determination of the object states can legitimately be overridden in order to "rescue and emancipate" strangers. But in this case, to presume that such consent exists is for the intervening government to take a highly paternalist leap of faith.

The second key problem, which follows immediately from the first, is that while domestic paternalism operates within a shared set of cultural norms that exist between the paternalizers and the paternalized, no such condition obtains between the international paternal interventionists and the paternalized. This is obviously most apparent in those interventions undertaken by the West in the non-Western world. That is, intervention in non-Western societies which subsequently leads to the imposition of Western cultural values and institutions might often override those of the object societies. Equally, in this case, to presume that the object/target society desires to be culturally converted to a new set of cultural and institutional norms is, once more, to take a giant paternalist leap of faith in believing that the paternalist society's norms and institutions are so universal that it is merely axiomatic that the people in the object society would naturally wish to give up forthwith its own identities, culture, and institutions.

All in all, then, it is these two issues, I want to argue, that render international paternalism highly problematic, if not illegitimate, on the one hand, and a form of liberal imperialism on the other (though, for the purposes of my overall argument, it should be understood that by liberal imperialism I am referring not to the exploitation of the objects but to their cultural conversion to liberal norms of behavior that are deemed by the paternalizers to be in the *real* interests of the object peoples). Even UN sanction for humanitarian intervention does not render it properly legitimate because the target people are not asked to give consent and, arguably, UN sanction reflects the problem of paternalist pronouncement by those outside of the object society. Moreover, as I mention in the chapter's conclusion, I would charge any form of international paternalism – Marxist, liberal, or otherwise – as a form of imperialism (understood in the terms described above). In this chapter, I shall elaborate these twin problems by focusing on liberal humanitarian-interventionist theory, given that it is this which provides the core theoretical rationale for the form of international paternalism that has become predominant in world politics mainly since the end of the Cold War. As such, this produces a rather different inflection to many of the other chapters in this volume, given that their focus is often on the actual implementation of interventionism in the "real world," by people on the ground.

The chapter proceeds through four sections, the first of which argues that liberal humanitarian theory today is nothing new but propels us back to the future of its putative nemesis: the pre-1945 era of Eurocentric liberal-imperialism. The second section then extracts the key properties of pre-1945 liberal-imperial theory before these are traced in contemporary liberal humanitarian theory in the third section, while the fourth section draws out the key properties of Eurocentric international paternalism as it plays out within liberal humanitarian theory.

A "Brave New Progressive World" or Back to the Future of the "Dark Old World" of Paternalist-Eurocentric/ Racist Imperialism?

While many liberals would concede that liberal international paternalism often entails various negative aspects – for example, aerial bombing and accidental civilian casualties (that usually goes by its sanitized term, "collateral damage") – equally, many would conclude that the benefits outweigh the costs. More generally, since the end of the Cold War, the cause of humanitarian intervention has become celebrated as one that emancipates humankind from the dark days of the nineteenth century when racist imperialism constituted the key modus operandi of world politics. Typically, the prominent liberal constructivist theorist, Martha Finnemore, characterizes the new liberal humanitarian discourse as one "by which non-white, non-Christian populations became 'humanized' for the West," given her claim that only white Christians had been the subject of nineteenth-century Western humanitarian interventions.[1] And supposedly this properly "humanized" (non-Eurocentric/non-racist) discourse is operationalized very differently to that of the nineteenth-century interventions insofar as humanitarian intervention today must meet the new global normative standard which prescribes multilateralism and proscribes colonialism.[2] Interestingly, Finnemore claims that today it is now a norm or a matter of common sense to believe that failing to intervene to protect non-white and non-Christians abroad reflects an unacceptable racist predisposition, for an indifference to saving strangers is tantamount to denying their innate humanity.[3]

[1] Martha Finnemore, "Constructing Norms of Humanitarianism," in *The Culture of National Security*, ed. Peter J. Katzenstein (New York: Columbia University Press, 2003), 153–85, 157.
[2] Martha Finnemore, *The Purpose of Intervention: Changing Beliefs about the Use of Force* (Ithaca: Cornell University Press, 2003), ch. 3.
[3] Finnemore, *Purpose of Intervention*, 85–140.

Finnemore's analysis feeds into the general assumption held by many
IR scholars, especially of a liberal persuasion, that after 1945 the old
era of Eurocentrism and racism came to an abrupt end such that the
subsequent era of decolonization witnessed the replacement of racial
intolerance with a more tolerant and benign discourse of racial equality which was coupled with the delegitimization of empire in world
politics.[4] Most significantly, 11/9 – the fall of the Berlin Wall in 1989 –
was an event that was perceived by many Western observers to be as
dramatic and world-changing as 1945 was, much as 9/11 would be
just over a decade later. While 1945 supposedly broke with the old
era of racist and Eurocentric imperialism, 1989, we are told, projected
us into yet another new era in which globalization and the demise
of the "Soviet Empire" enabled the recalibration of world politics
along progressive liberal-humanitarian lines and whose theme song
is "things can only get better." In this intellectual imaginary, then, the
bright new post-1989 liberal humanitarian world stands in stark contrast to the dark and oppressive era of nineteenth-century Eurocentric/
racist-imperialism.

This common mantra of contemporary liberal humanitarianism
relies on an "all-change idiom," in which world politics is represented
along a progressive evolutionary timeline punctuated by significant
moments of radical discontinuity that issue progressive normative
transformations (as in a "punctuated equilibrium" or "cladogenetic"
evolutionary model of change). However, I want to argue that this
is problematic insofar as it elides or obscures the many continuities
that exist between the nineteenth-century and post-1989 eras. Indeed,
the picture of radical discontinuity relies on two interrelated constructions of "temporal othering." These effect the construction of a
"twin-temporal binary" in which first, the "temporal other" of the
nineteenth century is represented as highly Eurocentric and racist so
that the post-1989 "temporal self" can be (re)presented as more tolerant, culturally pluralist and progressive than it is;[5] and second, the

---

[4] E.g., R.J. Vincent, "Racial Equality," in *The Expansion of International Society*,
eds. Hedley Bull and Adam Watson (Oxford: Oxford University Press, 1984),
239–54; Gerrit W. Gong, *The Standard of "Civilisation" in International
Society* (Oxford: Clarendon, 1984), 69; Audie Klotz, *Norms in International
Relations* (Ithaca: Cornell University Press, 1995).
[5] Robert J.C. Young, *Colonial Desire: Hybridity in Theory, Culture, and Race*
(London: Routledge, 1995).

nineteenth-century "temporal other" is represented as highly imperialist so that the post-1989 "temporal self" can be (re)presented as more non-imperialist than it is. Deconstructing – or "decolonizing" – these conjoined temporal binaries enables us to reveal the paradox of liberal humanitarianism: that, in both its pre-1945 and post-1989 incarnations, it embodies a politics of liberal-imperialism which is embedded within a paternalist-Eurocentric monism rather than a "tolerant" cultural pluralism. By no means is this meant to deny that various normative changes have indeed taken place in the last two centuries, but the crucial normative discourse of paternalist-Eurocentrism has not only remained, but its *aggregate depth* is probably more dominant today given that the "benign" purpose of nineteenth-century imperialism was often inflected beyond paternalist Eurocentrism by the impact of the harsher modes of scientific racism (which chimes with Michael N. Barnett's claim that the purpose of paternalism has become deeper over time; see Conclusion, this volume).[6] Moreover, while normative changes indeed might have "made colonialism taboo and respect for human rights essential,"[7] this misses the point that imperialism has been rehabilitated in the very practice that supposedly represents its nemesis: humanitarian interventionism.

Drawing out the paternalist aspect of post-1989 LHIT (or what I call "liberal humanitarianism 2.0") is nothing new since it has been highlighted by Michael N. Barnett in one of the finest and subtlest works I have seen in this literature, or anywhere else for that matter.[8] He claims that "the post-war paternalizers are not [defined as] superior because they are closer to God, come from the right Western country, or have the right skin color ... [but] because they have the right kind of training, education, and knowledge."[9] However, this technocratic cloak of the paternalizers, I want to argue, masks a liberal-imperialist mindset, for the fact is that the paternalists remain largely Western,

[6] Or as one authority puts it: "Nor did paternalism die out with colonialism. In fact, if humanitarian governance has grown, which it has, and if paternalism is alive and well, which it is, then paternalism is perhaps more prevalent today than it was during its presumed heyday during colonialism. Paternalism has been and remains central to the constitution of the global order." Michael N. Barnett, "International Paternalism and Humanitarian Governance," *Global Constitutionalism* 1, 3 (2012): 485–521, 487.
[7] Finnemore, *Purpose of Intervention*, 144.
[8] Michael N. Barnett, *Empire of Humanity* (Ithaca: Cornell University Press, 2011).
[9] Barnett, *Empire*, 516; see also Barnett, Conclusion, this volume.

Christian by name if not by conviction, almost always white, and
thought to be blessed with superior rational (or "expert"), Western
knowledge. Accordingly, this points to a Eurocentric mindset that is
reminiscent of pre-1945 imperialist, paternalist-Eurocentrism. Indeed,
the "expert knowledge" they bring turns out to comprise Western civilizational norms rather than something which is politically and ideologically neutral. Or put differently, in this imagination, such particu-
laristic Western norms are (re)presented, or masquerade, as universal
specialist/expert knowledge. And it is precisely when we are told that
norms are ideologically neutral or simply technocratic that we need to
be most on our guard.

For various reasons, however, most liberals would reject any comparison between liberal humanitarianism 2.0 and pre-1945 liberal-
imperial theory (or what I call "liberal humanitarianism 1.0"). The
first distinction drawn is that in the case of humanitarian interventionism, Western states seek neither to occupy nor to colonize the object
society so much as to undertake a rapid surgical strike in order to ter-
minate the immediate gross violation of human rights. But as Michael
N. Barnett points out, liberal humanitarianism 2.0 is girded with the
means to deal not simply with the violent symptoms of human rights
abuse, but with their "root causes." Thus a key property of liberal
humanitarianism 2.0 is that of "liberal peacebuilding," which emphasizes "the importance of markets, democracy, and human rights for
curing states of their ills and creating more peaceful and progressive
societies." Moreover, "[l]iberal peacebuilding is a highly invasive project; the expanded list of factors associated with a stable peace means
that nearly all of the features of state and society have become objects
of intervention."[10] Or as David Chandler put it, in the context of EU
enlargement, "[s]tatebuilding involves no less expenditure of resources
than empire, in fact, if anything, statebuilding is more invasive and
regulatory."[11] Thus it is precisely this which points up not only the
paternalist aspect of liberal humanitarianism 2.0 but, above all, the
associated imperial project of *culturally converting* Eastern states and
societies entirely along Western civilizational lines. Liberal humanitarians might reply by rhetorically asking how else Eastern states and

[10] Barnett, *Empire*, 164.
[11] David Chandler, "EU Statebuilding: Securing the Liberal Peace through EU
Enlargement," *Global Society* 21, 4 (2007): 593–607, 594.

societies could be rendered stable and safe for their own populations. Though by no means an unreasonable response, it merely confirms the point that I am making: that cultural conversion to the Western standard of civilization constitutes the very hallmark of liberal humanitarianism 2.0 (much as it did for liberal humanitarianism 1.0). And it is this which takes us directly into imperialist-ideational territory.

A second objection is articulated once again by Barnett who, though sympathetic to such a comparison, nevertheless claims that,

> Although humanitarian governance has the characteristics of empire, it differs in at least one critical way: it is dedicated to its own destruction. It is an empire of humanity, and humanity matters. In contrast to empires that fight for their immortality and whose decline we attribute to misadventure and self-defeating miscalculation, humanitarian governance hopes to put itself out of business. Empires might not mind – and might even enjoy – helping others as they help themselves, but the fundamental purposes of empire is to further the interests of the core, not the periphery.[12]

To this I have two responses, the first of which is that a critical property of pre-1945 liberal-imperial theory was precisely its dedication to the future destruction of Western imperialism. Thus imperialism was intended merely as a temporary catalyst of Eurocentric trusteeship, the function of which was to kick-start the development of Eastern societies so that their peoples too could come to enjoy the privileges of human rights and the political, social, and economic benefits that these entail. The paternalist-Eurocentric thinker, Gilbert Murray, expressed this idea thus:

> With regard to the general hegemony of the white races, our Liberal position is clear. It is expressed in Article XXII of the Covenant [of the League of Nations]. We do not believe in the equality of all nations; we believe rather in a certain hierarchy, no doubt a temporary hierarchy of races, or, at least, of civilizations.[13]

Thus, once these societies had been re-tracked onto a Western modernization path, imperialism, rather like Marx's socialist state once it

---

[12] Barnett, *Empire*, 222–3.
[13] Gilbert Murray (1925), cited in Jeanne Morefield, *Covenants Without Swords* (Princeton: Princeton University Press, 2005), 215.

had prepared the groundwork for communism, should simply wither away (though certainly the praxis of empire as performed by the various Western states belied this "noble" intention). Moreover, this is exactly commensurate with liberal logic given that the suspension of the Eastern individual's autonomy during the civilizing mission phase is necessarily temporary precisely because its sole purpose is to recalibrate Eastern societies along Western liberal lines so as to enable an unalloyed conception of Eastern individual autonomy to fructify in the future.

My second response is that Barnett's statement does not compare like with like. While the *practice* of liberal imperialism conducted by states and Great Powers before 1945 was indeed concerned with enhancing the colonizer society's self-interest, this was, however, very much a betrayal of liberal-imperial theory given its insistence that altruism, rather than self-interest, be the principal objective of imperialism. The left-liberal Leonard Woolf's words were typical when, in the context of European imperialism in Africa, he insisted that "the [old] belief that the State should use its power to promote the economic interests of Europeans would have to give place to the belief that its position was merely that of trustee for the native population and that its duty was to promote the interests, political, social and economic, of the Africans."[14] Or as the left-liberal imperialist writer J.A. Hobson put it, with respect to his theory of "sane imperialism," the Natives "should be gainers, not losers" and that "the direct gains of development should pass on equal terms to all the world and not to the capitalist exploiters of a single nation."[15] Likewise, liberal humanitarian theory today insists on precisely the same altruistic objective such that it would be unfair to dismiss the theory simply because states and Great Powers insert national self-interest into the humanitarian-interventionist mix. To argue that liberal humanitarians before and after 1945/1989 always need to be aware of the gap that inevitably exists between the theory and practice of humanitarianism is not,

---

[14] Leonard Woolf, *Empire and Commerce in Africa* (London: George Allen & Unwin, 1920), 362.

[15] J.A. Hobson, *The Recording Angel: A Report from Earth* (London: George Allen & Unwin, 1932), 78. For a discussion of Hobson's imperialist posture see John M. Hobson, *The Eurocentric Conception of World Politics: Western International Theory 1760–2010* (Cambridge: Cambridge University Press, 2012), 45–51.

however, to call into question the aspirations and logic of the theory in its own right.

Most generally, if we view all this through a purely international legal lens, then the twenty-first century looks quite different to its nineteenth-century predecessor. And it is this view which has sustained the liberal humanitarian belief that today we live in a bright new world that stands as the antithesis of the dark, racist, imperial past. The logic goes as follows: while in the nineteenth century sovereignty was the preserve of Western imperialist Great Powers and was denied to Eastern polities, the League of Nations Mandate System exhibited a shift in which Great Power imperialist interests were trumped by international law, a shift that culminated in the UN General Assembly Declaration on the Granting of Independence to Colonial Countries and Peoples (Resolution 1514), wherein colonialism was outlawed. There is no question that legal norms have changed and that formal colonialism is no longer an option on the Great Power menu, and there is no doubting that this is not an insignificant shift. But ultimately, what has shifted is the modus operandi of imperialism. Thus, despite all the liberal hopes at the time, the Mandate System nevertheless ultimately served to legitimize the various national imperial projects. And while the granting of sovereignty to once-colonized states was undoubtedly important, the post-1989 liberal humanitarian normative shift to "conditional sovereignty" marks a step back to the imperial past, constituting the means by which Western states can legitimately intervene in Eastern societies once more. Moreover, humanitarianism's logic of state-building/state reconstruction/liberal peacebuilding that follows the initial intervention marks precisely the same logic of the civilizing mission which demands the cultural conversion of Eastern societies to the Western standard of civilization. But this imperial dimension is missed by liberal IR scholars partly because of their tendency to reify international law and partly because they conflate imperialism with exploitation.

This leads directly on to an issue raised by Barnett who, when pointing out various parallels between humanitarianism and imperialism, suggests that "[h]umanitarian governance occasionally has a chummy relationship with the very empires that it supposedly resists. Powerful states generously fund humanitarian organizations, and the agendas of Great Powers and humanitarian groups have overlapped for decades."[16] Such a point equally feeds into a realist critique of humanitarian intervention.[17] But my critique of liberal humanitarianism as a paternalist-Eurocentric imperialist ideology is not reliant upon rooting out any convergent practices between Great Power imperialism and humanitarian organizations or, equally, any divergences between them that compromise or contradict humanitarian theoretical logic. Nor, I might add, is my critique based on the arguments made by those, such as Mark Duffield and David Chandler, who believe that imposing liberalism on Eastern societies leads inherently to the *infraction* of the very long-term autonomy of individuals that liberal peacebuilding is supposed to secure, although their fascinating claims certainly would add fuel to my critique.[18] Instead I focus specifically on the logic of the theory of liberal humanitarianism/LHIT and its international paternalist modus operandi on its own terms.

What is interesting here is that while most liberal humanitarians deny the linkage between humanitarian interventionism and paternalist imperialism, some have sought to bring the "E-Word" (empire) out of the liberal closet. Michael Ignatieff proclaims the liberal-humanitarian mission to be a fundamental component of a benign US neo-imperialism, to wit: "what is exceptional about American [humanitarian] messianism is that it is the last imperial ideology left standing in the world, the sole survivor of imperial claims to universal significance."[19] And it is no coincidence that Ignatieff's conception of "empire-lite" was first articulated in a piece entitled "The Burden."[20] Moreover, Robert Cooper portrays imperialism today in terms that are highly reminiscent of the nineteenth-century conception of the civilizing mission: "one [that must be] acceptable to a world of human rights and cosmopolitan values ... an

---

[16] Barnett, *Empire*, 222.

[17] Jeremy Moses, "Sovereignty as Irresponsibility? A Realist Critique of the Responsibility to Protect," *Review of International Studies* 39, 1 (2013): 113–35.

[18] E.g., David Chandler, *Empire in Denial* (London: Pluto, 2006); Mark Duffield, *Development, Security and Unending War* (Cambridge: Polity, 2007).

[19] Michael Ignatieff, "Introduction: American Exceptionalism and Human Rights," in *American Exceptionalism and Human Rights*, ed. Michael Ignatieff (Princeton: Princeton University Press, 2005), 16.

[20] Michael Ignatieff, "The Burden," *New York Times Magazine*, January 5, 2003, www.nytimes.com/2003/01/05/magazine/05EMPIRE.html?pagewanted=all (accessed November 7, 2015).

imperialism which, like all imperialism, aims to bring order and organization but which rests today as the voluntary principle ... [based on] the lightest of touches from the centre."[21] Indeed, even "liberal-realists," such as Niall Ferguson, have sought to reclaim the term "liberal-empire" by arguing that US imperialism today, just like its British predecessor, is beneficent in that it delivers free trade, liberal capitalism, and democracy to the world.[22] The task of the next section is to extract the humanitarian interventionist properties of liberal-imperial theory that existed prior to 1945 before the final section reveals their presence in contemporary liberal humanitarianism 2.0.

The Paternalist-Eurocentric Politics of "Liberal Humanitarianism 1.0"

Elsewhere I have argued that "Orientalism" is a highly complex archipelago of discourses which comprises paternalist and anti-paternalist Eurocentric institutionalism, on the one hand, and imperialist and anti-imperialist scientific racism, on the other.[23] Because this chapter is concerned mainly with paternalist Eurocentrism I shall first consider how "paternalist liberal humanitarianism 1.0" was constructed in the nineteenth century before revealing how it finds its expression in contemporary "paternalist liberal humanitarianism 2.0" in the next section.

First and foremost, what I call "Eurocentric institutionalism" locates difference in terms of institutional/cultural factors (as opposed to scientific racism which focuses on genes, environment, and climate). As it emerged after 1750, and developed into its complete form during the nineteenth century, Eurocentric institutionalism posits that *all* humans and *all* societies have recourse to universal reason and that *all* are capable of progressing from savagery through barbarism into civilization. Nevertheless, paternalist Eurocentrism posited that the rationality of Eastern societies was only latent and that they were mired in backward and irrational institutions which ensured the continuing poverty, repression, and inhumane treatment of their peoples. This rests on the

---

[21] Robert Cooper, "The New Liberal Imperialism," *Observer*, April 7, 2002, www.theguardian.com/world/2002/apr/07/1 (accessed November 7, 2015).

[22] Niall Ferguson, *Colossus: The Rise and Fall of the American Empire* (Harmondsworth: Penguin, 2004), 169–199, and 286–302.

[23] Hobson, *Eurocentric Conception*, ch. 1.

general Eurocentric move that sets up a binary construction in which the Western "self" enjoys *rational* institutions – democracy, the rule of law, bureaucracy, liberalism, individualism, science, etc. – all of which ensure Western progressive development into capitalist modernity while, conversely, the Eastern "other" endures *irrational* institutions – Oriental despotism or the state of nature, patrimonial bureaucracy or the absence of bureaucracy, authoritarianism, collectivism, and mysticism, etc. – all of which ensures Eastern stagnation and the repression of its peoples. In short, paternalist-Eurocentrism constructs a "civilizational frontier" that separates the civilized and "exceptional" West from the uncivilized East.

However, as Figure 3.1 reveals, overlaid upon this binary construction was a three-worlds meta-geographical conception of the world based on the social construct of the Western "standard of civilization." At the top of this discursive hierarchy stands the civilized West. Below this stands the second world of barbarism that was said to be governed by repressive Oriental despotism, with the third world of savagery residing at the bottom, living in an anarchic domestic state of nature. This, in turn, generated a schizophrenic construction of sovereignty. For the idea of the standard of civilization, which formed the basis of positivist international law but which emerged outside of it, deemed that only civilized states are worthy of sovereignty. This was famously advanced by John Stuart Mill:

To suppose that the same international customs, and the same rules of international morality, can obtain between one civilized nation and another, and between civilized nations and barbarians, is a grave error ... In the first place, the rules of ordinary international morality imply reciprocity. But barbarians will not reciprocate. They cannot be depended on for observing any rules ... In the next place, nations which are still barbarous have not got beyond the period during which it is likely to be for their benefit that they should be conquered and held in subjection by foreigners.[24]

The final part of this quote leads from the paternalist-Eurocentric norms of international law to a fully imperialist rationale insofar as Eastern polities/societies must also be denied sovereignty so that a

[24] John Stuart Mill, "A Few Words on Non-Intervention," in *Collected Works of John Stuart Mill*, XXI, ed. John M. Robson (Toronto: Toronto University Press, 1859/1984), 118.

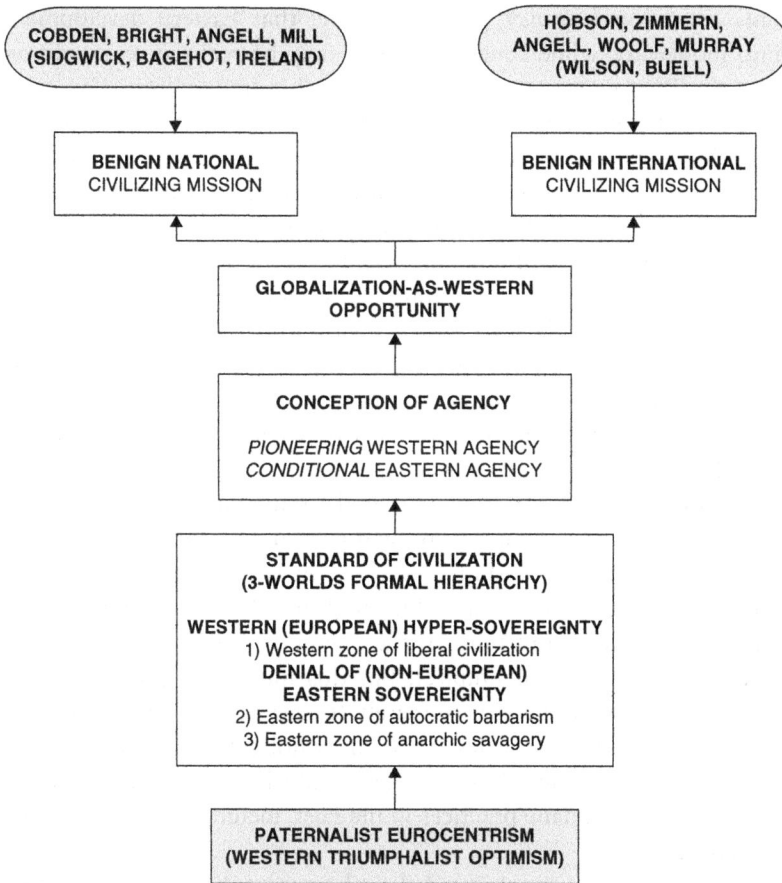

Figure 3.1 *Pre-1945 Liberal Humanitarianism 1.0 as Promoter of Western civilization*

discursive space can be opened up for Western imperial interventionism. Specifically, here we encounter a schizophrenic construction of sovereignty, wherein civilized Western states were rewarded with the privilege of "hyper-sovereignty" and the mandate of humanitarian-imperialism, while non-Western societies were denied the privilege of sovereignty in order to open them up to such imperial emancipation. And moving up one box in Figure 3.1, this rested on the paternalist-Eurocentric assumption that Western societies enjoy a *pioneering agency*, such that they can auto-generate or auto-develop into modernity while conversely, Eastern societies are said to endure only *conditional agency*, given the belief that Eastern development into modernity, while conceivable, can only be realized *on condition* that the West intervenes through paternalist imperialism. Critically, then, for liberal paternalists, imperialism is a civilizing mission which, by bringing to the surface the latent rationality of Eastern societies through the deliverance of the requisite rational institutions, enables them to subsequently develop into modernity. Such a civilizing mission constitutes a "vehicle of humanitarian intervention" which can rescue the inferior Eastern peoples from the inhumane treatment, poverty, and suffering that their irrational institutions had previously delivered. All in all, then, paternalist-liberal imperialism creates a "Genesis effect," wherein the "civilizational frontier" moves ever outwards, gutting Eastern societies in its path, and refurbishing them with bright new Western civilizational features.

Of course, it might be replied that the humanitarian aspect of the civilizing mission was the exceptional part and was limited to only a few "relatively minor" instances, such as the British termination of the Hindu practice of *Sati* (widow-burning), the Western termination of female foot-binding in China, or the saving of white Christians (principally in the Ottoman Empire). But this misses the point that, for liberal-paternalists, these were merely the tip of a vast humanitarian iceberg, wherein nothing less than the wholesale transformation of Eastern societies along Western lines would be affected so as to put an end to *all* inhumane practices in the East, including gross abuses of human rights.

Equally, it might be objected that the paternalist-Eurocentric discourse of the "white man's burden" was merely a thin ideological veneer applied *after* imperialism began in order to recast it in a morally legitimate light, and that, as such, it was but a sideshow to the real theater of imperial action where repression and economic exploitation stood center-stage (as many anti-imperialist/anti-paternalist liberals, such as Immanuel Kant and Herbert Spencer, argued). But this misses the point that the paternalist-Eurocentric thinkers, many of whom were liberals, were entirely sincere in prescribing the civilizing mission as a means to heal Eastern societies by enabling them to progress into a democratic-capitalist Western future so that they too could enjoy full human rights and the civilized benefits of individual autonomy (in exactly the same way that modern liberal humanitarian interventionist theorists argue for today). They were no less adamant that such intervention should *not* be undertaken with Great Power self-interest in mind, as I noted with respect to Leonard Woolf (even though, of course, the *practice* of imperialism always contradicted or disturbed this criterion). This noble-humanitarian sentiment was advanced by the likes of John Stuart Mill, Norman Angell, Alfred Zimmern, and, perhaps most surprisingly, Richard Cobden and John Bright.[25] But it also found its expression in the works of left-liberals, "new liberals" and British idealists, including J.A. Hobson, Leonard Hobhouse, William Robertson, and John Muirhead, as well as socialist and Fabian writers, including Ramsay MacDonald and Leonard Woolf. And equally, a similar formula found its expression in the works of some liberal scientific racists, including Woodrow Wilson, Raymond Buell, Alleyne Ireland, Henry Sidgwick, George Bernard Shaw, and David Ritchie (who are placed in brackets in Figure 3.1).[26] As indicated in Figure 3.1, some called for *national* forms of liberal-imperialism while others called for "international imperialism" (where an independent body contained within the League of Nations would supervise the various national empires in order to ensure that they worked in the interests of the Natives). Indeed, it was precisely because the Great Powers had often twisted imperialism to suit their own self-interest that many liberals embraced the League of Nations Mandate System. Typical here was David Mitrany, who argued that the Mandate System constituted a victory of international law over Great Power interests when he concluded that the Great Powers "have accepted of their own free will a restriction of rights acquired by conquest and placed their new acquisitions under the control of the League."[27] And recall that Article 22 of the League Covenant stipulated that "there should be applied the principle that the well-being and development of [colonized] peoples form a sacred trust of civilization and that securities for the performance of this trust should be embodied in this Covenant." Equally, when it failed to achieve these ends many liberals turned their backs on it.[28]

---

[25] See Hobson, *Eurocentric Conception*, ch. 2.

[26] See Hobson, *Eurocentric Conception*, chs. 2, 5, and 7.

[27] David Mitrany, *The Progress of International Government* (London: George Allen & Unwin, 1933), 79.

[28] E.g., J.A. Hobson, *Problems of a New World* (London: George Allen & Unwin, 1921).

Finally, and somewhat surprisingly, all pre-1945 paternalist-Eurocentric liberals were aware of what today we call "globalization," but which, back then, was usually referred to as global "interdependence" (or, according to racist-realists, the "closing of the world").[29] Critically, such liberal thinkers in effect constructed "globalization-as-Western opportunity" to remake the world along progressive Western civilizational lines.[30] That is, globalization brought all societies close together such that they were all tied into a collective world-community of fate and that, as such, the West was primed or charged with the mandate of ensuring the *cultural conversion* of all societies along Western lines for the betterment of the world. The question now becomes: how does such a discourse find its expression in modern "liberal humanitarianism 2.0"?

The Paternalist-Eurocentric Politics of "Liberal Humanitarianism 2.0"

In this section I argue that "liberal humanitarianism 2.0," which emerged after 1989, is founded on the same paternalist-Eurocentric base as that of "liberal-humanitarianism 1.0." The various Eurocentric categories are represented in Figure 3.2. The bottom left box's designation of paternalist-Eurocentrism can be elaborated by considering each of the subsequent categories in turn. I shall not discuss what I call "Western-realism," which has also been represented in Figure 3.2, but it serves at least as an implicit point of comparison.[31]

Reconstructing the Tripartite Eurocentric Global Hierarchy and the Standard of Civilization

Moving up one level within Figure 3.2, I argue that, like its nineteenth-century predecessor, "Western-liberalism," which is broadly synonymous with "liberal humanitarianism 2.0," in effect constructs a "civilizational frontier," on one side of which stands

[29] E.g., H.J. Mackinder, "The Geographical Pivot of History," *The Geographical Journal* 23, 4 (1904): 421–37.

[30] See Hobson, *Eurocentric Conception*, esp. 331–7.

[31] "Western-realism" is an umbrella term that comprises a wide array of theorists who include the likes of Robert Kaplan, Paul Kennedy, Samuel Huntington, and William Lind; see Hobson, *Eurocentric Conception*, ch. 11.

WESTERN–LIBERALISM
Things can only get better

WESTERN LIBERAL–REALISM/
REALIST–LIBERALISM
Things could get better or bitter

WESTERN–REALISM
Things can only get bitter

CIVILIZING THE BARBARIANS
AND SAVAGES

The Coming Peace and the
Universalization of Western
Civilization

The End of History
Obsolescence of war in the West/
Democratic peace theory
Liberal-Cosmopolitanism

Responsibility to protect/
Humanitarian interventionism
IFI pacification/neo-liberal conversion

Neo-trusteeships/
Decertification of failed
states

Anti-Immigration/Safe
return

Duty to Prevent
Pre-emptive/
Preventive Defence
(Bush Doctrine 2002)

Concert/League of
Democracies

"Benevolent" US
hegemony/Unipolar
moment

CONTAINING THE BARBARIANS

The Coming Anarchy and the New
Barbaric Threat
Eastern demographic time-bomb,
tribal warfare, terrorism, displaced
warfare, exodus of refugees,
the Yellow Peril

THE BARBARIAN TROJAN HORSE
INSIDE THE WESTERN CITADEL
Fears over non-Western immigrants
and the multicultural threat to
Western civilization

GLOBALIZATION-AS-WESTERN
OPPORTUNITY
Globalization as diffuser of Western
norms and civilizer of the East

GLOBALIZATION-AS-EASTERN
(BARBARIC) THREAT
Globalization brings the Eastern peril
onto the doorstep, and inside the
gates, of the Western citadel

STANDARD OF CIVILIZATION
(3-WORLD FORMAL AND INFORMAL HIERARCHY)

WESTERN HYPER-SOVEREIGNTY
1) Western zone of liberal *pacific civilization*

EASTERN CONDITIONAL-SOVEREIGNTY
2) Eastern zone of *autocratic barbarism*
(Oriental despotism)
3) Eastern zone of *failed states* (anarchic savagery)

PATERNALIST EUROCENTRISM
(WESTERN TRIUMPHALIST
OPTIMISM)

OFFENSIVE/DEFENSIVE
EUROCENTRISM
(WESTERN PESSIMISTIC ANGST)

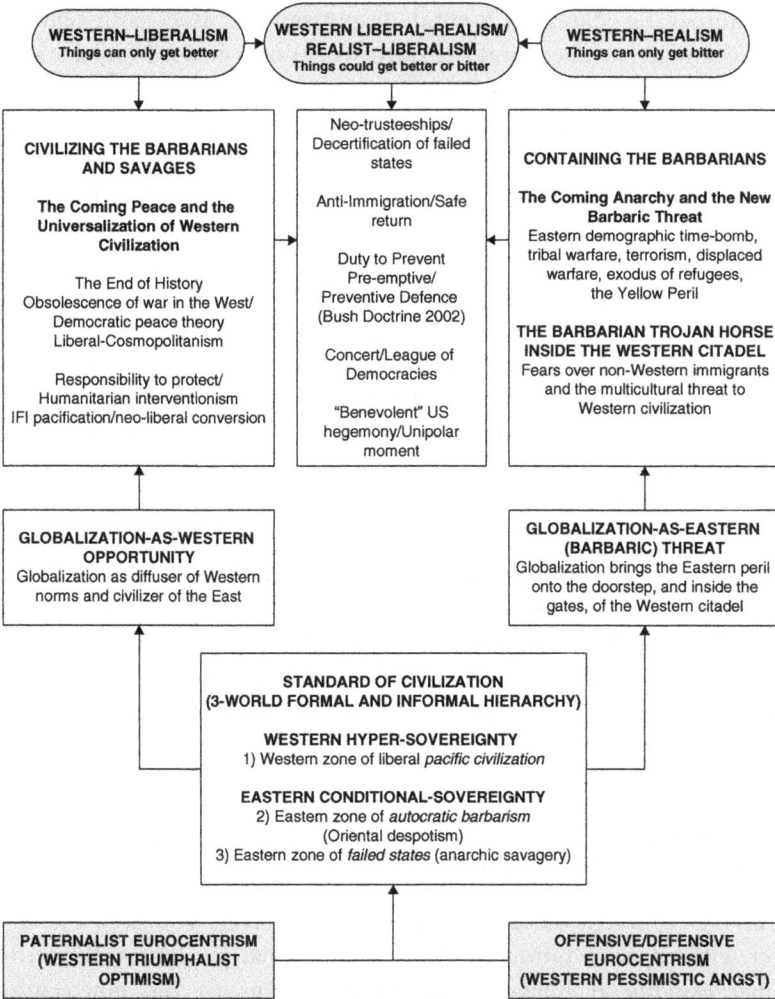

Figure 3.2 *Post-1989 Liberal Humanitarianism 2.0 as Promoter of Western civilization*
Source: J.M. Hobson, *The Eurocentric Conception of World Politics: Western International Theory* (Cambridge: Cambridge University Press, 2012), p. 260.

the "civilized West," while the "uncivilized East" languishes on the other side. Overlaid upon this is, once again, a three-worlds hierarchical meta-geography that derives from the idiom of the standard of civilization/standard of statehood. The first world comprises "civilized liberal" states, which is contrasted with the second world of autocratic states ("Oriental despotism" in nineteenth-century Eurocentric parlance) and the third world of collapsed/failed states ("savage" anarchical societies in nineteenth-century Eurocentric parlance). An obvious example of this is found in the work of John Rawls who divides the world into civilized liberal states, "outlaw states" (based on aggressive and repressive Oriental despotisms in the second world), and "burdened societies" (akin to savage societies residing in a domestic state of nature within the third world).[32] Equally, Robert Cooper differentiates three worlds, with European "postmodern states," which have created a civilized zone of peace occupying the first world. European states owe their peaceful relations to an "honest" and civilized "moral consciousness" which rejects war (or more specifically, war between civilized states); a position that was articulated previously by the liberal scholar, John Mueller.[33] The second world comprises "modern states," located principally in Asia, which engage in old-style relations involving Machiavellian (and Oriental despotic) principles of *raison d'état* and warfare, while the third world comprises "pre-modern states" – specifically failed/collapsed states – which are reduced to a (savage) anarchic state of nature torn apart by a Hobbesian war of all against all.[34] It is critical to note that this is not simply an innocent description but is politically loaded.[35]

Reconstructing Western "Hyper-Sovereignty"/Eastern "Conditional-Sovereignty"

Having separated out East from West and having endowed the latter with superior rational politico-institutional properties, Western-liberalism/liberal humanitarianism returns us to the nineteenth-century *bipolar* formal hierarchical conception of world politics that I discussed earlier with reference to John Stuart Mill's maxim.

---

[32] John Rawls, *The Law of Peoples* (London: Harvard University Press, 1999).
[33] John Mueller, *Retreat From Doomsday* (New York: Basic Books, 1989).
[34] Robert Cooper, *The Breaking of Nations* (London: Atlantic Books, 2004).
[35] Nevertheless, it is important to concede that while the Second World is represented by the likes of authoritarian Middle Eastern polities and Chinese autocracy, it is also true that there is an intra-Western dimension here, represented by quasi-authoritarian Russia. Accordingly, not all aspects of Western-liberalism can be captured perfectly within the framework that I deploy here.

A similar, albeit modified, trope is applied within liberal humanitarianism 2.0. Here it is argued that Eastern polities should not be granted sovereignty in a once-and-for-all move. Rather, such theorists argue that sovereignty in the non-Western world should have a "conditional status" whereby sovereignty should only be recognized or "allowed" when a state acts in a "civilized way"; that is, when it treats its own population fairly by respecting human rights contained within a democratic form of governance. The difference between this conception and that held before 1945 boils down simply to one of context: contemporary liberals are working within a post-colonial world, such that Eastern states have already been awarded sovereignty following decolonization. Thus, unlike their ancestors, liberal humanitarians today cannot do away with Eastern sovereignty altogether, for it is now a done deal. Instead they insist on *conditional* Eastern sovereignty, wherein sovereignty can be temporarily withdrawn through a "decertification process" should civilized conditions fail to prevail domestically.[36] Accordingly, the paternal-imperialist song remains the same.

Nevertheless, the similarity becomes yet closer when we recognize that some liberal humanitarians demand the *absolute* withdrawal or termination of Eastern sovereignty. Robert Keohane, for one, argues in relation to "troubled societies" (which are reminiscent of Rawls's "burdened societies") that they "may have more or less of it, but the classic ideal-type of Westphalian sovereignty should be abandoned even as an aspiration." And he insists that even once these troubled societies have been refurbished with a Western form of state, they should still be denied full sovereignty in favor of "gradations of sovereignty,"[37] thereby returning us to the nineteenth-century imperialist-hierarchical conception of a "procession of sovereignty." Either way, though, "conditional sovereignty" is the vital prerequisite or normative trigger for Western neo-imperial intervention much as the absence of Eastern sovereignty was for nineteenth-century paternalist-liberalism. In short,

---

[36] Jeffrey Herbst, "Let Them Fail: State Failure in Theory and Practice – Implications for Policy," in *When States Fail*, ed. Robert Rotberg (Princeton: Princeton University Press, 2004).

[37] Robert Keohane, "Political Authority after Intervention: Gradations in Sovereignty," in *Humanitarian Intervention: Ethical, Legal and Political Dilemmas*, eds. J.L. Holzgrefe and Robert Keohane (Cambridge: Cambridge University Press, 2003), 276–7.

Eastern *conditional sovereignty* is the flip-side of the coin that sports Western state imperialist *hyper-sovereignty* as its heads-side.

Reconstructing Globalization-as-Western Opportunity

Moving up another level in Figure 3.2, while "Western-realists" construct *globalization-as-Eastern threat*,[38] Western liberals construct *globalization-as-Western opportunity* to remake the world along civilized Western lines. Certainly Western-liberals (like Western-realists) also emphasize the "dark side" of globalization – for example, ecological crisis, nuclear weapons proliferation, terrorism, the democratic deficit, and the flood of refugees/emigrants from failed states. But these social diseases can be cured with the antidote of Western interventionism. Thus globalization is thought to enable the West to diffuse and universalize its civilizational norms (economic, political, cultural, and ethical) around the world in order to *culturally convert* all states along Western lines, much as it was for liberal humanitarianism 1.0.

The question now becomes: what is international paternalism and how is it informed by imperialist-Eurocentric thinking?

The Paradoxes and Properties of International Paternalism

Moving up to the final level of Figure 3.2, we encounter a series of Western-liberal/liberal humanitarian theories advocating the need to "civilize the barbarian and savage societies" (though, of course, these terms go by labels that dare not speak their name, such as autocracies/rogue states, failed/collapsed states, the "axis of evil," etc.). The impetus to this thrust was reflected in Francis Fukuyama's "end of history" thesis, which appeared on the eve of 11/9 and acted as virtual midwife in the birth of post-Cold War Western-liberalism, proselytizing Western liberal capitalist-democracy as the final stage of human history.[39] It

[38] E.g., Paul Kennedy, *Preparing for the Twenty-First Century* (New York: Random House, 1993); Robert D. Kaplan, "The Coming Anarchy," *Atlantic Monthly*, February, 1994, www.theatlantic.com/magazine/archive/1994/02/the-coming-anarchy/304670/ (accessed November 7, 2015).
[39] Francis Fukuyama, "The End of History?" *The National Interest* 16 (1989): 3–18. That this rehabilitation of Hegel entails a Eurocentric move reflects the latter's well-known claim that "[t]he History of the World travels from East to West, for Europe [i.e., the West] is absolutely the end of history, Asia the beginning." G.W.F. Hegel, *The Philosophy of History* (Kitchener: Batoche Books, 1837/2001), 122.

was, however, not just the end of the Cold War and the demise of the Soviet Union that created this discursive space for the emergence of new paternalist liberal imperialism. For even more important was the point that Western liberals, having overcome the racist colonial-guilt syndrome that had gripped much of the Western imagination between 1945 and 1989, were now girded once more with the messianic desire not to conquer the world but to culturally convert it to the norms of Western civilization for the betterment of all peoples and races. Larry Diamond characterized this sentiment thus: "Not since the end of World War I have the Western democracies had such an opportunity to shape the political nature of our world. By promoting democracy abroad, the United States can help bring into being for the first time in history a world composed mainly of stable democracies."[40]

More specifically, the Responsibility to Protect (R2P) is usually thought of as a strategy which enables Western states to intervene in Third World states only when the gross abuse of human rights occurs. On first viewing, this idea appears to differentiate R2P from the old liberal-imperial discourse, whereby the latter involves a "semi-permanent" occupation of the backward Eastern society, as opposed to the former's surgical strike modus operandi. But, as I noted in this chapter's introduction, the similarities emerge more clearly in the subsequent phase of humanitarian intervention which advocates the rebuilding of Eastern polities along Western liberal lines – otherwise known as liberal peacebuilding/state reconstruction. Thus, once again, humanitarian intervention constitutes a "weapon of mass deliverance" wherein the "civilizational frontier" expands outwards, ever eastward, as the Rest is culturally converted to the Western standard of state-hood/civilization through the "Genesis effect." Such a grand imperial design is articulated by one of the theory's most visible proselytizers, Fernando Téson, who argues that "[h]umanitarian intervention is one tool to help move the quantum of political freedom in the continuum of political coercion to the Kantian center of that continuum away ... from the extreme lack of order (anarchy), and ... from governmen-tal suppression of individual freedom (tyranny)."[41] And this applies

---

[40] Larry Diamond, "Promoting Democracy," *Foreign Policy* 87 (Summer, 1992): 29.

[41] Fernando Téson, "The Liberal Case for Humanitarian Intervention," in Holzgrefe and Keohane, *Humanitarian Intervention*, 97.

equally to Keohane, Ignatieff, Rawls, and many others, as already noted. Critically, a key ingredient of this neo-imperial project lies with its paternalist modus operandi. Or, put differently, the paternalist modus operandi of humanitarian interventionism provides the cue for revealing the theory's imperialist properties.

Here I develop further some of the criticisms of international paternalism that Barnett makes,[42] while simultaneously linking this discourse to the imperialist mindset of the pre-1945 paternalist-Eurocentric thinkers (as well as some liberal imperial-*racists*). I also follow Barnett's definition provided in the Introduction and Conclusion to this volume that international paternalism comprises "one actor's substitution of his judgment for another on the grounds that it is in her interests, welfare or happiness." I would also concur with the expanded definition that Barnett advances elsewhere, in which "international paternalism exists when one actor interferes in the affairs of another actor without its consent and justifies such interference on the grounds that it improves the subject's welfare, interests, or utility."[43] With this in mind, I single out eight core properties of international paternalism, five of which are core or primary properties and three of which are secondary. These are as follows:

Primary Properties of International Paternalism

1. The "duty" or "mandate" to assist "inferior" societies that are *unable to help themselves*.
2. The *intervening subject knows best* what the object society's interests are given that the object society *suffers from false consciousness*.
3. The intervening subject acts according to his/her own *notion of the political good* which entails a *sense of self-righteousness*.
4. The *intervener's self-righteousness* means that obtaining the *consent of the object* for the necessary reforms is unnecessary and is indeed best avoided given the object's false consciousness and that only the subject can see into the object's future.
5. A power relationship of control (rather than one of exploitation) in which the object's individual autonomy is suspended.

---

[42] Barnett, "International Paternalism," 485–521.
[43] Barnett, "International Paternalism," 500.

Secondary Properties of International Paternalism

6. The object's perception of a patronizing and hypocritical attitude on the part of the subject which fuels the latter's performance of double standards.
7. The subject's *non-reflexiveness* and *self-delusion* nurtures an unalloyed messianic zeal for undertaking future interventions.
8. The subject's assumption that there is a *one-to-one correspondence* between benign-humanitarian intentions and outcomes.

I shall take the primary and secondary properties in turn. First and foremost, while international paternalism is unequivocally a *discourse of benevolence* rather than one of oppression or exploitation, nevertheless the subject society is self-mandated to assist deeply troubled Eastern societies, thereby reconvening the idiom of the "white man's burden," which requires the intervening *subject* to act "on behalf of" the weak/inferior *object* in ways that are not open to the latter. Here I differ from the argument made by Aisling Swaine (Chapter 6, this volume). She follows the definition of paternalism advanced by Christophe Salvat, wherein one property of paternalism comprises actions that serve only the interests of the paternalist intervener, for the paternalist logic of intervention is premised on the paternalizer's genuinely benign desire to serve only the interests of the paternalized. The point, though, is that this benign desire or obligation reconvenes the paternalist-Eurocentric idiom of "pioneering" Western agency and "conditional" Eastern agency (or Western capacity versus non-Western incapacity), wherein the civilizing mission becomes the Western humanitarian vehicle given that only the West can *uplift* inferior peoples/societies that are bereft of the very rational institutions which could enable them to help themselves. Thus to adapt Samuel Smiles's famous dictum, "liberal peacebuilding helps those [ultimately to] help themselves." Such paternalist ideas informed much of the discourse of "trusteeship" found in the League of Nations Mandate System, which was based on the idiom of "the sacred trust of civilization" and whose rationale was for Western states to intervene paternalistically in order to prepare the inferior societies that were not yet able to stand on their own feet for future self-determination.[44]

---

[44] William Bain, *Between Anarchy and Society* (Oxford: Oxford University Press, 2003).

No less noteworthy is that while the imperial-discursive rationale of
this system originated with the 1884 Berlin Conference that sought to
prepare the basis for the imperial carve-up of Africa by the Western
Great Powers, nevertheless the very idea of trusteeship was the core
component of paternalist imperial theory in general, and of British
imperialism in particular. Still, one does not need to infer an imperialist political underbelly to liberal humanitarianism 2.0 here, given
that many of its advocates explicitly advance the cause of "benevolent
neo-trusteeship" as a means to "emancipate" the irrational East, as
do many "Western-realists" as well as "Western liberal-realists" and
"Western realist-liberals."[45]

Most importantly, we find lurking beneath this discourse of benevolence a series of assumptions that challenge the cardinal liberal axioms
of individual autonomy, free will, and agency.[46] Chief among them is
the second key property of international paternalism – the assumption that the *intervener always knows best* and that he or she knows
better than the object of what his/her interests comprise, given that
the latter in effect suffers from false consciousness. Thus because the
Rest does not know what its real interests are, it is incumbent upon
the West to tell the Rest of what its interests comprise given that the
"West knows best." And while it is true that the West has moved most
recently to the idea of "partnership" in many of its humanitarian

[45] Gerald Helman and Steven Ratner, "Saving Failed States," *Foreign Policy*
89 (1992–3): 3–20; Peter Lyon, "The Rise and Fall and Possible Revival
of International Trusteeship," *Journal of Commonwealth & Comparative
Politics* 31, 1 (1993): 96–110; Stephen Krasner, "Sharing Sovereignty: New
institutions for Collapsed and Failing States," *International Security* 29,
2 (2004): 85–120; James Fearon and David Laitin, "Failed States and
Protectorates," *International Security* 28, 4 (2004): 5–43; Francis Fukuyama,
"Building Democracy after Conflict: 'Stateness First'," *Journal of Democracy*
16, 1 (2005): 84–8; Lene Mosegaard Søbjerg, "Trusteeship and the Concept of
Freedom," *Review of International Studies* 33, 3 (2007): 457–88; Herbst, "Let
them Fail"; Keohane, "Political Authority after Intervention."
[46] This is a contested idea given that a minority position rejects the point that
paternalism infringes upon the liberty of the individual; e.g., Bernard Gert
and Charles M. Culver, "Paternalistic Behavior," *Philosophy and Public
Affairs* 6, 1 (1976): 45–57. For the majority position see: Gerald Dworkin,
"Paternalism," *The Monist* 56 (1972): 64–84; Michael D. Bayles, "Criminal
Paternalism," in *Limits of Law Nomos XV*, eds. James R. Pennock and
John W. Chapman (New York: Lieber-Atherton, 1974), 174–88; Donald
H. Regan, "Justifications for Paternalism," in Pennock and Chapman, *Limits*,
189–210.

forms of intervention, these too betray a certain paternalism,[47] a point which raises the thorny issue of whether humanitarian intervention can ever take the form of a non-paternalist modus operandi. Either way, though, both these interrelated points emanate from the assumption that the intervening subject is armed with a "superior rational-civilized culture" that presupposes an inferior or irrational mindset on the part of the object-peoples, as was the case with liberal-imperial theory 1.0.

Third, paternalism, though undoubtedly motivated by benign and the very best of altruistic intentions, operates according to the *intervener's own conception of the "political good."* Indeed it is axiomatic that this conception is superior to any that the object society might hold, all of which entail a notion of "self-righteousness" on the part of the subject. Moreover, this furnishes the paternalist subject with the "will to demand" of the object that it follows to the letter all the requirements imposed (given that "father knows best"), whether these actually help out or not.

Fourth, this sense of the subject's self-righteousness is such that gaining the consent of the object is deemed either unnecessary or to be positively avoided because the object is unable to recognize its own "real" interests given its supposed false consciousness. It is this problem which is brought out in many of the chapters in this volume, especially those which are dedicated to examining the mentality of those who intervene on the ground.[48] Moreover, a strong sense of self-righteousness is functionally required to arm the subject with the necessary determination to push through the requisite reforms of the object society. For while paternalist intervention undoubtedly infringes on the liberty, and often the dignity, of the object, this is not infrequently ignored by the paternalist subject on the grounds that curtailing the short-term freedom of the object society is functionally necessary so as to make possible its long-term freedom (though I don't doubt that this attitude is one that preys on the conscience of some of those who intervene on the ground as is made clear in some of the chapters in this volume; see especially Swaine, Chapter 6). And in any case, one should expect object societies to

---

[47] Maria Eriksson Baaz, *The Paternalism of Partnership* (London: Zed, 2005).
[48] See, e.g., Autesserre, Chapter 5, this volume; but cf. Swaine, Chapter 6, this volume.

complain once intervention begins, given Rudyard Kipling's warning to his American audience in 1899 when reading out the "White Man's Burden" – that the paternalist-imperialist should expect to receive only "the blame of those ye better, the hate of those ye guard" (a point which is reinforced in Séverine Autesserre's chapter, where she insists that listening to the complaints of the object peoples should very much preoccupy the conscience of the interveners if they are to transcend their own paternalism). Nevertheless, the logic of liberal humanitarian theory, as opposed to some of those who engage in humanitarianism on the ground, requires that the paternal-imperialist must plow on even in – or particularly in – the face of such short-term recalcitrance on the part of the seemingly ungrateful, short-sighted object precisely because the paternalist intervener is blessed with the unique property of being able to see into the object's beneficent future.

A fifth property of international paternalism flows from the fourth: that international paternalism entails a *power-relationship of control* (as opposed to a power-relationship of exploitation). This is a necessary property of liberal international paternalism because of the fundamental presumption that the object is helpless and requires rescuing by the intervening object, thereby rehabilitating the nineteenth-century trope of (the Eastern) Sleeping Beauty being awakened and saved by the kiss of her dashing and heroic imperialist (Western) prince. Still, a controlling element is necessary given that the object often resists such paternalist intervention owing to its "false consciousness" and that the program of intervention often goes against the immediate (irrational) preference-set of the object. Accordingly the object is best "seen but not heard." Nevertheless, because the paternalist is so convinced of the righteousness of his/her own values, coercion might in extreme cases be necessary in order to impose his/her benign plan (given the paternalist dictum that one sometimes "needs to be cruel to be kind"). Moreover for many paternalists, not to mention maternalists,[49] the "will-to-control" is often a kind of aphrodisiac for the intervener, which makes intervening so attractive in the first

[49] For the Eurocentric/imperialist dimension of Western feminism see Chandra Talpade Mohanty, "Under Western Eyes: Feminist Scholarship and Colonial Discourses," *Boundary 2* 12, 3 (1986): 333–58; Gayatri Chakravorty Spivak, "Three Women's Texts and a Critique of Imperialism," *Critical Inquiry* 12, 1 (1985): 243–61.

place (though I do not doubt for one moment the sincerity of Aisling Swaine's efforts at distancing herself from the element of control that paternalism entails; Chapter 6, this volume). Either way, though, it is notable that such a trope is placed at the center of Edward Said's conception of Orientalism.[50] And also of note is that the highly controlling nature of some paternalists/maternalists is "justified" by the fact that they are, after all, undertaking a noble, if not the very noblest, "mission of care" for which the subject should be nothing other than humbly, dutifully, and eternally grateful.

The upshot of this is that liberal humanitarianism's cardinal axioms of individual autonomy and consent are suspended in the case of all forms of international paternalist/maternalist interventionism in the East on the grounds that the object lacks a sufficient degree of rationality to be allowed the short-to-medium-term autonomy to make his or her own decisions (indeed, this premise holds by definition within the logic of the theory for if it did not, then there would be no humanitarian crisis in which to intervene in the first place). It is this idea which gives rise to one of the fundamental tropes of all imperialist-Eurocentric theory – what I call the *bipolar construction* of the international. This entails the notion that Westerners should treat each other with dignity and respect each other's sovereignty, whereas in their relations with the non-Western world they can and must readily intervene imperially on the grounds that the non-Western peoples/ societies lack sufficient rationality and hence the basic ingredients of "civilization." Above all, then, Western-centric paternalism (and maternalism) provides the lowest common-denominator of the liberal side of imperialist theory from Angell to Hobson, Reinsch to Wilson and thence on to Rawls, Cooper, Ignatieff, Nussbaum, and many of their contemporaries.

In addition to these primary properties, there are three secondary aspects that are important to note. A sixth property, unrecognized by the paternalist but often perceived by the object, is a patronizing attitude on the part of the subject, one which sometimes appears to evince a strong degree of hypocrisy and the performance of a series of double standards. Though most liberal humanitarians fail to recognize these double standards given their propensity for imperial self-denial, one

---

[50] Edward Said, *Orientalism* (New York: Pantheon Books, 1979); see also Young, *Colonial Desire*.

such liberal who has sought to bring the "E-Word" out of the liberal closet proclaims precisely that:

The postmodern [European] state ... needs to get used to the idea of double standards. Among themselves, the postmodern states operate on the basis of laws and open co-operative security. But when dealing with more old-fashioned kinds of state outside the [Western] post-modern limits, Europeans need to revert to the rougher methods of an earlier era – force, preemptive attack, deception, whatever is necessary for those who still live in the nineteenth-century world of every state for itself. In the jungle, one must use the laws of the jungle.[51]

But Cooper is one of several exceptions such that, for the most part within liberal humanitarianism, the West's double standards remain ignored.

In turn, this imperial self-denial derives from the seventh property wherein the paternalist subject's *non-reflexiveness* and *sense of self-delusion* are functionally required in order to prevent the intervener from recognizing the negative, and often unintended, aspects of intervention precisely so that (s)he can continue to undertake such "civilizing missions of care" in the future. That is, a certain sense of self-delusion alloys the subject's messianic zeal for future paternalist interventions (though again, I do not doubt the sincerity of those people who are engaged at the humanitarian coal-face and who most definitely do grapple with this issue, as many of the chapters in this volume bear ample testimony). My point is simply that at the level of *humanitarian theory* "self-delusion" seems to be an inbuilt characteristic.

Ei1ghth and finally, at the level of theory, paternalism rests on the assumption that the implementation of its benign plan will exhibit a perfect correlation with the actual outcomes – that there is a one-to-one correspondence between benign intentions and outcomes. But this ignores the attendant unintended consequences of such "grand planning" which, in whatever guise it takes – Marxist, fascist, or liberal-humanitarian – always in practice creates a whole set of additional problems that did not exist previously.[52] And this problem is exacerbated further if we run with the arguments made by Mark Duffield

---

[51] Cooper, *Breaking of Nations*, 61–2.
[52] E.g., David Chandler, "State-Building in Bosnia: The Limits of 'Informal Trusteeship'," *International Journal of Peace Studies* 11, 1 (2006): 17–38.

and David Chandler. Still, when practiced by the Great Powers in particular, these harmful consequences are quickly forgotten once the fanfare of the humanitarian intervention rapidly fades away as the humanitarian circus uproots and moves on with renewed fanfare to a new location to start the whole process anew in a kind of never-ending *Groundhog Day* scenario.

Conclusion

While this chapter has developed a critical theoretical take on liberal humanitarianism, it is interesting to note that some variants of critical theory also support international paternalism. In particular, Marx and Engels embraced a paternalist-Eurocentric conception of Western imperialism.[53] And, while most subsequent Marxists have rejected imperialism, some have maintained a commitment to a strong conception of domestic and international paternalism. Indeed what could be more paternalist than Vladimir Lenin's conception of the "revolutionary vanguard party"? For Lenin, the vanguard party is charged with the noble mandate of having to force through the overthrow of capitalism against the short-term, self-deluded interests of the working classes so as to secure their "real" long-term interests, given their alleged "false consciousness" which derives from them having been "bought off" by "economism." Moreover, this paternalism was extended into the international sphere when Lenin argued that the white racial vanguard party must act on behalf of non-whites across the world in order to deliver them to the promised land of the communist free world. Still, this parallel is instructive in that Marxist international paternalism is virtually identical to the liberal version, the only difference being that the final set of institutions sought are of a stateless-communist nature for Marxists and a capitalist-democratic one for liberals.

This similarity between the international paternalist stances of various Marxists and liberals emerges from the point that both theories are not simply Eurocentric but have universalist pretensions. Accordingly, I believe that it is problematic, if not damaging, for liberal humanitarians (as much as Marxists) to presume that their approach is founded on a pristine and noble universalism that nourishes their messianic zeal to "save" the East, when it turns out to be

---

[53] See Hobson, *Eurocentric Conception*, 52–8.

a form of paternalist-Eurocentric provincialism masquerading as the universal. For liberal humanitarianism ultimately rejects cultural pluralism and, in refusing the possibility of mutual inter-civilizational dialogue, offers up merely a Western monologue. Accordingly, in adopting a Eurocentric monism, the liberal humanitarian ultimatum is issued: only when the Eastern Other has been completely assimilated into the Western empire of civilization can it bask in the bright sunshine of liberal-humanitarian freedom. The East, therefore, has no alternative, for no "Other" worlds are viable.

The upshot of this is that international paternalism will continue as a perennial of world politics so long as the "civilization/barbarism" discourse remains, as much as it will only come to an end once the West moves away from Eurocentric monism in favor of a more genuine non-Eurocentric pluralism. This is not to say that paternalism is the only manifestation of Western foreign policy, for anti-paternalist, non-interventionist politics are also a product of Eurocentric identity, but it is to say that the door to international interventionism will remain open so long as Eurocentrism remains alive. It is this deeper discursive property of Western identity which ultimately constitutes the well-spring of international paternalism, and it is this which is rendered invisible by liberal humanitarian theorists who choose to look at a range of other factors concerning changes in international law, the shift to multilateralism, and surface-changes in norms, the most notable of which are human rights and anti-colonialism. For while these are by no means superficial, nevertheless they constitute changes that effervesce on the surface of what turns out to be a deep Eurocentric ocean.

In the light of this I shall close by noting two entwined and deep ironies that emerge from my analysis: first, at the very time when many Westerners believe we have entered a unique and entirely new cosmopolitan era – one that is based on the rise of an "international culture of care" which is radically differentiated from the dark past of paternalist-Eurocentric imperialism, we find ourselves going back to this very future, delivered through the time machine of international Eurocentric-paternalism. And second, the elevation of human rights to a global normative standard by the United Nations, which was designed in part to close out the era of colonial imperialism, finds itself as the key discursive vehicle delivering the neo-imperial Eurocentric mission of Western humanitarian interventionism today. In fact, this emerges as a double irony, for while it was the Eastern push at the United Nations after World War II that was so key to establishing the Universal Declaration of Human Rights in 1948 in order to bring a close to Western imperialism,[54] today we find that the Eastern peoples are back on the receiving end of a Western liberal imperialism delivered in the very name of the human rights regime for which they themselves had fought so hard.

[54] Philip Cunliffe, *Legions of Peace* (London: Hurst, 2013); Paul Gordon Lauren, *Power and Prejudice* (Boulder: Westview Press, 1996); Paul Gordon Lauren, *The Evolution of International Human Rights* (Philadelphia: University of Pennsylvania Press, 2003).

4 | The New International Paternalism: International Regimes

DAVID CHANDLER

It is taken as a truism that today we live in a globalized and interconnected world, but what has been less analyzed are the implications that this has for liberal modernist understandings of political and ethical responsibility. Particularly problematic today is the distinction between public political responsibility and personal moral responsibility. The boundaries between the public and the personal, and the political and the ethical, appear much less clear in a world in which we are all more interconnected and interdependent. This blurring is crucial to understanding the emergence of new paternalist approaches to international regimes. Paternalist approaches imply that some actors have a duty of responsibility or a duty of care for others. In formal paternalist regimes this duty is formalized in law and formal powers and responsibilities are constituted (see the Introduction to this volume). New paternalism claims concern an informal understanding of a duty of care and can thus be made over a wide range of issues or problems, including concerns over the environment. The key point of this chapter is to highlight that this approach implies a very different technique of governance that works on the basis not of assumptions of direct duties and responsibilities but of indirect ones.

The paternalist duty of responsibility for others is less likely to be applied directly through formal political and legal authorization but indirectly through consideration of the unintended outcomes of policy frameworks and social interactions. However, it is important to analyze these discussions of more mediated forms of policy influence which are both part of the process of reshaping and legitimizing the paternalist discourse of international policy responsibilities and the duty of governance over others. Whereas direct paternal duties involve governance over the other and deny to the other the formal rights of equality and autonomy, indirect paternal duties involve a different technique of governance, operating on the basis of a reflexive, responsive governance of the self through a new sensitivity or awareness of the embedded, relational consequences that our self-governance has for others.

New paternalism puts the other at the center of the ethico-political duties of international regimes and international actors but does not imply the problematic claims of Western moral and political superiority, nor incur the resistance, which old paternalist techniques of governance incite (see Autesserre, Chapter 5, this volume). In this sense, this form of paternalism is both new and very effective as a policy discourse that legitimizes Western authority but denies traditional forms of political and moral accountability. It is the self-reflexive claims to awareness of power inequalities and embedded interconnections which legitimize new international paternalism and which facilitate forms of intervention, direction, and control that do not formally seek to undermine the legal and political rights of non-Western states and societies. Because new paternalism works on the basis of informal and indirect techniques of governance, and because new paternalism works through auto-critique – the critical, reflexive "awareness" of the unintentional problems of liberal regimes of law, contract and universal assumptions – new paternalism has the moral and political legitimacy that traditional forms of direct paternalism increasingly lack. In fact, as we shall see below, the advocates of new paternalism seek to problematize the means and methods of traditional paternalist approaches while maintaining discourses of Western or international "duties" and "responsibilities" that seek to exercise governing authority through the ethics of care in indirect rather than direct ways.

Modernist framings of political responsibility have been challenged by new institutionalist understandings in economics and the social constructivist frameworks of institutionalist sociology and international relations, which have highlighted the problematic nature of rationalist conceptions of the subject. Rather than strict, liberal, binary approaches separating subjects from the world around them, the social world is understood as mediated by institutional frameworks shaped by historical experiences and the social contexts in which actors are embedded.[1] In these increasingly dominant post-rationalist framings,

---

[1] Exemplified in the rise of new institutionalist understandings, for example, Douglass C. North, *Institutions, Institutional Change and Economic Performance* (Cambridge: Cambridge University Press, 1990); B. Guy Peters, *Institutional Theory in Political Science: The New Institutionalism*, 2nd edn

the individual is no longer seen as an isolated actor but rather as a socially, environmentally, and materially embedded subject. It is also argued that our social and material embeddedness means that the consequences of our decisions take on greater importance as our actions are inserted into powerful processes of complex global interaction, extending the impact of our individual actions and choices.[2]

In a globalized world, the most important impacts of our choices and decisions are held to be their unintentional consequences – their "side effects" (in the language of Ulrich Beck) evidencing our materially networked "entanglements" (according to French social theorist Bruno Latour) – which mean that "externalities," previously excluded from the calculations of politics and the market, are now considered as central.[3] In this way, global interdependence and interconnectivity are held to pose substantial problems with regard to judging where political responsibility lies for events and situations that concern us. In a global world, political responsibility tends to be reformulated to take account of the fact that the consequences of our actions are dependent upon the socio-material processes into which they are inserted.[4] This new sociological field, which has opened up in the last two decades, has major implications, enabling the rearticulation of international paternalist framings. The field of ethical and political responsibility is therefore defined less by the formal public sphere of representation – democracy, rights, and sovereignty – and more by our embeddedness in emergent chains of causality.[5] In a global relational ontology,

(London: Continuum, 2005); James Mahoney and Kathleen Thelen, eds., *Explaining Institutional Change: Ambiguity, Agency, and Power* (Cambridge: Cambridge University Press, 2010).

[2] Ulrich Beck, *World at Risk* (Cambridge: Polity, 2009); Anthony Giddens, *Runaway World: How Globalisation is Reshaping Our Lives*, 2nd edn (London: Profile, 2002); John Dewey, *The Public and its Problems* (New York: Swallow Press, 1927); Bruno Latour, *Politics of Nature: How to Bring the Sciences into Democracy* (Cambridge, MA: Harvard University Press, 2004).

[3] Ulrich Beck, *The Reinvention of Politics: Rethinking Modernity in the Global Social Order* (Cambridge: Polity, 1997); Bruno Latour, "Is Re-Modernization Occurring – And If So, How to Prove It? A Commentary on Ulrich Beck," *Theory, Culture & Society* 20, 2 (2003): 35–48, 37.

[4] See further, the discussion in David Chandler, "Democracy Unbound? Non-Linear Politics and the Politicization of Everyday Life," *European Journal of Social Theory* 17, 1 (2014): 42–59.

[5] William Connolly, "Method, Problem, Faith," in *Problems and Methods in the Study of Politics*, eds. Ian Shapiro, Rogers M. Smith, and Tarek E. Masoud

our political-ethical responsibilities stem from the unintended consequences of our relational embeddedness and our duty to become
reflexively aware of this. This very distinct and, I argue, problematic
reformulation of ethical responsibility is conceptualized here as enabling a "new paternalist" reflection upon international regimes and
institutions.

This chapter seeks to stake out a series of claims with regard to
the rise of the relational ethics of new paternalism, premised upon
our embeddedness in complex chains of global interconnection.[6] First,
it is concerned with drawing out how understandings of relational
responsibility have become increasingly central to mainstream policy
and academic thinking, highlighting the conceptual links between the
ontological or "new materialist" turn in social theory and the rise of
post-rationalist or post-Rawlsian thinking more broadly. Second, it
highlights how the ethics of global relational embeddedness redis-
tribute ethical and political responsibility in ways that rather than
challenging power inequalities, appear to affirm or reify them. New
paternalist ethics rearticulate "Western responsibility" for global outcomes on the basis of indirect chains of causal interaction, rather than
superior liberal values or institutions, and rearticulate the outcomes
of market relations in terms of the embedded relational choices of
individuals.

The following section considers the rise of these "ontological,"
materialist understandings of ethical and political responsibility
as a shift away from the liberal "top-down" constructions of the
1990s, in which the West increasingly assumed traditional paternalistic duties and responsibilities. "Top-down" global ethics worked
on the basis of direct responsibilities, assuming direct (traditional or
liberal forms of) political and legal paternal authority over subjects

---

(Cambridge: Cambridge University Press, 2004), 332–9; Jane Bennett, *Vibrant
Matter: A Political Ecology of Things* (London: Duke University Press, 2010);
Erika Cudworth and Stephen Hobden, *Posthuman International Relations:
Complexity, Ecologism and Global Politics* (London: Zed Books, 2011).

[6] As I make clear elsewhere, my problem with "new materialist" social ontologies
lies less with the ontological assertions of complex social embeddedness
and attention to the contingent nature of our social world, than to the
normative philosophical, political, and ethical conclusions derived from these
understandings. See further, David Chandler, "The World of Attachment? The
Post-Humanist Challenge to Freedom and Necessity," *Millennium: Journal of
International Studies* 41, 3 (2013): 516–34.

who were denied equal rights.[7] The following sections discuss the evolution of "new paternalist ethics," which works on the basis of indirect assumptions of paternal responsibility – not on the basis of direct or formal legal, moral, or political responsibility, but on the basis of our relational embeddedness: the understanding of indirect side-effects caused by our associational connectivity in a complex and globalized world. On the international level, powerful Western states take responsibility for the unintended or indirect outcomes of market forces and their institutional frameworks. However, it is important to stress that this type of "responsibility" cannot be properly understood in either the political or moral terms of liberal constructions (outlined in the Introduction to this collection and the subject of John Hobson's excellent historical analysis in Chapter 3). New paternalist ethics fit with neither Weber's "ethics of responsibility" nor his "ethics of conviction."[8] Instead, we see the rise of a relational, material, or ontological ethic: a sociological recognition of the side-effects of complex global associational interconnections and their emergent properties.

This chapter seeks to problematize this shift by arguing that at the heart of new paternalist ethics is the rearticulation of power hierarchies and the reification of market relations and outcomes. The sociological framing of global complexity tends to understand the inequalities and conflicts that exist in the world as products of unintended consequences in a world in which modernist rationalities no longer operate. In other words, they highlight that the outcomes of liberal frameworks of political and legal freedoms and market exchange, in a world of difference and clashing temporalities, can reproduce inequalities and become a barrier to progress. In this perspective, Marxists are therefore right that the market is irrational and can reproduce inequality; where they are held to be wrong is in the assumption that we can somehow stand outside the associational interconnections of a globalized world. The sociologization of the market, as a self-emerging complex and adaptive process of indirect chains of connection and causation in which we are all embedded at different levels with different consequences,

[7] See, for example, William Bain, *Between Anarchy and Society: Trusteeship and the Obligations of Power* (Oxford: Oxford University Press, 2003).

[8] Max Weber, "Politics as a Vocation," in Max Weber, *The Vocation Lectures* (Indianapolis: Hackett Publishing, 2004), 32–94.

removes the liberal understanding of direct political or ethical responsibility for our choices.

The ethical and political duties emerging from these indirect responsibilities operate on a different register from the traditional liberal framing of law, sovereignty, rights, and intervention as, for the sociologically embedded subject, there is no assumption of pre-existing autonomy. Two examples of this framing of indirect responsibility are analyzed in the work of Paul Collier and Thomas Pogge. These authors are taken as heurist examples to demonstrate the ontological framings that enable the construction of indirect understandings of responsibility today. In conclusion, I will suggest that the flatter (but not flat) ontology of indirect responsibility replaces a liberal framing of formal political rights and responsibilities. In our relational embeddedness we become responsible for the world but capable only of working to change the world indirectly through working on our awareness of our own relations to others, leading to both political reflexivity and ethical self-growth. In this sense, new paternalist ethics work beyond the liberal political theory problematic of equal rights and the exceptions that justify their formal denial, well elucidated in Michael N. Barnett's framing chapter.[9] It is this evasion of liberal political concerns with formal equality, rights, and self-government that is the particularly alarming aspect of new paternalism; how this works is drawn out in the sections below.

New Paternalist Ethics

Under discourses of global interdependencies and social relationality, power relations can easily evaporate into complex processes of indirect interconnection, where responsibility for the actions of governments, as much as the actions of individuals, are seen to be shared much more equally. This process of dismantling frameworks of individual and collective responsibility often appears as an enlightened, socially rich, actor-networked perspective.[10] These richer social ontological approaches – highlighted in the rise of assemblage theory, new materialism, and post-humanism – tend to

---

[9] Michael N. Barnett, Introduction, this volume.

[10] See, for example, Bruno Latour, *Reassembling the Social: An Introduction to Actor-Network-Theory* (Oxford: Oxford University Press, 2007).

work on the basis of "flat" or "bottom-up" ontologies of interconnection.[11] Here, agency is distributed away from the formal centers of political power (the focus of liberal ontologies) and toward the margins or the "everyday," where the "tactics" of ordinary people contest and disrupt the strategies and understandings of the powerful.[12] In these more fluid ontologies, governing or personal intentionality is much less important than the complex ontological reality of social interconnectivity. The more broadly the connections are drawn, the more diverse are the actors and agents that need to be drawn in to provide an adequate explanation of concrete policy outcomes.[13] The focus upon the social relational embeddedness that produces concrete realities, rather than upon the abstract or metaphysical constructions of human purpose and intention, also enables agency to be redistributed beyond purely human or anthropomorphic constructions of intentionality.[14]

However, it is important to note that new paternalist ethics do not merely problematize the understanding of individual responsibility and bring the contingency of assemblages of interconnection into play, but they also articulate a new framing of international hierarchy which builds upon these ontological understandings of associational embeddedness.[15] This is because new paternalist ethics work through establishing the ontological power of social relational interconnection but then rearticulate the gap between conscious intention and concrete outcomes in terms of the ethical demand for self-reflexivity. New paternalist ethics work back from the appearance of the world to enable an embedded ethical reflexivity to guide the subject's own

[11] Manuel DeLanda, *A New Philosopy of Society: Assemblage Theory and Social Complexity* (London: Continuum, 2006), 28, 32.
[12] See, for example, Michel de Certeau, *The Practice of Everyday Life* (London: University of California Press, 1988).
[13] See, Latour, *Reassembling the Social*.
[14] For example, William Connolly, *A World of Becoming* (Durham, NC: Duke University Press, 2011); Bennett, *Vibrant Matter*.
[15] This challenges the presumption of some new materialist or actor-network theorists that the more interconnectivity can be established, the greater the contingency of outcomes and the more even the distribution of agency. New paternalist ethics understand connectivity as giving rise to the ethics of self-reflexivity precisely because agency remains unevenly distributed; see, for example, Noortje Marres, *Material Participation: Technology, the Environment and Everyday Politics* (Basingstoke: Palgrave Macmillan, 2012), 33; Chandler, "The World of Attachment?".

self-transformation.[16] In this framing, the problems of the world can be reinterpreted as ethical lessons for self-growth and self-awareness. The indirect ethical responsibility derived from self-reflexivity can thereby be neither understood as instrumental (it is the self-reflexive responses to outcomes which are important rather than the outcomes per se) nor as deontological (ethics are derived from external consequences). In this way, in a more interconnected world, Western agency can be rearticulated in terms of this distinct form of indirect ethical responsibility. Western powers can claim responsibility for the world, but rather than these claims of responsibility generating moral opprobrium or demands for political accountability, they can be used to produce new, reflexive forms of ethico-political authority.

To explain how this inversion works, it is worth recalling a point emphasized in the work of Hannah Arendt on how agency works in relation to "guilt." As Arendt noted, when we claim that "we are all guilty" we are actually expressing "solidarity with the wrong-doers" rather than the wronged.[17] This is the mirror-opposite of direct relations of political solidarity with the wronged, which suggests that we support their challenge to power in righting those wrongs. I wish to draw out, in particular, how this inversion works in relation to capitalism or market relations. In modernist framings, political solidarity was often demonstrated in understanding a common cause of struggle against market relations and its enforcement through the coercive political power of capital. In today's understandings of embedded associational responsibility for the unintended consequences of our actions, we are more likely to see our lifestyle or consumption choices as responsible for inequalities, conflict, or environmental problems.[18] In an age of political complexity, when it is "easier to imagine the end of the world than the end of capitalism,"[19] in effect, responsibility is

16 See Connolly, *A World of Becoming*, 145–6; see also David Chandler, "Resilience and the Autotelic Subject: Towards a Critique of the Societalization of Security," *International Political Sociology* 7, 2 (2013): 210–26.
17 Hannah Arendt, *Responsibility and Judgement* (New York: Schocken Books, 2003), 148.
18 See, for example, Andrew Dobson, *Citizenship and the Environment* (Oxford: Oxford University Press, 2003); Pheng Cheah and Bruce Robbins, eds., *Cosmopolitics – Thinking and Feeling Beyond the Nation* (Minneapolis: University of Minnesota Press, 1998).
19 Fredric Jameson, "Future City," *New Left Review* 21 (2003): 65–79; Slavoj Zizek, "Slavoj Žižek Speaks at Occupy Wall Street: Transcript," *Impose*

recast or internalized, displacing capitalism as the problem through vicariously seeing ourselves as responsible: understanding capitalism as merely a complex emergent process of exchanges in which we are embedded to differing extents and therefore indirectly responsible. In an age where the overthrow of capitalism seems unimaginable, capitalism is transformed as the sociological vehicle of connection, displacing the conscious and direct chains of politics.

If we were to trace a genealogy of new paternalism as a technique of governance, which only enters the field of international regimes in the 1990s, we would therefore need to start with the rise of corporate social responsibility, whereby economic actors needed to demonstrate an awareness of the indirect or unintentional consequences of their economic actions. Discourses of corporate social responsibility blur the line between economic, political, and ethical concerns, recasting large corporations as social and embedded actors with chains of embedded causality impacting their social and environmental context, not merely their workers or direct suppliers and consumers. Discourses of embedded and relational responsibility thus "politicize" actors, actions, and relations which were previously excluded from the political sphere in traditional liberal or modernist understandings. This process of politicization has no "natural" spatial or temporal limits; how far and how deeply the indirect consequences of large corporations extend through multiple chains of production and consumption is a matter of contestation.

It is important to highlight that indirect responsibilities have no inherent limits and are the product of awareness of these embedded relations. This "awareness," at the center of blurring the spheres of ethical, political, economic, social, and environmental responsibility, is itself a process of producing and contesting information and understandings. Which links of connection are considered important and which are not is itself a matter of political, ethical, and scientific dispute. There is no neat division between disciplines, as scientific "matters of fact" become transformed into political "matters of concern,"[20]

Magazine, September 17, 2013, www.imposemagazine.com/bytes/slavoj-zizek-at-occupy-wall-street-transcript (accessed November 7, 2015).

[20] Bruno Latour, "Why Has Critique Run out of Steam? From Matters of Fact to Matters of Concern," *Critical Inquiry* 30 (2004): 225–48.

in order to bring these relations to the surface, both for claims of "responsibility" to be made and for these claims to be denied, for some links to be the subject of regimes of transparency and for others to be hidden from view. Since the 1990s, the international sphere has become awash with the extension of social, economic, environmental, and political responsibilities, which are linked to all manner of international institutions and actors. The heuristic point, which this flags, is that the "responsibilities" involved are not those of direct governance over environmental, social, or political matters, but of reflexive self-awareness of how corporations (and other actors) should govern themselves on the basis of these indirect and unintended consequences.[21]

New paternalism is thereby not a technique of directly governing others, but of indirectly governing others through the governance of the self (through the awareness of the fact that the governance of others needs to reflexively inform the governance of the self). It is precisely in this inversion, in this shift of political responsibility from social structures and political frameworks external to ourselves to the recognition of our own indirect social or societal responsibility as complicit through our own choices and actions, that new paternalist ethics operates. New paternalist ethics redistributes responsibility and emphasizes the indirect, unintended, and relational networks of causality. The more these interconnections are retrospectively revealed though the work of self-reflexivity and self-reflection, the more responsibility governments, other actors, and individuals acting in the world, have. We learn and learn again that we are responsible for the world, not because of our conscious choices or because our actions lacked the right ethical intention, but because the consequences of our relational embeddedness cannot be known and understood without work on developing our knowledge, our responsivity, and our awareness. In a complex and interconnected world, few events or problems evade appropriation within this framing of new paternalism, providing an opportunity for recasting and redistributing responsibility in these ways.

---

[21] See, for an excellent study, Andrew Barry, *Material Politics: Disputes along the Pipeline* (Chichester: John Wiley & Sons, 2013).

New Paternalist Ethics and International Relations

In the international sphere, the articulation of political and ethical responsibilities has become transformed since the end of the Cold War. In the early 1980s, US President Ronald Reagan controversially described the Soviet Union as the "Evil Empire" in an attempt to reinvigorate the ideological certainties of the geopolitical divide, but no one in the West assumed that Western governments or citizens were in any way responsible for the acts of the Soviet Union or for those of other governments or societies. The concept of Western moral or ethical responsibility for the actions of others only began to arise in the 1990s, initially with the articulation of global moral or ethical understandings underpinning the liberal internationalist foreign policies of Western governments and giving content to the doctrines of humanitarian intervention and human rights enforcement. Discussions of humanitarian atrocities from Rwanda to Srebrenica focused on individuals and elites held to bear individual moral and political responsibility for war crimes and human rights abuses,[22] but also on the West's responsibility to intervene to prevent these atrocities and to protect basic human rights. While the West was not held to be responsible, it was held that there was complicity through non-intervening, which was seen as allowing the crimes of human rights abuse in sub-Saharan Africa or the Balkans. It was argued that the globalized world was increasingly becoming one community with shared norms and values and that foreign policy was not merely about national interests but liberal universal concerns of laws and rights as well.[23]

In the 1990s, the ethical or political responsibility of the West was generally cast in the direct terms of intervention to prevent human rights abuses by "others." The articulation of responsibility in a global world was couched in the universal rationalist terms of liberal discourse. Crimes of war or of human rights abuse were held to

---

[22] See further, Kirsten Ainley, "Individual Agency and Responsibility for Atrocity," in *Confronting Evil in International Relations: Ethical Responses to Problems of Moral Agency*, ed. Renee Jeffery (Basingstoke: Palgrave Macmillan, 2008), 37–60.

[23] See, for example, Andrew Linklater, *The Transformation of Political Community* (Cambridge: Polity, 1998); David Held, *Democracy and the Global Order* (Cambridge: Polity, 1995); Richard A. Falk, *On Humane Governance: Toward a New Global Politics* (Cambridge: Polity, 1995).

constitute an ethical and political "right" of intervention (even if this right was not formally upheld in international law).[24] The liberal discourse of rights and law pitted intervention directly against rights to sovereignty.[25] Western states not only acquired the new rights of intervention, to take responsibility for preventing human rights abuses, but were held to acquire new paternalist duties to enable their new charges to reconstruct their states and societies. The liberal internationalist discourses of the 1990s thereby made claims of exceptionalism, based on the incapacity of states and their loss of rights to sovereignty, to justify both intervention and post-interventionist protectorate or semi-protectorate regimes, clearly manifested in the international powers over Bosnia, Kosovo, and Timor-Leste. The liberal internationalist understanding of political and ethical responsibility was sharply bifurcated: responsibility for war crimes and human rights abuses was restricted to individuals or discrete groups of "others"; responsibility for the outcomes of intervention was restricted to the international "saviors" bringing peace, development, and democracy.[26]

After the 1990s, this linear, liberal framing became increasingly hollowed out with responsibility, both for crimes and interventionist outcomes, distributed more equally. In the sphere of international relations, the sociological logic of indirect responsibility – of new paternalist ethics – initially emerged in distinction to the rationalist logic of international liberalism, for example, in work in the tradition of the English School. In Robert Jackson's influential study, *Quasi-States: Sovereignty, International Relations and the Third World*, published in 1990, the discursive logic of societal interrelations is clear. It is the conceptualization of indirect responsibility that I wish to heuristically focus upon here. Jackson did not argue for the return of colonial paternalism, but for what might be seen as a new type

---

[24] Simon Chesterman, *Just War or Just Peace? Humanitarian Intervention and International Law* (Oxford: Oxford University Press, 2001); Jennifer M. Welsh, ed., *Humanitarian Intervention and International Relations* (Oxford: Oxford University Press, 2004).

[25] Mary Kaldor, *New and Old Wars: Organized Violence in a Global Era* (Cambridge: Polity, 1999).

[26] Anne Orford, *Reading Humanitarian Intervention: Human Rights and the Use of Force in International Law* (Cambridge: Cambridge University Press, 2003); Mahmood Mamdani, *Saviours and Survivors: Darfur, Politics and the War on Terror* (London: Verso, 2009).

of informal "paternalism":[27] a recognition that the problems of post-colonial states were not merely of their own making but a problem of emergent causality – a "side-effect" of the attempt to instigate an international constitutional order on the basis of equal sovereignty. This international constitutional order was held to have stacked the deck against domestic development and democratization and was argued to have encouraged despotism.

Jackson was not in favor of the return to traditional paternalist understandings and argued against the idea, popular at the time, that the West should take formal "moral or legal responsibility" for post-colonial states on the basis of their incapacity.[28] Instead, the new problematic that emerged in his work was one of recognizing the unintended consequences of institutionalist frameworks, held to be a barrier to development and democracy in these states. The key point about the emergence of new paternalist ethics is that in recognizing "responsibility" for the problems caused by the "side-effects" of shared institutional frameworks, there was an understanding of a new type of material ethical responsibility. This was neither moral nor political – the institutions were established for the best of reasons (for example, in the case of the United Nations and the UN Charter's enshrining of non-intervention, the prevention of war) – but an associational, networked, or indirect and unintentional "ontological" responsibility. Moreover, the consequences of this new relational and indirect responsibility were not clear until actors became "aware" of them long after their initial institution.

With this new type of "responsibility" comes an imperative to ethically reconsider international institutions in the knowledge that the institutional framework shapes the possibilities and actions of others (in this case, "quasi-states"). Once the associational link is established, through the connective framework of effects, then it is argued that Western states and actors have the ethical/political responsibility to reflexively consider a different set of institutional

[27] Robert H. Jackson, *Quasi-States: Sovereignty, International Relations and the Third World* (Cambridge: Cambridge University Press, 1990), 187. See also Richard H. Thaler and Cass R. Sunstein on "libertarian paternalism," *Nudge: Improving Decisions about Health, Wealth and Happiness* (London: Penguin, 2009), 5.

[28] Jackson, *Quasi-States*, 187.

practices which may more positively affect the outcomes in post-colonial states. New paternalist ethics argues that, like it or not, powerful states shape international institutions and therefore bear responsibility for their unintended consequences. The argument then follows that if international institutional frameworks have a deleterious effect on "quasi-states," others should be considered which could have a positive effect. While not assuming political responsibility for post-colonial states, as in the top-down paternalism of colonialism or of 1990s liberal internationalism, the associational responsibility confers upon the West the right to intervene *indirectly*, through the institutional framework, to positively affect the outcomes at the level of the post-colonial state. This is neither the old paternalism of colonialism nor the equal sovereignty of the post-colonial period but the recognition that inequality (the fact that powerful states shape the international institutional frameworks) gives Western states responsibility because they indirectly shape the outcomes for other (weaker) states.

In the framework of new paternalist ethics, there is therefore no such thing as non-intervention. Intervention is no longer understood as the formal undermining of sovereignty, as in colonialism. Intervention is seen to take place indirectly through the institutional frameworks and agreements of the international arena, and therefore the West is understood to be always indirectly intervening in the domestic politics of the post-colonial world through the institutional shaping of both economic and political relations. It is on the basis of this understanding that Western states and their citizens then have the ethical/political responsibility to reconsider this international institutional framework with regard to these outcomes. In passing, it should be noted that there is a similar new paternalist ethic at play in the argument that states have a duty to reflexively influence the private choices of citizens.[29] Once there is an assumption that in an interconnected world there is no sphere of autonomous choice making, there is then no barrier to the rise of the new paternalist ethics of intervention through indirect means.

---

[29] Thaler and Sunstein, *Nudge*; see also Peter John, Sarah Cotterill, Alice Moseley, Liz Richardson, Graham Smith, Gerry Stoker and Corinne Wales, *Nudge, Nudge, Think, Think: Experimenting with Ways to Change Civic Behaviour* (London: Bloomsbury, 2011).

The New Paternalist Ethics of Paul Collier and Thomas Pogge

It is important to highlight that the consequence of a more socio-logical approach – which understands responsibility as a product of associational links, actor networks, or assemblages – is that discourses of responsibility are neither political nor moral but ontological. Responsibility is ontologized, spread much more thinly but also in context-specific ways, so that responsibility is always a shared but fluid concept. This is very different to modernist understandings of responsibility, which operated to demarcate spheres of ethical understanding: political responsibility stopped with the sovereign or government, moral responsibility stopped with the private conscience. Ontological responsibility knows no political or private subjects, only subjects always and already embedded in fluid and complex networks of association. It is the networks of association that allocate the ontological responsibilities to actors. Responsibility no longer emerges from the decisions of the subject itself to be legitimized in instrumental or deontological terms. The ethical responsibility is indirect or secondary: to reflexively adapt to the unintended outcomes of structures and processes in which actors are embedded.

The sociological, institutionalist sensitivity articulated by Robert Jackson remained at a fairly abstract level, typical of the English School approach, concerned with drawing a sociological "third way" between the rationalisms of Realism and Liberalism in international relations theory. The sociological approach is heuristically drawn out in more depth below in an analysis of the conceptual frameworks deployed by two influential theorists: Oxford academic and World Bank policy advisor Paul Collier, and Thomas Pogge, a moral and political philosopher and Director of the Global Justice Program at Yale University.

Paul Collier's work is notable in that it removes the liberal rationalist ethics of responsibility from understandings of state collapse and human rights abuses by posing the problems of conflict and lack of development as matters of formal and informal associational connections, in effect reducing both politics and economics to sociological understandings of embedded context. Collier argues against the direct responsibility approach of liberal internationalism: Western or international actors cannot resolve problems by taking a traditional paternalist approach, telling others what to do, or by throwing aid money at them. Change "must come predominately from within; we cannot impose it on them."[30] However, we can help in terms of our own reflexivity about the international institutional frameworks which rich Western countries support and have established. Changing others "from within" can thereby be done if change also comes, reflexively, "from within," at the international level – rethinking the unintended consequences of trade regulations or of not having international agreements on extractive industries or the arms trade. This indirect approach of intervention works on the basis of Western states and international institutions reflexively working to address the unintended consequences of their actions rather than directly intervening or claiming the right of intervention in other states.

Collier, together with his Oxford colleagues, developed the "greed and grievance" model of conflict in the mid-2000s.[31] This model could be seen as a clear step back from the bifurcated framework of responsibility justifying liberal internationalist interventions in the 1990s. Collier's indirect framing of responsibility has a much richer model of social interaction, developing an understanding of post-colonial or post-conflict societies as shaped by the choice-making context in which actors are embedded. In their critique of theorists who sought to understand conflict in the rational terms of political rights (struggles over grievances), Collier and his team sought to analyze conflict in terms of the institutional constraints upon individual choice making. In this framing, political causation no longer becomes an explanatory or a legitimating factor; rather, it is the opportunity for rebellion that has explanatory value. Essentially, if finance is easily available (for example, due to easy access to primary commodity exports) and there is little opportunity cost (i.e., few other avenues to earn income, if access to secondary education is low and the economy is stagnant), then conflict "entrepreneurs" will arise who do not necessarily have any stake in furthering the interests or needs of their alleged constituents.[32]

---

[30] Paul Collier, *The Bottom Billion: Why the Poorest Countries are Failing and What Can be Done About It* (Oxford: Oxford University Press, 2007), xi.

[31] Paul Collier and Anke Hoeffler, "Greed and Grievance in Civil War," *Oxford Economic Papers* 56 (2004): 563–95; Paul Collier, Anke Hoeffler, and Dominic Rohner, "Beyond Greed and Grievance: Feasibility and Civil War," *Oxford Economic Papers* 61, 1 (2009): 1–27.

[32] Collier and Hoeffler, "Greed and Grievance in Civil War."

Political or ethical responsibility for conflict and war crimes is radically redistributed in the new institutionalist model put forward. For Collier's project, "where rebellion is feasible, it will occur without any special inducements in terms of motivation";[33] "motivation is indeterminate, being supplied by whatever agenda happens to be adopted by the first social entrepreneur to occupy the viable niche."[34] Once conflict is understood as the product of the societal context, shaping the choices of individuals, the possibility of reshaping the formal and informal institutional context, and therefore the outcome of decision-making, arises. This approach of indirectly influencing the conduct of communities and of individuals, on the basis of the international influence upon these frameworks, highlights the indirect consequences of associational connections at the expense of the political responsibility of both local actors and international interveners.

The work of Collier and his team has been highly influential on the policy developments of the World Bank, which, keen to take up new positions of reflexive responsibility, has been focusing on unintended consequences of institutional structures in a world of political complexity, rather than political or ideological concerns.[35] On an international level, Collier's sociological framing works in a very different register to liberal debates on intervention and sovereignty where Western responsibility recalls traditional paternalist understandings, formalizing inequality, and a denial of rights, such as the Liberian government's subordination of financial control to a coterie of international donors[36] or the "Responsibility to Protect" (R2P) doctrine, a "full-frontal assault on the concept of national sovereignty."[37] Here,

[33] Collier *et al.*, "Beyond Greed and Grievance," 19.
[34] *Ibid.*, 20.
[35] Tomonori De Herdt and Séverin Abega, "Capability Deprivations and Political Complexities: The Political Economy of Onions in the Mandara Mountains, Cameroon," *Journal of Human Development* 8, 2 (2007): 303–23; Verena Fritz, Kai Kaiser, and Brian Levy, *Problem-Driven Governance and Political Economy Analysis: Good Practice Framework* (Washington, DC: International Bank for Reconstruction and Development/World Bank, 2009); *The Political Economy of Policy Reform: Issues and Implications for Policy Dialogue and Development Operations*, Report No. 44288-GLB (Washington, DC: International Bank for Reconstruction and Development/World Bank, 2008).
[36] Paul Collier, *Wars, Guns and Votes: Democracy in Dangerous Places* (London: Vintage Books, 2010), 216.
[37] *Ibid.*, 218.

there is not intervention (as legally and politically conceived) merely "interference": the reflexive understanding of associational interconnection. Such institutional reforms of the international order do not directly undermine sovereignty but seek to "interfere" in ways that support progressive ends rather than work against them, for example in contractual relations to deter coups where there is a democratic mandate, support for financial probity, or in linking aid with military spending.[38] This sociological framing, Collier argues, takes us beyond the liberal rights framings contra-positioning intervention and sovereignty and enables "a compromise between positions that are currently deadlocked."[39]

The importance of Collier's work is in the clarity of articulating indirect ethical responsibilities and the practices flowing from these, in distinction to the direct interventions of liberal internationalism, for example as expressed in the politics of conditionality of the World Bank and the International Monetary Fund, which sought to paternalistically bend post-colonial states to their will in terms of particular policy outcomes.[40] Collier argues along similar lines to Jackson that the international institutional framework unfairly makes reform or development difficult. Despite the fact that change can only come from within, international states, institutions, and private economic actors can assist in ensuring that in their associations with these states they facilitate progress rather than shore up corrupt and failing regimes. In effect, the self-reflexive ethics of new paternalism politicizes all associational connections between external actors and the states viewed as problematic or failing. It does this through the ethic of sociological association: that any contact or connection, no matter how indirect, has unintentional effects. These connections, which previously would not have been understood as political, but as private contractual relations of trade, are then "politicized" in terms of where the wealth goes and how it is distributed. From the sociological perspective of embedded relationality there is no limit to the ethical injunction to reflect upon how one's associational connections "interfere" with others.

Collier's problematic of responsibility insists that "they" in the failing or post-colonial states are not entirely to blame for conflicts

---

[38] *Ibid.*, 202–27.
[39] *Ibid.*, 226.
[40] Collier, *The Bottom Billion*, 67.

and underdevelopment but neither are "we" in the rich West.[41]
However, he goes on to argue: "I am now going to pin some blame
on citizens of the rich world, who must take responsibility for their
own ignorance about trade policy and its consequences."[42] The
blame upon Western states and citizens is one of a lack of self-
reflection upon unintended consequences. Addressing these unintended consequences means, for example, becoming aware of the
impact of tariff protections, which prevent less-developed countries
from diversifying their production[43] and of the refusal to strengthen
institutional frameworks, which could diversify state monopolies
over wealth and resources or guarantee intervention if a democratic
regime is overthrown. From Collier's perspective, the struggle of
the poorest bottom billion "is not a contest between an evil rich
world and a noble poor world. It is within the societies of the bottom billion, and to date we have largely been bystanders."[44] The
intimation is that we in the rich West have an indirect responsibility for the outcomes, that our actions and choices at the moment
favor the side of corrupt elites, conflict, and poverty, and that we
could make other choices which would favor the side of progress
and development.

Collier's work denotes a very important shift in understanding,
one which privileges the importance of indirect or unintended consequences over those that are intended. Rather than advocating a set of
direct policy interventions, which would formally or informally recon-
stitute a relationship of paternalism, Collier argues that Western states
and international actors need to first reflexively consider the unintentional effects of their relational embeddedness, first of all in terms of
the unintended effects of formal institutional arrangements based on
abstract notions of universal equality, and second in terms of the externalities of economic trade and financial arrangements. Essentially,
Collier is arguing that formal political understandings and the respect
for the economic and financial relations of contract are not adequate.
Awareness of global interdependencies means that political agreements and economic contracts do not exist in separate, self-contained
worlds but have chains of causal effects that have previously been

[41] *Ibid.*, 157.
[42] *Ibid.*
[43] *Ibid.*, 160.
[44] *Ibid.*, 192.

excluded from calculation and consideration. Just as large corporations were called upon to draw up agreements of social, environmental, and human rights responsibilities and to account for externalities,
so should international institutions and other international actors, no
matter how large or small.

Thomas Pogge goes further than Collier in the sociological or ontological understanding of responsibility through associational connection. For this reason, his work has been used to challenge Collier's view
that "citizens of the rich world are not to blame for most of the problems of the bottom billion."[45] The irony, of course, is that Pogge's work
on the international regimes of property and resource rights, which
the international sovereignty regime enforces (and in which, therefore,
citizens in the West are complicit), uses a very similar framework to
Collier's sociological understanding of indirect causality as the basis
for the extension of ethical responsibility through market relations.
What is interesting about Pogge's work is that he is concerned to point
out how global institutional frameworks – both formal and informal –
institutionalize global inequalities.

Pogge argues that it is ethically desirable that there should be the
spread of democracy and human rights in the international sphere.
Reflexively understanding the "side-effects" of both personal and
institutional choices could thereby achieve a transformation of international norms, rules, and regulations, which at present create a problematic framework of environmental choices for the less-developed
world. His work is possibly the clearest example of how new paternalist ethics have developed. This is perhaps most usefully articulated in
his 2011 comment article, "Are We Violating the Human Rights of the
World's Poor?"[46] Pogge goes beyond liberal rationalist or contractual
understandings of rights and duties by asserting the importance of the
indirect consequences of our actions and inactions. The key point is not
the rationalist "interactional" liberal framing of government duties to
protect rights, nor our own duties to respect these rights, but the relational understanding of how the indirect consequences of our actions
may "facilitate" the promotion or violation of rights.[47] In his 2002

---

[45] Paul Segal, "Review of Paul Collier's *The Bottom Billion*," *Renewal* 16, 2 (2008).
[46] Thomas Pogge, "Are We Violating the Human Rights of the World's Poor?" *Yale Human Rights and Development Law Journal* 14, 2 (2011): 1–33.
[47] *Ibid.*, 12.

book, *World Poverty and Human Rights*, Pogge argued that we should
reject the liberal interactionalist understanding entirely,[48] but in the
second edition of 2008, this has been amended to an understanding
that there are two varieties of human rights violation.[49] However, the
concern is with the distinction between the two and the importance
of highlighting the understanding of indirect relational responsibility:

There is the interactional variety, where individual or collective human
agents do things that, as they intend, foresee, or should foresee, will avoidably deprive human beings of secure access to the objects of their human
rights. And there is the institutional variety, where human agents design and
impose institutional arrangements that, as they intend, foresee, or should
foresee, will avoidably deprive human beings of secure access to their human
rights.[50]

Once we lose the understanding of the autonomous, liberal subject
and instead understand the morality of the world on the basis of formal and informal institutional structures, in the everyday reproduction of which we are all complicit, then it is clear that responsibility for
human rights infringements has a much broader, flatter, or democratic
ontological basis. We are all then, to differing extents, responsible for
what might appear, not as the commissions or remissions of others
(the concern of Arendt),[51] but as indirect market outcomes, outside
any individual's direct responsibility:

Duties to facilitate constitute then a crucial addition which highlights the
vital importance that the design of institutional arrangements has for the
fulfillment of human rights ... The purely interactional analysis of human
rights deficits must then be complemented by an institutional analysis which
traces such deficits back not to wrongful conduct of individual and collective human agents, but to injustice in the design of social institutions: in the
rules and procedures, roles and agencies that structure and organize societies and other social systems.[52]

[48] Thomas Pogge, *World Poverty and Human Rights: Cosmopolitan
Responsibilities and Reforms* (Cambridge: Polity, 2002), 65.
[49] Thomas Pogge, *World Poverty and Human Rights*, 2nd edn (Cambridge:
Polity, 2008).
[50] Pogge, "Are We Violating the Human Rights of the World's Poor?" 18.
[51] Arendt, *Responsibility and Judgement*, 147.
[52] Pogge, "Are We Violating the Human Rights of the World's Poor?" 13.

Once we understand that indirect responsibility lies in the framing of social institutions and social systems – societal interrelations, with their unending chains of complex causal connection – the responsibility for human rights abuses is inevitably transformed, minimizing the importance of the liberal or modernist understanding of political or ethical responsibility. To take an example of Pogge's, if you were blackmailed for the ransom of your child by a kidnapper, your moral responsibility would not be merely to ensure that you maximize the prospects of your child's safe return by giving in to extravagant demands, as this would clearly encourage further kidnapping attempts on your children, but more importantly would also affect the kidnap risk to which children other than your own are exposed, as it "may attract more people to a career in the kidnapping business."[53] There is a clear indirect impact as individual choices and decisions constitute the choice-shaping institutional framework in which others decide whether or not the kidnapping business constitutes a viable career alternative. What is particularly important to note is that we are not all equally embedded in these interactive processes, clearly the more power, wealth, and influence we wield, and the more that this influence is extended by the technological and socio-material context in which we act, the more indirect responsibility we bear, and the more reflexive we need to become.

We may be pursuing what appear to be entirely rational and morally correct choices but be producing irrational and potentially immoral outcomes. The more power we wield within these socio-material contexts, the more responsible we are for these outcomes. The irrationality of the world or of the market system is thereby a product of our lack of reflectivity upon the unintended consequences of our embeddedness in these relations of interconnection, but this responsibility is unequally distributed. Here, responsibility for poverty and welfare problems cannot reasonably be seen to be that of those people living in these benighted states and seemingly lacking the capacities to resist,[54] nor necessarily with their cash-strapped and dependent governments; it lies elsewhere, with the extent to which we are embedded in the complex international system for which we are

---

[53] Thomas Pogge, "Achieving Democracy," *Ethics & International Affairs* 21, S1 (2007): 249–73, 253.
[54] Pogge, "Are We Violating the Human Rights of the World's Poor?" 17.

all in part responsible. If the market, and its institutional framing, is to blame through indirect links of causation, so therefore are we. The reason for this is that we make the market, we reproduce it, and, in so doing, have the capacity to shape it: to expand or contract the profitability of the kidnapping business, for example.

It is these indirect outcomes which constitute our unequal personal contributions to ethical or moral problems either by our commission or omission. For Pogge, the extension of ethical responsibility to indirect and institutional frameworks of social relations provides an avenue for linking personal citizen and consumption choices in the West with the morally problematic role of transnational regulatory institutions. Once the "interactive" link between individuals or collective actors and rights violations is broken, then it is the institutional context which increasingly bears the responsibility as the framework of incentivization or of environmental choice shaping. This approach clearly challenges liberal understandings of both individual and collective responsibility. In Pogge's work, the international level is the center of attention, and it is the institutional frameworks shaping market exchanges, in an era of globalization, which are alleged to bear an increasing responsibility for the level of democracy, development, and human rights in the non-Western world. Even where there is development, such as in India and China, it is highly unequal, and Western-enforced global regimes such as the World Trade Organization (WTO) and the 1994 Trade-Related Aspects of Intellectual Property Rights (TRIPS) Agreement reinforce these inequalities.[55]

Pogge's work does not merely focus on the impact of global market relations as framed by international agreements on trade and property rights but also on the formal regimes of international law, in particular the principle of sovereign equality – the bulwark of international law – seen to make it more difficult for non-Western states to achieve democratic and developmental stability. The reason for this is that:

[T]he developed countries are the chief upholders of the might-is-right principle. It is they who insist that the mere fact that someone holds effective power over us – regardless of how he came to power, of how he exercises

---

[55] Pogge, "Are We Violating the Human Rights of the World's Poor?" 26; Thomas Pogge, "Responses to the Critics," in *Thomas Pogge and His Critics*, ed. Alison M. Jaggar (Cambridge: Polity, 2010), 175–250, 177.

power, and of the extent to which he is opposed by the people he rules –
gives him the right to incur legally binding international obligations on our
behalf.[56]

International law's international sovereignty regime is seen to constitute an international institutional framework that makes democracy
and human rights much more difficult for non-Western states, leaving
them at risk of military coups or violent sectional conflict. Although
Pogge shares with Collier the view of the indirect responsibilities of
Western states and international actors through institutional frameworks of choice making, he extends the links of association much
more deeply, down to the level of the Western citizen as an individual
actor or agent.

Pogge's work, as a moral philosopher, rather than an economist or
an international relations theorist, is probably the best articulation of
new paternalist understandings and marks the clearest distinction from
the liberal ethics of cosmopolitan internationalism of the 1990s. In this
framework, global interdependence means that responsibility is shared,
but it is always indirect and it is always unequal. It is the ontology
of associative connection which constitutes the ethical need for self-
reflexivity of Western states and citizens who are encouraged to become
more ethical in their choice making. Having established the "collaboration" or complicity of Western citizens in ethically unfair regimes supported by their governments, he suggests that there is a moral duty to
reflect upon the indirect consequences of our embeddedness in Western
societies and in global markets. The solution, in terms of new paternalist thinking, is not necessarily that of joining a political party to change
policies or offer solidarity with the resistance of the poor and oppressed
but to consider how we as individuals might "compensate for our fair
share of the avoidable human rights deficit."[57] One such way is through
charitable giving: "Citizens can compensate for a share of the harm for
which their country is responsible by, for example, supporting effective
international agencies or non-governmental organizations."[58]

The new ethics of indirect responsibility for market consequences
can be seen clearly in the idea of environmental taxation, both state-
enforced through interventions in the market and as taken up by

[56] Pogge, "Achieving Democracy," 266.
[57] Pogge, "Are We Violating the Human Rights of the World's Poor?" 32.
[58] *Ibid.*

both firms and individuals. The idea that we should pay a carbon tax on air travel is a leading example of this, in terms of governmental intervention, passing the burden of such problems on to "unethical" consumers who are not reflexive enough to consider the impact of package holidays on the environment. At a broader level, the personalized ethico-political understanding that individuals should be responsible for, and measure, their own "carbon footprint" shifts the emphasis from an understanding of broader interrelations between modernity, the market, and the environment to a much narrower understanding of personal indirect responsibility, linking all aspects of everyday decision-making to the problems of global warming.[59]

Unlike the traditional paternalism of liberal internationalists in the 1990s, Pogge's concern is neither directly with the formal responsibility of leading Western states and institutions, nor with the ostensible "victims" in poor or underdeveloped countries. The concern of new paternalism is not even with the responsibilities of the "poor or poorly educated citizens" at home in the West. As Pogge states:

> I can suspend judgement about such cases because what matters is the judgement each of us reaches about ourselves. I believe that I share responsibility for what my country is doing in the name of its citizens, and I explain what human rights deficits I hold myself co-responsible for, and why. You must judge for yourself whether you find these reasons compelling or whether, on reflection, you find yourself sufficiently immature, uneducated, or impoverished to be exempt from the ordinary responsibilities of citizenship.[60]

New paternalism uses the problems of the global world to facilitate new forms of self-reflexive governance and of responsible citizenship. This is a far cry from the politics of resistance or of traditional forms of political contestation. For Pogge, the governance of the self does not involve political or public campaigning as much as individual reflexivity about the unintended consequences of our social embeddedness: "Each of us should ... do enough toward protecting poor people to be confident that one is fully compensating for one's fair share of the human rights deficit that we together cause."[61] When asked in

---

[59] See, for example, Noortje Marres, *Material Participation: Technology, the Environment and Everyday Politics* (Basingstoke: Palgrave Macmillan, 2012).
[60] Pogge, "Are We Violating the Human Rights of the World's Poor?" 3.
[61] *Ibid.*, 33.

an Internet magazine interview how his view of ethical responsibility worked, Pogge made a similar statement in terms of a rejection of existing structures or an attempt to change them from within. The answer was very clarifying: "There is a third way. I call it the 'Oskar Schindler solution': You remain within the system and try to compensate for the human rights deficits that are caused by the system because of your contribution to it. If you simply retreat from the system, nobody benefits."[62]

It is interesting to note the secular trend involved in the extension of the ethical world through the logic of association. It seems that the more responsibility is spread, the less interest there is in the specific problem itself and the more attention there is to the ethical self. In the bifurcated liberal ethics of responsibility in the 1990s, the attention was squarely on the problem of human rights abuse and war crimes, problems which non-Western "others" were morally and politically responsible for and therefore lost their rights to political and legal equality in the instantiation of paternalist regimes of intervention and the abnegation of sovereign rights. In the work of Collier, political responsibility is eroded through being sociologized: they are less responsible for the contexts in which choices are made and external interveners share less responsibility as direct intervention shifts to indirect "interference," which does not undermine formal legal and political rights. However, the problems of the world, for example, of the "bottom billion," are still at the forefront of political and ethical concern. With the radical social relationality of Pogge, new paternalism emerges much more clearly as a technology of governing the self rather than of governing others, where, in effect, populations in the West (particularly the more wealthy and educated) become increasingly "responsible" for the crimes and abuses of the world, and there is no real need to distinguish specific problems or specific agents of responsibility.

Conclusion

The "new paternalist" ethics of both Collier and Pogge emerge clearly in their desire to "interfere" more reflexively through the

---

[62] Thomas Pogge, "We Must Be Opportunistic in the Pursuit of Justice," *The European*, December 14, 2011, www.theeuropean-magazine.com/thomas-pogge–2/374-global-justice (accessed July 14, 2016).

indirect mechanisms of international institutions. They both reject the paternalism of direct responsibility as well as the idea that the West does not have the responsibility to act on the problems of non-Western states. In both these frameworks, Western wealth and power – the fact that Western states and institutions set the international agenda and shape the possibilities for the progress and development of non-Western states – are used to argue that there is an indirect responsibility for the outcomes in non-Western states and societies. The key point is that this form of new paternalist responsibility operates as a form of self-critique and as a technology of self-governance. On the basis of concerns with democracy, development, and human rights, international regimes extend not only in terms of their indirect impact on non-Western states but also in the construction of new regimes of transparency and ethical codes, monitoring and regulating a broad swath of international actors and their activities.

Implicit in the ontological understanding of associational responsibility is also a license to "interfere" or to "enlighten" the private choice making of Western citizens, often seen to lack the required reflexivity in their lack of understanding of their own complicity in, and responsibility for, these problems. New paternalism works on the basis of generating awareness of indirect connections and consequences and thus relies not merely on the generation of information, research, and transparency in order for citizens and other actors to reflect upon their choices and actions, but also depends on the inculcation of a community of ethico-political activists, advocates, and researchers. In this way, new paternalism builds a new political constituency and a new political discourse based upon a consensus that becoming aware of the problems of others enables us to govern ourselves on the basis of both political responsibility and ethical responsivity. While critiquing traditional forms of paternalism, it inculcates and generalizes a paternalist sensitivity as a technique of the governance of the self.

PART III

The Social Relations of Paternalism

5 | Paternalism and Peacebuilding: Capacity, Knowledge, and Resistance in International Intervention

SÉVERINE AUTESSERRE

A European diplomat once explained to me the logic behind his government's approach to the Democratic Republic of Congo: "It is a bit like with a teenager – someone who is 18 or 20; you want to help them, but you have to mind your manners and build the trust that enables you to do so." Indeed, the diplomat and his international colleagues – other diplomats, African Union and UN officials, and members of NGOs – all wanted to help a much-affected population by facilitating the re-establishment of peace on Congolese territory. However, not only did these foreign interveners regularly forget to "mind their manners and build trust," but their perception that Congo was like an adolescent who needed to be manipulated into accepting assistance often precluded them from treating the Congolese people as equal partners in the peace process. When the United Nations elaborated a plan to stabilize eastern Congo in 2008, for instance, its expatriate staff designed the strategy without actually involving national or local representatives in the drafting process. The implementation of this initiative suffered multiple setbacks, as well as considerable resistance from local authorities and communities, but UN officials still neglected to invite Congolese stakeholders to participate in the meetings devoted to discussing and revising the stabilization strategy. It took three years for the United Nations to finally do so.[1]

This mode of operation is not limited to Congo. According to several interviewees, there was a similar situation in Timor-Leste for several years after the 2006 riots. International interveners met on a

---

[1] This anecdote is based on the author's confidential interviews and field observations in Congo between June 2010 and July 2011.

I am grateful to Michael N. Barnett, Chuck Call, two anonymous reviewers, and the other contributors to this volume for their very helpful feedback. I also thank Erik Lin-Greenberg, Antonia Miller, Meena Roldan Oberdick, Alexandra Russo, and Stephanie Schwartz for their excellent research assistance.

bi-weekly basis in the UN compound. There, they planned the future of the country without communicating with, or involving, any local partners.[2] A Kosovar government official and a Sri Lankan civil society leader deplored similar phenomena in their own countries, where international actors coordinated among themselves without inviting any members of the host population.[3]

What all of these anecdotes have in common is that they show international interveners acting with the best of intentions – to improve the welfare of others by re-establishing peace in conflict zones – but without the input or consent of the intended beneficiaries. In other words, they are textbook examples of international paternalism as defined by Michael N. Barnett in the Introduction to this volume, and of "soft paternalism" as analyzed by Didier Fassin in Chapter 2.[4] Importantly, these actions are often perceived as such by the intended beneficiaries of international efforts, not only in Congo, Timor-Leste, or Kosovo, but also in many other conflict zones. Time and again, across all of my field sites, I, along with other researchers, heard the same kind of criticisms levied against interveners: Our local interviewees would complain that international peacebuilders were "arrogant," "condescending," and "paternalistic."[5]

These stories underscore a tension that recurs throughout theaters of intervention between the discourse and the practice of

---

[2] A non-confidential source for this anecdote is the author's on-record interview with Ben Larke, Dili, Timor-Leste, February 2012.

[3] CDA Collaborative Learning Projects, "The Listening Project Issue Paper: Structural Relationships in the Aid System" (Cambridge: CDA Collaborative Learning Projects, 2010), 9.

[4] Henry Richardson would argue that these actions are "only in the ballpark of paternalism," as they are not solely justified on the basis of the intervenees' good (see Chapter 1 in this volume). Ilana Feldman presents a convincing rebuttal – and develops an argument very close to the approach I use in this chapter – in the introduction to Chapter 9.

[5] For public sources, see Mary B. Anderson and Lara Olson, *Confronting War: Critical Lessons for Peace Practitioners* (Cambridge, MA: The Collaborative for Development Action, Incorporated, 2003), 39; Mary B. Anderson, Dayna Brown, and Isabella Jean, *Time to Listen: Hearing People on the Receiving End of International Aid* (Cambridge, MA: CDA Collaborative Learning Project, 2012), 27–8; Ishbel McWha, "The Roles of, and Relationships between, Expatriates, Volunteers, and Local Development Workers," *Development in Practice* 21, 1 (2011): 33; and Ole Jacob Sending, "Why Peacebuilders Fail to Secure Ownership and Be Sensitive to Context," *Security in Practice* 1 (2009). See also Henry Richardson's analysis of arrogance and international humanitarian aid in this volume (Chapter 1).

international peacebuilding. That is, the values that interveners claim to have and the theories of effective peacebuilding that they aim to follow are at odds with actual practice on the ground. "Consent" is supposed to be a prerequisite for any kind of UN engagement in conflict zones, but local people regularly complain that UN initiatives are imposed on them.[6] Scholars and practitioners routinely emphasize that solutions fostered domestically are much more likely to be effective and sustainable than arrangements that are externally dictated, but the latter prevail in many conflict zones.[7] Why do interveners continually behave in ways that conflict with their own values and discourses? How do they justify their own imposition? How does domination interact with compassion in international peacebuilding?

An interview I conducted with Ben Larke, a peacebuilder with twelve years of experience working for a variety of UN agencies and NGOs in Timor-Leste, illuminates the process through which interveners come to adopt a series of behaviors and attitudes that differ from and, at times, oppose the ones they aim for.[8] No matter how hard Larke and his colleagues tried to use "the most empowering methodologies," the "classic, almost paternalist thinking" that permeates aid efforts "crept into the psychology of everyone." To Larke, this patronizing attitude was rooted in the very fact that he and his colleagues were "brought

[6] On consent, see "Principles of UN Peacekeeping" on the UN website (available at www.un.org/en/peacekeeping/operations/principles.shtml) for an official statement and Lise Morjé Howard, *UN Peacekeeping in Civil Wars* (New York: Cambridge University Press, 2008) for an analysis. On imposition: Séverine Autesserre, *Peaceland: Conflict Resolution and the Everyday Politics of International Intervention* (New York: Cambridge University Press, 2014), ch. 3; and Andrea Kathryn Talentino, "Perceptions of Peacebuilding: The Dynamic of Imposer and Imposed Upon," *International Studies Perspectives* 8, 2 (2007): 152–71.

[7] Timothy Donais, "Empowerment or Imposition? Dilemmas of Local Ownership in Post-Conflict Peacebuilding Processes," *Peace and Change* 34, 1 (2009): 10–11; and Carolyn Hayman, "Local First – a Proposal for Development in the Twenty-First Century," in *Local First: Development for the Twenty-First Century*, ed. Kate McGuinness (London: Peace Direct, 2012), 23–5. For concrete illustrations, see the case studies on Congo and Burundi in Kate McGuinness, *Local First: Development for the Twenty-First Century* (London: Peace Direct, 2012), respectively 44–64 and 65–84, and my own work on various conflict zones around the world in Autesserre, *Peaceland* (notably chs. 2 to 4).

[8] Author's on-record interview, Dili, February 2012.

in from the outside with the idea that [they were] here to help – that
people [were] needy and lack[ed] capacity."

My own findings confirm Larke's analysis. As the first section of
this chapter explains, two main elements are at the root of the paternalistic attitudes that recur in international peacebuilding: first, the
idea that local populations need help because they lack capacity and
expertise, and second, the belief that international actors have the
capacity and the knowledge required to provide this help. The next
section of this chapter locates the source of these two recurrent narratives in the politics of knowledge at work in international peacebuilding and clarifies how this politics of knowledge legitimizes international interference. The third section identifies the most important
on-the-ground consequences of such a paternalistic approach: the
fact that host populations regularly resist, challenge, or reject the
international programs that are meant to help them. Throughout,
I note exceptions to the dominant practices and highlight the benefits
inherent to these alternative approaches. By way of conclusion, the
last section identifies the three main obstacles to changing and ending
these widespread practices: the role of accountability structures, the
dilemma that international interveners face in balancing the inclusion
of local actors with the hurdles that such inclusion often creates, and
the detrimental byproducts of the politics of knowledge at work in
the peacebuilding field.[9]

This chapter underscores two points that are critical for this volume. First, in international peacebuilding, paternalism manifests itself
in the process, rather than the goals, of intervention. Second, both
"Western" and "non-Western" actors use the everyday practices, routines, and narratives I analyze. In other words, in contrast to John
Hobson who argues that international paternalism is but an extension
of Western liberal imperialism, I maintain that African, Asian, Middle
Eastern, and Latin American interveners engage in the everyday paternalism I describe just as much as European and North American
peacebuilders.[10]

---

[9] The analysis presented in the subsequent sections extensively draws on – and
at times reproduces – the arguments formulated in Autesserre, *Peaceland*.
For more details and examples on the analysis presented in the first and last
section, see *Peaceland*, ch. 6; the second section, see *Peaceland*, part 1, notably
ch. 2; and the third section, see *Peaceland*, ch. 3.
[10] See Chapter 3 in this volume.

I develop this argument based on several years of ethnographic inquiry in conflict zones around the world. I spent these years embedded in the transnational community of expatriates who devote their lives to building peace in foreign countries. As I have demonstrated elsewhere, these individuals have extremely varied geographical origins, professions, and organizational affiliations, but they all inhabit a metaphorical world with specific customs, rituals, cultures, structures, beliefs, and taboos – a world that I call "Peaceland."[11] At times I studied Peaceland from the inside, as a fellow intervener, and, other times, from the outside, as an academic researcher.

I base my analysis on more than 640 in-depth interviews as well as three and a half years of field observations, most of which offered extensive participant observation opportunities. I collected this data primarily in Congo (where I traveled regularly between 2001 and 2014), but I also draw on research visits to other theaters of intervention, including Afghanistan (in 2002), Burundi (during several visits between 2003 and 2012), Cyprus (in 2011), Israel and the Palestinian Territories (in 2012), Kosovo (in 2000), Nicaragua (in 1998), South Sudan (in 2011), and Timor-Leste (in 2012). In addition, I build on participant observations and interviews conducted in the New York headquarters of various international and non-governmental organizations as well as interviews in African, European, and North American capitals (between 1999 and 2015).[12]

Insiders' and Outsiders' Capacity: The Dominant Narratives

The first source of the interveners' paternalistic attitudes is the view that intended beneficiaries lack the capacity and expertise necessary to solve their own predicaments – which justifies the need for foreigners

---

[11] Autesserre, *Peaceland*.

[12] Virtually all of my interviewees and contacts asked to remain anonymous due to the personal and professional risks involved in providing information for this chapter. They also requested that I maintain the same level of confidentiality for all the material gathered through field and participant observations. For this reason, I cite in full only that data which I obtained through on-record interviews and from public sources. All of the information and quotations for which I do not provide complete references come from confidential interviews, participant observations, and field observations. To ensure their reliability, I have triangulated all the statements that I make in this chapter, including those that I could not fully reference.

to help host populations. A few vignettes from my fieldwork will illustrate how this view plays out on the ground.

A French NGO intervener deployed in eastern Congo explained to me that leaders in the country are unreliable – "state structures are very weak," "there is a lot of poor governance," and authorities must strike shady deals just to survive – "so only the ... foreigners are capable of enacting reforms." I heard these kinds of pejorative statements about Congolese populations and authorities from interveners of all national, professional, and organizational backgrounds. Many interviewees – including African contacts – deemed local and national authorities incompetent, uneducated, corrupt, dishonest, insensitive to the sufferings of their populations, and incapable of long-term planning. In addition, some of them described the Congolese people as poorly educated, lazy, self-centered, violent, or untrustworthy; these negative perceptions also extended to Congolese associations and civil society organizations.[13]

In all of the conflict zones in which I worked, certain foreign peacebuilders expressed some form of this same dismissive attitude. Some interveners painted the South Sudanese people as lazy, inept, hopeless, and aggressive, while others branded Timorese nationals as backward, corrupt, and incompetent. Such derogatory comments were also widespread in Afghanistan, Burundi, and Nicaragua; my contacts described the same phenomenon in Albania, Azerbaijan, Chad, and Rwanda; a fellow researcher observed it in Liberia; and Ilana Feldman's chapter in this volume includes similar examples from the Palestinian Territories.[14] Admittedly, expatriates and immigrant communities often criticize the citizens of the foreign countries in which they live, whether in America, Europe, or Africa. However, criticisms are particularly harsh and widespread among interveners deployed in conflict zones, regardless of these individuals' geographic origins, professions, or organizational affiliations.

That international peacebuilders come to belittle their intended beneficiaries so pervasively is puzzling given the blatant contradiction

---

[13] See also Gabrielle Dietze, "Mythologies Blanches: Découvreurs et Sauveurs du Congo," in *Repenser l'Indépendance: La RD Congo 50 Ans Plus Tard*, ed. Pole Institute, *Regards Croisés* (Goma, DR Congo: Pole Institute, 2010).

[14] On Liberia: Ole Jacob Sending, ed., *Learning to Build a Sustainable Peace: Ownership and Everyday Peacebuilding* (Bergen: Chr. Michelsen Institute, 2010), 26–8.

between such attitudes and the values to which the vast majority of interveners claim to subscribe. The behavior surprises – and distresses – even the individuals who themselves engage in it. During a party I attended with other interveners in eastern Congo, a friend of mine went on a lengthy rant about how he could not stand the local people anymore. After a while, he paused, became very sad, and remarked on how he had changed in the year that he had spent in the field. All his ideals of equality, respect, and fairness had crumbled. He had become the very kind of person he used to hate. Only leaving the intervention world, he thought, would enable him to return to normal.

Not all interveners who engage in such self-reflection decide to change careers. Most of them, instead, try to fight the dominant discourse. In each of my field sites, I met expatriates who contested the dominant narratives and tried to rein in these types of careless comments. They reminded their colleagues that blanket statements about entire populations were bound to do injustice to many people. They pointed to the numerous local individuals they knew who defied the stereotypes and who had proved competent, intelligent, selfless, reliable, honest, hardworking, and fully dedicated to bettering the lives of their fellow citizens. They emphasized that despite the failings of state structures, many of their local counterparts had knowledge, expertise, and skills essential to peacebuilding. However, at best, these interveners were able to prevent one conversation or another from getting out of hand. They rarely managed to improve the overall image of local people.

The flipside of this discourse, which holds that host populations lack capacity and expertise, is the assumption that interveners have the knowledge necessary to compensate for local deficiencies – as I further explain in the next section. Together, these two narratives justify international imposition. This is evident in Aisling Swaine's analysis of the nexus between humanitarian agencies' perceptions of Darfuri women as utterly powerless and their exclusion from decision-making.[15] The words of a development worker I interviewed similarly encapsulate this dynamic. For over seventeen years, this expatriate had seen thousands of peacebuilders arrive in the city of Goma (eastern Congo). She explained that, although there are exceptions, the general perspective of interveners in crisis situations is that "these poor,

---

[15] See Chapter 6 in this volume.

helpless, catastrophic people need our expertise," so "we will do this for [them]." As people who live in conflict and post-conflict settings are in situations of extreme vulnerability and in need of help, "almost automatically there is [a] power imbalance." Owing to this attitude, foreign peacebuilders "totally disregard capacities already here on the ground." She concluded, "It is like 'these people have no power, so they have no voice'."

Main Source of Paternalism in Peace Interventions: The Politics of Knowledge

Thematic and Local Expertise

The idea that outsiders have the capacity that host populations lack is rooted in the politics of knowledge that characterizes international peace-building. In short, there is an ongoing dispute over which (and whose) knowledge matters most for effective peacebuilding. There are two principal contenders for this title. The first, which I refer to as either "local knowledge" or "country expertise," is based on a strong familiarity with specific places, whether countries, like Congo, or sub-national areas, like districts or villages. The second is a category that I call "thematic knowledge" or "technical expertise," and it relies on an in-depth understanding of particular aspects of intervention work. These may be general aspects, such as conflict resolution, development, or humanitarian aid, or they may be specialized ones, as in project management, public finance, or agricultural engineering. Both expatriate and local actors possess each type of knowledge to varying degrees, and they employ various strategies to demonstrate the importance of their particular expertise.

As other researchers have demonstrated, to be effective, peace interventions must draw on the local and thematic knowledge of both insiders and outsiders.[16] Whether they are local stakeholders with thematic

---

[16] Anderson and Olson, *Confronting War*, ch. 5; Susanna Campbell, "Independent External Evaluation – Peacebuilding Fund Projects in Burundi" (New York: UN Peacebuilding Fund, 2010), notably 11, 14, 16, 25, 52–9, and 69; CDA Collaborative Learning Projects, "The Listening Project Issue Paper: The Role of Staffing Decisions" (Cambridge: CDA Collaborative Learning Projects, 2010), 2–5; McGuinness, *Local First*, 182–3 and throughout the book; and Roger Mac Ginty, "Indigenous Peace-Making Versus the Liberal Peace," *Cooperation and Conflict* 43, 2 (2008), notably 141–3. For an overview of these arguments, see Autesserre, *Peaceland*, 64–7 and 71–3.

knowledge, expatriates with country knowledge, or vice versa, peace-builders with various competencies each contribute different "perspectives, networks, assets, and leverage with particular constituencies," all of which are essential to peacebuilding.[17] These various interveners make the greatest contributions to peace when they work together, each challenging the biases of the other.[18]

Unfortunately, a clear imbalance exists in the current international system. Just like Aisling Swaine has documented for humanitarian aid, the professionalization of the peacebuilding field has led to "the genesis of high-end knowledge which lends authority to the external experts vis-à-vis the knowledge of the 'local' person."[19] In peacebuilding, the most valued expertise is that of foreign interveners who are trained in conflict-resolution techniques and who have extensive experience in a variety of conflict zones. By contrast, and although there are exceptions, country knowledge is much less valued, and the knowledge of local people is usually trivialized.[20]

Recruitment practices embody the valorization of thematic expertise over local knowledge. The "career" pages of non-governmental and international organizations' websites show that peacebuilding organizations recruit operational experts, such as "Civil Affairs Officer," "Financial Controller," or "Election Specialist."[21] They rarely hire anthropologists, historians, or other kinds of country-experts who can help interveners gain an in-depth understanding of their work environments, and they virtually never ask for a specialist on, for example,

---

[17] Anderson and Olson, *Confronting War*, 35.

[18] *Ibid.*, 42.

[19] See Chapter 6 in this volume, citation from p. 221. On the professionalization of peacebuilding, see Autesserre, *Peaceland*, 75–9.

[20] Anderson *et al.*, *Time to Listen*, 27–8 and 31; Raymond Apthorpe, "Who Is International Aid? Some Personal Observations," in *Inside the Everyday Lives of Development Workers: The Challenges and Futures of Aidland*, eds. Anne-Meike Fechter and Heather Hindman (Sterling, VA: Kumarian Press, 2011), 200 and 202; Pierre Englebert and Denis Tull, "Postconflict Resolution in Africa: Flawed Ideas About Failed States," *International Security* 32, 4 (2008): 134–5; and Sending, "Why Peacebuilders Fail to Secure Ownership," 8–14.

[21] Representative examples include, among many others: www.aucareers.org/vacancies.aspx (African Union); http://employment.sfcg.org (Search for Common Ground); https://careers.un.org/lbw/home.aspx?viewtype=NCE (UN recruitment exam); and http://web.worldbank.org/WBSITE/EXTERNAL/EXTJOBSNEW/0,contentMDK:23122244~menuPK:8680050~pagePK:84543 06~piPK:7345678~theSitePK:8453353,00.html (World Bank).

Sudan or the Baucau district of Timor-Leste. Foreign ministries and
diplomatic missions similarly privilege thematic expertise over local
knowledge in the recruitment of their staff.[22]

As always, there are variations and exceptions to this trend. Some
recruiters value local expertise more than others. In contexts like
Afghanistan and the Palestinian Territories, country specialists have had
more success in demonstrating the relevance of their knowledge to the
overall intervention. This adjustment of knowledge hierarchies was evident in the comparatively larger proportion of expatriates I met whom
had been hired based on their pre-existing familiarity with the area.
However, even in such theaters of intervention, my contacts confirmed
that peacebuilding agencies still prioritized thematic expertise over local
knowledge in the recruitment and promotion of their employees.

This predilection for thematic knowledge has numerous consequences for international efforts, which I have analyzed elsewhere.[23]
Most relevant for this chapter is that it legitimizes outside interference
and leads to an outsider bias.

Legitimization of Outside Interference

Valuing thematic expertise over local knowledge justifies the interveners' claim that they have the capacity necessary to resolve the host
populations' problems. Foreign peacebuilders have technical expertise,
which is often attested by degrees from prestigious universities and
reinforced by work experience in multiple conflict zones – all of which
local counterparts rarely possess.

As a result, in virtually all aid and peacebuilding agencies, whether
diplomatic, international, or non-governmental, expatriates hold the
management positions, while local employees serve as staff. Very few
local people make it into leadership positions in their countries of origin. To move up in the hierarchy, they have to go abroad and become
expatriates themselves. In fact, most intervention structures value the
expertise of local people only at the level of implementation, if at all.[24] An

[22] See for instance www.diplomatie.gouv.fr/fr/ministere_817/emplois-stages-
concours_825/index.html (for France) and www.state.gov/careers (for the
United States). For assignment-specific recruitment, see for example www.
btcctb.org/fr/offres-demploi (Coopération Technique Belge).
[23] Autesserre, *Peaceland*, Part I.
[24] For a public source on this issue in Liberia and Sudan, see Sending, *Learning
to Build a Sustainable Peace*, 5, 24–5, 28–9, and 31–4; and on the Palestinian
Territories, see Chapter 9 in this volume.

agency may recruit a local staff member familiar with a specific theater in order to facilitate the execution of given strategies and projects, but it will not involve this person in the design of these initiatives. Similarly, as various interviewees and I experienced in UN agencies, diplomatic missions, and international NGOs, the role of the national staff is usually limited to collecting information that expatriates later analyze. Very few agencies build on local analytical capacity. This unequal relationship also prevails in the interactions between international and local NGOs, as the latter are "rarely" involved "in shaping strategy."[25]

There are only a few exceptions to this widespread practice: isolated efforts by select individuals, project staff (notably those working on community-driven reconstruction initiatives), and organizations (such as Caritas; Peace Direct; Catholic Relief Services in Bosnia, Serbia, and Timor-Leste; the Life and Peace Institute in Congo; and the Eastern Congo Initiative).[26] The common characteristic of these otherwise diverse people and organizations is that they base their actions on in-depth local knowledge and reject universal approaches to peacebuilding. The most innovative among them rely on local employees supervised by a few foreigners (who often have extensive pre-existing country knowledge). In these exceptional cases, local staff and counterparts are in charge of conceiving, designing, and executing the projects. The expatriates view their roles as "providing technical support, resources, and international connections" to the plans formulated by the local stakeholders.[27]

Apart from these exceptions, the marginalization of local input is widespread. While interveners often bemoan the lack of participation

---

[25] Keystone Accountability, "NGO Partner Survey 2010" (London: Keystone Accountability, 2011), citation from p. 5; details on pp. 17–20 and 48. Also Keystone Accountability, "Development Partnerships Survey: Headlines for International Development" (London: Keystone Accountability, 2013), 6.

[26] On Peace Direct, see McGuinness, *Local First*. On Catholic Relief Services in Bosnia and Serbia, see Chip Gagnon, "Catholic Relief Services, USAID, and Authentic Partnership in Serbia," in *Transacting Transition: The Micropolitics of Democracy Assistance in the Former Yugoslavia*, ed. Keith Brown (Bloomfield: Kumarian Press, 2006). On the Life and Peace Institute, see www.life-peace.org/what-we-do/guiding-principles/. On the Eastern Congo Initiative, see www.easterncongo.org/about. For additional examples, see Monica Kathina Juma and Astri Suhrke, *Eroding Local Capacity: International Humanitarian Action in Africa* (Uppsala: Nordic African Institute, 2002), 9.

[27] Gagnon, "Catholic Relief Services," 172.

and "buy-in" by local populations, they cannot, or do not, locate its source in their own practices. Tellingly, several interveners emphasized that "we cannot pacify Congo" (or Sudan, or Burundi) without the Congolese (or the Sudanese, or the Burundians), since "they are the ones who have the solution." To anyone outside of Peaceland, such a remark would have sounded like a truism. My interviewees, however, presented this argument as a profound conclusion born out of their long experience in conflict zones. To me, their statements highlighted just how ingrained paternalism is in the everyday practice of peacebuilding.

The dominance of thematic expertise does not solely influence power relationships within peacebuilding organizations; it also shapes the overall structure of an intervention. It generates an outsider bias, as Dennis Tull and Pierre Englebert trace in their study of state reconstruction in Africa. They convincingly demonstrate that "the very nature of international reconstruction efforts suggests that the knowledge, capacity, strategies, and resources of external actors are crucial ingredients for success."[28]

Combined with the negative view of local counterparts detailed earlier in this chapter, this pro-outsider bias entices international interveners to substitute themselves for local partners and, at times, to act without their consent. Aisling Swaine documents this problem with regards to emergency relief efforts,[29] and my contacts provided numerous examples from peacebuilding organizations. They told of expatriates fighting against injustice themselves instead of training grassroots activists to do so, drawing up action plans for elections themselves instead of letting opposition leaders design their own electoral strategies, or carrying out state reconstruction projects themselves without consulting state authorities. In conclusion, one of these interviewees offered a striking remark: "With all their self-confidence, [interveners] think that they can construct the Congo without the Congolese."[30]

There were exceptions within all organizations – people who tried, at their own level, to value country knowledge and local expertise

[28] Englebert and Tull, "Postconflict Resolution in Africa," citation from pp. 134–5, demonstration throughout the article.
[29] See Chapter 6 in this volume.
[30] Author's on-record interview with Onesphore Sematumba, Pole Institute, Goma, November 2010.

and to give their local partners as much responsibility as possible. However, these individuals all emphasized the rarity of their approach. Although other expatriates were aware of the problems inherent in their tendency to substitute themselves for their local partners, they explained that the low capacity and potential biases of these counterparts left them with little choice. My contacts stationed in states with weak capacities, such as Congo and Sudan, presented their dilemma as a catch-22: Either they did capacity building, which took an enormous amount of time and resulted in poorly executed programs – while intended beneficiaries continued to suffer from the continuation of violence in the meantime – or they imposed ideas and implemented the initiatives themselves, which was more effective in the short term but unsustainable in the long term. Throughout conflict zones, foreign peacebuilders also worried that, if they relied too much on local input, local stakeholders would manipulate the projects and bias them in favor of their political or ethnic groups. By contrast, foreign interveners viewed themselves as objective parties able to implement impartial programs that would maximize benefits for all stakeholders.[31] As a result, the outsider bias persists, and it creates some of the most significant problems for international peacebuilding: accusations of arrogance, local feelings of imposition, and, in consequence, resistance to and rejection of international programs.

Main Consequences: Adaptation, Contestation, and Resistance

Existing research has shown that, in every country, elite and ordinary citizens interact with interveners through a wide variety of strategies, which reflect the host populations' infinitude of goals, beliefs, customs, and attitudes.[32] For this reason, local reactions to international

---

[31] See also Anderson and Olson, *Confronting War*, 32. For illustrations of this self-perception, see the websites and charters of international peacebuilding agencies – for instance, the principles of UN Peacekeeping as presented on the UN website, www.un.org/en/peacekeeping/operations/principles. shtml#impartiality.

[32] This paragraph draws on Amitav Acharya, *Whose Ideas Matter? Agency and Power in Asian Regionalism* (Ithaca: Cornell University Press, 2009); Anderson *et al.*, *Time to Listen*, i, 1, 6, 21, and throughout the report; Michael N. Barnett and Christoph Zürcher, "The Peacebuilder's Contract: How External Statebuilding Reinforces Weak Statehood," in *The Dilemmas of Statebuilding: Confronting the Contradictions of Postwar Peace Operations*, eds. Roland Paris and Timothy Sisk (London: Routledge, 2009); Roger Mac

initiatives depend on the given project as well as the country, province, or village in which it takes place. Nevertheless, common patterns
recur throughout areas of intervention. Some actors, varying in number depending on the context, cooperate with certain aspects of the
intervention, either because they believe in the programs or because
they use the international initiatives to reach their own goals. In many
cases, however, local reactions to peace interventions also include
much less supportive responses such as non-engagement, subversion,
contestation, cherry-picking, outright resistance, and rejection.[33]

Other scholars have identified multiple reasons for these less supportive responses, including the local partners' poor understanding of
international strategies, the presence of vested interests, the impact of
financial and logistical constraints on the projects, and the Western
and liberal characters of the programs.[34] Local interviewees also often
complained that, because foreign peacebuilders ignored local expertise
and input, interveners implemented programs ill-adapted to local situations – programs that occasionally worsened local conditions and
that intended beneficiaries had to combat.[35] My research suggests an
additional factor, which can be even more influential than the factors
cited in existing literature, and which brings us back to the topic of
international paternalism. In my analysis, the varying degrees of non-
acceptance are due to the very act of imposition.

As one Congolese intellectual described:

Ginty, *International Peacebuilding and Local Resistance: Hybrid Forms of
Peace, Rethinking Peace and Conflict Studies* (London: Palgrave Macmillan,
2011); Oliver Richmond and Audra Mitchell, *Hybrid Forms of Peace: From
Everyday Agency to Post-Liberalism* (New York: Palgrave, 2011); and
Béatrice Pouligny, *Ils Nous Avaient Promis la Paix: Opérations de l'ONU
et Populations Locales* (Paris: Presses de la Fondation nationale des sciences
politiques, 2004). See also Chapter 9 in this volume.

[33] This sentence paraphrases Roger Mac Ginty, *No War, No Peace: The
Rejuvenation of Stalled Peace Processes and Peace Accords* (London: Palgrave
Macmillan, 2006), 17.

[34] See the sources listed in footnote 32.

[35] Other authors who have also documented this issue include, among many
others: Anderson *et al.*, *Time to Listen*, 24–5, 28, 31, and ch. 5; Tanja Hohe,
"Clash of Paradigms: International Administration and Local Political
Legitimacy in East Timor," *Contemporary Southeast Asia* 24, 3 (2002); Mac
Ginty, *No War, No Peace*; Roland Paris, *At War's End: Building Peace after
Civil Conflict* (Cambridge: Cambridge University Press, 2004); Roland Paris,
"Saving Liberal Peacebuilding," *Review of International Studies* 36, 2 (2010);
and Pouligny, *Ils Nous Avaient Promis La Paix*, especially 133–6 and 293.

The programs are often good, if you read the documents from the UN and all the others – at the core they have good intentions. That is not the problem, really. The problem is the bad set-up; things are badly set up from the start, so they cannot work. People here, the supposed beneficiaries, are not consulted; they do not participate in anything. When [interveners design] a project, it is as if it fell on the heads of people here.[36]

This quote reflects what I heard throughout my interviews with all kinds of Congolese people. Local employees of international agencies explained that they felt excluded from the decision-making process within their organizations. Intellectuals and authorities regularly complained that interveners tried to impose their ideas, values, and standard operating procedures with no consideration of local knowledge and customs. All of these local actors deplored their lack of influence over international strategies. Some of them overlooked these problems in order to benefit from the resources that interveners might provide (such as a steady salary or access to international networks), but others instead reacted by generating obstacles to the implementation of the international programs. For instance, local staff and partners dragged their feet by canceling meetings, forgetting to attend them, or creating state structures for the sole purpose of pleasing international donors but then never using them.

Interviewees recalled witnessing similar dynamics in Burundi, the Palestinian Territories, and South Sudan. A former government official complained about interveners arriving with external systems and ideas that disregarded existing Burundian ones; he explained that this practice led to "revolt" by local people, either through violence or through "a certain lack of discipline."[37] An American attorney working in the Palestinian Territories explained how her counterparts would listen to what she said, and then "do things their own way, ignoring the instructions or advice with which they disagreed." As her Palestinian colleagues themselves confirmed, they thought, "how dare she tell [them] what to do" in their own country, of which she knew nothing. Ilana Feldman's chapter on aid in the Palestinian Territories emphasizes a similar point.[38]

[36] Author's on-record interview with Jean-Pierre Lindiro Kabirigi, Pole Institute, Goma, July 2011.
[37] Author's on-record interview with Jean-Marie Ngendahayo, August 2010, Bujumbura.
[38] See Chapter 9 in this volume.

In her analysis, one of the main reasons why refugees might refuse aid is the United Nations' attitude towards them. As Feldman explains, all these refugees' demands were about respect and engagement, about the fact that they had the capacity to know what they wanted and needed. Likewise, a Sudanese civil society activist reported that "friction between the donor's perception of how things should look and the communities' perceptions" resulted in various local communities "reject[ing] the intervention," saying "to hell with their money."[39] Or, as Aisling Swaine documents in her chapter, intended beneficiaries would openly criticize international agencies and request a change of strategy. Alternatively, my Sudanese interviewee explained, communities "abandoned the project, worked against [it] by creating lots of obstacles," or simply let it collapse when the donor left. He concluded that "this is why some projects fail: because communities have never owned them, they were always owned by donors. ... It is very common."

Andrea Talentino reports a finding analogous to mine.[40] Through an in-depth study of local perceptions of eleven ongoing peace operations, Talentino demonstrates that "actors resist change, even when they might objectively agree that it is positive, if it seems forced upon them."[41] In all of her cases, even those where interveners were initially welcome (like in Kosovo and Liberia), she documents resentment at the imposition from at least some local groups – whether they were spoilers, elites, citizens, social groups, or a combination thereof.[42] Just like I have argued, Talentino also shows that this resentment results in pervasive obstructionism. Reyko Huang and Joseph Harris's analysis of capacity building by UN officials in Timor-Leste underscores a similar point. Expatriates making "direct or indirect attempts to impose" their ideas on national staff were met with "frowning and resistance," which compromised peacebuilding efforts.[43]

---

[39] Author's on-record interview with Edmund Yakani, Community Empowerment for Progress Organization, Juba, April 2011.

[40] Talentino, "Perceptions of Peacebuilding."

[41] *Ibid.*, 153. Also Laurie Nathan, "No Ownership, No Commitment: A Guide to Local Ownership of Security Sector Reform" (Birmingham: University of Birmingham, 2007).

[42] Talentino, "Perceptions of Peacebuilding," 161, especially Table 2.

[43] Reyko Huang and Joseph Harris, "The Nuts and Bolts of Post-Conflict Capacity Building: Practicable Lessons from East Timor," *Journal of Peacebuilding and Development* 2, 3 (2006): 83.

Interestingly for the debate on paternalism, these local reactions rarely take the form of open, obvious contestation or outright rejection. Instead, the large majority are subtle attempts at resisting without antagonizing international actors or causing them to leave. Numerous contacts noted that, in most theaters of intervention, whether due to poverty or low state capacity, local stakeholders have so few resources – financial, logistic, or otherwise – to accomplish their goals that they rely on outside help to obtain the material assets needed to complete their work. A Filipino city official and a Kenyan peacebuilder used the same words to describe the resulting dynamics: "beggars cannot be choosers."[44] In Haiti, for instance, the government has to comply with donors' conditions and suggestions because that is the only way it can get the financial resources it needs to govern.[45] Similarly, in Congo, the needs are so high that Congolese officials told me they "have to agree to anything" in the hope that it might "get [them] out of the ditch."[46] Interveners can thus – in the words of one of them – "set any kind of unreasonable rule [they] feel like" and impose the projects they want on their local counterparts. To make matters worse, the international peacebuilders deployed on the ground – those who meet regularly with local actors and set these seemingly unreasonable rules – are often individuals in their twenties or thirties.[47] The mere act of such young people arriving to advise seasoned, usually much older and much more experienced, ministers is inherently paternalistic – something that the interveners are often aware of and uncomfortable with. But again, most local elites will defer to these outsiders so as not to offend the people who can influence the distribution of material assets. Young interveners therefore feel that their advice is welcomed and their knowledge valued.

These various dynamics create a vicious cycle. Local appeals for assistance weaken the position of local elites and strengthen that of the intervening organizations, which then perceive themselves to be

---

[44] The Filipino city official is cited in Anderson *et al.*, *Time to Listen*, 61. The citation from the Kenyan peacebuilder comes from the author's confidential interview.

[45] Sending, *Learning to Build a Sustainable Peace*, 18.

[46] The citations comes from an author's on-record interview with Michel Losembe, vice president of the Fédération des Entreprises du Congo, June 2011, Kinshasa.

[47] Thanks to Stephanie Schwartz (Ph.D. candidate, Columbia University) for emphasizing the ideas I develop in the rest of the paragraph.

taking on the core responsibilities of the state and civil society and, as a result, operate with increasing arrogance. Local NGOs and authorities often respond by behaving deferentially toward representatives of these organizations in an attempt to secure their financial, logistical, and political support. To obtain funding, even the strongest and most respected civil society organizations regularly allow outsiders to set their agenda, rather than challenging international interveners on what they see as the country's priorities. Such conduct further undermines the authority of local stakeholders and fuels the interveners' beliefs that they know more than their local counterparts, which in turn reinforces the international tendency to value external knowledge over local input. At the same time, the increased arrogance and tendency toward imposition leads to amplified, but often covert, opposition. As a result, the interveners think that the beneficiaries consent to their projects, while these beneficiaries are instead engaging in passive or concealed resistance. The dissonance was clear in interviews I conducted with local and foreign actors working on the same initiative: In numerous cases, the interveners would explain that they had full cooperation from their partners or staff, while the staff complained of what they perceived as paternalistic behavior on the part of the expatriates, and then went on to explain how they adapted, distorted, or created problems for the international efforts.

In contrast, the exceptional individuals and organizations who fight the trends documented in this chapter, involve local stakeholders in the design of the international programs, build on local knowledge, and solicit local input throughout the course of the project face fewer of the obstacles analyzed in this section and eventually achieve much greater success. Extensive research by Mary Anderson and her co-authors in twenty-one conflict zones around the world found that "when people participate in all phases of an aid effort, from conception of the idea, to the design and planning, to implementation, and through final evaluation, they will 'own' the process and therefore be more likely to maintain the results."[48] A quantitative analysis of local involvement and international reconstruction efforts in Bosnia-Herzegovina (from 1991 to 1995) and Somalia (from 1987 to 1997) substantiated this evidence. The study found that "phases in the peacebuilding process with high local participation [were]

[48] Anderson *et al.*, *Time to Listen*, 67–8.

associated with lower levels of hostility, while phases with little local involvement tend[ed] to be associated with escalating violence."[49] Local communities in Cambodia, Ethiopia, Kenya, Thailand, and Zimbabwe told similar stories: They worked harder to ensure that a project succeeded and persisted when they viewed it as "theirs," while they did not "put [in] as much effort" when they perceived it as a donor's or NGO's initiative.[50]

Adam Moore reached a similar finding in his analysis of the United Nations' and the Organization for Security and Co-operation in Europe's peacebuilding efforts in the Brčko district of Bosnia-Herzegovina. The differing success of two consecutive international attempts at integrating schools in post-war Brčko illustrates the importance of soliciting and integrating local input, as well as the problems that occur when interveners fail to do so.[51] The first initiative occurred in 2000 "with little input from district officials or public discussion with concerned parents." It generated "massive protests" that "resulted in the temporary closure of the schools until changes were reversed." The second attempt took place a year later. It started with extensive consultations of district citizens, teachers, and officials, to discuss their concerns and gain their support for the proposed change. The subsequent implementation of the reform proceeded smoothly with minimal incidents or public protest. Beyond school integration, international staff based in Brčko worked on a daily basis with their local counterparts and took their suggestions into account. In Moore's analysis, the cultivation of local officials as partners in the peacebuilding process was one of the reasons for the success of reforms in this district, while efforts in the rest of the country widely failed.[52]

---

[49] Theodora-Ismene Gizelis and Kristin E. Kosek, "Why Humanitarian Interventions Succeed or Fail: The Role of Local Participation," *International Peacekeeping* 40, 4 (2005), citation from p. 363, demonstration throughout the article.

[50] CDA Collaborative Learning Projects, "The Listening Project Issue Paper: 'Discuss Together, Decide Together, Work Together' " (Cambridge: CDA Collaborative Learning Projects, 2008), 4–5; also Anderson *et al.*, *Time to Listen*, 68–9 and 74.

[51] This paragraph is based on – and the quotations come from – Adam Moore, *The Dynamics of Peacebuilding Success and Failure in Post-War Bosnia* (Ithaca: Cornell University Press, 2013), 122–4.

[52] *Ibid.*

Conclusion: Obstacles to Change

Two main elements are at the source of the paternalistic attitudes and behaviors that international peacebuilders routinely adopt when working on the ground in conflict zones. The first is the claim that host populations lack the capacity to resolve their own predicaments, and the second is the belief that international interveners possess this capacity. Both narratives are rooted in the politics of knowledge at work in the peacebuilding field, where thematic expertise is much more valued than country or local knowledge. The paternalistic attitudes and behaviors, when added to the narratives that justify them, antagonize host populations and generate widespread resistance and rejection, creating significant obstacles for the international programs.

Paternalism is thus embedded both in the everyday practice of intervention on the ground and in the very nature of the international peacebuilding system. As Ilana Feldman also emphasizes in her chapter,[53] it is from the moment that we identify a population or a person as needing help that the dangers of paternalism first appear. This moment, when interpreted through the dominant international peacebuilding lens, divides people into helpers (those experts who are brought in from the outside because they have the required knowledge and capacities) and those in need of help (those non-experts who are on site and lack capacity). From then on, there is a risk that paternalism may color any and all interactions between interveners and host populations.

Thankfully, there are exceptions to common paternalistic practices. The experiences of these exceptional individuals and organizations show both that another way of conducting international peacebuilding is possible and that these alternative approaches promote greater intervention success. They demonstrate that paternalism is not over-determined by the structure of the international peacebuilding system, no matter how ingrained it is in practice. Each intervener can contest the narratives and practices dominant among his or her colleagues, and in doing so, each of these individuals can challenge the structure of the overall system.

In fact, even among the foreign interveners who follow the dominant modes of operation, many individuals are aware that imposition

---

[53] See Chapter 9 in this volume, 291–314.

and the resulting lack of local buy-in to the international programs are problematic. These people and their agencies have therefore tried to take steps to mitigate these issues. "Local ownership" is now a buzzword in development and peacebuilding circles, and interveners regularly consult with area authorities. Sometimes, they even organize local focus groups when developing a new program. These actions are crucial to moderating the worst aspects of paternalism on the ground, but three elements counteract the broader efforts toward change.

The first element is that international peacebuilders face a dilemma. On the one hand, there are normative and practical reasons to encourage local participation and to avoid imposition. The idea of integrating host populations fits well with the liberal norms dominant on the international stage. The core idea of democracy (which the leading intervening organizations claim they want to spread) means participation of – or at the very least consent from – local stakeholders.[54] The practical dimension is just as clear: most interveners know that local "participation leads to ownership [which in turn] leads to sustainability."[55]

On the other hand, integrating local stakeholders may worsen the situation. To begin with, participation can slow things to a standstill. The more numerous the parties to a negotiation, the more difficult it becomes to reach an agreement and the higher the likelihood that local spoilers will find an opportunity to hinder or even stall the peace process.[56] Furthermore, local stakeholders regularly "game"

[54] On the dominance of liberal norms and the attempts to spread democracy, see (among many others): Susanna Campbell, David Chandler, and Meera Sabaratnam, eds., *A Liberal Peace? The Problems and Practices of Peacebuilding* (London: Zed Books, 2011); Mac Ginty, *No War, No Peace*; Paris, *At War's End*; and Oliver Richmond, *The Transformation of Peace, Rethinking Peace and Conflict Studies* (New York: Palgrave Macmillan, 2005).

[55] Anderson *et al.*, *Time to Listen*, 68. For a review of the main scholarly arguments emphasizing the importance of local ownership, see Sending, "Why Peacebuilders Fail to Secure Ownership," 4. For the policy perspective, see Anderson and Olson, *Confronting War*, 32–3; and the Organisation for Economic Co-operation and Development's *Paris Declaration* (2005) and *Accra Agenda for Action* (2008) (available at www.oecd.org/dac/effectiveness/34428351.pdf).

[56] For instance, Roberto Belloni, "Civil Society in War-to-Democracy Transitions," in *From War to Democracy: Dilemmas of Peacebuilding*, eds. Anna Jarstead and Timothy Sisk (Cambridge: Cambridge University Press, 2008), 182–3 and 192–3; and Jens Narten, "Dilemmas of Promoting 'Local Ownership': The Case of Postwar Kosovo," in *The Dilemmas of Statebuilding: Confronting the Contradictions of Postwar Peace Operations*,

the international system, interacting with interveners strategically in order to extract as many resources from outsiders as possible and to maintain or increase their existing power.[57] Thus, as explained earlier in this chapter, foreign interveners often worry that privileging local demands may lead to policy capture.[58] In addition, governments and civil society groups do not necessarily try to promote the welfare of the population. As a result, partnering with national and local elites may actually reinforce existing problematic structures rather than promote peace.[59] Finally, in a number of situations, interveners also face irreconcilable differences with the local or national elite, whose perspectives on contentious issues (like democracy and women's rights) may elicit demands that are unacceptable for many foreign and local peacebuilders.

Interviews with two donors, one based in South Sudan and the other in Congo, encapsulated the resulting dynamics. When we spoke, the first noted the problems inherent to imposing foreign ideas and mentioned that he and other interveners tried to involve their local counterparts in the design and implementation of international programs. He then explained why they regularly abandoned these efforts: Often expatriates get so frustrated at the behavior of their counterparts (like their abuse of power, resource embezzlement, and disregard for the plights of their fellow citizens) that they eventually stop trying to involve them or even get their consent. The second interviewee described the same dynamics in much harsher terms. In her words, the "contempt for local actors" that most of her expatriate colleagues shared made it seem appropriate for interveners to "manipulate" local counterparts and try to impose programs and ideas on them. Whether framed in harsh or sympathetic language, the process is the same and

eds. Roland Paris and Timothy D. Sisk (London: Routledge, 2009), 261 and 276.

[57] Barnett and Zürcher, "The Peacebuilder's Contract."

[58] See *ibid.* for an explanation of how this may happen.

[59] Anderson *et al.*, *Time to Listen*, 84–7 and ch. 7; Barnett and Zürcher, "The Peacebuilder's Contract," 24 and 31–6; Tanja Chopra, "When Peacebuilding Contradicts Statebuilding: Notes from the Arid Lands of Kenya," *International Peacekeeping* 16, 4 (2009); Donais, "Empowerment or Imposition," 14; Mac Ginty, *No War, No Peace*, 51–3; Paris, *At War's End*, 159–69; and Claudia Simons and Franzisca Zanker, "Questioning the Local in Peacebuilding" (paper prepared for the New Frontiers of Peacebuilding Conference, Manchester, 2012), 7–11.

so are the results: The dilemma international peacebuilders face reinforces their incentives to impose programs on host populations.

The second element that counteracts efforts toward change is that, for all interveners, accountability structures are oriented toward external entities, not toward beneficiaries.[60] NGOs are accountable to their donors, which are UN agencies, other international organizations, European and North American states, or private funders from abroad. Likewise, government donors are accountable to their taxpayers and legislators. Peacekeeping missions report to the UN Security Council, UN agencies report to their headquarters in New York and Geneva, and these headquarters report to the UN member states. Even academic researchers prioritize publication of their findings in prestigious journals and presses, which are overwhelmingly located in Europe or North America, over dissemination to local populations in order to maintain their positions at universities.

Admittedly, numerous intervening organizations have signed on to international charters aimed at improving downward accountability such as the Humanitarian Accountability Partnership and the Accountability Charter for International NGOs.[61] Some of these agencies have also developed mechanisms to gather feedback from stakeholders about their efforts, including participatory evaluations, complaints and response systems, perceptions studies, community scorecards, citizen report cards, and story-telling.[62] However, these various initiatives are isolated, often incomplete, and they remain

---

[60] Alex Jacobs and Robyn Wilford, "Putting New Approaches to NGO Accountability into Action" (paper prepared for the Development's Futures Conference, NUI, Galway, 2007) presents a very useful review of the scholarly literature on this problem. For analyses on peacebuilding, see Autesserre, *Peaceland*, ch. 6; and Chiyuki Aoi, Cedric De Coning, and Ramesh Chandra Thakur, *Unintended Consequences of Peacekeeping Operations* (Tokyo: United Nations University Press, 2007), part V. On the perception of host populations: Anderson *et al.*, *Time to Listen*, 91–3 and ch. 5.

[61] On the Humanitarian Accountability Partnership, see www.hapinternational. org. On the Accountability Charter for international NGOs, see CDA Collaborative Learning Projects, "Feedback Mechanisms in International Assistance Organizations" (Cambridge, MA: CDA Collaborative Learning Projects, 2011), 1 and throughout the report.

[62] *Ibid.*, 2, 9–10, 14–19, and 22–3; and IRIN, "Are They Listening? Aid and Humanitarian Accountability" (Geneva: Integrated Regional Information Networks, 2012), 7–10. See also the material available on the website Listen First (http://listenfirst.mango.org.uk).

the exception rather than the rule.[63] The resulting predominance of upward rather than downward accountability deprives interveners of incentives to obtain the consent of their intended beneficiaries, and it deprives these beneficiaries of the power to request an end to paternalistic practices.

The last obstacle to change arises from the detrimental byproducts of the politics of knowledge at work in the international peacebuilding field, which make it exceptionally difficult to move away from standard intervention routines. The experiences of the NGOs (such as International Alert and the International Rescue Committee) that have tried to promote local authorship and ownership by implementing community-driven reconstruction programs are telling.[64] According to my interviews with the staff working on such initiatives, local communities are so used to seeing foreigners arrive with a bossy attitude and set ideas that it becomes challenging to implement the new approach. Instead of giving their opinions and requesting what they actually need, a number of grassroots communities construct their appeals to reflect what they think the expatriates want to hear, as a way of ensuring access to funding and help. In other words, despite considerable efforts, these interveners still often end up facing problems similar to those of their colleagues who use less progressive methodologies.

International paternalism thus persists virtually unhindered, a vicious cycle of imposition without consent and passive acceptance without appreciation. The actions of resistant local stakeholders and exceptional interveners may start to mitigate the worst consequences of paternalism on the ground, but they are unlikely to eliminate paternalism for good.

[63] Also Anderson *et al.*, *Time to Listen*, i.
[64] See Elisabeth King, "A Critical Review of Community-Driven Development Programmes in Conflict-Affected Contexts" (London: DFID and International Rescue Committee, 2013) for an analysis of these initiatives across various countries and organizations.

6 Enabling or Disabling Paternalism: (In)attention to Gender and Women's Knowledge, Capacity, and Authority in Humanitarian Contexts

AISLING SWAINE

In 2006, working with an international aid agency in Darfur, Sudan, I was part of a large yet very constrained humanitarian response operation. Having worked in many prior operations globally, this was somewhat different. Humanitarian operations established in response to the Darfur crisis were severely and deliberately hampered by the Sudanese government. In an attempt to thwart international attention to a situation that was increasingly being noted for extensive human rights violations, international and national organizations were subject to a very effective intimidation campaign. It was so successful that international agencies performed operations as if walking on eggshells. There was a tacit consensus among agencies that the best-case scenario was to strive to maintain the provision of basic services, even where this meant working around, and saying little publicly about, the rights violations that were occurring within and outside the camps.

I was working on what might have been considered the most sensitive issue in that context at that time – the prolific use of sexualized violence, particularly rape, against women by parties to the conflict in Darfur. Sexualized violence in wartime is generally understood as a gendered violence, primarily impacting women and working off of gendered norms of power and inequalities between men and women. The prolific use of sexualized violence by armed actors became synonymous with the Darfur conflict in the global media in ways that had not been seen since the wars in the former Yugoslavia. The image of the raped female victim also became ubiquitous with Darfur and in many ways became a cornerstone of the multiple global advocacy movements that arose to decry what was happening there.

In this highly charged political situation, the act of rape and other kinds of sexualized violence took on hyper political significance. With the eyes of the International Criminal Court on the Darfur situation at the time, and the US government also making noise about possible genocide, the act of rape, formerly prosecuted as a component of genocide in the International Criminal Tribunal for Rwanda, invoked political significance for a government that could be held culpable. With the potential for rape to be charged as a war crime, allegations of rape were consistently denied by the Sudanese government. Any reference by international agencies to sexualized violence of any form was impossible by virtue of the potential repercussions from the government, i.e., cessation of agency operations and expulsion from the country. It became impossible to speak of this issue in any way publicly, both by the agencies involved, and by the women and girls who were subjected to these abuses. There was an accepted understanding among agencies that to make a loud noise about this issue would place women, as well as the overall humanitarian operation, at further risk.[1] This status quo created an incredible sense of discomfort. Not only were women's bodies subject to armed men's violence on a mass scale, services to them were also being restricted by the same actors responsible for those harms. It felt at times as if we were colluding with the perpetrators.

The context was so tense that when I entered Sudan, rather than have the correct title of program manager of my agency's violence against women program, I had to adopt a generic title that occluded the specific nature of my job. While the government knew well that this agency was providing services to women affected by violence (their intelligence operations knowing more about our work than we did at times), our official claim to not be doing so appeased tensions and allowed services to continue under the radar. As long as it remained that way.

My role was to oversee the covert delivery of sexual assault services to women and girls. Services were made available through women's centers that we had established in the camps. The centers provided broader education and support programs to women and girls, while

---

[1] For more on this see: Colum Lynch, "The Silence in Sudan: Why did the United Nations Stop Reporting Atrocities in Darfur?" *Foreign Policy*, May 7, 2012, http://foreignpolicy.com/2012/05/07/the-silence-in-sudan/ (accessed November 7, 2015). Human Rights Watch, *Darfur: Humanitarian Aid Under Siege* (New York: Human Rights Watch, 2006). Michael Kleinman, "Tough Choices for Agencies Expelled from Darfur," *Humanitarian Practice Network*, May 6, 2009, http://odihpn.org/blog/tough-choices-for-agencies-expelled-from-darfur/.

simultaneously acting as a front to work through established informal women's networks to make available confidential sexual assault
response services. About six months after I had taken up my post in
Darfur there was a spate of attacks against women outside one of the
camps I was working in. These attacks were unusual. As time had
passed, attacks on women by parties to the conflict had declined compared to the reports of endemic violence being experienced by women
and girls inside the camps. Increasing numbers of women began trick-
ling into the women's center we had established, reporting that they
had been raped early that morning. The number of women coming
in to report increased over subsequent days. The women informed us
that a large band of militia had made camp nearby and were attacking
them as they went searching for firewood.

We reported it to camp management, to the United Nations, and
to others, hoping for help to deal with this. I met with the head of
the African Union (AU) peacekeepers working to secure the location
of the camp. I explained what was going on and that a response was
needed to secure the area outside the camp. I also explained that the
women knew where the militia was camped and the attacks were happening, and I explained where this was. Curiously, he refuted what
I said, questioned the validity of the reports and was little interested
in hearing about where the women said the threat was coming from.
According to him there were no security threats in the vicinity of the
camp; if there were he, as the commander, would know about it. The
power of the local knowledge of these women, and the power of the
knowledge that they had passed on to me which I was now trying to
share, was completely negated. He said that his men knew better than
any of us about what was going on in the camp. Nonetheless, when
pressed, he agreed to look into it.

The aid professional in me was dumbfounded to leave that meeting feeling as if nothing I said had been taken seriously. It was clear
that as a woman representing other women (even where the politics
of race and neo-colonialism and my "expert" position as a humanitarian professional might have [uncomfortably and inappropriately]
counted) critical issues arose. Even where it could possibly be considered as local "intelligence," the information I was sharing was not
considered as valid as that produced by his men. Of course, the function of military operations relies on the gathering of intelligence that is
reliable and corresponds to their standards of credibility. Documented

in many contexts however is the value of engaging with women who, positioned in the midst of family and community, have direct access to and may be involved in what is happening at micro levels in respect of conflict dynamics. More obviously, they also know what they want and need and what is feasible for them within their own contexts.[2] I have no doubt that there was genuine sentiment on the part of everyone I approached that these rapes should be stopped. However, what was clear, and which I will elucidate further below, was that the value of information coming from women, who were living their lives at the front lines of this conflict, did not count in ways that men's information did.

The spike in rapes became common knowledge in the camp and was a topic at the security meeting for international organizations that followed soon after. An AU representative stood up at the meeting and explained that they had spoken with the male leaders in the camp and would be establishing a joint committee with these men to discuss and deal with the recent attacks against women. The peacekeeping men, in conjunction with the leading men in the camp, were going to address the problem. I was again dumbfounded. Women were being raped by men with guns. On the part of the international system, other men with guns (peacekeepers) were responsible for their protection. This set of men with the authority to "protect" considered another set of men, those who "rightfully" occupy roles of political, community, and public-sphere leaders, responsible for women's protection on behalf of the community involved.

In this triad, there was no mention, space, or regard for the women themselves, except as victims that required this male-centered response. The fact that these women, through me, had been the first to raise the alarm, had known more about what was happening with antagonistic parties to the conflict in the vicinity of the camp before the peacekeepers did, and brought this intelligence to the AU in the first place was not acknowledged. Nothing was said about engaging with these women themselves. No moves were made to come back to me or to

---

[2] Nordic Centre for Gender in Military Operations, ed., *Whose Security? Practical Examples of Gender Perspectives in Military Operations* (Stockholm: Nordic Centre for Gender in Military Operations, Swedish Armed Forces, 2015).

use the women's center as a way to safely engage with the women, or to connect with these women and verify what they were saying for their own intelligence purposes.

In her analysis of the intersection of gender, violence and security, Laura J. Shepherd has stated that "gendered violence is the violent reproduction of gender."[3] In this case, one set of men were enacting gendered violence on women for strategic political ends (militia), and in response another set of men (peacekeepers) were colluding with yet another set of men (community members) to protect women from the first set of men. As noted by Sara Poehlman and Felicity Hill, "women are seen as victims that need to be protected and helped, instead of participants in their own protection."[4] What was evident in all of this was a reproduction and reinforcement of the gendered norms and tropes which made women vulnerable to these kinds of attacks in the first place. In effect, it demonstrated how, in practice, men are "associated with the position of male head of household as protector of the family, and, by extension, with masculine leaders and risk takers as protectors of a population."[5]

Despite this, there was little evidence of what this committee would practically do given that none of these men, neither AU nor male camp dwellers, would go willingly to the places that these women ventured each day. None of these men were planning to go out to the places that the women went where they were being repeatedly attacked, and none were planning to openly address the probable source, ultimately the same body that was responsible for curbing these attacks, the Sudanese government. In effect, despite being the nominated protectors of these women, it was a protection that in this context came with an explicit lack of risk taking on their part, with continuing risk for these women. Still, the role of male-protector was upheld. This may have been out of necessity – Darfuri men leaving camps were under threat of being killed, and perhaps the AU was sensibly keen to avoid a situation of possible military engagement with the militia. Regardless, at least

[3] Laura J. Shepherd, *Gender, Violence & Security* (London: Zed Books, 2008), 51.
[4] Sara Poehlman-Doumbouya and Felicity Hill, "Women and Peace in the United Nations," *New Routes: A Journal of Peace Research and Action* 6, 3 (2001): 2.
[5] Iris Young, "The Logic of Masculinist Protection: Reflections on the Current Security State," *Signs: Journal of Women in Culture and Society* 29, 1 (2003): 1–25.

publicly, it seemed that this protectionism was infused with an ineffectual micro-level response which maintained a "below the radar" status quo satisfactory to ensuring minimal attention to what was happening and thus deemed to be in the best interests of everyone.

At a camp management meeting in the camp itself the following day, the Sheikah, the women's representative, responded to the AU's explanation of its approach by standing up and shouting angrily. Neither she nor other women had been consulted, nor had they agreed that this was how they wanted the situation dealt with. She then turned her attention to the international aid agencies that had a role in managing and delivering services in the camp. She did not hold back, but vehemently shouted at those she saw as responsible for acting at public levels and asked why the attacks were not being reported on the BBC news that they listened to avidly every day. She asked why the international community was not speaking out about it and doing something. Why were we not acting in pronounced and visible ways to deal with and prevent the attacks? In her utter indignation at not being asked what she thought should be done, and in her frustration at being perceived as a victim and being attributed little power to influence what was and was not being done, she completely shamed and denounced what she saw as a high-handed, exclusionary, and impotent response by international actors.

As developments unfolded, the male leadership in the camp later asked to meet with me and the camp management team. They were unsatisfied with the international response. They could not understand why these violations were being dealt with so furtively, were not making wider news and why our response was so muted. They were angry that we were operating in a way that we thought best – maintaining our own safety of operations. They wanted to go public; to them that was more important and far more in their interests than in pretending it was not happening.

There were more reports of attacks the following morning. That afternoon, a large group of women entered the women's center en masse and asked to speak to me. We went into an enclosed space and sat down on the floor to speak. I counted them. There were one hundred women. All of them had experienced attack and threat in previous days. Their spokesperson began describing the increased attacks to which they were being subjected outside the camp. Several other women spoke up and described their attack, their attackers and how many of them had been stripped and forced to walk back to the camp completely naked. They had been given messages by their attackers for delivery to their male family members, attempting to entice the men out of the camps to fight, to protect their women, to defend their honor. As has been documented in multiple conflicts globally, women's bodies are used as a means to communicate messages between men, in particular as a means to "deliver the message that they were unable to protect their women."[6] Here was another example of a conversation between men about men, with women at its center, and at the same time only and once again as victims. They asked me, as a representative of the international community, to go to those with clout at higher levels and ask them to do something. They explained that they would continue to take risks and leave the camp to collect fuel for cooking, that their male family members would be killed if they went out. The risk of rape was the "choice" that these families were left with.

I asked them about the possible repercussions of speaking out about what had happened, about the further dangers and targeting they could be subjected to if their reporting of the rapes became known. If we as international agencies spoke out and our operations were stopped, where would that leave them? What level of protection would be left? There would not only be a gap in service provision to the camp population that could be detrimental, the protection that was made possible through our very presence there could suddenly be gone. In many ways my questions followed my sincere concern for their safety, as I had already on multiple occasions witnessed harmful actions by the government on the camp population – disappearances, intimidation, arbitrary arrests. And I also knew that the work I was doing was certainly under microscopic scrutiny and any moves I or my organization made would be intercepted. In another way I was also guilty of following the line of the climate of humanitarianism into which I had become absorbed: that of refraining from poking the (not so sleepy) giant and incurring its wrath, i.e., the possible expulsion of expensive humanitarian operations by the Sudanese government.

---

[6] Nadine Puechguirbal, "Women and Children: Deconstructing a Paradigm," *Seton Hall Journal of Diplomacy and International Relations* 5 (2004): 5–16, 12.

These women were adamant that they wanted something to be done. They argued that they had survived earlier attacks, had survived the process of displacement and were enduring further attacks now too. How could it get worse than this? They reiterated their demand for a visible response from the international community aimed at stopping the attacks. If they could not go out to collect fuel, they could not provide for their families. This was their priority, a very different one from that of agencies wishing to fulfill this need but only in a way tailored to the political climate.

On the basis of the women's ideas, together we organized a "hearing" on what had been happening. We invited high-level representatives of the AU police and peacekeepers, of international governments, the UN and its agencies to come to the women's center and hear the testimonies of these women. We all knew that among the crowd would be government agents. Much more fearless than any of the international organizations present, these women gathered. One by one they told their stories publicly. They explained that it was their imperative that we take steps on their behalf in a political and public way and affirmed their will to deal with any consequences.

The stand taken by the humanitarian community in situ, myself included, had been utterly flawed. Not only had we made assumptions about what was the best approach to take, we had done so without consulting the very people affected. The peacekeepers, when they became involved, followed suit and, in addition, completely ignored the possibility that the women being attacked had anything to say about it or anything to add to a response. Their open resistance, a risk in itself, was the only means these women had to have their voices and sentiments heard and perhaps responded to. It was the only means that these women had to try and overcome the block that the humanitarian community had become to their ability to decide and determine for themselves what should happen.

The attacks stopped shortly after. There may be much more to this story than I am privy to, the goings-on behind the scenes, who pulls strings where to maintain or to cease these kinds of attacks. I can only presume that the government representatives, of the United States and others who attended the hearing, did what they could at national political levels. I learned subsequently that the AU did a helicopter fly-over of the area that I had described, where the women said that they had been attacked. The presence of the militia camp was confirmed. This I heard through back-channels. Not one representative of the AU peacekeeping force approached me or any of the women I was working with to speak with us again, to gain our insights and guidance on what we thought would be best to do, nor to confirm that the knowledge we had shared was in any way valid. I was under a lot of pressure from partner agencies about the risk we had taken to our and everyone else's operations, as well as a lot of criticism – we made many mistakes along the way. When I and others were temporarily moved out of that particular site for safety and precautionary reasons, no one was surprised.

It was a complex event with multiple repercussions for everyone involved, much of which I little understand to this day. Any and each decision to act or not act had repercussions, for someone or some entity, most likely negative and potentially harmful. However, what was evident was that, at a micro level, these women knew what they wanted to happen. In effect, they were expressing what they perceived to be best for them and what should be done in their interests in response to the situation they were facing. They were willing to take the kinds of action and risks that the international community would not take on their behalf, even when presuming to act in their best interests. These women wished for risks to be taken and for the power to decide that themselves.

This is possibly one of the only moments in my experience in humanitarian work where the "we know what's best" sentiment of humanitarian assistance was trumped by the resistance of the objects of that assistance. Despite the abundance of "experts" available on the ground, including myself, these women knew what was best for them and let us know that. It was only through them reaching a state of acute frustration and anger that it became obvious that the cautious protectionism of our operations delivered in their name and in their apparent best interests was obscuring and making irrelevant the decisions they might make about their own lives. Decisions on this matter were being taken elsewhere, in the offices of the AU peacekeepers and international organizations on the ground (including my own), while the opinions of the real experts were overlooked. While similar to the examples shared by Ilana Feldman and Séverine Autesserre in their discussions in this volume of refusals by the subjects of humanitarian aid,[7] this case also differs in many ways. These women took an open

---

[7] See Chapters 5 and 9, this volume.

and overt stand to what was happening. They made it clear to the humanitarian community that the (in)actions taken in their name were not what they wanted nor in their best interests at all.

In the case just described, a number of dynamics are evident. In relation to the broader operation, the humanitarian actors decided what was best to ensure a relationship with the Sudanese government that enabled operations to continue. It may be that the humanitarian organizations' sense of duty, and their own interpretation of what that duty entails in respect of delivery of care, informed and became their modus operandi. In this scenario, however, that sense of duty overrode any alternative preferences that the affected population may have held. In turn, the incidents of rape, and particularly our response to them, were kept under the radar in an effort to prevent interruption to operations and to mitigate the necessity for political engagement with the state. A similar dynamic informed a lack of consultation with the specific women concerned. The potential autonomy of these women to have a preferred response to the spike in rape was derided. "Protectionism," a concept deeply embedded with masculinist and paternalist overtures, reared its ugly head throughout these events. The actions taken by the stakeholders involved demonstrated a lack of consideration that these women might be able to make any judgment at all over their own lives. Invisible yet ubiquitous in all of this is a "we know what's best" sentiment, wholly paternalist in sentiment and action, and felt as such by these women (and by myself at times, even though I was also part of it). This signals not only the presence of paternalism within humanitarianism, but also how problematic paternalism might be in actions taken in the guise of the caring role. Related, another thread runs throughout this incident, that of power relations and arising inequalities between all of the actors present. In this one scenario, multiple forms of inequalities are evident – the weight given to Western expertise versus that of "locals," issues of race and neocolonialism and who is perceived to hold the knowledge required to make decisions, the credibility of the knowledge of the "hard" security actors versus those of the "softer" social care work of aid workers, and ultimately that of gender and gender inequality.

Gender is a concept that makes visible the way that privilege and power operate and how they are available in various ways depending on one's gender identity in context. It runs right through all of the events that I have just described, and it is a dynamic inherent to the range of inequalities I have just identified. In this scenario women's sexed bodies were the locale of attack in a war between men; my role as "an authority" (as per that outlined in the introductory chapter to this volume) was negated in favor of the men whose knowledge was deemed superior to mine; the most powerful men worked with the next set of powerful men to make decisions about women's protection and security; all of these men were deemed to know more about what was happening than the women who were themselves being attacked; and all of the actors failed utterly to even ask one of these women what they thought should happen. In the nexus between women's security, protection, and the paternalist response of international actors, one's gender is given meaning. These dynamics signal just how infused with gender paternalist actions may be.

In line with Feldman's contribution to this volume, I wish to take this "in the instance" example and explore its paternalist hues. My intention through this reflection is not only to contribute to this volume and its endeavor of exploring contemporary paternalism. It is also an attempt to identify the gendered hue of the paternalism in this case to shed light on gendered dynamics of paternalism more broadly, which has inevitable consequences for an ethic of care that treats the female as infantile, possessing little knowledge and in need of masculinist protection.

I undertake this inquiry as a former aid worker, as someone who once performed humanitarian work in the context I now examine and the actions I critique. In line with Feldman, I fall into an ethnography that draws from empirics.[8] However, I am not simply a researcher spending time in a context under scrutiny, but someone who has been part of the very system which I now examine and critique. I offer this in the spirit of reflexivity, a cornerstone of feminist approaches to praxis and research, within which I situate my chapter. I attest to a sense of uneasiness as I critique the aid world, my own role in it, and its potential to be paternalist. To invoke the idea that paternalism is a feature of the modern and dynamic humanitarian architecture that is in place today is not without controversy. It is particularly difficult for someone who has spent a significant amount of time working in the system, believing in its merits of goodwill, to propose that this is the case. To nominate

[8] See Feldman, Chapter 9, this volume.

paternalist values to a system understood to be rooted in global altruism also calls up blatant contradictions. How can initiatives that are principally framed by a mandate to help and assist be perceived or felt as condescending or authoritative? As explored in the other chapters in this volume, it could, in fact, be very easy to label the powerful, swift, and often forceful actions taken by international organizations as paternalist. However, doing so, applying this label, without attention to the multifaceted nuances of these contexts, the intricacies of the difficult decisions that need to be made, and the urgency of their execution, ignores the utter complexity that lies at the heart of humanitarian action. As I critique this field, I acknowledge, and later explore, that the mode of caring might be an earnest and sincere sentiment on the part of those caring enough to act, and it might be because of that sincerity and sense of duty that high-handed actions arise through paternalist means. To be "accused" of paternalism is wholly undesirable and goes against much of the motivation and purpose of the work that I, and others like me, have stood for and pursued. Paternalism could be perceived as anathema to the virtues of humanitarianism and to the rectitude of the humanitarian professional. This is why, however, I engage in this inquiry: to explore where those positive motivations of care for others might cross over, through the mode of practice within humanitarianism, to a space in which the knowledge and autonomy of the object of humanitarian relief is derided, and to consider whether this might hold a particular dynamic concerning women.

From here, I use the case study I have just outlined to pursue an inquiry into paternalism in humanitarian action. I use the example shared to assess and critique what this story can tell us about the concept of paternalism and its possible gendered hues. First, I lay out my understanding of the concept of paternalism, to establish its use in this chapter. In doing so, I engage in an analysis that draws the concept of paternalism together with that of gender, exploring and mapping how both concepts intersect. Through this analysis, I weave in the ways in which theory on paternalism and gender can be related to the case study itself and why both are relevant to consider together. I then move on to identifying and analyzing three thematic issues in the Darfur story that demonstrate the gendered hues of paternalism. I use these to set out what the case study tells us about the gendered dynamic of paternalism. I conclude by underlining the ways in which gender inextricably features in paternalism and paternalist actions, and the fact that both are active in aspects of humanitarianism. The challenge for humanitarianism is to find ways to operate that reflect its goal of solidarity, where the knowledge, capacity and abilities of its client population, rather than that of the humanitarian "experts", are central to operations. Central in such an approach is overcoming paternalist and protectionist assumptions that place women as subject to, rather than authors of, how humanitarianism operates in their name.

The Nexus of Paternalism and Gender

Commonly neglected across much of the literature on paternalism, whether in relation to humanitarianism or otherwise, is the glaringly obvious fact that the term itself, the very concept and quality of this idea, is highly gendered. This is a consideration which I wish to bring to this volume. How and in what ways can an understanding of paternalism, particularly in the sphere of humanitarianism, be advanced by assessing its potentially gendered root and hue? And what can this offer to an analysis of the story just outlined?

For the purposes of my discussion, I consider as paternalist actions that are authoritative and disempowering for the subjects of those actions, i.e., the ways that actions are carried out results in disenfran-chisement of the objects of that action from control over their own fate. It is my contention that actions might be paternal when they are decided upon in exclusive spaces, and when they do not involve the people who will be directly affected by these actions, reflect their express priorities, or take into account that the viewpoints of those others hold merit. The paternal actors deem the object to lack the capacity to make decisions or take actions that are in their own best interests. These actions invoke a relationship of superior/inferior, competent/incompetent, capacity/incapacity, where the dominant possesses the perceived authority and scope to make decisions over, or on behalf of, a subordinate and restrained other.

Paternalism is increasingly noted as a problematic aspect of the humanitarian world. It has even been referred to as the "ugly side" of this work by some who are involved in it.[9] Paternalism as such is

---

[9] See several online blog and discussion forums which feature debates on this issues, such as: "Paternalism in Development," *Bottom Up Thinking: The Ugly Side Of Conservation And Development*, May 12, 2011, http://bottomupthinking.wordpress.com/2011/05/12/paternalism-in-development/ and "Coming Out as a Feminist," *AidWatch*, May 6, 2011, http://aidwatchers.com/2011/05/bill-easterly-feminist-economist/.

a concept that is skirted around and rarely named in the humanitarian architecture, yet many of its characteristic features are those that the system is attempting to counter in its ongoing reform process.[10] The imperative of the humanitarian is to deliver humanitarian services to those in need. In the face of this urgency, while humanitarian actors may wish to ensure that all of their endeavors are in line with the best interests of the clients they serve, at times their actions do (sometimes inadvertently) run counter to the values that this system in essence wishes to uphold – that of ensuring the agency and independent choice making of its clients. Instead, as just outlined in relation to the Darfur case, the "authorities" (per introductory chapter of this volume), experts, and those who know best take over in an effort to manage and control the situation, to ensure that their imperative is fulfilled, i.e., provide and protect the provision of care. Its invisible yet ubiquitous presence signals how problematic paternalism as a notion is for the system itself, as well as for the individuals who inhabit it.

Humanitarianism, if indeed occupying a "global governance" status as espoused by Michael N. Barnett,[11] may be understood in ways similar to how Michael Runyan and V. Spike Peterson develop a gendered assessment of the system of "international relations": "as interconnected relations of inequality – among genders, races, classes, sexualities, and nationalities."[12] In any regular pre-crises context, women experience a pattern of gendered inequality and exclusion that, even if varying in context-specific multifarious ways, is a consistent feature of societies globally. Where an emergency arises, the empirics of that gendered order undoubtedly play a role in how women experience that crisis, exemplified in the Darfur case by the ways in which women's bodies were targeted for sexual brutalization by armed protagonists. That same gendered order will also undoubtedly inform how women experience a humanitarian operation, determining their access to, and decision-making power over, what becomes available to a community through aid (including an [in]ability to determine their own protection measures as described). The

---

[10] For an overview of the "Transformative Agenda?" being brought forward by the Inter-Agency Standing Committee on Humanitarian Action see, http://interagencystandingcommittee.org/node/2803.

[11] Michael N. Barnett, "International Paternalism and Humanitarian Governance," *Global Constitutionalism* 1, 3 (2012).

[12] Anne Sisson Runyan and V. Spike Peterson, *Global Gender Issues in the New Millennium* (Boulder: Westview Press, 2014), 1.

operations of humanitarian and peacekeeping organizations in themselves are highly gendered.[13] They are filled with the personal and professional baggage of the personnel coming from multiple socio-cultural contexts globally. They bring with them differing sex-gender identities and differing understandings of associated powers, and in turn, varying understandings of gender and gendered norms; they come from and constitute differing races and nationalities, which also may invoke variant notions of power and authority in practice. The concept of humanitarianism and its characteristic features in practice derive from that global system of international relations just described, i.e. it is infused with variant dynamics of inequalities present in the system of international relations from which it is described.[14] The range of gender inequalities and power relations inherent to the global system meets the gender norms and inequalities already embedded in the social context in which humanitarian operations become implemented. Conjointly morphing in response to each other and in respect to the conditions of the crisis, a new gendered order evolves establishing a hierarchy of power, authority and control, primarily evident in the relations between the outsider men and their engagement with the insider men. These "inter-connected relations of inequality"[15] are thereby critical to consider in respect of how and in what ways paternalism might arise in gendered ways for women.

The concepts of gender and paternalism find congruence in multiple ways. Both "characterize relations between individuals or between institutions and individuals or groups" and in so doing call up "familial relationships, particularly those traditionally existing between parent (or father) and child."[16] Paternalism is functionally rooted in the idea of the "paternal," articulated by John Stuart Mill, a decrier of

---

[13] Deborah Clifton and Fiona Gell, "Saving and Protecting Lives by Empowering Women," in *Gender, Development and Humanitarian Work*, ed. Caroline Sweetman (Oxford: Oxfam Publishing, 2002), 16–17.

[14] For further analysis of gender and international relations see: J. Ann Tickner, "Feminist Perspectives on International Relations," in *Handbook of International Relations*, eds. Walter Carlsnaes, Thomas Risse, and Beth A. Simmons (London: Sage, 1992); J. Ann Tickner, *Gender in International Relations: Feminist Perspectives on Achieving Global Security* (New York: Columbia University Press, 1992).

[15] Anne Sisson Runyan and V. Spike Peterson, *Global Gender Issues in the New Millennium* (Boulder: Westview Press, 2014), 1.

[16] John Kleinig, *Paternalism* (Manchester: Manchester University Press, 1983), 4.

paternalism,[17] as "the most natural authority of all."[18] Men's structural control over institutions of politics, law, and economics, and
"natural" role in determining socio-cultural, familial, sexual, and
religious values, characterizes women, in effect, as unfit to do so.[19]
Such natural authority is worked out through and echoes all of the
elements of patriarchy, a critical root concept in the understanding
of gender theory and gender relations. Patriarchy may be understood
as "a particular form of social ideology: protective attitudes towards
women, a reverence for the role of women as wives and mothers, and
an idealization of women as romantic love objects."[20] The paternal of
paternalism in particular relies on the legacy of the subjective positioning and infantilization of women, in turn reliant on patriarchy and
the ubiquitous way it informs relations of power and gender. Where
patriarchy is rationalized through "viewing women as not being fully
competent adults, legitimizing the need for a superordinate male figure,"[21] an entry point for "paternalistic rationales" arises.[22]

By identifying and working off of the constraints that are perceived
to affect the object, paternalism finds purchase. These constraints
may be understood by the paternalist as deriving from a range of
"lacking" characteristics – lack of knowledge or information, a lack
of freedom to act autonomously, and a lack of cognitive ability and
capacity (of variant forms). Arising out of this preponderance of
"lacking" qualities is a resulting lack of ability to know what is best
for themselves. "A woman's identity, or lack thereof, is established
outside of her scope of decision-making, such that her identity is
imposed from above, by society and/or the state."[23] In this fashion,
patriarchy informs much of what women are perceived to be lacking

---

[17] Christian Coons and Michael Weber, "Introduction: Paternalism – Issues
and Trends," in *Paternalism: Theory and Practice*, eds. Christian Coons and
Michael Weber (New York: Cambridge University Press, 2013), 1–24, 1.
[18] John Stuart Mill, *The Subjection of Women* (London: Longmans, Green,
Reader, and Dyer, 1878).
[19] Peter Glick and Susan T. Fiske, "The Ambivalent Sexism Inventory:
Differentiating Hostile and Benevolent Sexism," *Journal of Personality
and Social Psychology* 70, 3 (1996): 491–512, 492.
[20] *Ibid.*, 492.
[21] *Ibid.*, 493.
[22] Kleinig, *Paternalism*, 12.
[23] Gunhild Hoogensen and Svein Vigeland Rottem, "Gender Identity and the
Subject of Security," *Security Dialogue* 35 (2004): 155–71, 165.

(in this and other cases). Paternalism then may become wholly gendered in concept and in action, where superordinate males identify and act on the gendered constraints they perceive to be inherent in females. Almost by definition, paternalism is invoked in respect of women's lacking individual and autonomous identities, creating, in the Darfur example, the entry point for all-male decision-making in response to women's protection needs. By association, women are perceived to be lacking sufficient knowledge and capabilities, reinforcing the superior quality of knowledge and ideas of the men involved, and eliciting a gendered hue to the paternalist actions that are evident.

In the context of my discussion, the "power of gender"[24] directly determines a global humanitarian system where "hierarchical thinking in which those people and objects assigned masculine qualities are valued or given power over those assigned feminine qualities."[25] This has profound implications for women – most notably in how gendered power in favor of men works itself out and perpetuates itself through an ethic of sexism and an outcome of paternalist behavior. This is evident, and will be discussed more below, in respect to how, in practical terms, the feminine lends a tone of victimhood to women, while men take on the mantle of being the decision-makers and protectors. Whether women might be more susceptible to paternalist overtures is a strong possibility, particularly given the legacy of historical infantilization of women which is still felt today. I am not arguing that one necessarily needs to be female to be subject to paternalism, but rather that its root in paternal and patriarchal overtures means that in many contexts, there is a quality to paternalism that derives from, and gives meaning to, gender.

Critical Indicators of Gendered Paternalism

I now turn again directly to the example from Darfur. I use it to identify how the critical elements of paternalism evident in this case demonstrate how paternalist actions may have a gendered basis and hue. In order to explore this possibility, I examine three critical themes

---

[24] I borrow and use this term further in the paper, it is taken from: Runyan and Peterson, *Global Gender Issues in the New Millennium*, 7–8.
[25] *Ibid.*, 7–8.

which I earlier identified as indicating paternalism within the Darfur story. First is the tension between concepts and actions of caring and of duty, and how their critical intersection may give rise to humanitarian actions that are paternalist. In this, we see that women in particular become subject to acts of duty to protect on the part of male actors which are felt as paternalist by women subject to those actions. Second is the way in which the humanitarian community failed to consult with the women in question in order to identify and respond to the imperatives that the women had themselves identified and wished to pursue in respect of their own security. This lack of consultation may be felt as paternal for all, but when men are consulted and women are not, then a particularly gendered hue may be discerned. Third, women's knowledge and expertise about their own context and about what was needed in terms of their own protection was completely derided. In fact, women were not deemed capable of knowing what an appropriate response might be to what was happening, and again, there is a question about gendered, as well as hard and soft forms of knowledge that requires examination. I now explore these themes more deeply in respect of how these paternalist tendencies demonstrate a gendered dynamic as these organizations engaged with the security and protection needs and rights of women.

The Fine Line Between Duty, Care, and Control – and Paternalism Toward Women

As Michael Walzer has noted: "You can help desperately needy people in ways that disempower them and turn them into permanent clients, or you can help them in ways that promote their independence and enable them to help themselves."[26] As in the Darfur example, humanitarian action may be performed through methods that are disconnected from the people they are aimed at and, as a result, become, and are felt as, imperious in nature. In my experience, as described before, decisions and operations by humanitarian and peacekeeping actors are often run on a "we know what's best" basis. Such an approach is often not only essential but also critical to the efficacy of timely and

---

[26] Michael Walzer, "On Humanitarianism: Is Helping Others Charity, or Duty, or Both?" *Foreign Affairs*, July/August 2011, www.foreignaffairs.com/articles/2011-07-01/humanitarianism (accessed November 8, 2015).

life-saving measures, particularly in the acute stages of an emergency. I wish to use the Darfur example to engage with a critical tension that arises herein – the ways in which the humanitarian imperative may invoke much of what is paternalist about contemporary humanitarian response.

"The discourse of humanitarianism contains elements of both emancipation and domination."[27] In this example, the entire context of humanitarianism was teetering across a spectrum that captures elements of both emancipation (freeing women from harm) and domination (exclusionary modes of decision-making over what that freedom will be), of care (genuine care to protect women and preserve the delivery of services to a population strangled by an oppressive regime) and control (making operational decisions in ways that maintained agencies' control over what happened in that context). The imperative to serve, help, enable, and fulfill one's mandate can be exercised in multifarious ways which may advertently or inadvertently sit on opposing ends of a spectrum. A practice of care aimed at supporting and assisting may in fact move from a position of *solidarity with* to an assertion of *authority to and over*. The opening chapter of this volume elucidated this phenomenon as a binary of care and control. While it is implicit that control, on one end of the spectrum, is a complex phenomenon and largely where the paternalist end of action might be found, it is important to note that it does not act alone but gains admission to humanitarianism through the act of caring. At the care end of this spectrum is a more interesting and far more complex dynamic, however. It is that of the *caring humanitarian act* – which may not only be about *caring* or having a *concern* for others, but may also, for many, constitute a deeply felt *duty* and *imperative to act*.

The mode of the enactment of care is often the chief motif that is identified and critiqued in considerations of where and how paternalism arises. I am compelled to emphasize that, in the context of many humanitarian settings, the concept of "care" often falls short of fully capturing the magnitude of feeling experienced by an aid worker faced with the typical features of crises today. The sense of care turns into a sense of duty to act, which can be felt in a pressing and urgent way

[27] Michael N. Barnett, "Humanitarianism, Paternalism and the UNHCR," in *Refugees in International Relations*, eds. Alexander Betts and Gil Loescher (Oxford: Oxford University Press, 2011), 105.

by those witnessing mass atrocity and harm. It might become impossible to not feel some sense of duty toward fellow human beings in crises, and that duty might not necessarily be an adverse or paternalist sentiment. In addition, those who are witnesses often have access to echelons of power that those experiencing that atrocity do not. In such a context, a sense of duty plays a strong part in the act of caring. It can motivate, or not, the actions of international governments as well as individual aid workers in response to crises.[28]

While the fine line between care, duty, and control provides a lucid entry point for exploring paternalism, the examination of paternalism therein would be far too naïve and presumptive without acknowledgment of what the concept of care might look like in the humanitarian contexts of today. The overwhelming compulsion to respond in some way to the abject suffering of fellow human beings warrants acknowledgment in and of itself. In a context such as the one I have set out earlier, the genuine desire to serve and protect, to preserve the delivery of life-saving services to affected populations on the part of humanitarian organizations and to establish ways to protect women on the part of peacekeepers, must be acknowledged. The very presence of humanitarian actors as witnesses in such contexts can be a decisive factor in a population's survival. For many, it would be wrong not to try to preserve operations. If we did not act in some way in response to the suffering of others, and in ways that preserve their safety, where would humanity be? This is not to set humanitarianism up as a "more caring" or more altruistic profession than those sectors or actors which provide care in other ways within established care systems, such as for the elderly or hospice care for the sick. Rather, as we assess humanitarianism from the perspective of paternalism, the magnitude of what is occurring in a typical political crisis and the sheer compulsion to respond in a human way must be acknowledged. These contexts are acute. They are intense. The events and harms experienced by fellow human beings are often beyond many of our imaginations. The threat they are under from actors like the Sudanese government is very real. Aid workers themselves are consistently subject to threat, intimidation, and harm in many contexts. The need for provision of care and response is urgent. The situation itself is utterly compelling. It is in such a context, and one that may change from hour to hour,

---

[28] Walzer, "On Humanitarianism."

that humanitarian actors make decisions and take action. Often it is a case of making a bad decision among a set of even worse decisions. I can attest that despite the growing criticism that seems to assume that humanitarian workers are oblivious to the impacts of their own actions and decisions, most humanitarian workers are acutely reflexsive and self-critical of the system they are in. Ensuring that each act of care is undertaken in ways that are not controlling, but does fulfill the imperative to act through the provision of material and political support in appropriate ways, becomes a delicate act of conscious balancing. This does not always happen – which is why there is necessity for this inquiry into the potential for paternalism in humanitarian practice.

While the urgent and compelling nature of humanitarian crises requires acknowledgment in this critique, I also contend, like others in this volume, that the idea of feeling obliged to act corresponds with much of what may be paternalist about caring. The "duty" to care or to act might be interpreted as having a right to do so, or a conviction that stems from an oppressive righteousness, or even ethnocentricity. Autesserre in this volume, for example, describes how those working in peacebuilding invoked their superior knowledge and expertise as the root of their sense of duty to act. The lack of knowledge and expertise on the part of the population they are (apparently) serving is rationalized as the basis for their authoritative, high-handed, and we-know-what's-best attitude toward both their work and the population concerned. This is a highly problematic sentiment, as I explore.[29] In effect, this is the very sentiment that could be the facilitative factor in moving the concept of care toward that of control, and ultimately toward paternalism. The complexity and interconnection between the provision of care and this perceived duty to do so grants admission to paternalist overtures.

As demonstrated in the Darfur example, delivering care on the basis of presumed knowledge and expertise can result in the experience of that care as offensive and exclusionary. Such paternalism in action results in an authoritative ethic of care and a tendency toward making decisions isolated from the objects of that assistance, effectively, care expressed in dominant and paternalist ways. What we see in humanitarian action is the categorization of crisis-affected populations as

[29] Autesserre, Chapter 5, this volume.

"desperately needy," evoking an immediate hierarchy – that of the have and have nots, those in a position of need versus those who can provide and know how to provide, those who are the carers and thereby have the expertise and duty to care, and those who are in need of care. Again, I invoke Autesserre's argument that paternalism derives from the idea of access to expertise which has evolved within international humanitarian and peacebuilding work. This is evidently a critical driver in and indicator of paternalist tendencies. However, it is not only the issue of expertise and knowledge that informs paternalism in many of these contexts. As described by Lori Handrahan in respect of the peacebuilding and post-conflict arena:

This "international fraternity" – the community of decisionmakers and experts who arrive after a conflict on a mission of "good will" – holds the upper hand, morally, economically and politically. Its members are there to "enforce" UN mandates, international laws and norms. As individuals, they have significantly greater financial power than local people. Morally, they are the "saviours". They have been brought in because local males have "failed". ... The internationals also bring with them varying ideas of gender norms, which they may attempt, consciously or unconsciously, to impose.[30]

Just like Handrahan here, I earlier described a multiple range of inequalities and power dynamics evident in the situation in Darfur. These reflect the system and the people involved, which I also earlier described as coming from, and bringing in, a slew of variant identities, inequalities, and powers. Outside expertise is certainly a factor through which paternalist-style actions begin to take place, as described by Autesserre. However, the trumping of one expertise over another, thereby determining who is ultimately in control and holds the superordinate duty and imperative to act, finds further and much starker relief through a gendered analysis. The Darfur example demonstrated just how problematic paternalism in humanitarianism may specifically be for women. Where care becomes duty, and that duty is performed on the prize of the vulnerable victim woman, the gendered hue of paternalism becomes a critical consideration in respect to the humanitarian system and how it operates. It can work at multiple levels.

[30] Lori Handrahan, "Conflict, Gender, Ethnicity and Post-Conflict Reconstruction," *Security Dialogue* 35, 4 (2004): 429–45, 433.

First are the dynamics and inequalities that arise between the humanitarian actors themselves, in this case between the peacekeepers and me, on a gendered basis. Even where I was considered an "expert" on aid and sexualized violence care and response, and I came with specific intelligence on a critical security situation, my expertise and knowledge was derided by the fact that I was there to talk about security issues from a woman's, and gendered, perspective. That expertise and knowledge, and my proposal of what might be relevant and credible knowledge (i.e., a gendered analysis of what was happening) were clearly not as valid as that which was coming from the "hard" security experts. This kind of dynamic is evident in multiple contexts. Not only can I report that I and my work, as a gender adviser working on gender inequalities, have encountered derision and dismissal by humanitarian actors in multiple other contexts I have worked in, this is a consistent experience reported by many other gender advisers globally.[31] Traditional security actors persistently question whether women and gender issues have any relevance at all to humanitarian, peacekeeping, or security operations.[32] In humanitarianism itself, "gender" and work on community-based imperatives that are mainly staffed by women are not considered to be as relevant as the "hardware sectors of water, shelter, food aid and logistics which represent the backbone of humanitarian response, and command the greatest resources, [and] are mainly staffed by men."[33]

Another level where a gender analysis reveals its relevance is the level of interaction between the peacekeepers and the women in question. Even though the women who experienced the rape were the first to report it and have knowledge about the (in)security situation by the camp, their knowledge was never sought out or considered relevant to the design and execution of the modes of response put in place by the peacekeepers. Again, the expertise of

---

[31] Lucy Ferguson, "This Is Our Gender Person," *International Feminist Journal of Politics* 17, 3 (2015): 380–97; "Let's get with it! Sexism and Gender Equality Mainstreaming in the Humanitarian Sector," *The Cassandra Complexity Blog*, August 29, 2015, https://cassandracomplexblog.wordpress.com/2015/08/29/lets-get-with-it-sexism-and-gender-equality-mainstreaming-in-the-humanitarian-sector/; Clifton and Gell, "Saving and Protecting Lives by Empowering Women."

[32] Sahana Dharmapuri, "Just Add Women and Stir?" *Parameters* 41, 1 (2011); Clifton and Gell, "Saving and Protecting Lives by Empowering Women."

[33] Clifton and Gell, "Saving and Protecting Lives by Empowering Women," 16.

the security actors trumped those who were victims, despite the fact that those women were the only ones among any of us who encountered and had first-hand knowledge of the conflict parties and their whereabouts to which the peacekeepers were devising a response. As Handrahan further notes, "women's fundamental human rights and dignity are often caught in the middle of multiple male power struggles played out as identity norms."[34] She further cites Cynthia Cockburn who has argued that there is "one constant in a feminist gender analysis, whoever makes it: the differentiation and relative positioning of women and men is seen as an important ordering principle that pervades the system of power and is sometimes its very embodiment."[35] In effect, the multiple layers of gendered ordering and their interconnection in this one example evidence just how relevant gender relations and inequalities can be to an understanding and assessment of paternalism. My expertise is ranked on the basis of my gender and on the fact that my expertise is about gender itself. As for the Darfuri women? Well, their expertise simply disappears when those who consider themselves at the top of the expertise food chain do not see down to the lower levels, but instead sidestep to those in that context who are perceived to not in any way *lack* authority or expertise, the men of the community. In this fashion, patriarchy forms a bedrock out of which paternalist duty bearing arises. Described as a central tenet of patriarchy, the role of protector implies a superior role as "carer" on the part of the male. That caring role becomes duty, a duty to protect, that can only be performed on the basis of the expertise held by men.

While I have invoked women as the center point of the gender analysis that has informed my scrutiny of paternalism in this case, I pause to also acknowledge that patriarchy, and masculinity-derived basis of power, also affect men. "It is not men-on-top that makes something patriarchal. It's men who are recognized and claim a certain form of masculinity, for the sake of being more valued, more 'serious,' and 'the protectors of/and controllers of those people who

[34] Handrahan, "Conflict, Gender, Ethnicity and Post-Conflict Reconstruction," 434.
[35] Cynthia Cockburn, "The Continuum of Violence: A Gender Perspective on War and Peace," *Sites of Violence: Gender and Conflict Zones*, eds. Wenona Giles and Jennifer Hyndman (Berkeley: University of California Press, 2004), 28.

are less masculine' that makes any organization, any community, any society patriarchal."[36] Patriarchy is long acknowledged as operating to not only subordinate women, but to also privilege some men over other men. Thereby the status, knowledge, and expertise of some men will override that of other men. On the basis of gender and multiple other inequalities cited by Handrahan, the peacekeeping men in this case hold more authority and power over the men of the camp population, creating its own gendered dynamic of power, expertise, and knowledge.

In keeping with my assessment of gendered dynamics impacting women, it is clear that in respect of what this example shows, there is no more compelling a case that may be subject to the patriarchy of protection and humanitarian in-practice paternalism than the female victim who is deemed to hold little knowledge or expertise.

The Failure to Consult with Women

Enacted on the basis of a "politics of empowerment," humanitarian action derives its standing from an assumed consistency with the needs of the intended beneficiaries.[37] It may not always be the case that actions are taken at the behest of those for whom they are intended, however. In fact such actions might not be welcome at all, as was seen in the Darfur case. As described, in response to incidents of rape, women's representatives and wider community leaders openly criticized international actors for taking actions on their behalf that were based on the international actors' own assumptions of what was appropriate. It was evident that efforts by those seeking to act in the best interests of these women did so without the women's consent and divorced from the ways that the women wanted such issues addressed. The women who were subject to the harms playing out, i.e., sexualized violence, did not get to consent nor determine the quality or texture of the actions taken on their behalf. They were never consulted by the principal actors involved. The idea of consultation and enacting the politics of empowerment brings up critical considerations of how

---

[36] Carol Cohn and Cynthia Enloe, "A Conversation with Cynthia Enloe: Feminists Look at Masculinity and the Men Who Wage War," *Signs* 28, 4 (2003): 1187–207, 1192.

[37] Barnett, "International Paternalism and Humanitarian Governance."

actions on the part of others work off gendered conceptions of power and authority.

The exclusion of women from decision-making in operations undertaken by peacekeeping and humanitarian actors is not unusual. The strategy of "gender mainstreaming" was adopted by the UN in 1997 in an attempt to ensure that both men and women's interests and rights are addressed through global policy and programming.[38] It has been specifically applied to the humanitarian sector, lending a basis of normative persuasion as well as a practical imperative to the need to consult with women as a fundamental good and moral practice, as well as a requirement if aid is to be in any way fully effective.[39] Its effective adoption across the UN and by international organizations more broadly has been sporadic to date. Adopting a gendered approach to programming implies that actions will respond to the express and variant concerns, interests, needs, and rights of men and women (and boys and girls). It ensures that actions on behalf of those men and women take account of how their social, economic, and political positioning fare relative to the resources and benefits available through aid. It rests on an approach commensurate with inquiring and consulting, and thereby ensuring that men and women have a say in the actions that affect their lives.

The humanitarian arena has been particularly resistant to the idea that "gender" as a conceptual lens, up until recently tied to longer-term development approaches, holds any relevance to operations responding to crises. In situations of crisis, the "tyranny of the urgent" prevails and attention to gender issues is still considered by many actors to be a luxury item employed "when there's time," not a critical concern to a critical humanitarian situation. It also becomes conflated with women and women's rights. In many ways it is, of course, tied to those ideas, but only when a thorough consideration of gender norms and inequalities in a particular context identifies that women are at a disparity

---

[38] UN Economic and Social Council, 52nd Session, Agreed Conclusions 1997/
2, Supplement No. 3, *General Assembly Official Records*, New York, July
18, 1997.

[39] IASC, Gender Policy Statement. United Nations Interagency Standing
Committee on Humanitarian Action, New York, June 20, 2008; IASC,
Women, Girls, Boys and Men Different Needs – Equal Opportunities: Gender
Handbook in Humanitarian Action, United Nations Interagency Standing
Committee on Humanitarian Action, 2006.

that requires redress. This exclusion occurs because of approaches that are "neutral" and assumed to address the needs of a population. Crises, and any society broadly, cannot be considered gender-neutral; they are, in fact, infused by gendered norms and dynamics as earlier discussed. It is the non-neutral, gendered characteristics of a context which require attention if both men and women's needs are to be met and their viewpoints considered equally valid. The humanitarian actors' standpoint that "gender" is not necessary is paternalist in itself. As I have shown in the last section, gender expertise is relegated in favor of "real" expertise identified by the real emergency experts. Similar to the argument made by Autesserre in this volume, it is demonstrative of a superiority of knowledge assumed by the actors themselves. Accordingly, operations will be run according to that form of knowledge and expertise, and not in line with any alternate viewpoints that might exist among the population itself.

Where women might complain about not being listened to, humanitarian organizations' response is one which says "not now," the situation is too urgent right now to consider "women." I have heard this countless times in my work. Even where forums of consultation are created by humanitarian actors (such as camp committees), there have been consistent issues with the exclusion of women from them.[40] And still humanitarian actors across multiple sectors argue that gender considerations are not necessary, at least not now, even though consultation on operations and involvement in decision-making is possibly the principal way (and only way) that a camp population might have any power or say in what an international humanitarian organization is doing.

Where community and consultation forums are established, humanitarian actors usually engage with "community leaders" (read: men) of that community. It could be argued more generally, as well as specifically in

---

[40] An online blog by the Senior Gender Adviser at the UN Office for Coordination of Humanitarian Affairs notes, for example, that: "What's less widely acknowledged is that the humanitarian community continually fails to properly engage women and girls in the plans, responses and recovery efforts that are launched on their behalf. Their contributions and experiences are underplayed, taken for granted or, at worst, simply ignored." Njoki Kinyanjui, "The Invisibility of Women and Girls Affected by Humanitarian Crises," UNOCHA blog, March 11, 2015, https://medium.com/@UNOCHA/the-invisibility-of-women-and-girls-affected-by-humanitarian-crises-e7d66a7ed01f.

relation to this case, that this is a culturally appropriate and sound approach. The AU peacekeepers were in fact acting in a culturally appropriate way, engaging with the primary leaders of that community (i.e., the men) to take decisions on behalf of that community. Who decides who the primary and most significant leaders are however is a critical consideration in the potential for paternalist approaches to evolve even where consultation takes place.

Research by Devanna De La Puente, for example, underscores that the idea of men as the natural community leaders in the context of Darfur can be easily contested.[41] Her research describes a long preceding historical context to women's public leadership roles in Darfur before the conflict and its resulting crisis. Early royal Sudanese society had women in powerful political leadership roles. This changed in the early 1900s with the arrival of the British and the imposition of administrative structures which worked women out of the public and leadership picture, installing men in public roles. Further still, women historically played and continue to play significant leadership roles in the inculcation of cultural values and practices, substantively recognized in Darfuri society. As sheikhas, they continued to play leadership roles in the structures created in the newly formed conflict-time camps. De La Puente's research, conducted following the period in which the incident I shared took place, found that where women were part of consultation committees and meetings with humanitarian organizations, "it was not that sheikhas would not talk because they were not allowed; it was generally because they were not asked."[42] Work by Alex de Waal, which De La Puente also cites, has found that Darfuri women have contested Darfuri men's estimations that they are the natural leaders and protectors of women. In a meeting on this topic, one woman explained that "[t]here is a female sheikha who is also elected ... and by the way she gives birth to the male sheikh."[43] These women are not afraid to say what they think when it is needed, whether they are permitted to, of course, is what matters.

[41] Devanna De La Puente, "Women's Leadership in Camps for Internally Displaced People in Darfur, Western Sudan," *Community Development Journal* 46, 3 (2011).
[42] *Ibid.*,11.
[43] Alex deWaal, "Making Sense of Sudan: Could a Woman be a Sultan?" African Arguments, Blog. www.Africanarguments.org/category/making-sense-of-sudan (accessed July 20, 2016).

It is evident that in this particular context, women are and can be public leaders, something that I witnessed myself. While they experience discrimination in their own communities, they find opportunity and voice to play leadership roles in ways that they can (not dissimilar to many Western societies). De La Puente's research and my chapter here, evidences that the arrival of the aid operation is a critical factor in women's potential for power and equality in the context of the disruption that has occurred in their lives as a result of the conflict. An approach by humanitarian and peacekeeping actors which excludes women as relevant actors effectively mirrors that of the colonial era, where Darfuri men were placed in leadership positions and the views and inputs of women were rarely solicited. The importing of international patriarchy[44] has, over time, successively relegated women from positions of leadership, entrenching existing patriarchies. A critical question for humanitarianism is whether it acts to reinforce the power of local men over these women or takes the time to ensure that the existing power available to women is supported, further empowered and the inequalities present not entrenched by the attitudes and actions of these outside actors. Women's authority as "an authority" may be determined by *how* humanitarian actors undertake their work, and whether they feel that they know more than these women can about what their needs are.

When it came to this particular incident, it was evident that the AU peacekeepers were even less au fait with the gendered dynamics of leadership in this context, and how consultative approaches (that would include women) might inform their work. Again, this is not atypical of peacekeepers at that time (and even now), even though understanding of these issues is improving as the UN and troop-contributing countries become more adept at translating provisions of gender and peacekeeping into their operations. Since this event occurred, there has been a deluge of normative and practice attention to conflict-related sexualized violence internationally. Most notable are a set of eight resolutions adopted by the UN Security Council on "women, peace and security," four of which focus specifically on sexualized violence in conflict.[45] While portending

---

[44] Fionnuala Ní Aoláin and Michael Hamilton, "Gender and the Rule of Law in Transitional Societies," *Minnesota Journal of International Law* 18 (2009).

[45] These are: United Nations Security Council Resolution 1820, S/RES/1820 (2008); United Nations Security Council Resolution 1888, S/RES/1888 (2009); United Nations Security Council Resolution 1960, S/RES/1960 (2010); United Nations Security Council Resolution 2106, S/RES/2106 (2013).

to the best interests of women affected by armed conflict, the Security Council has effectively set out a new paradigm for how women's experiences of conflict and women's security concerns should be understood and addressed. While helpfully establishing that "gender is crucial to the story of how and why civilians are intentionally killed, raped or abused in war," the resolutions also demonstrate that "victimized women are the territory being fought over, and wartime rape is an attack on the property and pride of male/masculine enemies."[46] In effect, the predominant focus on the sexual vulnerability of women's bodies evokes a "binary universalism, 'celebrating' or romanticizing the victimhood of women."[47] The approach under which international operations now effectively respond to sexualized violence is one in which the Security Council has set out a clear remit for itself as "protector" of women,[48] and its peacekeeping mandates its operational arm of the same.

Coming to fruition under the "human security" banner, a vision of women's protection in humanitarian contexts has emerged. While it has made women's lives visible to the arena of security, humanitarianism, and peacekeeping, it has also created a very refined notion of that visibility. While lending a much-needed window on women's lives, these developments have also had the adverse effect of making women out to be the *most insecure* and thereby in need of the might of the patriarchal and paternalist international system. "Central to the logic of masculinst protection is the subordinate relation of those in the protected position. In return for male protection, the woman concedes critical distance from decision-making autonomy."[49] Little wonder that, in practice, humanitarian response and the provision of peacekeeping which these resolutions directly speak to follow through

---

[46] Laura Sjoberg and Jessica Peet, "A(nother) Dark Side of the Protection Racket," *International Feminist Journal of Politics* 13, 2 (2011): 163–82, 164, 166.

[47] Heidi Hudson, "'Doing' Security As Though Humans Matter: A Feminist Perspective on Gender and the Politics of Human Security," *Security Dialogue* 36 (2005): 155–74, 159.

[48] Diane Otto, "Power and Danger: Feminist Engagement with International Law Through the UN Security Council," *The Australian Feminist Law Journal* 32 (2010): 97–121, 109.

[49] Iris Marion Young, "The Logic of Masculinist Protection: Reflections on the Current Security State," *Signs: Journal of Women in Culture and Society* 29, 1 (2005): 1–25, 4.

on a practice of men protecting women from other men enabling and "justif[ying] the social dominance of masculinity."[50]

When it comes to the issue of women's security and protection, and humanitarianism and peacekeeping in action, I argue that a paternalist dynamic may acutely arise. Security is a space in which the gendered hues of paternalism might most easily be seen. "Through gender, we can make linkages from the individual to identity, and from identity to security. The adage that 'the personal is political' also rings true for security studies."[51] Indeed, "what is at stake is the definition of men (the protectors) versus women (the protected) who have little control over their own protection."[52] This is the case when women are not consulted about what that protection might be and mean. It is furthered, however, in the fact that in this particular case, the dominant male protectors consulted with the men whom they perceived to be next in line in terms of holding a protection role. Not only were women not consulted in any way by themselves, when a consultation structure on this very issue was organized, it actively excluded and discriminated against women.

In the emergence of security and humanitarianism, including peacekeeping practices, "[a] pattern can be clearly identified in the language used by the UN to talk about the situations of women that is closer to victimization than empowerment."[53] Protectionism invokes paternalist tendencies toward the needy female, the femme fatale, a bodily territory that the male holds a natural duty and authority to protect. With this practice of care and concern for women comes a domination and a reinforcement of the idea of masculinist protection and the paternal actor primarily responsible for the protective care of women.

In many ways, the women who feature in this example constitute what might be considered to be the good or exemplar victim. Women whose rights and bodies are brutalized. Those who are subject to higher and violent forces and are the perfect objects of the international community's preoccupation with the need to "protect." Those who protect are active, and those who are the objects of that protection, are the passive recipients. It allows us to see women's inequality

---

[50] Sjoberg and Peet, "A(nother) Dark Side of the Protection Racket," 168.
[51] Hoogensen and Svein, "Gender Identity and the Subject of Security," 163.
[52] Puechguirbal, "Women and Children," 6.
[53] *Ibid.*, 7.

of access to and decision-making power over the steps taken in their best interests, and how prevailing inequalities may be exacerbated by the work of international actors. It is little surprise that a paternalist ethic of care will flourish. Recognizing patriarchy in the mode of its own work as well as in that of the community it is assisting is critical if humanitarianism is to assess the degree to which it lends itself toward paternalism. Women can be consulted or excluded by humanitarian agencies, either creating or disabling the conditions for paternalism to arise.

The "Lacking" of Capacity on the Part of Women

As noted earlier, paternalist actions invoke a relationship of superior/inferior, competent/incompetent, capacity/incapacity where the dominant possesses the perceived authority and scope to make decisions over or on behalf of, and in the best interests of, the subordinate and restrained other. I move now to examining much of what this dynamic rests on, a perception that some actors may lack capacity and/or be incapable of knowing better than you do. Often, "paternalistic behavior is made worse by the fact that even if *they* know what is to be done, *they* can rarely insist on their point of view."[54] In the Darfur case, not only was there no opportunity afforded to women to express their view, given that they were women in need of protection, their capacity to know anything about what might be best for them in this situation was utterly disregarded by the protagonist actors (until they protested, of course).

In this instance there was a direct and "natural" collusion between male peacekeepers and male community leaders to protect women deemed unfit to know what should be done. Identifying women as utterly powerless and incapable obviously takes away any agency on their part and reinforces the "natural" authority attributed to men, rendering the affected women as "unfit" to articulate and determine what should happen. A critical moment that demonstrates this was when those actors ignored the local knowledge that the women, and I on their behalf, were offering to the peacekeepers. As Autesserre

[54] "Are NGOs Paternalistic? Why?" *Musings...of a Wanderer*, January 22, 2013, http://makarandimpressions.wordpress.com/2013/01/22/are-ngos-paternalistic-why/.

notes in her chapter, the most valued expertise in these contexts is that of the international actors, their knowledge and expertise trumping anything that is on offer locally.[55] As I explored before, this paternalist dynamic is further entrenched when it is gendered – the "hard" security knowledge of military actors trumps the "soft" knowledge of women. It is evident through this example that this is even the case when these same women are the only ones who have had more than a close encounter with the militia the military are looking for, have been raped by these militia, have been given messages for the men of their community by these militia, are the ones whose bodies have been used as a means of messaging between men and are the only ones among this range of actors that have been in the environs of the militia's camp and know where they are located. None of this seems to matter in the face of outside "real" expertise.

As Henry S. Richardson argues in this volume, the label of paternalism may be easily charged and is often erroneously applied to situations in which high-handedness or domineering practices arise.[56] As I argue for the relevance of gender to the concept and practice of paternalism, I realize that there is potential for actions that disregard women's capacity and power to be labeled as "merely" sexism and not the more controlling end of that spectrum that might be referred to as paternalism. The charge of sexism, rather than paternalism, might be one that arises for the case that I am discussing. I wish to unpack the possibility that the principal actors' actions were merely sexist. I would argue that they were indeed sexist. But they could also be considered paternalist.

Peter Glick and Susan T. Fiske describe the existence of a "benevolent sexism" which they define as "a set of interrelated attitudes toward women that are sexist in terms of viewing women stereotypically and in restricted roles but that are subjectively positive in feeling and tone (for the perceiver) and also tend to elicit behaviors that are typically categorized as prosocial (e.g., helping) or intimacy-seeking (e.g., self-disclosure)."[57] While "not overtly hostile"[58] and seemingly

---

[55] Autesserre, Chapter 5, this volume.
[56] Richardson, Chapter 1, this volume.
[57] Glick and Fiske, "The Ambivalent Sexism Inventory," 491.
[58] Miguel Moya *et al.*, "It's for Your Own Good: Benevolent Sexism and Women's Reactions to Protectively Justified Restrictions," *Personality and Social Psychology Bulletin* 33, 10 (2007): 1421–34, 1422.

enacted in positive undertones, for example in the interests of caring and protecting as I have described, they note that it is not a positive dynamic, but rather one that derives from masculine dominance. This might indeed be where the actions of the principal actors in this case could be deemed as sexist. The peacekeepers were acting in the best interests of these women. They went to the people they deemed to be their natural protectors to establish ways to jointly offer protection, all of this positive, benevolent, and perhaps an example of acting in good faith. It is also clearly sexist excluding women from the hard and tough decisions to be made by men.

It also moves toward paternalism, however, when the concept of dominance is understood as a performance of masculine *power over*, or *acting on behalf of*, when the subject is deemed to be *unfit to know what her best interests might be*. Herein, we find the basis for a tone of paternalism that is derived from the paternal, the patriarchal, and specifically directed toward women who are deemed incapable of agency. We then move quickly toward evaluating a critical conclusion – the added value of viewing men's dominance over women as not just sexist, but also, at times, paternalist. That there is a "backdrop of paternalism in gender relations"[59] is then clear, as is there evidence, on the basis of the Darfur example of gender operating within and informing paternalism in practice.

This example demonstrates where the actors in question "exhibit[ed] a willingness to limit the choices of others if those choices are seen as ill-informed."[60] The peacekeepers are convinced that they know best. They are also convinced that they have a better understanding than these women of the security concerns of the camp population. They not only determined their own recourse to make decisions on behalf of the population in question, they also self-determined their own ability to make decisions that were "better" than those that might be made by the object whose freedom is perceived as so constrained. In doing so, what was evident was the lack of value and power afforded to the "local" knowledge of those women. Instead, the peacekeepers sought out and secured the engagement and endorsement of the men of the community, reinforcing the inability of those women to make decisions akin to those of the male leaders. In all, the "security" knowledge

---

[59] *Ibid.*, 1421.
[60] Barnett, Introduction, this volume.

of the peacekeepers trumped that of the knowledge offered by those women, and together with local men's knowledge, a much "better" form of knowledge emerges. Thereby their decisions, combined with the male leadership of the camp, will be the best ones to reinstate that security.

On the part of the humanitarian community, the tacit agreement to not "rock the boat" with the Sudanese government was taken in the exclusive spaces of organizational offices, on the ground and in headquarters that are very far away. There was a conviction that maintaining operations was the best scenario for this population. It was evident that these women thought differently, a view that only became evident when they forced those with power to listen. In effect, it seemed that for both sets of actors relying on what these women thought and wanted would "lead to an inferior outcome or quality of life,"[61] an element of paternalism identified in the introductory chapter. In all, this scenario is exemplary of the definition of paternalism that frames this volume. The peacekeepers and humanitarians enacted a "substitution of [these women's] judgment" for judgment by those they felt knew better.

There is a reality to concretely consider. The agencies in question in Darfur could easily argue that the women concerned were not fully au fait with all of the circumstantial evidence in hand. The population in question may not have fully understood the pressures that humanitarian agencies were under by the Sudanese administration, nor that their speaking out could actually result in no provision of basic services for the entire camp population. Nor, perhaps, could they understand that there are moments where the rights of the few may be overridden in the interest of the many. Whether these women, or the wider population, understood any or all of this was never really ascertained, at least in this specific instance. They were never asked by those making the decisions, nor was the possible solution to the problem debated and discussed with them. Inevitably a hierarchy of inference prevails in many contexts, with the expertise of outsiders trumping the knowledge of insiders. Solidarity with is replaced by an authoritative knowledge and power over. The expertise of humanitarian hegemony negates the need for women's voices to be heard and privileges the fast-acting, "hard," and masculinist "save the day" mentality. There is, after all, little room

[61] *Ibid.*

for gender considerations in fast-paced humanitarian action, yet this very instance was entirely gendered and paternal.

In this, and in many cases, there may be a perception by outsiders that the women in question lack the power or capacity to act. Or that if they did or expressed a viewpoint, that it simply would not suit or fit with the view of the experts on what they thought should happen. What is problematic is not the intention to act, but rather doing so on the basis of "knowing better" than and by virtue of this negating the relevance of the efforts of the subjects of that action. The international actors undertook actions for the welfare of others in a style that was authoritative and exclusionary; the relation between the agencies and the women concerned was configured along a dynamic of "we know better" and what's best for you; and the actions were premised on an assumed superiority of knowledge and capacity on the part of the paternal over those assumed to be dispossessed of such capacity due to the confines of their situation.

In this context, the melding of patriarchies reinforces inequality and promotes protectionist approaches to women. The international actors undertook actions for the welfare of others in a style that was authoritative and exclusionary; the relation between the agencies and the women concerned was configured along a dynamic of "we know better" and what's best for you; and the actions were premised on an assumed superiority of knowledge and capacity on the part of the paternal over those assumed to be dispossessed of such capacity due to the confines of their situation and because of their gender. In such a context, there is much complexity to contend with. Whether that becomes an instinct to control what happens matters in whether the caring or duty roles played by humanitarian actors become and are felt as paternal. As Glick and Fiske further explain, "the exploited group's lack of competence to exercise structural power with self-serving 'benevolent' justifications ('We must bear the burden of taking care of them') ... allow members of the dominant group to view their actions as not being exploitative."[62] In the context of this example, this can be understood as manifesting in what they term as "protective paternalism."[63] Whether well meaning or not, what matters is that these women *felt* a protective paternalism in this instance, and expressed

[62] Glick and Fiske, "The Ambivalent Sexism Inventory," 492.
[63] *Ibid.*, 493.

an anger at not being consulted, at not being heard and at having their viewpoint displaced by viewpoints that were favored as more authoritative. Despite the express aim of international organizations to empower, to aim toward the emancipatory rather than the dominant end of the spectrum of aid delivery, the actions of those involved in this situation rendered women as incapable of making an informed and effective decision about what was best for them.

Conclusion

This case demonstrates the power of gender in inculcating paternalist rationales, and in associated actions that are infused with gender norms and paternalist assumptions. If paternalism is about relations between actors, institutions and otherwise, then gender infuses all of those dynamics. Gender and paternalism are inextricably linked, while both may be active in elements of humanitarianism.

The power of gender runs through all aspects of this example I have shared. That these women were attacked en masse as a group was not inconsequential. Here we see the power of gender acting to make harm meaningful, right behind, and central to, the actions of the violent aggressors targeting male paternal power over their women. The power of gender is evident in the humanitarian system itself as an element of the gendered global political order and with it ways of operating infused with paternalist tendencies. The power of gender is evident in the actions taken by the women their resistance made on a sex-gender basis, as a collective of women against a system of decision-making inherently patriarchal and paternal in nature. They shared powerlessness, anger, and resistance all on the basis of the female group identity.

Like the populations discussed by Feldman and Autesserre[64] in this volume, the resistance and complaints about the humanitarian response by the population cited in this case were about the express lack of respect for their knowledge, wishes, and demands; the lack of consultation with them about what should be done, and about the exclusionary decision-making that was happening. This community, men and women, wanted to shout out loud about the violations that they were experiencing. The humanitarian community wanted to dampen this, keep it all quiet so that their operations would remain

[64] Chapters 5 and 9, this volume.

uninterrupted. For many, this was an ethic of care toward the population they were serving (while for others also about self-preservation). The peacekeepers wanted to provide protection to women in the way that they thought best. In many respects, this population did lack the capacity needed to act, i.e., what was needed was a political resolution to the attacks, one which is impossible to render when one is at the bottom of the rung of the power plays in a conflict such as this. As the gatekeepers and the ones with the power to access the "outside world", i.e., the media, the military, the diplomatic community, the international criminal court, the humanitarian community they did little to ask them, is this how you want this situation that is impacting you and your life handled? They also did little to ensure that the population, and the women in particular, retained some semblance of the kind of micro-level power that was available to them in this highly constrained context – the power to express what they wanted and how they wanted it to happen. As Autesserre notes, "paternalism manifests itself in the process of intervention, not the goals."[65]

The professionalization of the humanitarian world has led to the genesis of high-end knowledge which lends authority to the external experts vis-à-vis the knowledge of the "local" person. As noted by Tonkens and Duyvendak, "a professional speaks on someone else's behalf because they are not considered to be an equal individual with an equal point of view."[66] It is this tendency that must be overcome if paternalism is to feature less in the work of humanitarian actors and if freedom for the objects of care to have autonomy over their lives is to become central to approaches taken by humanitarian organizations. A fluidity is required that responds to the privileging of differing kinds of capacity in differing circumstances. The capacity that external humanitarian expertise might offer will be required in one moment, while the expertise of own-knowledge and knowing what's best for oneself will be required in another. It is a back and forth that affords equal value to both sets of knowledge, and to the authority of knowledge generated and expressed by both men and women.

I contend that understanding paternalism as gendered exposes much of the assumptions that we make about social relations, actions

[65] Chapter 5, this volume, 164.
[66] Evelien Tonkens and Jan Willem Duyvendak, "Paternalism – Caught Between Rejection and Acceptance: Taking Care and Taking Control in Community Work," *Community Development Journal* 38 (2003): 6–15, 8.

and their meanings and provides justification for the ways in which protection and care are partied out by international actors. I borrow the words of Nadine Peuchguirbal to conclude that, "Maybe we could suggest that women would be better protected if they were seen as autonomous actors in charge of their own lives, thus being in a position of asserting their own rights and fighting back."[67] Maybe indeed. However, that might not occur until the gendered hues of humanitarianism and of paternalism in practice are exposed and acknowledged. Humanitarian actors simply need to do more so that their *express goal* of solidarity with becomes an actual solidarity with *in practice*. That practice must reflect an approach that values women's capacity and ability to express their own interests and lead responses to their own protection, so that ultimately protection from men is not the most urgent priority in women's lives.

[67] Puechguirbal, "Women and Children."

7 The Limits of Consent: Sex Trafficking and the Problem of International Paternalism

SALLY ENGLE MERRY AND VIBHUTI
RAMACHANDRAN

Take up the White Man's burden, Send forth the best ye breed
　　Go bind your sons to exile, to serve your captives' need;
To wait in heavy harness, On fluttered folk and wild—
　　Your new-caught, sullen peoples, Half-devil and half-child.

Take up the White Man's burden, Have done with childish days—
　　The lightly proferred laurel, The easy, ungrudged praise.
Comes now, to search your manhood, through all the thankless years
　　Cold, edged with dear-bought wisdom, The judgment of your peers!
　　　　　　　　"The White Man's Burden," Rudyard Kipling, 1899

Sex trafficking is commonly represented by the image of a young girl, kidnapped and sold from hand to hand until she ends up in a brothel in a large city, or sold by impoverished parents to a criminal network. She disappears into a world of sex work where she services thirty men a night. Such stories have elicited an active rescue network, invading brothels, rescuing women, sending them to shelters, and sometimes repatriating them to their countries of origin if they moved across national borders. But the situation is far more complicated. Social scientists studying trafficking report that there are many paths into brothels in addition to those depicted in popular literature on trafficking. Many women who go into prostitution are seeking a better life or an escape from an intolerable one. Many are married to abusive husbands, or face starvation unless they migrate away from their community. Some go for the adventure and the money they can earn.

We are grateful to the Law and Social Sciences Program and Science, Technology and Society Program of the National Science Foundation for support for this research, #SES-0921368. Most of the research in India was carried out by Vibhuti Ramachandran.

224

Despite this complexity, many of the activists in the contemporary anti-trafficking movement, which include NGOs, journalists, faith-based groups, radical feminists, liberal feminists, and humanitarians more generally, tell a simpler story, one that recycles the classic images of imperial-era paternalism. For example, Nicholas Kristof, the *New York Times* Pulitzer prize-winning correspondent who has been increasingly interested in covering sex trafficking in Asia over the past decade, writes newspaper columns in which he characterizes sex trafficking as a brutality that is largely the lot of the developing world, and from which it must be "saved." His writings focus on the vulnerable victimhood of the Third World Prostitute.[1] In 2004, Kristof staged a journalistic intervention that cast him in the role of the white "savior" of two young Cambodian girls whose freedom he purchased from their brothel-owners. Kristof's descriptions of rescuing these girls from a "wild brothel town" are full of stereotypes about the pitiable state of women as "second-class citizens" and "21st-century slaves" in Third World countries.[2] While Kristof justifies his act of buying these girls partly as drawing attention to the perversity of sex trafficking in Cambodia, he makes no attempt to hide the affective dimension of his role as savior in the intervention. For instance, he recounts that one of the girls who grabbed at him in the street, pulling him toward her brothel, "looked so young and pitiable that I couldn't help thinking that she really wanted me to tug her away."

As with "human rights" reportage and stories about HIV/AIDS in the Third World, such instances of intervention by prominent journalists from the global North are inevitably laced with assumptions about race and Third World victimhood. Makau Mutua deconstructs the "grand narrative" of the human rights paradigm itself, which is predicated on a sharp, racially marked divide between "victims" and "saviors."[3] He locates the roots of this subtext in a Western colonial

---

[1] Nicholas Kristof, "Slavery in Our Time," *New York Times*, January 22, 2006, http://query.nytimes.com/gst/fullpage.html?res=9903E3D6123FF931A15752C0 A9609C8B63 (accessed November 8, 2015).

[2] Nicholas Kristof, "Girls for Sale," *New York Times*, January 17, 2004, www. nytimes.com/2004/01/17/opinion/girls-for-sale.html (accessed November 10, 2015) and Nicholas Kristof, "Going Home, With Hope," *New York Times*, January 24, 2004, www.nytimes.com/2004/01/24/opinion/24KRIS.html (accessed November 10, 2015).

[3] Makau Matua, "Savages, Victors, Saviors: The Metaphor of Human Rights," *Harvard International Law Journal* 42 (2001): 201–45.

urge to save and redeem the Third World "other," coupled with a missionary zeal to "help those who cannot help themselves." Mutua sees this combination of attitudes reflected in the language of human rights reports that suggest the need for outside intervention to save Third World victims.

Thus, the gendered and raced tropes of Kipling's famous poem, characteristic of the paternalism of nineteenth- and early twentieth-century colonialism, appear in subtle ways in the discourse of the modern anti-trafficking movement. This movement similarly depicts oppressed and suffering people who await rescue by those in more affluent countries, even though they may not welcome such help. In both cases, the helper knows best. While the gendered dimensions are now more nuanced, the prevailing victim is a sexually exploited young woman, usually in a poor country. The problem of sex trafficking, which is increasingly referred to as "modern-day slavery," is imagined as a feature of poor countries while the interveners are often from rich countries. Remnants of the racial dimensions of the old paternalism also appear, since rescuing countries are largely white while victims are often brown.

Sex workers sometimes resist these interventions, and scattered data suggests that they often return to the same form of work. The rescuers, like the imperialists of Kipling's day, are nevertheless understood as engaging in heroic work that contributes to the betterment of society. It is assumed that the victims do not understand their best interests and are unable to help themselves. In this volume, Michael N. Barnett claims that "Paternalism can be broadly understood as the substitution of one actor's judgment for another's in order to improve the object's welfare, interests, and happiness."[4] Thus, the anti-trafficking movement has features of classic paternalism as it was practiced during the colonial era.

Yet, this framing of the trafficking problem fails to consider the complicated problem of consent. It assumes that trafficking victims are coerced or tricked into the positions that they are in, or that they are too young to choose. Under these conditions, the rescuer need not explore whether the victim wishes to be rescued or has chosen this path given whatever constraints she faces in her life. Instead, given the

---

[4] Conclusion, this volume.

assumption of enslavement and force, the rescue, while paternalistic, need not question whether it overrides the choice of the rescued person.

Humanitarian interventions, as Michael N. Barnett points out, sit at the conjunction of care and control. In practice, care and control are inseparable since the helper makes his own decisions about the victim's best interests. As Barnett notes, there is wide variation in the way care and control come together in paternalism. The anti-trafficking and "modern-day slavery" movements that focus on rescues assume that victims have not consented to their exploitation, so that both care and control are necessary to liberate them. Yet, even individuals who are in such situations have sometimes consented in some fashion. They may find themselves in forced labor conditions through a combination of coercion and consent. Consent may be reluctantly extracted under difficult life circumstances such as violent marriages or frustration with a limited, hard life. Thus, the anti-trafficking movement can be seen as occupying a curious position within humanitarianism, promoting rescue whether or not it is desired in the name of a bygone model of white male heroes protecting sexually vulnerable women. Defining trafficking as recruitment into exploitative labor without consent, and even as a form of slavery, ignores the complicated conditions under which consent and coercion merge. In order for the anti-trafficking movement to present itself as caring rather than controlling, it is necessary to construct victims as non-consenting. Only then are rescues justified that do not question whether or not the person wishes to be rescued. Yet the act of helping those defined as child-like and unable to determine their own best interests, described so vividly in Kipling's poem, is the essence of the older version of imperial paternalism.

Defining Human Trafficking

Trafficking generally refers to movement by force, fraud, and coercion for commercial sex, or if a person under eighteen is induced to perform the sex act, or if a person is subjected to involuntary servitude, peonage, debt bondage, or slavery. According to the most widely used definitions, from the United Nations and the United States, trafficking involves both a mode of recruitment and exploitation of labor, but the fundamental element is coercion.[5] In fact, according to the widely referenced 2010

[5] Paola Monzini, *Sex Traffic: Prostitution, Crime and Exploitation* (New York: Zed Books, 2005), 50, fn. 11, 56–7; see Kay B. Warren, "The 2000

report by the US Department of State on trafficking, a person need not be physically transported to be a trafficking victim, but can be considered trafficked if there is exploitation of labor.[6] Thus, a lack of consent is a central dimension of trafficking, as currently understood.

Determining which events are instances of trafficking and which individuals have consented is fraught with ambiguity. As the focus of concern shifts from recruitment and movement to exploitative labor conditions, the ambiguity simply grows. Yet, modes of measuring and assessing violations require certainty. Through an examination of efforts to count victims of trafficking and the rates at which traffickers are prosecuted and international mechanisms for assessing violations, such as the US State Department Trafficking in Persons Report, this chapter argues that measurement systems inevitably simplify the question of consent in order to generate quantitative data on the extent and nature of the problem. This data is useful to draw attention to the issue and to pressure countries to change their policies. However, it fails to separate consenting from non-consenting victims or to interrogate the complex conditions under which individuals become involved in exploitative labor, thus reinforcing the assumption that all those who are counted as trafficked had no choice. The chapter is based on an analysis of laws and practices and Vibhuti Ramachandran's ethnographic research on trafficking in three cities in India.

Since the year 2000, global interest in sex trafficking as a form of "modern-day slavery"[7] and organized crime[8] has expanded astronomically, with the distinction between prostitution and its exploitative dimensions often elided.[9] There are ever more media reports about trafficking, more laws and policies, more anti-trafficking programs,

UN Human Trafficking Protocol: Rights, Enforcement, Vulnerabilities," in *The Practice of Human Rights: Tracking Law between the Global and the Local*, eds. Mark Goodale and Sally Engle Merry (Cambridge: Cambridge University Press, 2007), 242–70.

[6] United States Department of State, *Trafficking in Persons Report, 10th edn* (Washington, DC: US Department of State, 2010), 8.

[7] Kevin Bales, "Slavery and the Human Right to Evil," *Journal of Human Rights* 3, 1 (2004): 55–63.

[8] UN Protocol to Prevent, Suppress and Punish Trafficking in Persons Especially Women and Children, supplementing the United Nations Convention against Transnational Organized Crime (2000), www.ohchr.org/EN/ProfessionalInterest/Pages/ProtocolTraffickingInPersons.aspx (accessed July 6, 2016).

[9] Carole Vance, "States of Contradiction: Twelve Ways to Do Nothing about Trafficking While Pretending To," *Social Research* 78, 3 (2011): 933–49.

and overall more public distress about the extent of the problem and the suffering of the victims. Institutionalized in law-making and law enforcement agendas in the United States and, increasingly, in other parts of the world, anti-trafficking campaigns have gained much traction through an emergent global media interest in depicting the issue in this vein.[10] Sex trafficking evokes human rights concern because it is an activity that imagines women as vulnerable and passive victims of sexual assault.[11]

The growing concern about sex trafficking has produced a spurt in humanitarian rescue missions, built on the trope of a vulnerable, innocent young girl sold to a "Third World" brothel, abused and exploited, and eager to be saved from sexual exploitation.[12] Such images create the conceptual framework through which "trafficking" is understood and acted upon, as media coverage, research reports, government documents, and nonprofit literature feed into each other.[13] The image of the sex trafficking victim is one who has not consented to the labor she is doing.

Debates about sex trafficking typically focus on the question of consent to prostitution. If a woman knowingly enters into sex work, even if it is exploitative, has she consented? If she was driven to do so by poverty or some other form of vulnerability, has she consented? Is poverty a form of coercion that precludes consent?[14] Do any women

---

[10] Girish J. Gulati, "News Frames and Story Triggers in the Media's Coverage of Human Trafficking," *Human Rights Review* 12, 3 (2011): 363–79.

[11] Sealing Cheng, "The Traffic in 'Trafficked Filipinas': Sexual Harm, Violence, and Victims' Voices," in *Violence and Gender in the Globalized World: The Intimate and the Extimate*, eds. Sanja Bahun-Radunovic and V.G. Julie Rajan (Burlington: Ashgate, 2008), 141–56; Sealing Cheng, *On the Move for Love: Migrant Entertainers and the US Military in South Korea* (Philadelphia: University of Pennsylvania Press, 2010); Carole S. Vance, "Innocence and Experience: Melodramatic Narrativesof Sex Trafficking and their Consequences for Law and Policy," *History of the Present* 2, 2 (2012): 200–18; Kay B. Warren, "Troubling the Victim/Trafficker Dichotomy in Efforts to Combat Human Trafficking: The Unintended Consequences of Moralizing Labor Migration," *Indiana Journal of Global Legal Studies* 19, 1 (2012): 105–20.

[12] Kristof, "Slavery in Our Time."

[13] Julietta Hua, *Trafficking Women's Human Rights* (Minneapolis: University of Minnesota Press, 2011); Ronald Weitzer, "The Social Construction of Sex Trafficking: Ideology and Institutionalization of a Moral Crusade," *Politics & Society* 35 (2007): 447–75.

[14] For further elaboration on this question, see Rajeswari Sunder Rajan, "The Prostitution Question(s): (Female) Agency, Sexuality and Work,"

230   *Sally Engle Merry and Vibhuti Ramachandran*

voluntarily consent to prostitution, or are they all coerced in some fashion? Is prostitution inherently coercive and degrading to women, so that her consent is irrelevant? If women are coerced into sex work, should they be rescued? Although this debate has not generally used the language of paternalism, the link is clear. Any intervention that assumes that an adult sex worker cannot consent to such "degrading" labor, has consented only under duress, or has consented but does not understand that this work is against her best interests, is paternalistic. The paternalistic approach does not ask her opinion or interrogate whether she has exercised agency in choosing the work. It argues that this work is itself destructive to her well-being and therefore she needs to be protected. Moreover, it is not always possible to draw definite conclusions about whether or not someone consented to sex work. Trafficking exists within the context of international and intra-national economic migration and labor smuggling,[15] with the overlap between the processes sometimes making it difficult to discern and assess the extent of violations.

A significant segment of the anti-trafficking movement, including many feminists, argues that prostitution is inherently exploitative and violent to women and therefore consent does not diminish the exploitation. Other feminists say that adult women can consent to sex work, which can be seen as an acceptable form of labor. The definition of paternalism in the Introduction, "paternalism occurs when one actor interferes in the choices of another without her consent and on the

Reproductions 2 (1999): 12. On a related note, Svati Shah argues against all-too-easy conflations of poverty with a lack of agency. Svati Shah, "Distinguishing Poverty and Trafficking: Lessons from Field Research in Mumbai," *Georgetown Journal on Poverty Law and Policy* XIV, 3 (2007): 442. Shah is critical of discourses about human trafficking that translate the economic vulnerability of the poor to mean an absence of consent in adopting illegal and underground strategies for economic survival.

[15] Radhika Coomaraswamy (Special Rapporteur on Violence against Women), *Report on Trafficking in Women, Women's Migration and Violence Against Women*, UN Doc. E/CN.4/2000/68, February 29, 2000, www.unhchr. ch.html/menu2/7/b/mwom.htm 1242000; Melissa Ditmore and Marjan Wijers, "The Negotiations on the UN Protocol on Trafficking in Persons," *Nemesis* 4 (2003): 79–88; Jacqueline Berman, "Biopolitical Management, Economic Calculation and 'Trafficked Women'," *International Migration* 48, 4 (2010): 84–113; Sverre Molland, *The Perfect Business? Anti-Trafficking and the Sex Trade along the Mekong* (Honolulu: University of Hawai'i Press, 2012).

grounds that it is in her best interest,"[16] accurately describes the view of those who think sex work is beyond consent and requires rescue. In the fierce debates surrounding how to handle sex trafficking and prostitution more generally, whether or not to adopt a paternalistic stance toward sex workers and under what conditions is a core issue.

The two dominant approaches to sex trafficking fall out on this point. One opposes all prostitution as inherently degrading to women and therefore seeks to abolish prostitution as well as coerced movement into prostitution. Consent does not matter since it does not obviate the exploitative nature of the relationship. This has been called a radical feminist or abolitionist perspective, which views prostitution itself as a form of violence against women.[17] It is supported by conservative and religious groups and conforms to state agendas for stricter border control.[18] The second position is that sex work is a form of labor to which a person can consent, and that those who do should benefit from the same protections accorded to all workers. This position is advocated by sex workers' rights groups, who see commercial sex as a form of work and seek to improve the conditions of labor.[19] It is also supported by certain human rights and labor rights activists and public health workers concerned with protecting sex workers and their clients from STDs, including HIV/AIDs, among others.

Within this second perspective, most recognize that there are some areas where consent is not possible. These include sex work by children, by people who have been tricked or forced into sex work, and by those who work in slave-like conditions of exploitation. This is a position more in tune with liberal theories of individualism and autonomy in that it recognizes the possibility of agency, but it still retains a protectionist perspective with regard to coercion through movement,

---

[16] This volume, 5.

[17] Kathleen Barry, *Female Sexual Slavery* (New York: New York University Press, 1979); Sheila Jeffreys, *The Idea of Prostitution* (Melbourne: Spinifex Press, 1997).

[18] Elizabeth Bernstein, "Militarized Humanitarianism Meets Carceral Feminism: The Politics of Sex, Rights, and Freedom in Contemporary Anti-Trafficking Campaigns," *Signs: Journal of Women in Culture and Society* 36, 1 (2010): 45–71.

[19] Jo Doezema, *Sex Slaves and Discourse Masters: The Construction of Trafficking* (London: Zed Books, 2010); Gayle Pheterson, ed., *A Vindication of the Rights of Whores* (Seattle: Seal Press, 1989).

childhood vulnerability, or labor conditions. Thus, advocates of the second position vary in how they conceptualize the conditions under which a sex worker can voluntarily consent to her situation but assume that under certain conditions, consent is possible. In contrast, advocates of the first position see prostitution and commercial sex work as inherently degrading so that it is always a violation of the person, and those who consent are suffering "false consciousness."

Ideological and institutional factors separate the two groups. The two international coalitions of NGOs working on sex trafficking are the Coalition Against Trafficking in Women (CATW), which condemns prostitution as a violation of women's bodies, persons, and rights, and the Global Alliance Against Traffic in Women (GAATW), which sees sex work as a form of work and advocates better working conditions and protections for those providing it.[20] While condemning coerced participation in commercial sex, it respects the right of individuals to choose this work. A third approach argues that the harm of prostitution is the product of moral condemnation and criminalization of the activity and that decriminalization and a human rights framework that includes migrant and labor rights is preferable, a position advocated by the Network of Sex Work Projects.[21]

The two major global legal documents defining trafficking differ in significant ways in how they demarcate the space of agency and the scope of consent. Both laws were created in 2000, one by the US Congress and the other by the United Nations. While similar in many ways, they differ in the conditions under which a person can perform sex work and not be considered trafficked. The UN law, the Protocol to Prevent, Suppress and Punish Trafficking in Persons, Especially Women and Children, generally called the Palermo Protocol, is attached to a major international crime convention, the Convention against Transnational Organized Crime. It was written under the auspices of the Commission on Crime Prevention and Criminal Justice in

---

[20] See Global Alliance Against Traffic in Women, *Collateral Damage: The Impact of Anti-Trafficking Measures on Human Rights around the World* (Bangkok: GAATW, 2007).

[21] Cheng, *On the Move for Love*, 200; Shohini Ghosh, "Decriminalizing Sex Work," *Seminar* 583 (2008), www.india-seminar.com/2008/583/583_shohini_ghosh.htm.

2000 and came into force in 2003.[22] By 2015, it had 166 states parties. It operates as a multilateral convention, binding on those states that ratify it.

The Palermo Protocol offers the most widely used international definition of trafficking.[23] It defines trafficking as coerced recruitment intended for the purpose of exploitation. Article 3 (a) of the Protocol to Prevent, Suppress and Punish Trafficking in Persons, Especially Women and Children defines trafficking in persons as:

(a) the recruitment, transportation, transfer, harbouring or receipt of persons, by means of the threat or use of force or other forms of coercion, of abduction, of fraud, of deception, of the abuse of power or of a position of vulnerability or of the giving or receiving of payments or benefits to achieve the consent of a person having control over another person for the purposes of exploitation. Exploitation shall include, at a minimum, the exploitation of the prostitution of others or other forms of sexual exploitation, forced labour or services, slavery or practices similar to slavery, servitude or the removal of organs.[24]

Article 3 also defines the scope of consent within the definition of trafficking.

Article 3 (b). The consent of a victim of trafficking in persons to the intended exploitation set forth in subparagraph (a) of this article shall be irrelevant where any of the means set forth in subparagraph (a) have been used;

(c) The recruitment, transportation, transfer, harbouring or receipt of a child for the purpose of exploitation shall be considered trafficking in persons even if this does not involve any of the means set forth in subparagraph (a) of this Article.

(d) Child shall mean any person under eighteen years of age.

---

[22] Warren, "The 2000 UN Human Trafficking Protocol."

[23] For detailed discussions of how the political and ideological differences between the two contrasting feminist/activist positions played out during the framing of the Palermo Protocol, see Ditmore and Wijers, "The Negotiations on the UN Protocol on Trafficking in Persons."

[24] United Nations Office on Drugs and Crime, *Protocol to Prevent, Suppress and Punish Trafficking in Persons, Especially Women and Children* (2004), www.unodc.org/documents/treaties/UNTOC/Publications/TOC%20Convention/TOCebook-e.pdf, Art. 3 (a).

Thus, the consent of the victim of trafficking is irrelevant where forms of coercion listed in Article 3 (a) have been employed. Forms of coercion include the broad category of "abuse of a position of vulnerability," a concept that could stretch from poverty to domestic violence. Moreover, children under the age of eighteen cannot consent to exploitation. Thus, anyone who enters the sex trade because they are poor, female, disabled, or in an abusive relationship could theoretically be in a vulnerable position and consequently coerced rather than having chosen the work. Even if a person is not tricked or beaten, she can be perceived as pressured through her vulnerability to do commercial sex, and consequently not seen as consenting. The ambiguity of the reference to abuse of a "position of vulnerability" in the UN definition has proved difficult to work with. As a result, the UNODC has initiated a series of expert group meetings and reports to delineate the meaning of the phrase more clearly and to examine how it is being used in specific countries.[25]

Thus, the Palermo Protocol stresses the vulnerability of the victims of trafficking, portrayed repeatedly as "women and girls," and downplays consent or agency.[26] Indeed, inserting the phrase "abuse of a position of vulnerability" into the list of factors that define a person as a victim of trafficking was a major triumph for anti-prostitution feminist activists since it is a move toward establishing all prostitution as exploitative labor. The use of this condition expands the scope of people who can be considered trafficked and shrinks the number who can be considered as having consented to sex work and other exploitative labor conditions.[27]

In 2000, the US Congress passed a similar law against trafficking that was attached to the Violence against Women Act (VAWA), called the Trafficking Victims Protection Act (TVPA). The law has been revised and renewed several times, most recently in 2013. It defines severe forms of trafficking in persons as:

[25] Anne T. Gallagher, *Issue Paper: Abuse of a Position of Vulnerability and other "Means" within the Definition of Trafficking in Persons* (Vienna: UN Office of Drugs and Crime, UNODC, 2012).

[26] Warren, "The 2000 UN Human Trafficking Protocol," 12.

[27] Anne Gallagher, "Improving the Effectiveness of the International Law of Human Trafficking: A Vision for the Future of the US Trafficking in Persons Reports," *Human Rights Review* 12, 1 (2011).

(a) sex trafficking in which a commercial sex act is induced by force, fraud, or coercion, or in which the person induced to perform such act has not attained 18 years of age; or

(b) the recruitment, harboring, transportation, provision, or obtaining of a person for labor or services, through the use of force, fraud, or coercion for the purpose of subjection to involuntary servitude, peonage, debt bondage, or slavery.[28]

While quite similar to the Palermo Protocol, the TVPA does not include "abuse of power or of a position of vulnerability" in the definition of conditions of recruitment. It does specifically mention sex trafficking rather than incorporating it into the broader field of trafficking of (b).

The TVPA law included a mandate to publish annual reports on trafficking in persons that assessed the extent to which countries around the world are working to diminish trafficking. Although the early *TIP Reports*, first published in 2001, focused on the movement of trafficked victims across international borders, the later *TIP Reports* shifted to exploitation rather than movement. The 2012 report says, "A victim need not be physically transported from one location to another in order for the crime to fall within these definitions."[29] People can be considered trafficked if they were born into servitude, previously consented to work for a trafficker, or participated in a crime as a direct result of being trafficked.[30]

The 2012 report recognizes that consent may change over time. It says that initial consent to prostitution does not mean a person is not a victim of trafficking. "A person's initial consent to participate in prostitution is not legally determinative: if one is thereafter held in service through psychological manipulation or physical force, he or she is a trafficking victim and should receive benefits outlined in the Palermo Protocol and applicable domestic laws."[31] As the report says, "At the heart of this phenomenon is the traffickers' goal of exploiting and enslaving their victims and the myriad coercive and deceptive practices they use to do so."[32] Thus, the US approach to trafficking increasingly

[28] United States Department of State, *Trafficking in Persons Report*, 13th edn(Washington, DC: US Department of State, 2013), 8.
[29] United States Department of State, *Trafficking in Persons Report*, 12th edn(Washington, DC: US Department of State, 2012), 8.
[30] *Ibid.*, 33.
[31] *Ibid.*, 33.
[32] *Ibid.*

targets the exploitation of labor rather than recruitment or transportation, paralleling the growing use of the framework of slavery to define trafficking.

Both the UN Protocol and the TVPA limit the conditions under which a person can consent to exploitative labor, despite some differences in the two laws. From the perspective of the anti-prostitution activists, the addition of "abuse of a position of vulnerability" in the UN Protocol expands the scope of conditions under which a person could be considered coerced into prostitution, thus broadening the field of women who are defined as victims of trafficking. From the perspective of sex work advocates, this phrase shrinks the number of women who could be said to consent, since many enter sex work because it is better than something else. Such decisions could well be motivated by being in a position of vulnerability. Should those who enter sex work because they are in a vulnerable position be considered trafficked victims or adults making hard choices? Do they need to be rescued or given better labor rights? Both the UN Protocol and the US TVPA and *Trafficking in Persons Reports* circumscribe the agency of the person entering sex work, but neither attends to the messiness of determining what constitutes consent.

Measuring Responses to Trafficking

With the growth of sex trafficking as a global crisis have come demands for data on the number of trafficking victims. But counting the number of victims requires determining, at least in theory, whether or not they have consented to engaging in prostitution or other forms of exploitative labor or been coerced. It is clearly very difficult to count the number of people in exploitative labor at all, given its illegal and shadowy status, and assessing how they moved into this mode of work is yet more challenging. However, since trafficking victims are defined as those who did not consent to exploitative labor, determining consent is, at least in theory, a fundamental part of the process. For those who see prostitution as inherently exploitative, on the other hand, it is enough to count the number of prostitutes. Whether or not they were forced into prostitution is irrelevant.

The dominant global mechanism for assessing the size and scope of trafficking, the US State Department's *Trafficking in Persons Report*, places very little emphasis on the issue of consent. Although it covers both sex trafficking and labor trafficking, the major concern, especially during the Bush administration (2000–2008), was sex trafficking. During that period, under the influence of conservative religious groups, the office took a strong anti-prostitution stance, defining it as slavery and refusing funding to any organization that did not take an anti-prostitution pledge.[33] Consequently, consent was deemed irrelevant to determining if a person working in commercial sex was trafficked or not.

The United States has been at the forefront of global concern around human trafficking (and sex trafficking in particular) through the TVPA and its Trafficking in Persons initiative, corralling its political and financial wherewithal to influence how other countries respond to the problem.[34] The TVPA law required the US State Department to publish an annual report on the status of efforts by governments across the world to control trafficking. This report, published every year since 2001, uses a system of categorical ranking that differentiates countries by their efforts to prevent trafficking. With a system of carrots and sticks, the United States offers rewards, in the form of high ranks and grants to anti-trafficking NGOs, to countries it deems successful and imposes sanctions on countries that fail to work to improve their trafficking records according to US standards. As of 2013, the report classifies 188 countries according to a four-tiered scale of how well they are working to control trafficking. Initiated by the TVPA, the *TIP Report*, published by the G/TIP office in the State Department, was envisioned as a way for the United States to focus on the efforts of "sending" countries to help stem the flow of trafficked victims into the United States. The law, passed in conjunction with a renewal of the Violence against Women Act, built on experience in combating domestic violence and sexual assault. In addition to the report, the G/TIP office funds many anti-trafficking NGOs. Despite its origins

---

[33] Jayne Huckerby, "United States of America (USA)," in *Collateral Damage: The Impact of Anti-Trafficking Measures on Human Rights Around the World* (Bangkok: Global Alliance Against Traffic in Women, 2007), 230–56, 237; Elizabeth Bernstein, "Sexual Politics of the New Abolitionism: Imagery and Activism in Contemporary Anti-Trafficking Campaigns," *Differences: Journal of Feminist Cultural Studies* 18, 3 (2007): 128–51.

[34] Janie Chuang, "The United States as Global Sheriff: Using Unilateral Sanctions to Combat Global Trafficking," *Michigan Journal of International Law* 27 (2006): 437–94, 438.

in concerns about women trafficked for sex work, it has increasingly
focused on all forms of forced labor, recently expanding to include
child soldiers. In addition to ranking countries' efforts to control trafficking, the annual reports offer estimates of the size of the trafficked
population.[35]

The TVPA law sets minimum standards for the elimination of trafficking which are the responsibility of governments. The minimum
standards specify government obligations to prohibit severe forms
of trafficking and punish acts of trafficking, prescribe punishment
commensurate with that for grave crimes for both sex trafficking
and other forms of trafficking in persons – punishment that is sufficiently stringent to deter and that adequately reflects the heinous
nature of the offense – and to make "serious and sustained efforts
to eliminate severe forms of trafficking in persons."[36] Clearly, these
standards rely on vague and unspecified terms such as "severe" and
"grave."

The act then lists eleven factors to be considered as indicia of serious
and sustained efforts by governments. The first one specifies investigation, prosecution, conviction, and sentences for principal actors
in serious cases of trafficking, with a failure to provide information
creating the presumption that such efforts have not been made. The
second one requires the government to protect victims and ensure that
they are not inappropriately incarcerated, fined, or otherwise penal-
ized, which includes training of police on approaches that focus on
the needs of the victims. Other indicia are public education, cooperation with other governments, extradition of traffickers, monitoring
immigration and emigration for evidence of trafficking, prosecution of
complicit public officials, progress over the previous year, and efforts
to reduce demand for commercial sex and international sex tourism.[37]
Thus, the law sets out general principles for state action and develops
a series of more specific indices, most of which center on prosecution.
The underlying assumption is that the criminal justice system is the
best way to stop trafficking, and the reports talk mostly about prosecution and law enforcement rather than the complex set of conditions
under which people move into exploitative labor. Although they offer

[35] US Department of State, *Trafficking in Persons Report 2013*, 46.
[36] *Ibid.*, 410–11.
[37] *Ibid.*

estimates of the number of victims, there is little information about the source of the estimates.

The *TIP Report* uses these indicators to assess the performance of countries, providing a brief narrative for each one as well as ranking them into three tiers based on their compliance with minimum standards established in the TVPA law, with Tier 1 being the most compliant. A fourth tier, the Tier 2 watch list, was added in 2004. Countries that fall into Tier 3 face the possibility of sanctions by the United States, while a 2008 amendment consigns those ranked in the Tier 2 watch list for two consecutive years, beginning in 2009, to Tier 3 for the next year, unless there is a presidential waiver.[38] Sanctions include withdrawal of non-humanitarian aid and non-trade related foreign assistance, exclusion of government employees from funding for cultural and educational exchange programs, and opposition by the United States to assistance from international financial institutions such as the IMF and the World Bank.[39] However, sanctions may be waived by the US president if they are not in the national interest, including security interests, or if they would harm vulnerable populations such as women and children. Until 2010, the United States did not rank itself, but in response to global complaints, has now started to do so.[40]

Although the *TIP Reports* promote the three "p's" – prosecution, protection, and prevention – the major focus of the report is prosecution. Since 2004, the *TIP Report* has provided the annual numbers of prosecutions, convictions, victims identified, and new or amended legislation.[41] In 2013, this data was presented in tables both at the global level and regionally, divided into six regions, for the previous six years.[42] The tables describe prosecution and conviction figures, not the number of visas issued to trafficked people, the number who have found other livelihoods, or the number of people who received legal permission to travel and work so that they did not have to move illegally.

[38] United States Department of State, *Trafficking in Persons Report*, 10th edn(Washington, DC: US Department of State, 2010), 25.
[39] US Department of State, *Trafficking in Persons Report 2013*, 47.
[40] See US Department of State, *Trafficking in Persons Report 2010*, 1; Gallagher, "Improving the Effectiveness of the International Law of Human Trafficking."
[41] See US Department of State, *Trafficking in Persons Report 2013*, 46.
[42] *Ibid.*, 46, 57–62.

Such systems of measurement homogenize the complex populations of people who become victims of exploitative labor situations,
as well as the traffickers who take them there. Research on trafficking
has shown great variability in how and under what conditions people
become involved in forced labor and who is responsible for getting
them there.[43] The definitions discussed in the previous section conceptualize a victim of trafficking as a person who has not consented to his
or her labor situation. However, the question of whether or not a victim has consented is often difficult to answer. It inevitably takes place
within a social context in which a person must choose among a range
of options, the costs and benefits of which are socially, economically,
and sometimes culturally specified. Sex work may seem better than
starvation or living with a sexually abusive parent or violent partner.
A person may agree to travel to a city for sex work because she has
been invited by a friend to join her in an adventure. A person may
migrate and undertake miserable work to taste the excitement of the
city, provide support for family at home, or participate in modern consumer culture – or all of these together. The costs and benefits of going
clearly differ among differently situated people. Ethnographic studies
of sex work in India,[44] South Korea,[45] and Laos[46] all show that the
journey into sex work is a complicated blend of consent and coercion.

Both of the major trafficking laws specify that a child cannot
consent to exploitative labor, pegging the end of childhood at age
eighteen. However, societies differ greatly in the age at which they
understand a child to become an adult. For purposes of establishing
strong global standards, it is important to fix the age of adulthood;

---

[43] E.g., Laura Maria Agustin, *Sex at the Margins: Migration, Labour Markets,
and the Rescue Industry* (New York: Zed Books, 2007); Cheng, "The Traffic
in 'Trafficked Filipinas'"; Cheng, *On the Move for Love*; Molland, *The Perfect
Business?*; Denise Brennan, *What's Love Got to Do With It? Transnational
Desires and Sex Tourism in the Dominican Republic* (Durham, NC: Duke
University Press, 2005); Denise Brennan, *Life Interrupted: Trafficking into
Forced Labor in the United States* (Durham, NC: Duke University Press,
2014); Prabha Kotiswaran, "Born Unto Brothels: Toward a Legal Ethnography
of Sex Work in an Indian Red-Light Area," *Law & Social Inquiry* 33, 3
(2008): 579–629; Prabha Kotiswaran, *Dangerous Sex, Invisible Labor: Sex
Work and the Law in India* (Princeton: Princeton University Press, 2011); Svati
Shah, *Street Corner Secrets: Sex, Work, and Migration in the City of Mumbai*
(Durham, NC: Duke University Press, 2014).
[44] Kotiswaran, *Dangerous Sex, Invisible Labor*; Shah, *Street Corner Secrets*.
[45] Cheng, *On the Move for Love*.
[46] Molland, *The Perfect Business?*

yet, even determining a person's age, in the absence of documentation such as birth registration or other forms of identification, is difficult. When police and NGOs carry out brothel and workplace raids, in theory they can rescue anyone under eighteen, but making this determination is clearly difficult. Some people do not themselves know their numerical age and have no documented proof of it. This difficulty is rarely discussed in *TIP Reports* or other efforts to count the number of people who are trafficked.

Similarly, a "trafficker" is not a uniform entity who can be easily identified and prosecuted. A trafficker may be the head of a major organized crime ring, a diplomat bringing a domestic worker to another country, a former victim of trafficking who has learned to manipulate the system for herself, or a neighbor or relative of the person who is trafficked. In her study of trafficking in Southern and Eastern Europe, Rebecca Surtees points out that the dominant image of the typical trafficker tends to be a middle-aged man, unknown to the victim, who deceives her and traffics her into prostitution. In reality, however, Surtees finds that traffickers are far more diverse than represented in media and information campaigns. Traffickers include not only men but also women. Some were women who were encouraged by their recruiter/trafficker to invite their friends to work abroad also but were unaware of the intention to exploit. Other female recruiters were victims of trafficking who were obliged by their traffickers to return home and recruit other women, often under the scrutiny of people working for the trafficker to ensure compliance and prevent escape. Traffickers often promised to free victims if they could find someone to replace them. Some women may eventually develop affinity with their traffickers and become recruiters.[47]

Within this highly varied and complex world of trafficking and forced labor, the *TIP Report* seeks to build a coherent, global framework which defines the phenomenon and enables comparisons among countries about their efforts to combat these practices. The report presents its policy in terms of American values. It has adopted the language of slavery and freedom to describe trafficked victims,[48] often

[47] Rebecca Surtees, "Traffickers and Trafficking in Southern and Eastern Europe: Considering the Other Side of Human Trafficking," *European Journal of Criminology* 5, 1 (2008): 39–68, 44–5.

[48] Broadly deployed even in media and activist narratives, e.g., see Bales, "Slavery and the Human Right to Evil"; Kristof, "Slavery in our Time."

drawing close parallels between the United States' emancipation of
slaves and the current effort to free victims of trafficking. This framing of trafficking eliminates the question of consent, since a slave by
definition lacks freedom and is forced into that status. Rhetorically,
it frames the contemporary anti-trafficking movement within the historic US abolitionist movement and replicates the narratives of heroic
rescue and freedom of an earlier era. The 2010 report draws explicit
linkages between the abolition of slavery and the contemporary anti-
trafficking movement, including a quote from Frederic Douglass[49] and
a bill of release from slavery from 1819 in Virginia and from 2007
in India, where the incidence of bonded labor is assumed – without
analysis – to be the same as slavery.[50] The 2012 report's introduction, titled "The Promise of Freedom," noted that the American fight
against modern slavery stretched back to its historic fight against slavery and that the year 2012 was the 150th anniversary of Lincoln's
Emancipation Proclamation.[51] "A century and a half later, slavery
persists in the United States and around the globe, and many victims' stories remain sadly similar to those of the past." The report
estimates that there are as many as twenty-seven million victims of
trafficking worldwide and that the work of combating trafficking is
"fulfilling the promise of freedom: freedom from slavery for those
exploited and the freedom for survivors to carry on with their lives."
The report continues that this is now an international promise as
well, citing Article 4 of the Universal Declaration of Human Rights
and the Palermo Protocol.[52]

The 2013 *TIP Report* continues this theme, calling all forms of trafficking in persons modern slavery and connecting its work to the historic American fight against slavery and search for freedom.[53] In July
2013, the Ambassador at Large of the Office to Monitor and Combat
Trafficking, Luis CdeBaca, noted that the linkage between human trafficking and the fight against modern slavery had made it through the
transitions between the Clinton, Bush, and Obama administrations –

[49] US Department of State, *Trafficking in Persons Report 2010*, 5.
[50] *Ibid.*, 33.
[51] US Department of State, *Trafficking in Persons Report 2012*, 7.
[52] *Ibid.*, 7.
[53] US Department of State, *Trafficking in Persons Report 2013*, 7.

"I think this shows it is a bipartisan fight, it's quintessentially an American fight."[54]

In sum, the US *TIP Report* uses a criminal justice framework based on counting prosecutions and convictions to assess state compliance with a framework for trafficking based on American concepts of slavery. It allows a minimal space for consent, especially for commercial sex work, and takes a strongly protectionist approach based on state intervention. In the process of doing so, it inevitably homogenizes the complex set of motivations, conditions, and contexts within which individuals become involved in the kinds of labor defined as exploitative. Global comparison and quantification require such simplification.[55] Yet, a framework that ignores the possibility of consent to poor labor conditions turns policy in particular directions. In order to protect victims without agency – slaves – it promotes prosecution of traffickers. The failure to acknowledge consent steers policy away from approaches that build on alternative preferences and efforts, such as improved regulation of labor conditions, prosecution of employers, changing travel regulations that permit legal travel, or the development of more attractive work options. Instead, it encourages paternalistic policies that offer help but ignore the range of conditions under which people enter exploitative labor and the possibilities of navigating these situations. When paternalistic humanitarianism turns to the criminal justice system, it produces greater surveillance of young women and sometimes boys, more substantial authority by police and border patrol to stop and question, and the potential for more frequent state intervention into the lives of the poor and marginalized.

As we will see in the next section, in practice, sex trafficking incorporates a highly differentiated and contextually varied set of practices in which consent and coercion are deeply intertwined. Failure to recognize these complexities contributes to interventions that are paternalistic and that promote control as well as care.

[54] US Department of State, "Technology as a Tool in the Fight Against Human Trafficking," July 24, 2013, www.state.gov/r/pa/pl/cwa/212411.htm (accessed November 9, 2015).
[55] See Sally Engle Merry, "Measuring the World: Indicators, Human Rights, and Global Governance," *Current Anthropology* 52, no. S3 (2011): S83–S95; Sally Engle Merry, *The Seductions of Quantification: Measuring Human Rights, Gender Violence, and Sex Trafficking* (Chicago: University of Chicago Press, 2016).

Sex Trafficking in Practice

Clearly, in practice, consent is a murky issue. Sociological and anthropological research on sex work and trafficking shows that there are a wide range of factors that bring a woman into sex work and keep her there or allow her to move out. The move into sex work can be a complicated set of decisions which varies greatly by context. People may migrate in search of a job and end up doing sex work in exploitative conditions. A person's entry into sex work may be the enactment of a family tradition or caste-based practice, as in some parts of India,[56] or it may be a slippery slope from a few sexual encounters to a permanent mode of survival. Moving to a new location to do sex work is often a way to escape poverty, starvation, or an abusive family situation. But, as some researchers have shown, it can also be the product of a desire to travel and experience new places.[57] Sealing Cheng's study of Filipina entertainers in South Korea shows a complex series of paths by which women move into sexual labor, sometimes through friends or through the desire for money.[58] Their desires range from supporting their children to acquiring the consumer goods such as make-up and clothes that mark modernity. Cheng describes how many women who move for sex work hope to marry a man richer than those available at home, possibly allowing them to stay in the country where they worked or to go with them to their home country, such as the United States. Anthropologists have explored critical links between sex work and migration choices involving intimate partnerships,[59] global and local labor markets, and kinship networks,[60] offering multiple ways of understanding the identities and strategies sex workers engage with along a spectrum of socio-economic choices and constraints. The status of coerced worker can also change over time. As Prabha Kotiswaran shows in Kolkata, India, some brothels use trafficked women while others rely

---

[56] Anuja Agrawal, *Chaste Wives and Prostitute Sisters: Patriarchy and Prostitution among the Bedias of India* (New Delhi: Routledge, 2008).

[57] Agustin, *Sex at the Margins.*

[58] Cheng, *On the Move for Love.*

[59] Brennan, *What's Love Got to Do With It?*

[60] Kay B. Warren, "Troubling the Victim/Trafficker Dichotomy in Efforts to Combat Human Trafficking: The Unintended Consequences of Moralizing Labor Migration," *Indiana Journal of Global Legal Studies* 19, 1 (2012): 105–20.

more on local women.[61] Women can move from brothels that use trafficked women to those of local women over time, and gradually become property owners and rent to other sex workers. Some will eventually become brothel owners and may even work in running trafficking networks themselves.

Vibhuti Ramachandran found in her research in Mumbai that the police and judicial magistrates sometimes struggled to discern whether the Bangladeshi women rescued from brothels there were victims, illegal immigrants, or traffickers themselves. Sometimes, the same person had experiences that could fit into each of these categories. It was also observed that some women traveled back and forth between Bangladesh and India repeatedly. They were not necessarily victims of trafficking, though the factors leading to consensual or coerced border-crossing usually overlapped. Sverre Molland describes a similar pattern of movement and ambiguity along the Thai/Lao border.[62]

During rescue operations, it is often difficult to distinguish between trafficked victims and consenting sex workers. One solution is to focus on rescuing children, who according to the UN Protocol cannot consent to trafficking. However, it is often hard to know the age of young people, who typically lack reliable documents of their age. In our research in India in 2010, NGO activists working in the anti-trafficking field told us that those who are trafficked from villages rarely have reliable birth certificates or identity documents. In Kolkata, the courts and NGOs relied on bone ossification tests to determine a girl's age, using a doctor's certification to validate the test. However, the test cannot precisely pinpoint age and may vary by as much as two years.[63] Thus, it is impossible to determine precisely which women in a brothel are adults, and could consent, and which are children and, by definition, cannot.

In India, we found that those who introduced a woman to the sex trade were often relatives, neighbors, or friends. Once she has started working in commercial sex, a woman may have the opportunity to improve her situation. At a women's shelter in Mumbai, Ramachandran met a woman from Delhi whose friend had convinced her that she was

---

[61] Kotiswaran, "Born Unto Brothels."
[62] Molland, *The Perfect Business?*
[63] Jaisingh P. Modi, *A Textbook of Medical Jurisprudence and Toxicology* (Nagpur: LexisNexis Butterworths Wadhwa, 2013), 147.

"spoilt goods" after an affair with a man who was already married and took her to Mumbai knowing that she would provide him with sexual services. In this case, there was some degree of consent as well as some deception in the way she was recruited, making the distinction between trafficking and migration quite slippery. The spaces and conditions of the brothels to which the woman was initially taken were miserable, until she reached a point where she could contract herself out. She moved to a different location and started getting rich clients from the Gulf who lavished gold and fancy cell phones on her. She was planning to select one of them as a husband at the time her brothel was raided by the police and she was sent to a shelter.

People migrate both for sex work and for other kinds of work. A migrant may intend to take on one kind of work and find herself in the other, or go back and forth between both sex work and other forms of work depending on circumstances.[64] The line between labor migrants, sex work migrants, and victims of sex trafficking is vague and ambiguous. Sex trafficking is not easily distinguished from smuggling, forced labor migration, or traveling as bonded or contract labor. In practice, it is difficult to distinguish between voluntary and coerced migration, as people move under varying degrees of coercion.

Rescue is often promoted by anti-trafficking activists and legal frameworks (described in the previous section) as a solution for trafficked persons, particularly for women engaged in sex work. Like systems of measurement, rescue projects assume a greater degree of homogeneity than exists in practice. Many of the prominent US anti-trafficking groups, inspired by an interesting coalition of secular radical feminists and Christian faith-based groups, use the language of freedom to stage rescues from brothels and restore women to their families and/or facilitate their rehabilitation in low-wage service work.[65] The "rescue industry"[66]

---

[64] Agustin, *Sex at the Margins*; Kamala Kempadoo, "The Migrant Tightrope: Experiences from the Caribbean," in *Global Sex Workers: Rights, Resistance, and Redefinition, eds.* Kamala Kempadoo and Jo Doezema (New York: Routledge, 1998); Svati Shah, "Solicitation, Migration and Day Wage Labor: Gender, Sexuality and Negotiating Work in the City," in *Poverty, Gender and Migration,* eds. Sadhna Arya and Anupama Roy (New Delhi: Sage Publications, 2006); Shah, *Street Corner Secrets.*

[65] Bernstein, "Sexual Politics of the New Abolitionism"; Gretchen Soderlund, "Running from the Rescuers: New US Crusades against Sex Trafficking and the Rhetoric of Abolition," *NSWA Journal* 17, 3 (2005): 64–87.

[66] Agustin, *Sex at the Margins.*

is clearly paternalistic. Some NGOs, including faith-based ones, see rescue as part of their mission of redemption, a paternalistic project aided by the power of God and prayer. An installation on trafficking on display in New York City in 2010 dramatically represented the aspirations of rescue work for first-world audiences, incorporating the theme of redemption and rebirth. A series of box cars led the visitor first into a room with pictures of ordinary women, including a mirror where the visitor could see herself as one of such women, showing that anyone could be trafficked. After passing through a room designed to look like a brothel bedroom, the visitor walked through a dark space into the space of rehabilitation and freedom. The installation power-fully evoked the metaphor of rebirth to describe rescue.

Yet, brothel raids are difficult, women do not always wish to be res-cued, and many escape from the shelters where they are held pending their return home, rehabilitation, and/or testifying against traffickers.[67] In India, such raids are typically conducted by the police with NGO rep-resentatives present to provide counseling for the victims, which often entails encouraging them to testify against their traffickers. Shelters may hold women in prison-like conditions to prevent their return to sex work, to protect them from pimps and traffickers, and/or to ensure they will testify against their traffickers. Although ideally they are repatriated, in Kolkata we were told that it was difficult to repatriate Bangladeshi women across the border because the Bangladeshi government is unco-operative about receiving them. Besides, many women want to stay on in India and explore economic opportunities there (whether in sex work or through domestic work or other forms of labor). Both Indian and Bangladeshi women often spend months or longer at shelters in Kolkata and Mumbai, pending bureaucratic delays in releasing them or the lack of alternative dwellings or job prospects, prolonging many women's frustration at being rescued. Rescued women can be detained at these sites for long periods because of delays in medical examinations and court processes.[68] There are delays in the process by which NGOs, courts, and police determine the women's home backgrounds and the suitability of their families to be appropriate guardians. According to

[67] See Cheng, *On the Move for Love*; Soderlund, "Running from the Rescuers."
[68] Ratna Kapur, "India," in *Collateral Damage: The Impact of Anti-Trafficking Measures on Human Rights Around the World*, ed. Mike Dottridge (Bangkok: Global Alliance Against Traffic in Women, 2007), 114–42, 123.

the Indian law on "immoral traffic," this procedure is to be followed even for adult women.[69] This is a telling instance of paternalism, since it sees the women as non-agents, whose well-being lies in either state protective custody or the assumed idyllic life (and patriarchal protection) of their family lives back home. During a visit to a shelter in Kolkata where rescued women were taken, we found many of the women very eager to leave, but court orders and the NGO that ran it prohibited them from doing so. There are several reports of women escaping or going "missing" from government shelters in India.

Ethnographically, it is unclear what happens to rescued women. They are portrayed in general as being repatriated and/or rehabilitated, but the scant data available suggests that this is again an overly homogeneous picture. There is little information available about the rehabilitation dimensions of rescue work, as the women typically disappear.[70] Even if repatriated to another country, many return, often because of the same pressures that drove them to move in the first place. This tendency to return does not necessarily mean that these women would not prefer a different kind of work, but it may be that sex work may be the best or only available option. Cheng's depiction of migrant women's return home to the Philippines shows clearly how the pressures of money to support children and family, along with the desire for the consumer goods that mark modernity, drive women back into migration for entertainment and sex work.[71]

Along with rescues, prosecution is a major component of the solutions that the dominant legal frameworks discussed in the previous section prescribe to combat trafficking. Given the global push toward prosecution initiated by the UN Office on Drugs and Crime and the US State Department, NGOs consider rescued women valuable as key witnesses against traffickers. In cases of trafficking across national borders, it is common to require their participation in prosecution as

[69] Immoral Traffic (Prevention) Act, Statute No. 104 (India: Universal Law Publishing Co. Pvt. Ltd., 1956), Sect. 17.

[70] Kay B. Warren, "The Illusiveness of Counting 'Victims' and the Concreteness of Ranking Countries: Trafficking in Persons from Columbia to Japan," in *Sex, Drugs, and Body Counts: The Politics of Numbers in Global Crime and Conflict*, eds. Peter Andreas and Kelly M. Greenhill (Ithaca: Cornell University Press, 2010), 110–26; Warren, "Troubling the Victim/Trafficker Dichotomy in Efforts to Combat Human Trafficking."

[71] Cheng, *On the Move for Love*, 166–91.

the price of remaining in the country from which they were rescued.[72] As a result, some rescue-oriented NGOs focus on working with victims and training them to testify in court. In a conversation with representatives of a faith-based anti-trafficking group in India in 2010, we were told that rescued women were eager to testify against their traffickers and that the organization offered them training and support to testify. Some stayed in shelters when they testified, while others were repatriated to their homes and families and then brought back by the police and NGOs to testify against a trafficker.[73]

As Anne Gallagher and Elaine Pearson point out, a rights-based approach to trafficking demands that victims of trafficking be treated as more than criminal justice resources or as passive recipients of assistance.[74] Recognizing that the terms "victim" and "witness" should not be automatically equated, some scholars have called for an alternate approach to victim protection that does not mandate cooperation with law enforcement and prosecution.[75] While many women who migrate would like to stay in the country they have traveled to, this option is rarely available and if it is, often depends on helping to prosecute the trafficker.[76] In the United States, for example, trafficked persons are only eligible for immigration relief if they assist law enforcement or comply with "reasonable requests" to assist in investigation and prosecution.[77] The United States provides T visas to victims of trafficking, but fewer than half the annual allotment of 5,000 T visas a year have been approved since 2002.[78] In order to receive a T visa, which has nonimmigrant status, a person has to provide evidence that he/she was

[72] Global Alliance Against Traffic in Women, *Collateral Damage*.
[73] Occasionally, women have testified through video-conferencing. We heard of two such instances in Mumbai and Delhi.
[74] Anne Gallagher and Elaine Pearson, *Detention of Trafficked Persons in Shelters: A Legal and Policy Analysis*, Asia Regional Trafficking in Persons Project, 2008, http://ssrn.com/abstract=1239745 or http://dx.doi.org/10.2139/ssrn.1239745, 26.
[75] Hussain Sadruddin, Natalia Walter, and Jose Hidalgo, "Human Trafficking in the United States: Expanding Victim Protection Beyond Prosecution Witnesses," *Stanford Law & Policy Review* 16, 2 (2005): 379–416.
[76] Dina Francesca Haynes, "Used, Abused, Arrested and Deported: Extending Immigration Benefits to Protect the Victims of Trafficking and to Secure the Prosecution of Traffickers," *Human Rights Quarterly* 26 (2004): 221–72.
[77] Huckerby, "United States of America (USA)," 243.
[78] US State Department, *Trafficking in Persons Report 2012*, 15.

a victim of trafficking, is willing to cooperate with law enforcement in prosecuting traffickers (except for minors or especially traumatized victims), and would suffer extreme harm if removed from the United States.[79] Similarly, Australia offers assistance and rights to remain to those potentially useful in providing evidence to prosecute traffickers.[80] Sweden, a leader in criminalizing customers, extends limited residence rights to trafficking victims willing to testify against their traffickers.[81] The Netherlands offers an initial short visa to a trafficked victim to allow her to decide if she will testify against her trafficker and a longer one to those who agree to testify. The longer visa lasts until the end of the trial.[82] Thus, the ability to stay longer in the country to which a person has been trafficked is rarely permanent and is often contingent on assisting with prosecuting traffickers. However, there is often a gap between what criminal justice authorities want from trafficked women and what trafficked women are able and willing to give in light of the dangers posed to them if they agree to cooperate in a criminal investigation.[83]

Feminist critics of the new regime of anti-trafficking activism argue that it has increased the control that states and NGOs exercise over women and their expression of sexuality in the name of protection.[84] Sociologist Jennifer Musto argues that advocacy efforts to protect trafficked persons have been appropriated by the criminal justice system, merging the efforts of NGOs and law enforcement and creating a regime of "carceral protectionism" that joins criminal justice and social service interventions.[85] The approach of the *TIP Report*,

---

[79] *Ibid.*

[80] Elaine Pearson, "Australia," in *Collateral Damage: The Impact of Anti-Trafficking Measures on Human Rights Around the World* (Bangkok: Global Alliance Against Traffic in Women, 2007), 28–61, 29.

[81] Janet Halley, Prabha Kotiswaran, Hila Shamir, and Chantal Thomas, "From the International to the Local in Feminist Legal Responses to Rape, Prostitution/Sex Work, and Sex Trafficking: Four Studies in Contemporary Governance Feminism," *Harvard Journal of Law and Gender* 29, 2 (2006): 335–423, 396.

[82] *Ibid.*, 399.

[83] Jo Goodey, "Sex Trafficking in Women from Central and East European Countries: Promoting a 'Victim-Centred' and 'Woman-Centred' Approach to Criminal Justice Intervention," *Feminist Review* 76 (2004): 26–45.

[84] Ali Miller, "Sexuality, Violence Against Women, and Human Rights: Women Make Demands and Ladies Get Protection," *Health and Human Rights* 7, 2 (2004): 17–47.

[85] Jennifer Lynne Musto, *Institutionalizing Protection, Professionalizing Victim Management: Explorations of Multi-Professional Anti-Trafficking Efforts in the Netherlands and the United States* (Ph.D. dissertation in Women's Studies, University of California/Los Angeles, 2011).

blending its concern with victims' protection and prosecution of trafficking, embodies this approach to anti-trafficking. If the focus is on apprehending and convicting traffickers, victims will inevitably be subject to various forms of control.

Feminist legal scholars have coined the term "governance feminism" to describe the way certain feminists have moved into positions of political power to become part of political institutions, often working with civil society organizations or through litigation.[86] Halley *et al.* argue that governance feminism can be counterproductive for feminist concerns, as it validates a law enforcement approach due to their close alignment with a securitized state apparatus. In the context of sex trafficking, Halley *et al.* argue that through its conflation of prostitution with sex trafficking and sexual slavery, the governance feminist approach erases questions of labor and migration and reduces the issue to one that can be resolved by better policing. The equation of prostitution, trafficking, and slavery shrinks the space of consent so that sex workers are defined as victims rather than criminals, needing rescue rather than prosecution, but still denied the possibility of making their own choices. Nevertheless, governance feminist work on trafficking retains a paternalist approach, denying consent and focusing on control as much as care, but now carried forward by women as well as men. In contrast, the human rights approach that focuses on the well-being and choice of the victims puts greater focus on care, and could be described as a maternalist approach.

Paternalism and Nationalism

Underlying the paternalistic concern with protecting women's sexuality is a preoccupation with women's bodies as representatives of national identity and virtue. Why this nationalist concern has expanded to women from the global South is clearly an important question, perhaps related to the global expansion of empathy and humanitarianism, along with older ideas of the reformist capacity of the West embedded in imperialist ideas of rescue and uplift along with ideas of human rights protection.[87] The idea that women's bodies are

[86] Halley *et al.*, "From the International to the Local in Feminist Legal Responses to Rape, Prostitution/Sex Work, and Sex Trafficking."
[87] See further Nandita Sharma, "Anti-Trafficking Rhetoric and the Making of a Global Apartheid," *NSWA Journal* 17, 3 (2005): 88–111.

central to the identity of the nation and should be subjected to its patriarchal control has a long history. In late colonial Britain, the anxieties evoked by the figure of the "white slave," centered on the sexual violation of women's bodies, mapped on to equally trenchant concerns about regulating national borders and racial identities. The rising number of unaccompanied white women engaged in sexual labor in the British colonies threatened the stability of the racialized control of sexual relations in imperial expansion.[88] In the United States, the understanding of "white slavery" that informed anti-prostitution activism in the Progressive Era was based on concerns around the sexual violation of women's bodies. Middle-class abolitionist feminists in the United States were, like their British counterparts, invested in "rescuing" women in prostitution, while male purity reformers in the Progressive Era, as was the case in late colonial Britain, were concerned with the moral opprobrium "fallen women" might augur for American society.[89]

In India, as Partha Chatterjee argues, the middle-class nationalist Indian imagination of the woman as embodying the nation, as carrying the spiritual Indian tradition, was tied to the emergence of an Indian nationalism opposed to British colonial critiques of the "degenerate and barbaric" traditions of treating Indian women.[90] Veena Das describes the way India and Pakistan adopted a protectionist attitude toward women's sexuality during the post-Partition era in India.[91] In response to the widespread abduction of women by both sides during the war between India and Pakistan in 1947, along with allegations of forced conversions between Hinduism and Islam as women were abducted across religious lines, both states took responsibility for restoring these women to their original homes. Das argues that restoration of women and children became a matter of national honor, a state responsibility, rather than a question of women's own choices. Social workers sent women home

---

[88] Philippa Levine, *Prostitution, Race, and Politics: Policing Venereal Disease in the British Empire* (London: Routledge, 2003).

[89] Ruth Rosen, *The Lost Sisterhood: Prostitution in America 1900–1918* (Baltimore: Hopkins Press, 1982).

[90] Partha Chatterjee, "Colonialism, Nationalism, and Colonized Women: The Contest in India," *American Ethnologist* 16 (1989): 622–34, 622.

[91] Veena Das, *Life and Words: Violence and the Descent into the Ordinary* (Berkeley: University of California Press, 2007), 22–5.

even when they wanted to stay with men they had married and their children. The social workers felt that they knew better than the women themselves what the women wanted, but were also following national "Recovery" legislation. Administrative systems, including social workers, were empowered to return women to their families even when they did not wish to be returned. In this alliance between social work as a profession and the state as *parens patriae*, kinship norms of honor and purity were transformed into the law of the state.[92] Upholding the honor of women became the duty of the "civilized" state. The laws on abduction and restoration constructed the nation as a social contract between men acting to uphold the order of the household.[93] Ratna Kapur suggests that anxieties over the abduction and forced movement of women during the Partition continue to inform conflations between migrant workers and victims of trafficking in the anti-trafficking discourse of the post-colonial Indian nation-state.[94] It was as a protégée of the family and the state, and not as a migrant (whose movement might have entailed complex experiences including some elements of both consent and coercion), that the women displaced during the Partition were acknowledged as part of the Indian nation-state. Kapur draws a connection between Partition-era attitudes to gendered migration and the current reluctance of the Indian state to recognize the possibility of women being willing migrants.

In these cases, the protection of women's sexuality is translated into the need for nations to exercise control over their sexuality in order to appear "civilized." While not denying the violence and suffering sex trafficking causes, it seems likely that the preoccupation with controlling sex trafficking resonates with the above concerns as well as with ending the suffering of victims. Sex trafficking is perceived as both an abuse of women and an assault on paternalistic control over women's sexuality. However, in the Partition era and thereafter, it is important to recognize that even women who have been victimized may choose not to be rescued by a state that presumes to protect them.

---

[92] *Ibid.*, 25.
[93] *Ibid.*
[94] Ratna Kapur, *Makeshift Migrants and Law: Gender, Belonging, and Postcolonial Anxieties* (New York: Routledge, 2010), 7.

Conclusion

It is clearly important to consider to what extent policies toward victims of sex trafficking are paternalistic as well as humanitarian. One dimension of the paternalistic nature of the anti-trafficking movement is its focus on women and the sex trade. Although there are currently efforts to expand trafficking to include labor trafficking, the situation of women and girls still dominates the law and social movements. In South Asia, the dominant protocol against trafficking, the SAARC convention, applies only to sex trafficking. This emphasis conforms to the prevailing interest in protecting women's sexuality. Clearly, there is an undercurrent of paternalism in the choice of what constitutes a violation and where women's agency lies. The tendency to see women's bodies as symbolic of national honor reinforces the idea that the violation of a woman's sexuality is a violation of the nation.

US global interventions to save "Third World" women are a strange mix of imperialist impulse and a faith-based will to protect women's sexuality. Protecting women has considerable political power. The US invasion of Afghanistan was fueled in part by images of burqa-clad women who needed to be rescued and freed by the masculinist US state. As women are perceived as carriers of national identity and as their sexually vulnerable bodies appear violated and in need of protection by such a state, intervention becomes a national – and global – necessity. Agency disappears, and consent is irrelevant. Rescue is an obligation, and even if this involves preventing victims from making their own choices or subjecting them to increased surveillance in the name of protection, it seems worth it. As Kipling points out, the hero seeking to uplift the colonized may only be appreciated in his home country.

The technologies of measurement adopted by the US *TIP Reports* reinforce such simplified and coherent modes of thinking about trafficking. The system cannot accommodate the complexity of modes of trafficking and exploitation if it is to produce comparable data.[95] The question of consent is submerged in order to generate quantitative data on the extent and nature of the problem. This tendency toward homogenization in a system of measurement contributes to the paternalistic nature of interventions by its inability to assess the range of forms of coercion at play, their changes over time, and the

---

[95] See, Merry, *The Seductions of Quantification.*

need for a more wide-ranging and varied set of interventions. Under these conditions, interventions paint too broad a stroke and increase control without sufficient attention to agency. The TIP country rankings, which are credited with inspiring some countries to act more energetically to stem trafficking, fail to distinguish between degrees of coercion of victims or the extent of their consent. Moreover, the pressure to report prosecutions diminishes victim agency, since they must choose between staying and testifying or being deported.

In sum, our examination of the anti-trafficking movement suggests that the conversion of ambiguous data about complex social processes into unambiguous numbers and simplified narratives of capture, rescue, and prosecution has succeeded in eliciting paternalistic responses from the international community but by ignoring spaces of agency and consent, has increased paternalistic control in the name of humanitarianism.

8 | Modernity at the Cutting Edge: Human Rights Meets FGM

STEPHEN HOPGOOD

On the face of it, there is no cultural practice that demands international paternalism more than female genital mutilation/cutting (FGM/C).[1] It seems a paradigm case of "hard paternalism" where intervention is justified regardless of the wishes of those undergoing the cutting and those carrying it out.[2] In other words, for all but the most hardened cultural relativists, the practice of cutting the clitorises off prepubescent girls in their millions is indefensible. FGM/C trespasses on several deeply held norms treasured by liberals, stimulating the urge to protect the autonomy and integrity of the innocent person threatened by actions deemed barbaric (i.e., based in ignorance and tradition) and therefore the antithesis of the enlightened modern. Recall Gerald Dworkin's influential definition of paternalism, "interference with a person's liberty of action justified by reasons referring exclusively to the welfare, good, happiness, needs, interests or values of the person being coerced."[3] Could there be a better test case for this sort of paternalism than FGM/C, especially because children are its victims? The quintessential nineteenth-century liberal, John Stuart Mill, acknowledged three exceptions to the restriction on interfering with people's liberty: preventing harm to others, the protection of children, and what he called "backward states of society."[4] For many abolitionists, FGM/C brings all three of these exceptions together.

But things immediately become more complicated. For a start, intervention in most cases is a three-way relationship: intervener, mother,

---

[1] I discuss the politics of this term later. I mainly use FGM/C except when referring to the practice's most vocal opponents for whom only the acronym "FGM" will do.

[2] Joel Feinberg, *Harm to Self: The Moral Limits of the Criminal Law* (New York: Oxford University Press, 1986), 12.

[3] Gerard Dworkin, "Paternalism," *The Monist* 56, 1 (1972): 65.

[4] John Stuart Mill, *On Liberty* (A Public Domain Book), 7, 39. Also Dworkin, "Paternalism," 76.

child. Children are not only the classic targets of paternalistic action, their interests are the grounds for the claims to rightful authority of *both* interveners and parents.[5] We have, in other words, two competing claimants to the title "legitimate paternalist." The child does not get to define what her interests are; as with any child, her life up to this point has been one act of paternalism after another. She is already self molded by paternalistic acts – parental and social choices (embedded in socio-cultural norms) made for her on the basis that it's "for her own good." Now anti-FGM/C activists arrive to trump parental authority in time to prevent an irrevocable act of what's seen as wrongful paternalism, modifying or removing the child's genitalia, taking place.

To stop FGM/C these external interveners insert their judgment in place of the judgment of the girl's family, in particular her mother.[6] Because we are dealing with a child, the girl's consent (or lack of it) has little social, legal, or moral force.[7] Others compete to define and realize her interests. Given that the dividing line between "hard" and "soft" paternalism is largely about consent (in hard paternalism, whether or not you consented to be circumcised would not matter), and that parents have rightful authority over their daughters and in the majority of active cases continue to circumcise, why does their "consent" (that is, their paternalistic choice for their daughter) lack force? In the case of FGM/C, international paternalism overrules parental paternalism on the basis that cutting daughters is considered "presumptively wrong" because such acts "invasively interfere by transgressing independently specifiable moral principles e.g., it is presumptively wrong to kill, coerce, deceive and so on."[8] In short, FGM/C is considered both morally wrong in and of itself as well as being against the "real interests"

---

[5] Dworkin defines as "impure paternalism" situations ("two-party cases") where those whose liberty is being constrained (in this case mothers and midwives who circumcise) differs from those who will benefit: "Paternalism," 68. Joel Feinberg prefers the term "indirect" to impure; *Harm to Self*, 9–10.

[6] For a discussion of authority including the idea of surrendering one's judgement, see Joseph Raz, *The Morality of Freedom* (Oxford: Clarendon Press, 1988), chs. 3 and 4, and Seana Valentine Schiffrin, "Paternalism, Unconscionability Doctrine, and Accommodation," *Philosophy and Public Affairs* 29 (2000).

[7] See Francis Schrag, "The Child in the Moral Order," *Philosophy* 52, 200 (1977).

[8] Donald VanDeVeer, *Paternalistic Intervention: The Moral Bounds on Benevolence* (Princeton: Princeton University Press, 1986), 21.

of the child (as per Dworkin's definition above). In such a case, parental paternalism ("consent" to FGM/C) carries no weight and hard international paternalism is justified, for advocates, in trumping it. As we will see, this marks the anti-FGM strand of the global anti-FGM/C movement.

Soft paternalism differs from hard paternalism in that it "permits interference only in the absence of voluntariness or genuine consent."[9] This is particularly acute given the irrevocability of FGM/C. As Dworkin puts it:

Some of the decisions we make are of such a character that they produce changes which are in one or another way irreversible. Situations are created in which it is difficult or impossible to return to anything like the initial stage at which the decision was made.[10]

Thus the burden is high when it comes to the question of voluntary action. At the core of the anti-FGM/C campaign is the notion that circumcision is a coercive act, and that mothers who choose it and daughters who more or less willingly submit are both victims of false consciousness about the real interests they had *before* they were socialized to endorse FGM/C. Consent to circumcise can never, in this sense, be taken as genuine. But neither are all anti-FGM/C advocates happy with being labeled paternalists. As a result, significant effort goes into creating conditions in which consent will be forthcoming. Much turns on whether this constructive creation of consent is an offer that can be refused. There is an obvious resource imbalance between well-prepared and informed international interveners and local women. As a result, even at its most sensitive, such an intervention entails a degree, however attenuated, of structural violence (the power to turn up in a village thousands of miles from home and insist on changing long-established social norms). These local women will not be arriving in London or New York any time soon to take a look at how citizens in the United Kingdom and United States treat their children.

---

[9] Feinberg, *Harm to Self*, 15. Feinberg also terms this as "soft anti-paternalism" on the basis that it does not override genuine consent, the classic case of paternalism in action and the one for which he argues the term should be reserved.

[10] Dworkin, "Paternalism," 80.

As a social practice, therefore, and regardless of how we might define it, paternalistic FGM/C elimination cannot evade the context within which it takes place, one where a global set of institutions with a structural power advantage trump local claims to autonomy and parental authority. This is where human rights (and as part of that, women's and children's rights) comes in. Much work on paternalism talks about how a state or society can legitimately treat one of its own members. By claiming we are all citizens of the same universal society, the objection that we have not consented to "the rule of law" is avoided. We are all subject to natural law, and its customary and positivist embodiments, regardless of consent. This reflects a distinction I have made elsewhere between Human Rights and human rights, the former (upper case) universal, global, and monotheistic in voice (natural law), the latter (lower case) bottom-up, interpretive, and flexible in the hands of local people (democracy). Another way to see the generation of local consent by the "soft paternalists" of the FGM/C movement is as a way to make Human Rights into human rights. The end – Human Rights, that is, eliminating FGM/C – is not really negotiable, only the means and the timing of change.[11]

This "state of exception" will last until local people are able to enact their rights *appropriately* for themselves (until Human Rights become human rights). It is reminiscent of the moment Gayatri Chakravorty Spivak describes when "the protection of woman (today the 'third world woman') becomes the signifier for the establishment of a *good* society which must, at such inaugurative moments, transgress mere legality, and equity of legal policy." She goes on: "In this particular case [widow burning or *sati*], the process also allowed the redefinition as a crime what had been tolerated, known or adulated as ritual."[12] In just this way, paternalism trumps existing norms within local society to criminalize and eliminate the ritual of FGM/C in the name of moral progress as well as the good of the child. But soft paternalism goes even further: It creates not just the institutional site for choosing Human Rights (thereby changing behavior), it also seeks to construct (or "free") newly self-aware women who can then see their real

---

[11] See Stephen Hopgood, *The Endtimes of Human Rights* (Ithaca: Cornell University Press, 2013).

[12] Gayatri Chakravorty Spivak, "Can the Subaltern Speak?" in *Marxism and the Interpretation of Culture*, eds. Cary Nelson and Lawrence Grossberg (Urbana: University of Illinois Press, 1988), 271–313.

interests for themselves. There is a strong ideological commitment to the idea of the liberal subject at the heart of soft paternalism, in other words, a subject capable of demanding her right to choose. Once this sense of agency has taken hold, the state of exception can be lifted. To paraphrase Hannah Arendt, you once again have a place in the world and so regain *your right to have rights*.[13] In this way soft paternalism might be construed as more radically invasive than hard paternalism, as a major instance of what Barnett and Duvall call "productive power."[14]

For those, including queer theorists, radical feminists, anthropologists, postcolonialists, and poststructuralists, who are wary of totalizing narratives that justify intervention in the politics of female, African bodies, with all its colonial and patriarchal overtones, this is a problem. We have trodden this route before, say critics.[15] Furthermore, if we take a more radical view of subjectivity with Foucault (that one of power's first effects is to *make the individual*, rather than to act upon already constituted individuals), we see that closing off the option of alternative subjectivities until eighteen, for example, an age long past primary identity formation, makes the liberal subject's triumph a self-fulfilling process.[16] Paternalistic intervention in the case of FGM/C goes a lot deeper, in other words, than simply eliminating a dangerous and damaging ritual. It creates a sense of individual entitlement that is the basis for the liberal subject's claim for her rights against the state, against society, and against her parents. It is also the vanguard for new gender norms that challenge existing ideas of appropriate womanhood. The adult woman whose autonomy (that is, her Human Rights) must be protected from paternalism is herself the product of a

[13] Hannah Arendt, *The Origins of Totalitarianism* (New York: Harvest Books, 1973), 296.

[14] Michael N. Barnett and Raymond Duvall, "Power in International Politics," *International Organization* 59, 1 (2005).

[15] As Leslye Obiora puts it, "rescuing non-white women from the barbarity of the culture into which they had the misfortune of being born played an important role in justifying the imperial project," see Leslye Amede Obiora, "The Anti-Female Circumcision Campaign Deficit," in *Female Circumcision and the Politics of Knowledge: African Women in Imperialist Discourse*, ed. Obioma Nnaemeka (Westport: Praeger Publishers, 2005), 183.

[16] Michel Foucault, *Society Must be Defended: Lectures at the College de France, 1975–76*, eds. Mauro Bertani and Alessandro Fontana, trans. David Macey (New York: Picador, 1997), 29–30.

paternalism struggle waged years earlier rather than the pristine flowering of a natural self grown to maturity. She is made, not born, to paraphrase de Beauvoir.

The rest of this chapter explores these questions further. The first section is an introduction to the scale and scope of FGM/C and the second section looks at elimination politics historically and in the contemporary environment. In the third section I unpack the question of paternalism and human rights, examining hard and soft variants alongside the Human Rights/human rights distinction. I also ask whether less judgmental, more community-based trust-building interventions designed to eliminate FGM/C, and so-called "libertarian paternalism," are still paternalistic. In the fourth section I analyze in more depth the site of this normative battle. The thrust of elimination efforts is a familiar, colonial-style argument about the liberal subject not as constructed but as freed from "involuntary servitude" (women, nascent bearers of rights, having hitherto been imprisoned by culture). But this is simply the beginning. The argument that girls should be *free to choose* (that they are liberal subjects) is located within a set of claims about femininity, sexuality, and maternalism that contain strong further assumptions about appropriate identity choices. In addition, the freedom to choose is hampered by an economic context that makes many meaningful choices impossible. It is also marked by a great deal of liberal hypocrisy.

The Scale and Scope of FGM/C

FGM/C is widespread in as many as twenty-nine African countries stretching from Sudan, Somalia, and Kenya to Mali, Senegal, and Nigeria. Estimates of the number of girls and women who have undergone FGM/C until recently varied between about 100 million and 140 million, figures which confirm both its scale and legitimacy.[17] It was further

---

[17] The most recent detailed data available is found in: United Nations Children's Fund, *Female Genital Mutilation/Cutting: A Statistical Overview and Exploration of the Dynamics of Change* (New York: UNICEF, 2013), www.childinfo.org/files/FGCM_Lo_res.pdf (accessed July 12, 2016) and Charlotte Feldman-Jacobs and Donna Clifton, "Female Genital Mutilation/Cutting: Data and Trends Update 2014" (Washington, DC: Population Reference Bureau, 2014), www.prb.org/Publications/Datasheets/2014/fgm-wallchart-2014.aspx (accessed July 12, 2016). Note both these reports use the term "female genital mutilation/cutting."

estimated that about three million girls, the majority under fifteen years of age, undergo FGM/C every year (typically pre-puberty, aged seven or eight).[18] However, more up-to-date data from Southeast Asia, especially Indonesia, has led UNICEF to add an incredible seventy million to the total of girls and women thought to be cut, increasing the total figure to 200 million (although the severity of cutting in Southeast Asia is at issue, see below).[19] The majority of FGM/C cases continue to be in Africa although it is also found in the Middle East (e.g., in Iraq and Yemen) and is an increasing issue among migrant communities in Western states.[20]

Particularly in its most invasive form, infibulation, FGM/C carries several potential health risks including traumatic pain, infection, and serious complications with childbirth.[21] It is by no means the same

[18] Some evidence suggests the age is getting earlier in certain cases (Kenya, for example) in order to defeat legislation by circumcising the girls before they become more socially visible.

[19] On the 2016 UNICEF estimate, see "New Statistical Report on Female Genital Mutilation Shows Harmful Practice is a Global Concern," www.unicef.org/media/media_90033.html (accessed July 12, 2016).

[20] The National Society for the Prevention of Cruelty to Children in the United Kingdom has referred thirty-four cases of FGM/C to the police for prosecution: "Female Genital Mutilation Helpline Uncovers 34 Potential Cases," *Guardian*, September 5, 2013, www.theguardian.com/society/2013/sep/05/female-genital-mutilation-helpline-cases (accessed November 9, 2015). See also Alison Brysk, "Changing Hearts and Minds," in *The Persistent Power of Human Rights: From Commitment to Compliance*, eds. Thomas Risse, Stephen C. Ropp, and Kathryn Sikkink (New York: Cambridge University Press, 2013), 259–74, 265–7.

[21] There is considerable variety in the kinds of FGM/C which take place and almost all books on the subject include graphic accounts of the various "categories" (usually reduced to three or four): clitoridectomy, which involves the removal of part or all of the clitoris; excision, which subsumes clitoridectomy and also involves the removal of the labia minora; and infibulation (or pharaonic circumcision) which usually involves removing all of the external genitalia and, crucially, the stitching together of the vulval opening to leave only a small hole. Some types of clitoridectomy, known as *sunna* to mark them out as sanctioned by Islam, only involve the removal of the prepuce (hood) of the clitoris; see Nahid Toubia, *Female Genital Mutilation: A Call for Global Action*, 2nd edn (New York: Rainbo, 1995), 10–11, and Esther K. Hicks, *Infibulation* (New Brunswick: Transaction Publishers, 1993), 9–12. Most current studies refer to the four-fold World Health Organization description that includes the categories clitoridectomy, excision, infibulation, and "other" which encompasses "all other harmful procedures to the female genitalia for non-medical purposes, e.g. pricking, piercing, incising, scraping and cauterizing the genital area," a definition that not only opens up the question of comparison to male circumcision but also comparison with

operation across societies, however, differing between communities and within and between regions, countries, and ethnic/tribal groups in terms of the physical content of the operation, its social/cultural meaning, and the attendant long-term health effects. In much of Southeast Asia, for example, it seems the practice currently only requires witnessing "a single drop of blood" or, at worst, the removal of a tiny piece of flesh rather than the removal of any part of the girl's sex organs or re-stitching.[22]

In the Horn of Africa, where FGM/C's historical roots lie (in the Arab slave trade), infibulation appears to be perpetuated by beliefs about marriage prospects, the value ascribed to female chastity and virginity more generally, especially in a society where men are frequently absent, to fears about social acceptance, and (erroneously but effectively) that it is a practice required by Islam.[23] By contrast, in Southeast Asia, according to William Gervase Clarence-Smith, it is not only likely FGM/C was brought to the region by Islam in the thirteenth century, the Shafi'i school of Islam continues to be an important reason for FGM/C's continuation. As he puts it:

The Shafi'i school of law, widespread in the Indian Ocean, is unique in Sunni Islam in declaring female circumcision to be obligatory. In the fivefold ethical terminology of Islam, this ranks above the term for honorable or recommended, which is applied to female circumcision by the three other surviving Sunni schools of law, as well as by the Shi'a.[24]

In many parts of Africa (e.g., Kenya, the Gambia, and Sierra Leone), excision and clitoridectomy are the usual kinds of FGM/C. In these

---

numerous cosmetic genital procedures in the West. World Health Organization, "Female Genital Mutilation," Fact Sheet no. 241, 2013, www.who.int/ mediacentre/factsheets/fs241/en/ (accessed July 12, 2016).

[22] William Gervase Clarence-Smith, "Female Circumcision in Southeast Asia since the Coming of Islam," in *Self-Determination and Women's Rights in Muslim Societies*, eds. Chitra Raghavan and James P. Levine (Waltham: Brandeis University Press, 2012), 114. This may be changing, however, with the rise of a more radical version of Islam in Southeast Asia leading possibly to more girls being cut and more invasive forms of cutting: Clarence-Smith, "Female Circumcision in Southeast Asia since the Coming of Islam," 120.

[23] Hicks, *Infibulation*. On the role that marriage prospects play in FGM/C's perseverance, see Gerry Mackie's seminal article, "Ending Footbinding and Infibulation: A Convention Account," *American Sociological Review* 61 (1996): 999–1017.

[24] Clarence-Smith, "Female Circumcision in Southeast Asia since the Coming of Islam," 110–11. See also fn. 22 above.

societies, circumcision is a key ritual in the passage to womanhood which can be accompanied by celebrations, present-giving, feasting, and the inclusion and seclusion of girls in secret societies so they can be socialized in age-related groupings as female members of their communities. FGM/C has also been an ethnic (and national) identity marker; it was promoted, for example, in Kenya during the colonial liberation.[25] FGM/C's underlying structure is patriarchal (it privileges the position and interests of men) but ethnographic work confirms it is women who most strongly perpetuate circumcision. It is one area of social life over which they exercise significant control in societies where the status positions open to them are few. Circumcision is then reinforced by the powerful vested interests of midwives who usually perform circumcisions and who receive income and prestige from their high-status occupation.

The most extensive report so far produced on FGM/C was published by UNICEF in July 2013.[26] Based on statistical data from surveys going back twenty years, the report highlighted several key findings. First, prevalence rates differ greatly depending on religion, ethnicity, region, urbanization and education, even within countries. Second, while there remain many high-prevalence countries (more than 80 percent of girls and women of reproductive age have been cut in Somalia, Guinea, Djibouti, Egypt, Eritrea, Mali, Sierra Leone, and the Sudan), the trend in many countries, especially those with lower prevalence rates already, appears to be a (sometimes steep) decline in the practice. The primary evidence for this comes from comparing, in 2011, the percentage of women aged 45–49 who have been cut with those aged 15–19.[27] This yields a more promising result than just calculating overall prevalence among all age groups, including all the women between nineteen and forty-five. Third, in many countries a substantial majority of girls and women aged 15–49 who have been cut say they think FGM/C should be

---

[25] See most famously Jomo Kenyatta, *Facing Mount Kenya* (New York: Vintage Books, 1965). Also Alison Brysk, *Speaking Rights to Power: Constructing Political Will* (Oxford: Oxford University Press, 2013), 89. In a recent case, the village of Myabé in Chad, FGM/C was only introduced in 1980; Lori Leonard, "'We Did it for Pleasure Only': Hearing Alternative Tales of Female Circumcision," *Qualitative Inquiry* 6, 2 (2000): 212–28.

[26] UNICEF, "Female Genital Mutilation/Cutting."

[27] *Ibid.*, 99–101.

stopped.[28] These women are, in principle, less likely to cut their own daughters (thereby accelerating the rate of reduction in FGM/C) although the power of reinforcing norms about social acceptance, marriage, and virginity makes this only an assumption.[29]

There are as yet too few data points over time, and too much ambiguity in terms of reporting, to reach definitive conclusions. Nevertheless, it seems safe to say that where the practice is already at a lower prevalence rate decline has set in. This may not be irreversible but in the case of Kenya, Tanzania, Benin, Central African Republic, Iraq, Liberia, Nigeria, Ghana, and Togo, the trend is fairly clearly downward at a rapid rate. Burkina-Faso and Ethiopia, two higher-prevalence countries, have also seen notable declines.[30] What is not clear, however, is exactly why. It could be increases in education and wealth, or the adoption of anti-FGM/C legislation (e.g., in Burkina-Faso, although fear of legal consequences may also artificially boost the number of girls and women reporting they have not had FGM/C whatever the reality), or the widespread public education campaigns against the practice in many of the countries concerned. One important case is Senegal, where the organization Tostan pioneered a human rights-based "community empowerment model" that we look at in more detail below.

If a majority of girls and women, even if they have experienced FGM/C, would prefer that the practice cease, information and education would seem to have had a significant effect. This would be a major achievement because it tips the balance in favor of "consent" to elimination (although it masks significant national and ethnic differences). This has been facilitated by new communications technology, growing social mobility, and urbanization. Where FGM/C is already a minority practice, and where those who have been cut more frequently encounter uncut girls and women, wider cultural norms may simply be absorbing and assimilating local norms through the kind of process classic modernization theorists predicted. This is likely to be particularly effective where FGM/C is already a minority practice which in most cases means countries that are not majority-Islamic. In hard cases change is almost non-existent: Chad, Djibouti, Gambia, Guinea-Bissau, Mali, Somalia,

[28] *Ibid.*, 77.
[29] *Ibid.*, 80.
[30] *Ibid.*, 114–15.

Sudan, and Yemen. In the case of Djibouti, there has been a move toward a less invasive form of FGM/C. But in the main, prevalence rates remain high. Although not all are Islamic states, the impression that Islam requires FGM/C has an important reinforcing role among adherents.[31] Where almost all girls and women are circumcised, changing the basic social norm (whereby social acceptance requires FGM/C) to the opposite norm (social acceptance requires not subjecting young girls to FGM/C) is a formidable task.[32] Conflict, inaccessibility, and poverty make several of these countries difficult to access physically, especially in their interiors. Facing hostile governments in Somalia, Sudan, and Yemen does not help. The strategies that appear to have worked in many of the cases where FGM/C is declining may be of little use here.

FGM/C is also sustained by migrant communities outside Africa. Although FGM/C had been illegal in the United Kingdom since 1985 through the Prohibition of Female Circumcision Act, a further tougher Female Genital Mutilation Act was passed in 2003.[33] Despite evidence that young girls are sometimes sent back to their countries of origin to undergo FGM/C, it was only in March 2014 that the first prosecutions under the act were brought (both against men).[34] In France, by contrast, there have been more than one hundred prosecutions. Prominent women's rights campaigner Julie Bindel claims as many as 65,000 young girls in the United Kingdom are at risk from FGM/C.[35] In London, in particular, where there are sizeable populations of migrants from FGM/C-practicing parts of Africa, former mayor Boris Johnson established an FGM Taskforce. Even Malala, icon of a

---

[31] In Egypt the state has led efforts to challenge this claim as well as stress the health dangers of FGM/C, but the results are not promising; Amel Fahmy, "Can We Really Eliminate FGM in Egypt by 2030?," *openGlobalRights*, July 2015, www.opendemocracy.net/openglobalrights/amel-fahmy/can-we-really-eliminate-fgm-in-egypt-by-2030 (accessed July 12, 2016).

[32] To shift from a bad equilibrium to a good one, in other words: see Mackie, "Ending Footbinding and Infibulation."

[33] Note the name change.

[34] It was alleged in July 2015 that as many as fifty Somali girls born in the United Kingdom had been taken back to Somalia to be circumcised; "'Fifty girls' taken from UK to Somalia for FGM," *BBC News*, July 17, 2015, www.bbc.co.uk/news/uk-33572428 (accessed July 12, 2016).

[35] Julie Bindel, *An Unpunished Crime: The Lack of Prosecutions for Female Genital Mutilation in the UK* (London: The New Culture Forum, 2014). The evidence on the extent of FGM/C in Europe and North America is not good: UNICEF, "Female Genital Mutilation/Cutting," 17.

new generation of women's and children's rights advocates, has been enlisted to the cause, as has the Duchess of Cornwall. Current estimates in the United States suggest that more than half a million women and girls are at risk of FGM/C.[36] It seems reasonable to assume that these numbers will fall as young people within migrant communities are socialized to Western norms, as the law is enforced, and as those entering Western countries from FGM/C-practicing countries are less and less likely to have experienced FGM/C themselves (although many migrants are from the hard cases in the Horn of Africa).

The Global Campaign against FGM/C

In 2012, the UN General Assembly passed a resolution titled, "Intensifying global efforts for the elimination of female genital mutilations." This followed UN recognition of February 6 as "The International Day of Zero Tolerance on FGM," a date pioneered at the 2003 Inter-African Committee (IAC) on Traditional Practices Affecting the Health of Women and Children at its conference in Addis Ababa. By 2015, the proposed Sustainable Development Goals, successors to the Millennium Development Goals, included (as item 5.3): "Eliminate all harmful practices, such as child, early and forced marriage and female genital mutilations."[37] The United Nations' explicit commitment after two decades of work by activists to the global elimination of FGM/C is a milestone, making FGM/C a part of the United Nations' formal mission, not just an issue for its operational agencies.

This achievement came nearly ninety years after early anti-FGM/C campaigners, including Western missionaries, began a concerted effort to eliminate FGM/C in Africa.[38] In 1924, for example, all British district commissioners in the Sudan received a circular telling them to encourage "enlightened natives who had begun to abolish or

[36] Howard Goldberg, Paul Stupp, Ekwutosi Okoroh, Ghenet Besera, David Goodman, and Isabella Danel, "Female Genital Mutilation/Cutting in the United States: Updated Estimates of Women and Girls at Risk, 2012," *Public Health Reports* (Atlanta: Center for Disease Control and Prevention, 2016), vol. 131.

[37] "Open Working Group Proposal for Sustainable Development Goals," Sustainable Development Knowledge Platform, https://sustainabledevelopment.un.org/sdgsproposal (accessed November 9, 2015).

[38] On circumcision politics under colonial rule in the Sudan, see Heather Bell, *Frontiers of Medicine in the Anglo-Egyptian Sudan, 1899–1940* (Oxford: Oxford University Press, 1999), ch. 7, and Janice Boddy, *Civilizing*

modify the custom."[39] This moral crusade was actually an early form
of biopolitics, according to Janice Boddy: Concerned that infibulation
led to low birth rates and high infant mortality, colonial authorities targeted FGM/C as a way to increase the child-bearing potential of Arab
women.[40] At the same time as the colonial state tried to apply social
and political pressure for the elimination of infibulation, eventually
seeking an alliance, for example, with the Sudan's Islamic leader, the
Grand Mufti, the formidable matron of the Midwives Training School
in Omdurman, Mabel E. Wolff, and her sister Gertrude, were educating
trainee Sudanese midwives to practice a less destructive form of FGM/
C than infibulation. Despite her strong objection to "the barbarous custom," Wolff was well aware that a form of medicalization was far more
likely to show positive results in terms of the suffering of infibulated
Sudanese women.[41]

In London, meanwhile, two pioneering female MPs, the Duchess of
Atholl and Eleanor Rathbone, joined forces in 1929 on an all-party
Committee for the Protection of Coloured Women in the Crown
Colonies.[42] Spurred on by testimony from missionaries, Atholl and
Rathbone were soon active in trying to stop FGM/C in Kenya as well
as the Sudan.[43] In Kenya, attempts by the missionaries to coerce local
people into abandoning FGM/C (by refusing them communion, for
example) not only failed but led to a radicalization of the Kikuyu population. This was a foretaste of things to come during the independence struggles when FGM/C played a prominent role in the Mau Mau
rebellion, as well as being linked to the *Ngaitana* movement in which
young girls in Meru, Kenya, denied FGM/C by tribal elders who had
liaised with the British, went into the bush to circumcise themselves.[44]

Women: British Crusades in the Sudan (Princeton: Princeton University
Press, 2007). On Kenya, see, for example, Susan Pedersen, "National
Bodies, Unspeakable Acts: The Sexual Politics of Colonial Policy-Making,"
Journal of Modern History 63 (1991): 647–80, and Margaret E. Keck and
Kathryn Sikkink, *Activists Beyond Borders* (Ithaca: Cornell University Press,
1998), 67–72.

[39] Boddy, *Civilizing Women*, 173.
[40] *Ibid.*, 172.
[41] *Ibid.*, 196.
[42] *Ibid.*, 234.
[43] Pedersen, "National Bodies, Unspeakable Acts."
[44] Lynn M. Thomas, "'*Ngaitana* (I Will Circumcise Myself)': The Gender and
Generational Politics of the 1956 Ban on Clitoridectomy in Meru, Kenya," in
Gendered Colonialisms in African History, eds. Nancy Rose Hunt, Tessie P.
Liu, and Jean Quataert (Oxford: Basil Blackwell, 1997).

These early efforts made little progress but they did reveal that, handled badly, anti-FGM/C efforts could produce significant resistance. After decolonization, and the rapid departure of colonial officials from Africa and Asia, next to nothing occurred in terms of anti-FGM/C activities until the 1970s when there was suddenly an explosion of interest linked to the emerging women's movement. Some American feminists were very vocal about the "barbarity" of FGM/C from the start. In the words of the most prominent early American campaigner, Fran Hosken, FGM/C arose out of "contempt for the female of the species," where, "What are called 'cultural traditions' in reality are practices that support the ritual abuse of women, systematically damaging women's health and strength to make sure of their subordination to men."[45]

In an earlier version of her *Hosken Report*, Hosken had written: "It is evident that female genital mutilation can be abolished and wiped out in our lifetime. We are able to teach those who cling to distorted beliefs and damaging practices some better ways to cope with themselves, their lives, reproduction and sexuality. We know that everyone on earth has the capacity to learn."[46] Many African feminists objected deeply to the overt neocolonial paternalism of this sort of Western feminist dialogue.[47] Corinne Kratz contrasts the self-image of many Western feminists in the 1970s with their view of "third world women" who needed saving because they were without agency and thus "powerless, constrained by a tradition defined by men, unable to think clearly, and having only problems and needs, not choices."[48] In contrast to the strong paternalism of early American campaigners, an influential British report from 1980 struck a different, if no less patronizing, tone about African women working to end FGM/C: "They are beginning the delicate task of helping women free themselves from

---

[45] Fran Hosken, *The Hosken Report: Genital and Sexual Mutilation of Females*, 4th edn (Lexington, MA: Women's International Network, 1994), 9, 16; Claude E. Welch Jr., *Protecting Human Rights in Africa: Roles and Strategies of Non-Governmental Organizations* (Philadelphia: University of Pennsylvania Press, 1995), 104, fn. 4.

[46] Quoted in Boddy, *Civilizing Women*, 309.

[47] Brysk, *Speaking Rights to Power*, 90.

[48] Corinne Kratz, *Affecting Performance* (Washington, DC: Smithsonian Institution Press, 1994), 343. See also Chandra Talpade Mohanty, "Under Western Eyes: Feminist Scholarship and Colonial Discourses," *Feminist Review* 30 (1988): 61–88.

customs which have no advantage and many risks for their physical and psychological well-being, without at the same time destroying the supportive and beneficial threads of their cultural fabric."[49]

That the hard paternalism of these early efforts was a problem is evident. Despite facile efforts at demonization, the "perpetrators" of FGM/C are not sadists or pathological child abusers. Those who perpetuate the practice are mothers, grandmothers, and other village women who do it from an ethic of care and concern for their daughters. They have what they see as their daughters' best interests at heart. As Yoder *et al.* put it: "Mothers organize the circumcision of their daughters because that is considered part of raising a girl properly, of being a responsible mother ... women in central Guinea ... said that their religion required that parents do three things for their daughters: 'to educate them, to circumcise them, and to find them a good husband.' "[50] Consider Ellen Gruenbaum's description of a circumcision in Sudan: "Children dressed up with special ornaments and new clothes, a surgical procedure, ululations, small gifts and congratulations, no patriarchal authority figure overseeing and dictating the sequence of events."[51] Like many other major life events, this was a moment for celebration with family, friends, and neighbors rather than a matter for shame or regret, and women are its central actors.

Early anti-FGM/C efforts took place in the absence of any systematic reference to human rights for two reasons: as an international movement it was in its infancy at the time, and the movement's focus was almost exclusively civil and political, much to the irritation of women's rights and LGBT rights activists in the 1980s. From 1993 onward, following Vienna's World Conference on Human Rights, FGM/C was increasingly "reconceptualized as a human rights violation," that is, as gender-based violence against women and children.[52] Human rights were becoming the dominant frame, reflecting a shift in

---

[49] Scilla McLean and Stella Efua Graham, eds., *Female Circumcision, Excision and Infibulation: The Facts and Proposals for Change*, second rev. edn (London: The Minority Rights Group, 1985), 3.

[50] Stanley P. Yoder, Noureddine Abderrahim, and Arlinda Zhuzhuni, "Female Genital Cutting in the Demographic and Health Surveys: A Critical and Comparative Analysis," *DHS Comparative Reports No. 7* (Calverton, MD: ORC Macro, 2004), 13.

[51] Ellen Gruenbaum, *The Female Circumcision Controversy: An Anthropological Perspective* (Philadelphia: University of Pennsylvania Press, 2000), 59.

[52] UNICEF, "Female Genital Mutilation/Cutting," 6.

the late 1980s when the term "female genital mutilation" or FGM was coined by the Geneva-based IAC. Use of the term FGM soon became a marker of one's position on the advocacy spectrum. One of the earliest anti-FGM/C advocacy organizations, Equality Now, was founded in New York in 1992 (by, among others, former UN High Commissioner for Human Rights, Navi Pillay). It remains active on a whole array of issues concerning the treatment of women and girls; its total income in 2012 was nearly four million dollars.[53] Gloria Steinem, prominent in early anti-FGM/C campaigns, remains on its board. Equality Now's first anti-FGM/C newsletter, *Awaken*, published in 1997 in English, Arabic, and French, was subtitled, *Towards a better understanding and a more effective strategy for the eradication of all forms of female circumcision*. In its first issue, the editor wrote: "*Awaken* will not judge the material that appears on its pages by which term is being used by those who contribute to it."[54] FGM, FC (female circumcision) and genital surgery or genital cutting were all judged acceptable. But most letters and contributions from readers in subsequent issues used the term FGM until it became clear that for Western-based global advocacy only "FGM" would do.

This battle over naming had first burst into the open at 1980's Copenhagen UN Conference on women when African activists objected to the tone of Western feminists and, critically for paternalists, denied the very right of those Western women to lead elimination efforts.[55] As we have seen, UNICEF and some other operational agencies like the UN Population Fund have adopted the term FGM/C, as has the influential Washington, DC-based Population Reference Bureau. In its statistical report, UNICEF explicitly refers to having "tact and patience" and using "respectful terminology."[56] The World Health Organization and UN Women retain the "FGM" framing and the UN General Assembly's 2012 global ban explicitly uses that term.

In 1997, Somali-born supermodel Waris Dirie, herself circumcised, had become the "UN Ambassador for the Elimination of FGM," and

---

[53] See: www.equalitynow.org (accessed July 12, 2016).

[54] *Awaken* 1, 1 (June 1997).

[55] Nahid Toubia, *Program Guidelines for Integrating Activities to Eradicate Female Genital Mutilation*, USAID, May 1997, http://pdf.usaid.gov/pdf_docs/PNACB026.pdf (accessed July 12, 2016), Appendix A, 1–2.

[56] UNICEF, "Female Genital Mutilation/Cutting," 7.

in 1998 she published her bestselling autobiography *Desert Flower*.[57]
In the same year, USAID firmed up its position on FGM. While recognizing "the need for sensitivity to the perception of interference
in local cultural beliefs and practices," the "unequivocal consensus"
at the international level meant that, "there is now less reason to be
hesitant about openly committing to support for FGM eradication
programs."[58] In this report, written for USAID by prominent FGM/
C activist Nahid Toubia, the story of the 1990s – greater attention
to mainstreaming gender, the linking of health to individual human
rights, intense domestic pressure, and the succession of major international conferences at which women's rights were central (Vienna
1993, Cairo 1994, and Beijing 1995) – culminated in a detailed and,
crucially, *proactive* USAID elimination policy from 2000 onward.[59]

Human Rights/human rights

As argued above, all forms of anti-FGM/C advocacy rely on a human
rights frame to legitimate their intervention. Nevertheless, the international movement against female circumcision could broadly be seen to
divide along a Human Rights/human rights fault line which maps on
to the use of the terms FGM (Human Rights/hard paternalism) versus FGM/C (human rights/soft paternalism).[60] For the former, human
rights are an end in themselves, FGM another and particularly egregious example of a human rights violation – violence against women
and children – that must be stopped at all costs. For the latter, human
rights are one means among others to try to end the practice, the starting point being engagement with the communities concerned and a
reluctance to use demonizing language.[61] Here human rights follow

---

[57] We look in more detail at Dirie's activism in sections 3 and 4 below.
[58] Toubia, *Program Guidelines for Integrating Activities to Eradicate Female Genital Mutilation*, 9.
[59] Many American troops and officials returning from Operation Restore Hope in Somalia had also been exposed to FGM/C for the first time, and by the mid-1990s asylum cases were being heard where the risk of being subjected to FGM/C was the rationale for the granting of permanent leave to stay in the United States.
[60] See Hopgood, *The Endtimes of Human Rights*.
[61] There is a third category we might label *skeptics*. They are suspicious of the moralizing of the anti-FGM movement and seek to challenge advocacy myths about the health complications of circumcision and about the refusal to compare male and female circumcision in many cases. See, for

rather than lead; they need to be mapped on to existing beliefs. In the language of the 2013's UNICEF report:

> The abandonment of FGM/C is framed not as a criticism of local culture but as a better way to attain the core positive values that underlie tradition and religion, including "doing no harm to others". We have found that, addressed in this way, efforts to end FGM/C contribute to the larger issues of ending violence against children and women and confronting gender inequalities.[62]

As an example of the Human Rights position, take the report by Julie Bindel on FGM in the United Kingdom, titled *An Unpunished Crime*. This refers to "a procedure that belongs in the dark ages" and "a catalogue of torture." This pure paternalism takes us back to the 1970s. A campaign by major UK newspapers led by London's *Evening Standard* and the national newspaper, *The Times*, carries the message that the law must be implemented at all costs.[63] Bindel is forthright that sensitivity over paternalism is the main reason, in addition to problems of evidence gathering, for the failure of the British authorities to tackle FGM: "By far the most important factor … is excessive cultural sensitivity: quite simply, there is a reluctance to combat the practice of FGM for fear of appearing reactionary or prejudiced. Here, the laudable desire to show respect for other cultures has degenerated into a form of paralysis – a terror of taking vigorous action just because the practice occurs overwhelmingly in migrant communities."[64]

The absolutist Human Rights position recalls the discourse of civilization and infantilism by which colonial authorities treated their subjects as children who needed educating and disciplining. This is hardcore, pure paternalism. Human Rights on this understanding

example, Richard A. Schweder, "Symposium on German Court Ruling on Circumcision: The Goose and the Gander: The Genital Wars," *Global Discourse* 3, 2 (2013): 348–66, and Kirsten Bell, "Genital Cutting and Western Discourses on Sexuality," *Medical Anthropology Quarterly* 19, 2 (2005): 125–48. See also, The Public Policy Advisory Network on Female Genital Surgeries in Africa, "Seven Things to Know About Female Genital Surgeries in Africa," *The Hastings Center Report* 42, 6 (2012): 19–27.

[62] UNICEF, "Female Genital Mutilation/Cutting," iii.

[63] E.g., "It's Child Abuse that has Gone Mainstream," *The Times*, January 31, 2014, www.thetimes.co.uk/tto/news/uk/crime/article3991120.ece (accessed July 12, 2016).

[64] Bindel, *An Unpunished Crime*, 6–7.

are binary. They condense and submerge complexity under one all-encompassing normative standard of right against wrong. It is a seductive narrative for would-be saviors. To be progressive you must be *pro* human rights because there are only two sides. We see this clearly in the WHO's approach. From a position of more cultural sensitivity in the 1990s, the WHO in 2014 characterizes the campaign totally in Human Rights terms:

FGM is recognized internationally as a violation of the human rights of girls and women. It reflects deep-rooted inequality between the sexes, and constitutes an extreme form of discrimination against women. It is nearly always carried out on minors and is a violation of the rights of children. The practice also violates a person's rights to health, security and physical integrity, the right to be free from torture and cruel, inhuman or degrading treatment, and the right to life when the procedure results in death.[65]

For Human Rights advocates, the term *female genital mutilation* or "FGM" is a true description of the nature of the practice. This makes FGM/C a crime, amounting to child abuse and even torture. In the words of Waris Dirie:

FGM has to be eradicated, and it *will* be eradicated. It's barbaric: against children and women, against the law, against religion, against humanity. It has no place in a human society. It is a crime that seeks justice.[66]

This is archetypal hard paternalism. Mostly, Human Rights advocates have focused on extending legal punishment for FGM/C including threats of imprisonment.[67] The criminal law helps, it is argued, by

[65] See World Health Organization, *Female Genital Mutilation: A Joint WHO/ UNICEF/UNFPA Statement* (Geneva: World Health Organization, 1997), 1–2, www.childinfo.org/files/fgmc_WHOUNICEFJointdeclaration1997.pdf, and World Health Organization, "Female Genital Mutilation."

[66] Leyla Hussein, "Waris Dirie: 'Never Give Up. FGM Has to be Eradicated, and it Will be Eradicated,'" *Cosmopolitan*, July 1, 2015, www.cosmopolitan.co.uk/ reports/news/a36860/waris-dirie-fgm-leyla-hussein/ (accessed July 12, 2016).

[67] One of outgoing Nigerian president Goodluck Jonathan's last acts in office in May 2015 was to sign a statute outlawing FGM: Shyamantha Asokan, "Nigeria's Outgoing President Signs Off on Banning Female Genital Mutiliation," *Buzzfeed*, May 28, 2015, www.buzzfeed.com/ shyamanthaasokan/nigerias-president-signs-off-on-banning-fgm?responses#. ko1LgXXpe (accessed July 12, 2016).

giving advocates for abandonment an extra mechanism to exert lever-age. Even in Senegal, however, legalization and the threat of criminal punishment as a strategy in itself may be counter-productive, gener-ating resistance and driving FGM/C underground.[68] Human Rights advocates have yet to advocate systematically for the use of force but there seems little doubt that with available resources they would be open to that.

While acting paternally is associated historically with fathers, and therefore with men, acting *in a masculine way* implicates women too. Indeed, in relation to combatting FGM/C, the international movement has been dominated by female Western feminists. Yet it is vital to reit-erate that, despite being an ongoing legacy of structural patriarchy, it is women who continue the practice of FGM/C and that, to stop it in the here-and-now, the people who have to cease cutting girls are their mothers, aunts, and grandmothers. As we noted, the mothers who cir-cumcise their daughters do so from an ethic of love and care, not abuse and cruelty. Is this better described as a clash between paternalism and maternalism, with maternalism as a rival authority claim to paternal-ism, one that gives the existing rights of mothers a privileged position regardless of the content of those maternal claims (e.g., whether or not being a mother must mean to be "nurturing")? Paternalism would then be about voiding the authority claims of mothers in the name of morality. This echoes a familiar gender dynamic where paternalism is identified with rational rights-based moral action and maternalism with care-based emotional nurturing. But this way of thinking doesn't take us very far. The insistence of many mothers that their daughters be circumcised so they are not ostracized and can make good mar-riages is just as comprehensible as a form of paternalism.

Hard Human Rights paternalism has not only generated resistance, there has not been a terminal reduction, as UNICEF's figures show, in the prevalence of FGM/C, despite a century of activism. While Human Rights continues to be the dominant frame internationally, and in the

---

[68] Bettina Shell-Duncan, Yiva Hernlund, Katherine Wander, and Amadou Moreau, "Legislating Change? Responses to Criminalizing Female Genital Cutting in Senegal," *Law and Society Review* 47, 4 (2013): 803–35. See also Matilda Aberese Ako and Patricia Akweongo, "The Limited Effectiveness of Legislation against Female Genital Mutilation and the Role of Community Beliefs in Upper East Region, Ghana," *Reproductive Health Matters* 17, 34 (2009): 47–54.

West, within Africa itself what success there has been has come from a more pragmatic, engaged approach which concentrates less on the symbolism of specific cases and laws and more on incremental change in sympathy with the women concerned. For a time, strategies based on the negative health effects of FGM/C were marginalized by hard paternalists who feared this would lead to the legitimation of medicalization (as has to some extent happened in Egypt and Indonesia). But more nuanced, needs-related arguments quickly returned to complement Human Rights, as did the term FGM/C to provide a less judgmental label than FGM.[69]

This more pragmatic, "soft" paternalism legitimates itself not by overriding the liberty of women and their girl children as hard paternalists would but by arguing that "genuine consent" hasn't been forthcoming in the first place. Soft paternalists are all about producing consent. They pursue this end by stressing education based on an understanding of the reasons why FGM/C continues and sympathizing in a deep way with those who have been circumcised. In other words, they try to pursue change in partnership with the women concerned, as part of an open, discursive, negotiated process. Emphasizing health risks, for example, promotes change while maintaining the autonomy and dignity of the women concerned. This form of paternalism acknowledges the depth of feeling that undergirds FGM/C and the fact that women and girls are part of a meaningful community, rather than individuals waiting to be liberated from their cultural prison. The label FGM/C, FGC, or sometimes FC (female circumcision) reflects this commitment.[70]

Soft paternalism also creates incentives to act in a specific way rather than issuing moral demands. It seeks compliance rather than demands obedience. In their book on framing institutional choices, *Nudge*, Richard Thaler and Cass Sunstein call their approach "libertarian paternalism." This entails freedom of choice but choice in a world where "it is legitimate for choice architects to try to influence people's behavior in order to make their lives longer, healthier, and better."[71] This self-assigned right to change outcomes in the deeper

[69] Bettina Shell-Duncan, "From Health to Human Rights: Female Genital Cutting and the Politics of Intervention," *American Anthropologist* 110, 2 (2008): 225–36.

[70] The epitome of this approach is the UNICEF report, "Female Genital Mutilation/Cutting."

[71] Richard H. Thaler and Cass R. Sunstein, *Nudge: Improving Decisions About Health, Wealth and Happiness* (New York: Penguin, 2009), 5.

interests of persons resembles the "capabilities approach" pioneered by Amartya Sen and Martha Nussbaum.[72] The first step to realizing human rights for Sen and Nussbaum is to increase a person's capacity to make good choices. Giving people full information is critical, the assumption being that knowing alternative options exist will stop someone from choosing to undergo or propagate cultural practices like FGM/C that may cause them or their children significant harm.

These are exercises in institutional power, to be sure, in that they create conditions of choice designed to privilege some options and exclude others.[73] But in the *Nudge* example, you can still choose the bad option, you just have to expend more effort to get it. In other words, you can say no even to paternalism. This makes full information critical. What if you don't realize there's another option?[74] Is it paternalist to disguise someone's full range of options (we try to hide many things from children until we think they are able to choose wisely)? If holding back information and available choices is paternalistic, then giving someone more choice would presumably be its opposite? This would be Nussbaum's and Sen's position. And in many ways the enlightenment position as a whole: We are showing you there's another way, then it's up to you.[75] Or perhaps these are context-specific forms of paternalism, depending in each case on the circumstances? The most successful attempts to change FGM/C rely on a shared communication mechanism – giving people more information about the availability of alternatives (that not circumcising reduces health complications, reduces maternal mortality and childbirth pain, that women in the next village do not circumcise their daughters and still find marriage partners for them).

The epitome of this approach is outlined in a publication by UNICEF's social science-led Innocenti Research Centre, called *Changing a Harmful Social Convention: Female Genital Mutilation/Cutting*. In this report, ground-breaking work on harmful social

[72] Martha C. Nussbaum, "Symposium on Amartya Sen's Philosophy: 5 Adaptive Preferences and Women's Options," *Economics and Philosophy* 17 (2001): 83, and Amartya Sen, *The Idea of Justice* (Cambridge, MA: Belknap/Harvard University Press, 2009).
[73] See Barnett and Duvall on "institutional power" in "Power in International Politics."
[74] See Steven Lukes' second and third dimensions of power in *Power: A Radical View*, 2nd edn (London: Palgrave Macmillan, 2005), 20–8.
[75] We return to the question of choice and agency below.

conventions figures prominently in informing policy-making.[76] It is
based on the work of scholar Gerry Mackie who argues that what
sustains FGM/C (particularly infibulation), as with foot-binding in
China, is the prospect of making a good marriage. It is a self-enforcing
social convention that can (potentially) be changed quickly.[77] By getting parents and children to pledge not to circumcise their daughters,
and to allow their sons to marry uncircumcised girls, a critical mass
of those in non-FGM/C marriages will be reached and hopefully pass
"the tipping point" beyond which a new equilibrium is established
where FGM/C is no longer the dominant norm.[78] To get to this stage
requires information, public commitment (in pledging ceremonies)
and coordination within the community. Although there are other
FGM/C-reinforcing norms such as religion, rites of passage and female
honor and modesty codes, it is changing the marriageability norm that
matters most in Mackie's area of research and activism.[79]

This work has been an integral part of the most successful effort at
eliminating FGM/C. The "Tostan Model" was launched in Senegal in
1991 by American activist Molly Melching. The model now operates
in eight countries: Djibouti, Guinea, Guinea-Bissau, Mali, Mauritania,
Senegal, Somalia, and The Gambia.[80] The essence of the Tostan model is a
three-year "community empowerment program" in local languages that

---

[76] United Nations Children's Fund, "Changing a Harmful Social
  Convention: Female Genital Mutilation/Cutting," *Innocenti Digest* 12
  (New York: UNICEF, 2005), available at: www.unicef-irc.org/publications/pdf/
  fgm_eng.pdf (accessed July 12, 2016). See also Mackie's "Ending Footbinding
  and Infibulation."
[77] See Mackie, "Ending Footbinding and Infibulation," and Gerry Mackie
  and John LeJeune, "Social Dynamics of Abandonment of Harmful
  Practices: A New Look at the Theory," *UNICEF Innocenti Working Paper*,
  May 2009, www.polisci.ucsd.edu/~gmackie/documents/UNICEF.pdf (accessed
  July 12, 2016).
[78] Malcolm Gladwell, *The Tipping Point: How Little Things Can Make a Big
  Difference* (New York: Little Brown, 2000).
[79] Mackie and LeJeune, "Social Dynamics," 29–30.
[80] On Tostan, see also Yiva Hernlund and Bettina Shell-Duncan, "Contingency,
  Context and Change: Negotiating Female Genital Cutting in The Gambia
  and Senegal," *Africa Today* 53, 4 (2007): 43–57, Bettina Shell-Duncan, Yiva
  Hernlund, Katherine Wander, and Amadou Moreau, *Contingency and Change
  in the Practice of Female Genital Cutting: Dynamics of Decision-Making in
  Senegambia* (Seattle: University of Washington, 2010), and Charlotte Feldman-
  Jacobs, ed., *Ending Female Genital Mutilation/Cutting: Lessons from a Decade
  of Progress* (Washington, DC: Population Research Bureau, 2013), 16.

first promotes "positive traditions while encouraging discussion of how new ideas and practices can help build a healthier community," following which "participants learn to read and write in their own language, study basic math, and gain management skills."[81] The first year's discussions include "deliberation on democracy, human rights and responsibilities, problem solving and hygiene and health."[82] It is in these forums that "the tradition" usually becomes a topic of animated conversation.

To the suggestion that human rights are a Western imposition, Tostan argues that it encourages participants to "deliberate what constitutes human dignity and how it can be upheld: a term translated into local languages and one that people resonate with. The rights framework can then be used as an international framework which supports that idea of dignity developed within class."[83] Rights follow, they do not lead. The Tostan approach is more human rights not Human Rights, in other words. As activist Lucy Walker puts it:

To come to human rights in this way – to work out what a community wants and back it up using the framework of human rights – is rather different to the usual development rhetoric of going in and waving the declaration around and shouting about it! It develops internal agency – the understanding that we have rights and can bring these to our community.[84]

Similarly, Molly Melching stresses "the importance of non-formal education in national languages, the social mobilization work of people who were themselves affected by the practice, and an approach based on empathy and respect."[85] And the Tostan approach appears to be working. According to the Orchid Project:

[81] "Program Structure," Tostan, www.tostan.org/tostan-model/community-empowerment-program/program-structure (accessed July 12, 2016).
[82] This description is from a blog post by Lucy Walker, the Knowledge and Programmes Coordinator for an NGO called "The Orchid Project" that works with Tostan; see "Tostan's Human-Rights Approach to Community-led Development: the First TTC," Orchid Project, April 14, 2015, http://orchidproject.org/tostans-human-rights-approach-to-community-led-development-the-first-ttc/ (accessed July 12, 2016).
[83] *Ibid.*
[84] "A Chance to Experience Tostan Classes," Orchid Project, May 1, 2015, http://orchidproject.org/a-chance-to-experience-tostan-sessions/ (accessed July 12, 2016).
[85] See: "Les Contributions de Tostan vers L'abandon de L'Excision Soulignées par le Gouvernement du Sénégal et l'ONU," *Tostan Blog*, February 6, 2015,

The proportion of mothers [in Senegal] with at least one daughter who is cut has declined from 20% in 2005 to 6.2% in 2010 – a decrease of about 69%. Between 2005 and 2010, the number of Soninké women (the most vulnerable group in 2005) with at least one daughter cut declined by 86.1%. Along the same lines, Diola, Fula and Mandinka groups saw a decrease of 65.1%, 81.8% and 60.2% respectively. Among Christian women, the practice of FGC has nearly disappeared. In 2005, 11.2% of Christian women had a daughter who was cut. This has reduced to 0.9% in 2010, meaning a 92% decrease...On the other hand, Muslim women continue to practice, although there has been a significant decline. The number of women with a daughter who is cut decreased from 20.3% to 6.4% between 2005 and 2010 – a 68.5% reduction.[86]

By improving the social acceptance of not circumcising without damaging marriage prospects, rates of FGM/C have shown a rapid decline. These twin reinforcing pressures suggest that where most women one meets are circumcised rates of decline will be lower because the existing social norm is still strongly in favor of cutting. This would explain why in the hard cases, particularly in the Horn of Africa, prevalence rates remain extremely high compared with the minority who still circumcise in Senegal. And why where prevalence is lower elimination appears to be happening faster. Tostan's model has helped shift the norm by ensuring the involvement of local women at every stage, creating more and more advocates for abandonment who thereby spread the message and constitute visible evidence of an increasingly legitimate alternative norm.

This systematic and sustainable basis for change seems more likely to succeed than the more instrumental approach of Waris Dirie's Desert Flower Foundation which, under the title "Save a Little Desert Flower," agrees a contract with parents and provides financial support in return for not circumcising their daughters.[87] Not tackling

http://fr.tostan.org/news/les-contributions-de-tostan-vers-l'abandon-de-lexcision-soulignées-par-le-gouvernement-du (accessed July 12, 2016), and the interview at: Melinda Gates, "Melinda Gates: 5 Questions for Tostan's Molly Melching," *Impatient Optimists*, Bill and Melinda Gates Foundation, June 25, 2013, www.impatientoptimists.org/Posts/2013/06/Melinda-Gates-5-Questions-for-Tostans-Molly-Melching#.VZkWGngk_dl (accessed July 12, 2016).
[86] Lucy Walker, Personal Communication, The Orchid Project, May 1, 2015.
[87] "Our Achievements," Desert Flower, http://retteeinekleinewuestenblume.de/en/our-achievements.html (accessed July 12, 2016).

the social acceptance/marriage prospects issue collectively via community engagement is even less likely to work where prevalence is so high (e.g., 93 percent in Djibouti in 2013 according to UNICEF). Unsurprisingly, the families who sign contracts come under intense social pressure from their non-contracted neighbors who represent the dominant social norm. The mother of Safa, a Djibouti girl who acted as the young Dirie in a movie of her life called *Desert Flower*, expresses some regret for this very reason:

My husband and I signed this contract where we guaranteed not to have Safa circumcised. But to be honest I am not convinced that it was the right decision. The circumcision ritual is part of our tradition. We will never find a husband for Safa if she is not circumcised. She will never belong to our society like the other girls. So I am sure that one day we will have her circumcised anyway.[88]

Tostan-style education programs, and the provision of better information about the impact of circumcision and alternative choices (not to circumcise, or to circumcise less invasively), are explicitly designed to avoid this dilemma. They seem as light-touch a form of paternalism as one could envisage but in being based on a rejection of existing consent (that is, the status quo: consent to carry on the practice), they qualify as a form of soft paternalism. The efforts made to change choices, and shape the self-identity of the choosers, are part of a sophisticated project designed to change lives. They are not openly coercive, nor based on a deception, and they encourage dialogue, discussion, and a non-judgmental approach. But these forms of soft paternalism are justified by the lack of valid consent and they are not about to take no for an answer.

There is, of course, a paradox in doing nothing: Keeping the existence of a different option from women who cut their daughters might be seen to be just as paternalistic as intervening. Does the provision of information designed to change the status quo constitute paternalism, rather than a leveling up of the scales (against years of parental paternalism)? It is proactive – those who don't self-identify as having a problem are now told something they see as legitimate is

---

[88] This quotation comes from a fascinating and thoughtful account by Waris Dirie of her interactions with Safa's family in an extract from her book *Saving Safa*. Extract from *The Weekend Australian*, June 27, 2015, 28.

indeed a problem. Dworkin's original definition was about interference with a person's "liberty of action" (echoing Mill). But isn't community empowerment even more invasive than that? In the name of moral advance, it is problematizing an existing way of life without any request to do so. This is the true power of the Human Rights language – by claiming a universal solidarity it claims anyone's problems are everyone's problems, thereby legitimating unsolicited intervention. Even light-touch paternalism has traces of the claim to moral superiority built into it. In other words, any engagement in the lives of others that they would not necessarily choose for themselves as they are constitutes a form of paternalistic interventionism, however soft, in the name of the person they could become. Why should it be so difficult to acknowledge this as a legitimate demand for moral change that is obviously paternalistic?

Unless we see tribal and village life as hermetically sealed, with the tribe or village having a kind of transcendent ontological reality linked to a moral monopoly, is there a reason to privilege *what is* in favor of *what could be*? Cultural relativists and some conservatives would say yes against the emphatic no of liberals. To defend existing culture on principle requires an argument for why it should be protected and that opens up a discussion about what appropriate norms ought to be. In other words, cultural relativists would need to argue for the universal principle of "leaving other cultures alone regardless of their substantive social norms" thereby conceding the point that whether or not other cultures should be left alone must be the result of a moral discussion about how people ought to be treated. To refuse this conversation is just to absent yourself from it rather than to prevent it from happening (much less win it). It opens up the space in principle for universal, agreed norms. If all parties can engage in this discussion, as we have seen women in Tostan programs in Senegal do on more or less equal terms, then there is a kind of consent at work even if, in the absence of soft paternalism, such an option would likely never have been chosen.

And this consent is the prize because it effaces the moral drive that lies behind intervention and will not be denied. In this way, the similarities with the colonial practice of moral crusades against the cultural life of colonized peoples, especially women, can be disguised. There's no harm in the truth: anti-FGM/C missionaries in the 1920s in Sudan and Kenya would have seen many of these issues in exactly the same terms as we do today. In this way we understand that empire wasn't a phase so much as a structural relation that is always with us where the dominant seek to discipline, and even eliminate, "the other" in their midst. All that has changed is that we call missionaries and district officers "human rights and development activists" today. Unsurprisingly, therefore, the scope of paternalism goes much deeper than mere behavioral change, into subjectivity and identity itself. In other words, soft paternalism of the producing consent variety may have more far-reaching long-term effects than hard paternalism which seeks no more than a change in behavior.

FGM/C and the Subject of Human Rights

Evidence from many African countries suggests persistent support among many women for FGM/C's continuation as well as examples where a majority of men are opposed to the practice.[89] Circumcision is often celebrated as an essential social ritual for girls and a proud day for parents and extended families.[90] Testimony from some of the women who support abandonment, including midwives, show a variety of motivations including health consequences, religious beliefs, and human rights concerns. And most recognize that the community as a whole has to change for the norm to shift.[91] These cases show the importance of sensitive and supportive conversations with others in a shared language for creating the momentum for change. This is tougher to do in harder cases where a large majority still circumcises. Underlying the broader elimination campaign, therefore, is also a drive to liberate liberal subjects from their cultural prisons, a classic colonial urge.

The liberal subject (leaving aside the assumption that the universal gender of the subject is male) is well described by John Rawls: "the self is prior to the ends which are affirmed by it; even a dominant end must be chosen from among numerous possibilities." He goes on:

[89] There are several cases where more boys and men than girls and women want FGM/C to be eliminated (in Guinea, Sierra Leone, and Chad, for example). In Cameroon, 85 percent of boys and men surveyed thought FGM/C should stop: UNICEF, "Female Genital Mutilation/Cutting," 62.
[90] Gruenbaum, *The Female Circumcision Controversy*, ch. 2.
[91] "Meeting with 'Social Norms Entrepreneurs,'" *The Orchid Project blog*, May 15, 2015, http://orchidproject.org/meeting-with-social-norms-entrepreneurs/ (accessed July 12, 2016).

a moral person is a subject with ends he has chosen, and his fundamental preference is for conditions that enable him to frame a mode of life that expresses his nature as a free and equal rational being as fully as circumstances permit.[92]

Or, in the words of Marie Bassili Assaad, the head of an Egyptian taskforce on FGM/C whose 1980 report on Egypt was highly influential: "A woman's view of herself and her belief in old customs change in response to information, education, and social and economic opportunities. Educated women see that their status may be derived from roles other than those of wife and mother."[93] Contra Foucault, there is in these cases a self-conscious liberal subject with a pre-existing nature who freely chooses her own way of being human. For liberal paternalists it is this moral person whose interests must be represented. For Foucault, in contrast, such a narrow conception of what it means to be human – the individual liberal subject – closes off other as-yet undiscovered or tightly patrolled alternative ways in which one might be human.[94] Judith Butler extends this analysis by looking at the ways in which even some feminist theory assumes "women" exist as a natural subject needing representation. She argues that the legal and normative regimes which claim to represent "women's interests" are as much producers of the category "women" as representatives of it as a pre-formed, pre-social entity.[95] In other words, the formation of liberal subjects closes off as many options as it opens, and in particular it creates a certain kind of individual whose agency becomes about realizing her own interests and choosing her own identity.

We can see this in relation to conceptions of femininity, maternity, and sexuality. The control of female sexuality has been cited as a feature of many local justifications for FGM/C and several studies make note of it.[96] As the World Bank put it in 1994, its aim was to

[92] John Rawls, *A Theory of Justice* (Cambridge, MA: Harvard University Press, 1971), 560, 561.
[93] Marie Bassili Assaad, "Female Circumcision in Egypt: Social Implications, Current Research, and Prospects for Change," *Studies in Family Planning* 11, 1 (1980): 6.
[94] See Ben Golder, "Foucault and the Unfinished Human of Rights," *Law, Culture and the Humanities* 6 (2010).
[95] Judith Butler, *Gender Trouble: Feminism and the Subversion of Identity* (London: Routledge, 2006), ch. 1.
[96] See the survey carried out by an affiliate of the IAC, the National Committee on Traditional Practices in Ethiopia; *Awaken* 2, 2 (1998): 8. And also Amel

challenge "the social attitudes and beliefs that undergird male violence and *renegotiating the meaning of gender and sexuality* and the balance of power between men and women at all levels of society."[97] Or, in USAID's words: "The ultimate desired outcome of FGM/C projects is to eradicate the practice, to preserve women's bodies, and to empower them to make better choices regarding their sexuality and reproduction."[98]

Critical to this freeing of the liberal subject is preventing her natural self from being damaged in some permanent way by ritual. This includes not just threats to her life from FGM/C but also to her "normal" (that is, "natural") appearance and sexual functioning. Waris Dirie's foundation has even paid for reconstructive surgery for some infibulated women. As a Masai woman called Ntailan Lolkoki told an interviewer after the surgery: "I looked wonderful all of a sudden. As a kid you start to explore your sexuality but circumcision stopped that. After the surgery those feelings were restored. I would lie in my bed and I could feel everything. My neighbours could tell I had this sexuality."[99] Another woman, twenty-year-old Idriss, says: "After surgery I felt complete as a woman."[100]

But these views of normalness and naturalness, of femininity and sexuality, are not universal. In her work on the Hofriyat in Sudan, Janice Boddy argues that:

Fahmy, Mawaheb T. El-Mouelhy, and Ahmed R. Ragab, "Female Genital Mutilation/Cutting and Issues of Sexuality in Egypt," *Reproductive Health Matters* 18, 36 (2010): 184.

[97] Lori L. Heise, Jacqueline Pitanguy, and Adrienne Germain, *Violence Against Women: The Hidden Health Burden* (Washington, DC: The World Bank, 1994), my italics.

[98] Toubia, *Program Guidelines for Integrating Activities to Eradicate Female Genital Mutilation*, 24. UN High Commissioner for Human Rights, Zeid Ra'ad Al Hussein, says, in advocating for girls' education: "In addition to academic achievements, education must equip students with the tools to critically analyse and challenge rigid gender roles that limit choices and perpetuate women's subordination." "Girls' Education Key to Eliminating Discrimination," United Nations Human Rights, June 22, 2015, www.ohchr.org/EN/NewsEvents/Pages/GirlsEducation.aspx (accessed July 12, 2016).

[99] This led to some unwanted attention from some of the men around her as she recounts in the article. Rosamund Urwin, "Waris Dirie: The Supermodel Giving FGM Victims Their Sexuality Back," *Evening Standard*, July 1, 2015, www.standard.co.uk/lifestyle/london-life/waris-dirie-the-supermodel-giving-fgm-victims-their-sexuality-back-10357560.html (accessed July 12, 2016).

[100] *Ibid.*

By removing their external genitalia, female Hofriyati seek not to diminish
their own sexual pleasure – though this is an obvious effect – so much as
to enhance their femininity. Pharaonic circumcision is a symbolic act which
brings sharply into focus the fertility potential of women by dramatically
deemphasizing their sexuality.

Later, she adds: "Village women do not achieve social recognition
by behaving or becoming like men, but by becoming less like men,
physically, sexually, and socially."[101] Anthropologist Ellen Gruenbaum
recalls a conversation with a neighbor in Sudan who asked if women
in the United States were infibulated:

I told her, "No, we leave women 'natural,' with no circumcision at all." She
paused thoughtfully before her reply: "This is 'natural' for us."[102]

Other anthropological accounts record the amusement of women who
have been circumcised at the appearance of uncircumcised Western
women, as well as discussions of whether or not FGM/C prevents
women from experiencing sexual pleasure. Gruenbaum queries this
conclusion on the grounds that simply focusing on sex demeans the
importance of sensuality and love and ignores any psychological factors that may be present and inhibiting female enjoyment of sex, but
also that the data on sexual response post-FGM/C is ambiguous.[103]
Melissa Parker goes even further arguing that:

The apparent need for many people in the West to make sense of themselves
in terms that emphasise particular aspects of their sexuality, and to require
particular kinds of sexual gratification for their well-being, is not, of course,
universal. In other parts of the world, and indeed for some people in the
West, such ideas seem immoral, amoral or bizarre.[104]

---

[101] Janice Boddy, *Wombs and Alien Spirits: Women, Men, and the Zar Cult in
the Northern Sudan* (Madison: University of Wisconsin Press, 1989), 55, 56
(Hofriyat is a pseudonym used by Boddy). Boddy argues that biological sex –
as evident in the genitalia of babies – is an ambiguous indicator of a child's
future gender identity which, for the Hofriyati, is a matter of socialization
over subsequent years. As a result: "Genital surgery accomplishes the social
definition of a child's sex," for both boys and girls. *Ibid.*, 58.

[102] Gruenbaum, *The Female Circumcision Controversy*, 68.

[103] *Ibid.*, 132, 144, and ch. 5, *passim*. See also Bell, "Genital Cutting and Western
Discourses on Sexuality," 138.

[104] Melissa Parker, "Rethinking Female Circumcision," *Africa* 65, 4 (1995): 520.

Underlying elimination efforts is a conception of the liberal subject that reflects widely held views about the civilizational progressiveness of Western women as Mohanty has argued (referring to the view some Western feminists hold of Third World women):

This average third-world woman leads an essentially truncated life based on her feminine gender (read: sexually constrained) and being "third world" (read: ignorant, poor, uneducated, tradition-bound, religious, domesticated, family-oriented, victimized, etc.). This, I suggest, is in contrast to the (implicit) self-representation of western women as educated, modern, as having control over their own bodies and sexualities, and the "freedom" to make their own decisions.[105]

This view of poor women isn't restricted to the Third World. In her account of "professional middle-class maternity" in Britain, where she argues a neoliberal form of feminism is establishing itself, Angela McRobbie describes successful women as either stage-managers of the "family financial unit" and successful professionals in their own right, or as slim and youthful mothers whose lives revolve around "routines of play dates, coffee shops and jogging buggies." This conception of modernity eschews feminism's social democratic heritage and reinstates "new norms of middle-class hegemony against which less advantaged families can only feel themselves to be inferior or inadequate or else judging themselves as having not tried hard enough."[106] This conception of empowered maternity and femininity, consistent with the subject at the core of human rights, puts a high premium on autonomous individual choices. This is what allows FGM/C to be categorized as the crime of child abuse (i.e., bad or "non-maternal" mothering) and justifies a child being protected from her mother and other female relatives until she is old enough to make an informed choice for herself. In some ways this is the least visible but most important impact of paternalism. But the full panoply of neoliberal choices is not available, of course, to young girls in FGM/C-practicing societies; FGM/C is just one part of their lives along with many poverty-related concerns like lack of education and health care.

---

[105] Mohanty, "Under Western Eyes."
[106] Angela McRobbie, "Feminism, the Family and the New 'Mediated' Maternalism," *New Formations* 80–81 (2013).

Conclusion

In the campaign against FGM/C, I've argued, paternalism is an ever present. It's obviously there in relation to children, and it's present in a clash between parents and elimination advocates who would use the criminal law to stop it. But even the most sensitive strategies of the FGM/C movement reject the notion that the status quo of ongoing consent is legitimate. This consent is not genuine largely because of a combination of a set of existing patriarchal norms that disguise women's true interests and a lack of adequate information about alternatives. Choices are not being made in a defensible way. Soft paternalists rely on this lack of genuine consent for justification, but they also shape the making of choices in far more subtle ways than hard paternalists. In the end, this more subtle persuasion operates at a deeper level of paternalism, having radical effects on FGM/C-practicing communities and on the self-identities of the girls who grow up in them. Whether paternalism is justified through moral or welfare concerns, the scale of this involvement in the lives of others regardless of their own professed desires surely constitutes a powerful form of paternal action.

In conclusion I want to make four further points. The first is about the nature of the conversation. We can see structural power ("empire") at work in the fact that African women do not get to problematize and challenge Western norms about, for example, child raising. Paternalism is a top-down social practice. The women Tostan deals with don't get to come to London or New York and start a discussion about Western norms of gender, sexuality, and appropriate ways to treat children. If they did, what might they say about intensely competitive education (and the depression to which it increasingly leads), boarding schools, lack of play and risk appreciation, medication of behavior, overprotectiveness, lack of social responsibility, greed, poor consumption habits, obesity, weak impulse control, addiction to technology, sexualization of children and so on. They might accuse children in the West of being infantilized well into adulthood, overly entitled and anti-social and lacking in proper respect for their elders, rather than prepared for their adult lives by their parents within a functioning community.

This leads to the second point. Culture and community are often portrayed as playing a negative role in the case of FGM/C. In the words of Nahid Toubia:

The fear of losing the psychological, moral and material benefits of "belonging" is one of the greatest motivators of conformity. When the demands of conformity conflict with rationality or individual need, denial intervenes as a mechanism for survival. In this way, many women justify their own oppression.[107]

Safa's mother, quoted above, put this succinctly: "She will never belong to our society like the other girls." But we have seen the vital importance of community involvement in social change. In some ways, the authority of the community makes normative change easier. In the case of the United Kingdom, for example, changing a norm about appropriate civility in public life would require legal change and persuasion of each individual, in a sense, to abide by collective expectations. In the case of Senegal, in contrast, the community shifts the norm of acceptability and everyone, feeling the weight of community membership, follows. For many the lack of community support is exactly one of the ills of modern life. Hillary Clinton's 1996 book *It Takes a Village* was an attempt to argue that raising children in America was a social responsibility.[108] "It takes a village (to raise a child)" was said to be an African proverb.

But can modernity realize the vision of liberal subjects without disassembling the village? Is FGM/C a ritual that precisely consolidates the sense of shared identity and destiny that makes a village, a community, strong? In this sense, it is about high entry and exit costs. If you are circumcised then you are committed in a deep sense to remain amongst others who both share and understand the practice. The village keeps its young people and the families – and the family economy here is pivotal to survival – ensure its reproduction. In many ways, the liberal subject is fashioned to leave the village, to take her labor power and turn it into capital somewhere else for someone else's benefit rather than that of her relatives. She can see herself as a free agent, unencumbered by permanent identity and able to choose any sense of femininity and sexuality for herself. Are we so sure we are right that this is progress on the metric of human happiness if we measure it by a sense of security and belonging? This is not to

---

[107] Toubia, *Female Genital Mutilation*, 37.
[108] Hillary Rodham Clinton, *It Takes a Village, And Other Lessons Children Teach Us* (New York: Simon & Schuster, 1996).

defend FGM/C. If the Tostan model could be effective throughout Africa it would seem to be a net gain on any metric one might care to specify – what's right, what's good, harm to others, longevity, quality of life. It's hard to see what argument can be made against it beyond "it is tradition" which only opens up the debate about why any given tradition should (or should not) persist. But it is to ask what function such rituals play in community life, and what is lost as well as gained by eliminating them.

This leads to the third point: What *responsibility* goes along with pushing for radical cultural change? Does creating liberal subjects create a responsibility for making a liberal society to go with them? The women we have been hearing about are often living in conditions of great material scarcity and environmental vulnerability. They remain responsible for the long-term life prospects their daughters enjoy once the anti-FGM/C movement's gaze moves on. For many FGM/C-practicing communities, the imminent threat to life and health are greater from other causes – disease, violence, hunger – than from the negative consequences of FGM/C. As a result, seeing FGM/C within its "socioeconomic, political and cultural context" is essential.[109]

If we intervene in this significant way, do we not then take on a responsibility to see the job through? If we stop a parent abusing a child, if we create estrangement by educating the rising generation in a way that clashes with the values of their parents, if we introduce new consumption patterns, do we not retain some ongoing responsibility for the consequences? Surely this must be part of the paternalistic discussion? Is it really enough to undertake our experiment and then get back on the plane? When the rights of African girls are said to be our mission, then the fact they may be malnourished matters as much to them, as it should to us, as the fact that they face FGM/C. If we assume FGM/C is our responsibility, we should be asking what else will improve the life chances of the child concerned: health, education, work? Moreover, are we not obligated to address squarely the contradictions in our position? Isn't it the rights of children that concern us? In which case, all forms of physical interference with the genitalia

---

109 Obioma Nnaemeka and Joy Ngozi Ezeilo, "Context(ure)s of Human Rights – Local Realities, Global Contexts," in *Engendering Human Rights: Cultural and Socioeconomic Realities in Africa*, eds. Obioma Nnaemeka and Joy Ngozi Ezeilo (London: Palgrave Macmillan, 2005), 5.

of young children at whatever age should be part of the conversation, including male circumcision.[110]

Finally, the children themselves are almost entirely absent from this story. They are in Tostan's model: there is a separate track for adolescents separate from their parents although these are older children than the age at which circumcision takes place. But in general the voice of the child isn't heard on either side. For the parents, the child is not a liberal subject with rights against them but integrally part of "the family economy" and thus like all family members she has a role, obligations, and expectations placed on her that are defined in large part by the family's needs. For interveners, many of these children would choose circumcision given that their mothers and grandmothers, sisters and friends are all circumcised (and their brothers, there being few examples where male circumcision doesn't go along with female circumcision). The social implications of such a change in family dynamics, especially in poor, rural societies, are profound. If young people, for example, do not remain to tend the elderly, where will a social safety net come from? The state? Western aid agencies? And do children have a strong voice in our own societies? They certainly lack many of the formal mechanisms by which to represent their own interests (to vote, to appear in their own rights before the law, to marry, to have sex). These are all areas where we silence them but is it "for their own good" or ours? The very least we can do in eliminating FGM/C is take a hard look at our own attitudes and practices toward children and reflect on the many hypocrisies which mark the supposedly more developed and civilized societies of the West.

[110] Schweder, "Symposium on German Court Ruling on Circumcision"; Bell, "Genital Cutting and Western Discourses on Sexuality."

9 | Humanitarian Refusals: Palestinian Refugees and Ethnographic Perspectives on Paternalism

ILANA FELDMAN

The aim of this chapter is to develop an analysis of actually-existing paternalism. I mean this in much the same way that people talk about actually-existing cosmopolitanism,[1] neoliberalism,[2] and democracy[3] to suggest that an understanding of any of these concepts requires capturing the complexity of experience and building a theory of the concept from that complexity. From an "actually-existing" perspective, the contradictions and messiness of lived paternalism (or anything else) neither needs to be explained away as deviations from a model nor does it serve as evidence that a circumstance is not a case of paternalism. Rather, this experience provides the grounds for understanding what paternalism might actually be in the world. Thinking about actually-existing paternalism can help avoid a conceptual cul-de-sac wherein paternalism is defined so narrowly as to make it essentially unreal. If one can identify paternalism only in cases where the motives for intervention are entirely altruistic (not returning any kind of benefit to the intervener), for instance, then paternalism seems more like a unicorn than a horse: something that can be described, but never encountered in the world. To capture what paternalism actually is in the world, an ethnographic perspective is, if not vital, certainly extremely helpful. Ethnography, whether the face-to-face interactions of classical fieldwork or ethnographic readings of archives and other texts,[4] builds theory from the ground up. It starts, though does not necessarily end, with the subjects' perspective.

---

[1] Bruce Robbins, "Introduction, Part 1: Actually Existing Cosmopolitanism," in *Cosmopolitics: Thinking and Feeling Beyond the Nation*, eds. Pheng Cheah and Bruce Robbins (Minneapolis: University of Minnesota Press, 1998), 1–19.

[2] Neil Brenner and Nik Theodore, "Cities and the Geographies of 'Actually Existing Neoliberalism'," *Antipode* 34, 3 (2002): 349–79.

[3] Nancy Fraser, "Rethinking the Public Sphere: A Contribution to the Critique of Actually Existing Democracy," in *Habermas and the Public Sphere*, ed. Craig Calhoun (Cambridge, MA: MIT Press, 1992), 109–42.

[4] Ann Stoler, *Along the Archival Grain: Epistemic Anxieties and Colonial Common Sense* (Princeton: Princeton University Press, 2009).

Any consideration of paternalism has to think about the question of its subjects, even if these are often abstract rather than actual subjects. But most reflections on the ethics of paternalism begin from the perspective of the (potential) paternalist. It is the intervener who is the key actor in these concerns and the one who is asked to think about the ethics and politics of his or her actions and interventions. So even as the liberal theory of paternalism claims to start from a presumption of fundamental equality – each person posited as a rational actor who can expect non-interference – it is in fact ensconced in the hierarchies that make up actual people and relationships. In this chapter I offer a different perspective and begin from a different starting point: that of the experiences of people who are on the receiving end of possibly paternalist action. I begin here not just to account for and respect these realities (though that is important in and of itself), but because actually-existing paternalism is defined by the experiences of all its participants, and by the relations among them.

Ethnographic investigation of paternalism reveals a network of relations, rather than a collection of pre-formed, atomized persons who restrict (or not) other persons' liberty. Through this lens paternalism appears, not just as an ethical principle guiding action, but as a field of practice. In circumstances such as humanitarian crises and long-term humanitarian conditions[5] paternalism can be a crucial part of shaping life-worlds: subjects are formed through these practices (they do not simply enact them), relations are structured by them, political engagements are produced through these dynamics. An ethnographic account of paternalism also exposes paternalism as a field that contains multiple sorts of hierarchies. Where a classic discussion of paternalism appears dyadic – one subject restricting another subject's liberty – actually-existing paternalism contains a variety of imbalances and restrictions. In a humanitarian context these can include both large geopolitical inequalities across populations and intimate differentials in decision-making authority. It involves both international agencies and local expressions of patriarchy and other social hierarchies.

---

[5] Ilana Feldman, "The Humanitarian Condition: Palestinian Refugees and the Politics of Living," *Humanity: An International Journal of Human Rights, Humanitarianism & Development* 3, 2 (2012): 155–72.

The case I use to pursue this investigation is the Palestinian refugee experience of living with humanitarianism over the long-term. This instance spans more than seventy years (from 1948) and five fields of displacement and humanitarian apparatus (Jordan, Lebanon, Syria, West Bank, and Gaza Strip). After this long time, there are now five million refugees registered with UN Relief and Works Agency for Palestine Refugees (UNRWA). I use examples from a range of times and places in this experience. My interest here is not just in using this instance as a case-study to advance a more general argument about paternalism. This chapter also seeks to develop a better understanding of how Palestinian refugees (and aid providers) have responded to the assorted hierarchies that shape their life-worlds. It forms part of a larger research project in which I am investigating how humanitarianism helps define the features of a dispersed, but not dissipated, Palestinian community and am outlining the characteristics of long-term humanitarianism.

Palestinians are war refugees, displaced from their homes and homeland in the conflict over the establishment of the state of Israel and never, yet, permitted to return. The United Nations quickly commissioned a number of private agencies – the American Friends Service Committee and the League of Red Cross Societies among them – to deliver UN-provided assistance. These agencies, along with the governments of the countries to which refugees fled, managed the aid system until the creation of UNRWA – a recognition that the situation was not coming to a quick conclusion. Since UNRWA began working in 1950 it has been the premier aid agency for Palestinian refugees, but in every time and place other organizations have continued to operate.

The "birth of the Palestinian refugee problem"[6] essentially coincided with the creation of the post-war international humanitarian regime. And since this problem has not yet been solved, the trajectory of assistance to Palestinian refugees over the last seventy years provides a lens into the contours of this wider system over that time. There is much that is distinctive, even exceptional, about the Palestinian case – not least that there is a separate UN agency dedicated to the provision of humanitarian assistance to Palestine refugees, these refugees are excluded from the terms of the 1951 Convention on the Status

---

[6] Benny Morris, *The Birth of the Palestinian Refugee Problem, 1947–1949* (Cambridge: Cambridge University Press, 1987).

of Refugees, and they fall outside the jurisdiction of the UN High Commissioner on Refugees (UNHCR). Despite these significant distinctions, the character of humanitarian services and the structure of humanitarian relations are much the same as in other circumstances. What we can learn by considering the Palestinian instance has broad import.

The empirical focus of this chapter is how people who are on the receiving end of humanitarian intervention respond to procedures and relationships that often feel to them to be paternalistic and deeply hierarchical. I am particularly interested in responses that seek, in some way, to alter these dynamics. I investigate refusals of refugees to accede to the humanitarian order: sometimes by refusing to receive aid, sometimes by skirting the rules of such acceptance, and sometimes through proactive attempts to produce a qualitatively different kind of engagement in situations of need. These efforts and refusals are a response to paternalism not as a matter of considered policy, but as a practice on the ground and in the instance. These refusals also constitute an insistence that paternalism is a political as well as ethical matter, and that changing the relationships and practices that define a paternalist landscape has significant political import.

Paternalism as Framework for Thinking about Humanitarianism

Humanitarianism exerts a powerful claim on the global imagination. It appears to many as almost the ultimate form of doing good, a path to engagement across distance and difference that is governed by compassion and care, rather than by strategic alliances and cynical political calculations. But scholars investigating the experiences and effects of humanitarian interventions have described a more complicated picture. Among what Fiona Terry calls the "paradoxes of humanitarian action"[7] and David Kennedy describes as the "dark sides of virtue"[8] are the possibilities that humanitarian intervention may prolong conflicts that cause the suffering it seeks to alleviate; that principles of neutrality and

---

[7] Fiona Terry, *Condemned to Repeat? The Paradox of Humanitarian Action* (Ithaca, NY: Cornell University Press, 2002).

[8] David Kennedy, *The Dark Sides of Virtue: Reassessing International Humanitarianism* (Princeton: Princeton University Press, 2004).

confidentiality may impede calling perpetrators to account; that, in serving as gateways to assistance, procedures of refugee identification and registration may also impose restrictions on victims' actions; and that the need to mobilize international compassion to support humanitarian endeavors may involve some degree of exploitation of people's suffering.

The possibility that humanitarian intervention can impede resolution of the underlying causes of humanitarian need is of great concern to humanitarian actors. Few humanitarian agencies would consider it within their purview to work actively toward such a resolution, and indeed most see their recusal from involvement in political processes as crucial to their ability to accomplish their goals. At the same time, they hope that carving out a "humanitarian space" within which they can protect lives and alleviate suffering will provide local actors with the political space in which to conclude conflicts and adjudicate responsibility. That warring parties may use the breathing room – or even the services – that humanitarianism provides to extend their campaigns is a source of great anguish for these agencies.

Humanitarian action's impact on recipients of aid can be equally contradictory. It can reduce people to their victim status – in part by requiring them to appear as exemplary victims and not political actors in order to receive recognition of their suffering, and in part as a byproduct of mechanisms of aid delivery that restrict their capacities to act in other ways. Humanitarian agencies depend heavily on donations from governments, foundations, and individuals, and on the mobilization of compassion. The global circulation of images of suffering becomes a necessity for "transforming emotion into donations."[9] At the same time, there are ways in which humanitarian action, without meaning to, can serve as a space from which people can act politically and can provide a language to press such claims. Limit and possibility are linked in humanitarianism's effects on those it seeks to help.

Paternalism is not all that needs to be understood about humanitarianism and humanitarian relations. Humanitarianism is a space of political claim making,[10] of identity formation and the building of

[9] Rony Brauman, "Global Media and the Myths of Humanitarian Relief: The Case of the 2004 Tsunami," in *Humanitarianism and Suffering: the Mobilization of Empathy*, eds. Richard Wilson and Richard Brown (Cambridge: Cambridge University Press, 2009), 108–17.
[10] Feldman, "The Humanitarian Condition."

historical narratives,[11] of ethical labor for providers,[12] among other things. And it is a space of hierarchical relations that are mediated through the language and practice of care. Considering humanitarianism through the lens of (actually-existing) paternalism and paternalism through the dynamics of humanitarianism in practice reveals important features of each. How can the concept of actually-existing paternalism help us better understand humanitarian dynamics? Actors in humanitarian situations – both providers and recipients – grapple with questions about the character of these interventions, their effects on recipient societies, and the forms of hierarchy that are presumed and produced by this assistance. Precisely because good intentions are baked into the concept of paternalism,[13] it can provide an important perspective for analyzing the complex effects of the humanitarian terrain.

Paternalism provides a framework for thinking about humanitarian challenges that resists easy recourse to the language of hypocrisy, a charge which is inadequate for understanding humanitarian interactions. The language and practice of humanitarianism can provide a cover for imperial adventures and is certainly an exercise in global power, often reflecting the cynical calculations of distant politicians. But it is not only that, and the closer to the ground one gets – to the messy work of aid delivery, not the calculation about whether to intervene – the less it looks like that. The concept of actually-existing paternalism provides a means to understand the power dynamics, inequalities, and sometimes significant ill effects that result from humanitarian interventions regardless of how well intentioned those interventions are. When humanitarian actors grapple with the ethics of their interventions they are caught in this "double bind."[14]

Few scholars, aid workers, or recipients would disagree with the premise that humanitarianism is necessarily hierarchical. In the humanitarian context paternalism is both a condition and is sometimes expressed as a value, even if practitioners might not use the

[11] Liisa Malkki, *Purity and Exile: Violence, Memory, and National Cosmology among Hutu Refugees in Tanzania* (Chicago: Chicago University Press, 1995).
[12] Ilana Feldman, "The Quaker Way: Ethical Labor and Humanitarian Relief," *American Ethnologist* 34, 4 (2007): 689–705.
[13] Richardson, Chapter 1, this volume.
[14] Peter Redfield, "The Unbearable Lightness of Ex-Pats: Double Binds of Humanitarian Mobility," *Cultural Anthropology* 27, 2 (2012): 358–82.

word. It is a condition in the sense that the very circumstances that necessitate humanitarian intervention are either products of, or themselves produce, different opportunities and capacities. Some people need help, whether because of natural disaster, war, or other dislocation, and some people can help. These differences are the starting point for humanitarian work. But paternalism is also expressed as a value when humanitarian practitioners make clear in a variety of ways that the humanitarian mission of doing good for refugees relies on their capacity to know better. This capacity sometimes takes the form of technical expertise and sometimes of better judgment, the capacity to better understand the situation in which refugees live.

Humanitarian actors have responded to the felt paternalism of humanitarianism in a range of ways. Even when they recognize or claim a paternalistic relation to recipients, they are often also interested in mitigating some of the effects of this hierarchical condition. One of the idioms through which this goal is pursued is participation. Across the humanitarian and development world efforts toward recipient participation, community buy-in, and bottom-up planning have gained currency in recent years. This has certainly been the case in the Palestinian context. This interest in participation, and the ways this turn is perceived by refugees, further reveals the relevance of paternalism to lived humanitarianism.

Humanitarianism is a global system, involving actors in the centers of power and in the most peripheral of spaces. Much of what structures humanitarian work is, thus, shaped by factors distant from any particular circumstance. At the same time, on the ground humanitarianism is an often intimate endeavor. It brings providers and recipients into close, sometimes uncomfortable, relation. It is perhaps for this reason that the question of humanitarian attitude – the interpersonal, affective dimension of aid provision – seems such an important part of the question of humanitarian paternalism. I would suggest, though, that the question of attitude, while not insignificant, is not in fact the heart of the matter. The problem of paternalism (to the extent that there is a problem) cannot be solved through a change in attitude. And recipients are most concerned about the structural hierarchies that underlie the aid system, even when it is populated by entirely well-intentioned, sympathetic, and sensitive aid workers.

Refugee Refusals

How do Palestinian refugees live in relation to paternalism? How do they respond to the hierarchies that structure the aid relation, and therefore their lives? There is no single response, of course. Plenty of people accept the situation, in practice, even if not in principle, either seeing it as an unavoidable accompaniment to the aid they want or lacking the wherewithal to do anything other than live with it. Some, though, try to refuse this condition. Such refusal, which is not easy, takes multiple forms. Exploring forms of refugee refusal not only lets us see the variety of ways that recipients of humanitarian aid react to the hierarchies of this practice, but also to better understand the hierarchies themselves. As I suggested above, actually-existing paternalism is defined in part by the experiences and responses of those who are on its receiving end. I explore three of these forms here.

The most dramatic refusal I consider is a rejection of humanitarianism entirely. It should come as no surprise that it is also the least common. By refusing to participate in the humanitarian enterprise at all, people who take this path insist on their freedom of action, which in the dramatically constrained conditions of a humanitarian crisis can mean the freedom to remain exposed and at risk. This stance is a political one: it not only asserts the continued capacity for agency in the face of dramatic need, but also renders a judgment on the humanitarian enterprise. I look at this rejection by considering the refusal to register as a refugee. This refusal responds most directly to paternalism as a structuring condition (the uneven distribution of capacity) rather than to paternalism as a value or an attitude.

Another, much more frequent, form of refusal is a refusal within humanitarianism. This sort of refusal can take the form of demanding policy reforms, seeking to make changes in particular humanitarian practices. This kind of refusal constitutes an insistence on the part of refugees of their capacity for judgment – that they, as much as planners and practitioners, can have a say in the form of humanitarian practice. As such, this refusal within humanitarianism seeks to impose limits on the paternalism of the enterprise. Refusals within humanitarianism provide an especially clear window into the ways that paternalism structures relationships

Both the refusal *of* and the refusal *within* humanitarianism are forms of speaking back directly to this apparatus, its practitioners, and its claims. The third sort of refusal I consider is one that pursues an alternative to humanitarian dynamics by creating possibilities for living otherwise. Over the years Palestinian refugees have pursued a variety of paths toward non-humanitarian futures, including grassroots politics and military activity. Some of these paths have been ephemeral and experimental. Others have been organized and even codified. These are not direct refusals of humanitarianism, they bypass rather than confront it. This pursuit of alternatives seeks to alter the conditions that generate paternalist relationships, and in that sense move beyond a stance of refusal to one of innovation.

Refusing Registration

I begin my consideration of refugee refusals with the most dramatic, and the rarest form of refusal: the refusal of aid entirely. Thinking about instances of rejecting assistance means turning to threshold moments in the refugee, and therefore the aid, experience. With Palestinian displacement exceeding seventy years now, the humanitarian experience, and most of the refusals I explore, is of a *longue durée*. But most registration happens immediately after displacement, in the moment of crisis.[15] 1948 was the key time of displacement, followed by a second major wave in 1967, when Israel occupied the West Bank and Gaza Strip. Most Palestinian refugees not only accepted, but sought assistance, as evidenced by the fact that most displaced persons who were eligible, and some who were not, registered as refugees.[16] The rarity of refusal is further evidenced by its absence from the documentary historical records. I have encountered only a few references to this practice. I have heard about exceptional instances of refusal in the course

---

[15] I say most because children born to refugees are then registered as refugees themselves, so the registration process has never ended. What I am exploring are the instances of adult registration that happened when people were displaced.

[16] A much more common circumstance than refusal was that people who were not eligible for relief according to UN criteria (native poor in Gaza for example) found ways onto the ration rolls and families who were receiving rations did not report changes in life status (death, move, etc.) that would decrease the family's rations. On the challenges of defining a Palestine refugee and managing access to relief see Ilana Feldman, "The Challenge of Categories: UNRWA and the Definition of a 'Palestine Refugee,'" *Journal of Refugee Studies* 25, 3 (2012): 387–406 and Ilana Feldman, "The Quaker Way."

of ethnographic fieldwork and conducting life-history interviews in refugee camps. I have also heard expressions of frustration that it was not a more widespread choice. Instances of rejection not only provide a window into the significance of these choices, they also illuminate the conflicts that could emerge among refugees, and especially within refugee families, about such choices.

Why might people refuse aid? And why might people wish that more refusal might have been possible? One reason is the existential crisis that sudden need produces. It is well known that the experience of finding oneself suddenly dependent, in need when one had always been self-sufficient, is often humiliating. My research with Palestinian refugees makes this clear, as does research on crisis responses around the world. When humanitarian actors respond to these crises they are aware of these feelings, an awareness that further contributes to the imperative to keep intervention short term, even as conditions may make a quick end to aid impossible. Providing food to someone in need, even if receiving that food feels humiliating, seems like one of the clearest cases of the humanitarian imperative at work. To choose not to intervene, to privilege some notion of self-respect over the importance of saving lives, appears to most people – humanitarian actors, recipients, and observers alike – as an ethically untenable position. And hence it also seems to be one of the clearest instances of justified paternalism: the capable actor must save peoples' lives, no matter what their view on the matter. But since my perspective is ethnographic, the fact that such paternalism might be justified cannot be the end of my inquiry. I have to consider what might be at stake for refugees in refusing, or trying to refuse, the help they so evidently need.

The hierarchies of lives that humanitarian crises bring into relief – that some people are at risk and others in a position to save them – has been a source of concern for some humanitarian workers. Didier Fassin, for instance, describes the decision by Médecins San Frontières/Doctors Without Borders (MSF) workers to stay in Iraq as the 2003 American bombing campaign loomed as in part motivated by a desire to disrupt the "inequality between those whose lives are sacred and those whose lives may be sacrificed."[17] By choosing to stay, MSF staff

---

[17] Didier Fassin, "Inequality of Lives, Hierarchies of Humanity: Moral Commitments and Ethical Dilemmas of Humanitarianism," in *Government and Humanity*, eds. Ilana Feldman and Miriam Ticktin (Durham, NC: Duke University Press, 2010), 238–55, 247.

made a gesture toward exposing themselves to risk just as Iraqis were exposed. The difficulty, perhaps impossibility, of actually transforming this inequality was also revealed in this instance. And, after three team members were abducted, MSF left the country. As much as humanitarian workers may desire (and many, quite reasonably, would not so desire) to put themselves into positions of humanitarian vulnerability, they can never be as vulnerable as those they seek to help. Refugees who try to refuse these same hierarchies, may in fact deepen the vulnerability they already are experiencing. Rejecting humanitarianism's hierarchies may require, and has seemed to some people to require, rejecting humanitarianism *in toto*.

In the course of my research in the Jerash refugee camp in Jordan, a camp populated largely by people who were refugees to Gaza in 1948 and displaced a second time to Jordan in 1967, I heard several stories of refusing registration. The circumstance of double displacement means that the camp's residents experienced at least two threshold moments. Jamal, whose family is from the Beersheba region in southern Palestine, described an instance of post-1948 refusal. When the family was displaced to Gaza, his grandfather, as head of household, refused to register them with UNRWA because "he did not want to be a refugee." Since refugee status passes down to children, through the male line, this initial decision to refuse has had multi-generational consequences. Following UNRWA criteria, which reserves the official refugee category for 1948 displacement, Jamal's family are considered *nazihiin* (displaced) in Jordan, rather than *laj'iin* (refugees). This distinction has real consequences for their eligibility for humanitarian services.

In registration refusals such as that of Jamal's grandfather, several things seem to have been at stake. These refusals seek to make a change in existential and political conditions. They speak to the hierarchies of lives that make humanitarianism necessary and which its practice can further deepen. They can also make a claim about the politics of aid in the Palestinian instance, especially its relation to the larger questions of resolution, restitution, and return. In addition to what they try to effect, registration refusals also reveal the multiplicity of hierarchies that are present in Palestinian life, and in which humanitarianism is complicit.

Refusal to register speaks back to the hierarchy of lives and its relation to risk and exposure. As Jamal noted about his grandfather's choice, it was a refusal to accept his condition: to try to refuse to be (to become?) a refugee. To the extent that refusal to register is a rejection of paternalism, it is a rejection of paternalism as a condition, not as an attitude or even as a specific set of actions. This refusal entailed accepting, maybe even insisting upon, a certain degree of exposure and suffering in order not to acknowledge or be trapped by the categorical condition of loss. To this extent refusing registration is also a refusal of one of humanitarianism's central hierarchies: precisely the capacity to put oneself at risk. What we see in this case is an insistence on the part of victims of their capacity to remain exposed: to refuse the transfer of agency over life that humanitarian intervention entails. Humanitarianism seeks to remove people from threat, to save them from exposure. Refusing to enter the system, to accept assistance, to register as a refugee, is in part an effort, not simply to be exposed as displaced persons already are, but to choose exposure for a larger purpose. Such capacity is what is often denied refugees, both by their circumstances and by the structure of humanitarian practice. This is part of the paternalism, not so much of humanitarians, but of humanitarianism: that the aid system operates to remove the availability of bad choices from refugees.

In the Palestinian case, refugee registration was a family matter. So refusal was not only addressed to humanitarianism, it resonated within families. UNRWA's choice to have the head of household do the registering and to have status descend through the male line has meant that the humanitarian system is patriarchal,[18] and in this it resonates with gendered and generational hierarchies that are part of Palestinian society. Registration refusal does not disrupt these hierarchies, but rather reveals their effects. In Jamal's family's case the effect has been multi-generational. Another refusal story I heard in Jerash, this one about the 1967 second displacement to Jordan, shows how refusal could be a source of contention within families.

Im Taha, originally from Iraq Suwaydan in Palestine, described how Jordanian officials registered people coming across the Allenby bridge into Jordan – in the process switching their place of UNRWA registration from the Gaza Strip to Jordan. Her husband did not want to register because he was afraid that registering in Jordan would mean

---

[18] Christine Cervenak, "Promoting Inequality: Gender-Based Discrimination in UNRWA's Approach to Palestine Refugee Status," *Human Rights Quarterly* 16 (1994): 300–74.

they would not be able to go back to Gaza. His concern was not about being registered as a refugee per se (the family was registered), but with maintaining his status as a refugee registered in the Gaza field. As he sat at a distance from the registration, Im Taha, concerned first and foremost about getting help for herself and her children, registered herself as being the wife of another man – who she said had been missing for six months. In this way she got a tent and food supplies despite her husband's refusal. If part of what was at stake in Jamal's grandfather's refusal was a practical instance on the capacity to remain exposed, Im Taha appears to have refused precisely such exposure. This case was a secondary refusal in several senses: Abu Taha refused a second registration, one that would confirm his second displacement. Im Taha refused Abu Taha's refusal, choosing the immediate welfare of her family over a claim about principle. Abu Taha's refusal may have tried to disrupt paternalism, but it underscored patriarchy. Im Taha's refusal of his refusal intervened in this second sort of hierarchy.

These individual refusals of humanitarian categories and aid illuminate principles and politics of refugee action, but they were rarely articulated in precisely those terms. These minority actions have tended to fade into the background of the much larger story of refugee registration and the widespread and initially comprehensive aid system. Even as the effects lingered for individuals, they are not really part of the collective story of displacement. If anything the role that registration refusal plays in this collective story is precisely about its absence. In my conversations with Palestinian refugees over the years I have heard many people lament that there wasn't more refusal by Palestinian refugees to enter into the humanitarian system after 1948. This lamentation must be understood as part of the extremely conflicted feelings Palestinians have about humanitarian aid in general and UNRWA in particular. On the one hand, UNRWA's presence is viewed as an acknowledgment of the international community's responsibility for Palestinian suffering and its obligations to restore their rights. In this regard, people often say that UNRWA is not a humanitarian institution, if by humanitarian one means aid motivated by compassion, rather than governed by obligation. On the other hand, people identify the persistence of humanitarianism as an impediment to a political resolution, and some see it as part of a concerted plan to thwart Palestinian aspirations for independence and restoration.

Thus, when some Palestinians express an interest in a collective refusal to participate in the humanitarian apparatus, it is directed not just, or even primarily, at the hierarchies that are baked into the structure of humanitarian intervention (the saver and the saved), but at the geopolitical imbalances that render Palestinian claims unattainable. One person told me a story from the early days of UNRWA that was meant to underscore the point that the acceptance of UNRWA services was detrimental to Palestinian political aspirations. He told me about a friend of his who met an American working with UNRWA who tried to give him some political advice: "The American told my friend: 'this food you eat from UNRWA I want to tell you something but do not say that I told you. If you reject the provisions and do not eat and 20 people die because of hunger, then they will take you back soon to your homes'. But we did not have that awareness. If we told people to do so they would have refused." The very structure of the story highlights the imbalanced power and capacity that he thought refusal might have worked against: it was an American who offered the political insight. It was the Palestinians who lacked "awareness" and who would have refused the advice. In this case both aid and the possibility of refusing aid were part of paternalist conditions.

As something that happens rarely what can these rejections of humanitarianism tell us about Palestinian responses to paternalism? They illuminate the perceived stakes of participating in this dynamic and underscore how difficult it is to remain apart from the system. Each of these instances, with its radiating effects on other family members, down generations, and across community also provides a window into ways Palestinians judge themselves. As they experience and evaluate the humanitarian experience, the significance of its paternalism, and its consequences for the possibilities of their lives, refugees are not only concerned with what is being done to them, but with their, sometimes necessary, complicity in the process. Refusals at the very edge of possibility – which refusing aid in circumstances of acute need certainly is – can rarely change much, precisely because they are inevitably so rare. But they do enable us to better understand how recipients feel about humanitarian intervention.

Protesting Policy

If individual refusals of registration constitute a refusal of humanitarianism, refugee protests about policy, procedure, and services are refusals within humanitarianism. These efforts to change particulars about humanitarian procedures are in some sense a more narrow sort of refusal than rejections of registration: they seek reform, rather than revolution. They are a wider sort of refusal in their relative frequency. Contrary to registration refusals, protests are widespread, often collective, and reflected upon. Both the archival record and the ethnographic field are replete with them. Like registration refusals, they constitute an insistence on refugee capacity and judgment. The capacity at issue in these protests is not the capacity to choose exposure or safety, but rather the capacity to evaluate and weigh in on humanitarian procedure. This claim is also consequential. It refuses a slightly different aspect of humanitarian paternalism: the presumption that only humanitarian actors have the ability to make systematic evaluations, to see the big picture, and to look beyond immediate personal need. Refugee protests about policies reject these claims. These refusals within humanitarianism highlight the extent to which humanitarian paternalism structures relationships among people. It can produce imperious attitudes and angry responses. It can also create close connections and mutual empathy. It shapes the mechanisms through which participants in the humanitarian dynamic engage each other: protest and responses to it are clear forms of communication.

Frustration with paternalistic presumptions about refugee capacity for judgment is evident in a range of contexts. A series of interviews from the West Bank make this clear. Part of my larger research project, these interviews were conducted by a group of young refugees from camps in the southern part of the West Bank with whom I have been collaborating. In the context of this collaboration, they interviewed other camp residents about their experiences with humanitarian assistance. We developed the interview questions together, drawing both on the questions I have been asking in interviews in other fields of UNRWA operations and on the participants' own experiences and ideas about important subjects to address. One set of questions that they put on our list is: Has anyone asked you what you really need in the way of services and assistance? Or do they just give you what they think you need? The formulation of the questions emerges from the strong sense among this group of young people, and the wider refugee community, that humanitarian practice is a deeply unequal endeavor and that opportunities for involvement not just in delivery but in substantive planning of projects and programs are limited.

The interviewees' answers to these questions bear this out, as no one indicated that they are asked about their own perceptions of their needs. But this question and its answers exist in a context where UNRWA in particular (and other humanitarian organizations as well) expends considerable effort on community engagement and refugee participation. Whenever I talk with UNRWA officials they describe their work to engage refugees. And I think these efforts are sincere. So why this disconnect? Why might people feel they are not consulted when humanitarian actors believe themselves to be doing so? In part it is because the camp residents interviewed in the West Bank are acutely aware that what is being sought is their "buy-in" to policies that have been developed by others, not their participation in the formation of policy. By and large humanitarian efforts to mitigate hierarchy and the disempowerment of aid recipients are not, in fact, efforts to work against paternalism. Rather, they are structured by it. Refugees understand this fact and make judgments based on it.

Over the years, and in every field of UNRWA operations, refugees have protested about a wide range of matters, from early rejections of replacing tents with more permanent structures (out of concern that this indicated that their displacement would be permanent) to recent demonstrations in the West Bank and Gaza about cutbacks in the UNRWA emergency job creation program. Humanitarian workers respond to these protests in a range of ways, including sympathy, agreement, frustration, and outright condemnation. In most fields of UNRWA operation employees operate with an acute awareness that anything the Agency does to change policy or procedure will be scrutinized by recipients and could easily generate protest. Some UNRWA personnel see in many such protests a manipulation of refugees by local political actors (especially by the popular committees which mediate between the Agency and the population), but regardless of their view of their genuineness, everyone has to be prepared to deal with them.

An instance of refugee protest in the late 1950s in Lebanon – a boycott of Agency services – provides an opportunity to explore the terms in which protests are conducted and the extent to which they constitute a reaction to perceived paternalism. In December 1958 "The Palestine Arab Youth in Lebanon" called on refugees to refuse to receive rations and on UNRWA's refugee employees to refuse to work until a range of demands were met. These demands included removing certain UNRWA officials from their posts, restoring medical clinics that had been discontinued, "abolishing the new administrative procedures," improving school conditions and hiring more teachers, and that the Agency's activities be "confined to humanitarian field."[19] The meaning of this last statement is not made explicit in the call, but I take it to refer to a rejection of presumed or actual resettlement plans. As the strike got underway it was widely reported on by the Lebanese press, and UNRWA took careful note of these reports. According to one account: "The Palestine refugees have for the first time yesterday gone on a collective boycott to UNRWA in Lebanon and prevented the staff from exercising their work in camps; students have refrained from going to schools; and refugees stopped receiving rations, or any medical services."[20] The strike was a strategic refusal of humanitarianism in order to accomplish an improvement in humanitarian services, and to make a statement about humanitarian politics.

An article published in *Beirut al-Masa* highlighted the extent to which the strike was not just about particular policies, but was also about an Agency attitude toward refugees: an attitude which refugees saw as disregard.[21] The terms of these objections to the attitudes of some UNRWA staff make clear, though, that even complaints about attitudes were also (and perhaps at core) complaints about the presumed distribution of judgment. According to the article, strikers wanted certain officials removed, for instance, because "the refugees accuse [them] of defying their feelings and resisting their wishes." A further demand was for the appointment of "a number of educated Palestine young men who are well-known to the refugees" to work with UNRWA because "these alone can transmit the proper and just refugee wishes to those responsible in UNRWA, and cooperate with it in its humanitarian mission, provided that the mission does not exceed the limits of humanitarian affairs and does not at all interfere in

---

[19] UNRWA, Inactive Files Box 7, L/500/1 – Lebanon, Refugees, Boycott. Declaration from Palestine Arab Youth in Lebanon to Refugees, December 15, 1958.
[20] *Ibid.*, translation of article from Al Siyasa, December 18, 1958.
[21] Beirut Al-Masa, byline Fu'ad Nabil, December 18, 1959.

politics." A related demand was that UNRWA consult with Palestinian national organizations, such as the Arab Higher Committee.

These demands for the removal of some personnel and the employment of people from the camps clearly reflect a conviction that Agency personnel were not treating refugees with proper respect. To this extent they were about attitude. More than that, however, the paired demands indicate a rejection of an existing distribution of planning capacity (in the hands of foreign UNRWA personnel) and constitute a concrete proposal for a redistribution of this capacity (through the hiring of Palestinians). In thinking about problems with humanitarian dynamics it is easy to focus on matters of disrespect and high-handedness and, as I describe below, particular personalities can call attention to themselves. The glaring nature of certain acts of disrespect can make them seem like the locus of "bad" paternalism. I would suggest, however, that to focus on these problems to the exclusion of broader structural issues is to miss the point: both of the character of humanitarian paternalism and of refugees' complaints about it. Like most people, refugees would like to be well treated by their service providers. Even more, they would like the opportunity to shape the services provided to them.

The initial response of the UNRWA representative to Lebanon (one of the people whose dismissal was called for) was, though, a classic example of paternalism expressed in an imperious manner. In his recommendation to headquarters about how to respond to the strike DePage indicated his belief that the refugees did not in fact know what was right for them and that, furthermore, some of the issues they raised were simply none of their business. In regard to changes in administrative procedure he stated that some proposed changes had already been abandoned in the face of refugee opposition and that "the allocation of responsibility to my staff, and administrative measures for improving the efficiency of the setup intended to serve the refugees, does not come within the province of the Agency's beneficiaries."[22] On medical services: "the refugees fail to realize that although curative medicine is the branch of medicine which they consider the most important, preventative medicine ... also fall within the framework of the medical service." He argued that they were inappropriately fixated on the

[22] *Ibid.*, Summary of Events and Recommendations to HQ, From: UR/L – Dr. DePage, Dec. 23, 1958.

status of two medical clinics in the camps. On a change in the procedures for determining rations reductions, he said "I don't consider it
would be in the refugees' own interests to revert to the previous system." The comments continue in that vein, by and large rejecting the
demands of the strikers in the name of the refugees' interests.

The strike continued. At the end of January, a month and a half into
the strike, the Agency agreed to a number of changes that responded
to refugee demands. And correspondence among UNRWA officials
suggests that HQ thought that "misjudgment" by DePage had been a
big part of the problem and that the negative response by refugees to
his reorganization plans should have been responded to earlier.[23] The
boycotters suspended the strike to give UNRWA an opportunity to
implement the changes. Issues continued to arise, including complaints
about the quality of rations, but a March 1959 report from the new
UNRWA representative to Lebanon to HQ indicated that most of the
changes either had been or were being implemented. In this instance,
at least, refugee refusal to accede to policies they did not like and to
agree to the principle that such decisions were "not their province"
was successful.

It would be a mistake to overstate the consequences of such suc-
cesses. They do not eliminate the hierarchies that precede and are
produced by humanitarian action. Nor do they produce an even distribution of effective capacity. Regular protests by refugees do make
UNRWA officials aware that they cannot proceed simply as they see
fit. To this extent protests impose limits on unfettered paternalism.
These limits matter, both in the lives of refugees and in understanding how humanitarianism works in practice. Like most aspects of the
humanitarian encounter, paternalism is not a given, but is a site of
negotiation, contestation, and relation.

Experimenting with Alternatives

Palestinian refugees live in a long-term "humanitarian condition."[24]
They are not alone in this. Protracted refugee situations comprise

---

[23] *Ibid.*, Letter to Assistant Director, Department of Operations, UNRWA, Beirut,
sender unnamed, Jan. 31, 1959.
[24] Feldman, "The Humanitarian Condition."

a significant portion of the international humanitarian landscape.[25] Many decades old, with no end in sight, the Palestinian case is among the most extended instances of long-term displacement. Although many refugees continue to live in difficult economic and political circumstances which demand continued assistance, the longevity of displacement has meant that a sizable number of people have been able to exit the humanitarian system. Few have severed their connections entirely, as their recognition as refugees is seen as vital to any political resolution. But plenty live without a relationship to aid. In addition to the individual or family-based processes of creating alternatives to humanitarian paternalism remaining a key structuring aspect of life, at various moments and in various places across the displacement landscape, Palestinians have engaged in collective efforts to develop new possibilities for living.

These efforts constitute a refusal of humanitarian paternalism in quite a different way than either of the practices discussed above. Both registration rejection and policy protest respond directly to the terms and conditions of this felt paternalism, seeking in one way or another to rework the hierarchies and rearrange the relationships that make up this field. Experiments in alternatives instead bypass humanitarianism precisely through trying to create alternative possibilities. Some such experiments do so within a humanitarian world. They start from a recognition that humanitarian hierarchies may never be defeated directly. Humanitarian paternalism will never succumb to a full-frontal charge. Not only are humanitarian actors driven by a commitment to do good that is a powerful, even if sometimes destructive, force, the structures of aid are too deeply embedded to be easily dislodged. But by working in the open spaces within these structures – the spaces between donation and outcome – it may be possible to create a different experience for refugees who live in this world.[26]

---

[25] UN High Commissioner for Refugees, Protracted Refugee Situations: A Discussion Paper Prepared for the High Commissioner's Dialogue on Protection Challenges, UNHCR/DPC/2008/Doc. 02, November 20, 2008, www.unhcr.org/492ad3782.html.

[26] In this description I am thinking in particular of one project that has been a site for my research, the Campus in Camps project in Dheisheh refugee camp in Bethlehem. The aim of Campus in Camps is to find forms of engagement in and with the camps that break the mold of the usual donor-driven, development industry inspired, too often unproductive, NGO projects. For details on their work see: www.campusincamps.ps/en.

Other experiments in alternatives are self-consciously revolutionary
and insist that another world is possible. These sorts of projects are
necessarily tied to political analysis and organizing. The Palestinian
Liberation Organization (PLO) attempted to create such possibilities,
in part through its economic wing, Samed (Palestine Martyrs' Society).
These efforts are evident in Samed's operations in Lebanon in the years
prior to the PLO's departure from the country under Israeli assault.
Samed, which ran workshops in a number of refugee camps, producing furniture, clothing, and other goods, described its activities as a
key part of the Palestinian "revolution," the liberation struggle. It also,
precisely through providing employment and contributing to a vibrant
camp economy, had the effect of creating opportunities to bypass
humanitarianism. In 1981, Robin Wright reported in the *Christian
Science Monitor* that "with 6,500 full-time employees, and another
4,000 part time, the revolutionary group ranks as one of the largest
employers in Lebanon."[27] She quotes from a Samed booklet that
describes its aims as being "to create the nucleus for a Palestinian
revolutionary economy, to develop economic self-sufficiency for the
revolutionary and the masses, and to lay the foundation for the economic structure of the future Palestinian soviet." In addition to its
industrial activities, Samed had a film production department and,
beginning in 1978, published a monthly journal.[28]

The articles in the journal, which include descriptions of different workshops, interviews with Samed workers, and analyses of the
project, are propagandistic in tone, with liberal use of revolutionary
slogans and rhetoric. And they also provide a clear statement of how
leaders and participants in the organization understood the endeavor.
I turn to the pages of the journal to explore how this effort to develop a
"revolutionary economy" operates as a refusal of paternalism. Above
I described how humanitarian paternalism and cultural expressions of
patriarchy were intertwined. Samed's work took place on the grounds
of another intersecting set of hierarchies: of humanitarianism and
capitalism. An interview with a worker in a tailoring workshop in the
Burj Shamali camp in south Lebanon highlighted this multiplicity of

[27] Robin Wright, "PLO's Pinstripes, Money Behind Fatigues and Guns," *Christian Science Monitor*, October 1, 1981, www.csmonitor.com/1981/1001/100134. html (accessed May 20, 2014).
[28] Copies of this journal, *Samed Al-Iqtisadi*, are housed in the Institute for Palestine Studies library in Beirut.

targets.[29] Ghada contrasted Samed's workshops with ordinary "commercial institutions" who only care about "material gains." Samed was founded as an institution to improve the condition of the Palestinian people: "The work then has humanitarian and nationalist motivations." She then went on to talk about the conditions of work in the workshop: "We do not feel that we are employees. We own the work. The work is not for our sake; it is for the revolution and the revolution is for the people." As described here, Samed's aim was to make Palestinians self-sufficient not simply as individuals, but as a collective and as a nation: to refuse the hierarchies of humanitarian assistance and capitalist labor by creating alternative possibilities.

The journal includes many personal accounts that seem intended to convey the success of this project, not yet in liberating Palestine, but in transforming Palestinians. An account by a painter (the arts being another area supported by Samed) described her transformation from a life defined by the "struggle for life and a bit of bread" that began in 1948 to one where she struggled for the nation through her art.[30] Her first painting was of a humanitarian scene: children at an UNRWA school drinking ration milk. She said that she had refused to sell it to a foreigner who saw it at her exhibition because she felt he wanted to take pleasure in the pain of Palestinian lives. Rejecting this relationship was one declaration of Palestinian self-sufficiency, and a refusal of the relationships in which refugees were ensconced. She used another artist's words to describe her aims: "I paint my wounds and the wounds of my people. I paint my hopes and the hopes of my people." But her art was not just a form of personal expression, it was a means to change how foreigners engaged them. The article ends with a description of another exhibition in Germany and a quote from one of the guest-books: "I now understand why there all Palestinian fidayeen [guerillas]." By transforming the subjectivity and activity of Palestinian refugees, the article seems to suggest, it will be possible to change the international political landscape: to move people from pity to solidarity.

Other articles in the journal describe Samed's structure and method, underscoring that the organization was established for "the achievement of self-sufficiency regarding the needs of the revolution and the masses."[31] In a discussion with Samed's director, Abu Ala' (Ahmad

---

[29] *Samed* 1, 7 (1978).
[30] *Samed* 1, 9 (1978).
[31] *Samed* 1, 11–12 (1978).

Qurei'a), he described how this revolutionary institution "sees the human being as the most valuable means of production and the most valuable means of struggling as well." Through this structure and this transformation in the means of production, Samed was preparing for a liberated future:

[Samed] is an economic experience that will define the features of the society in the future ... This people has many qualifications and skills. These features are among the most important for the production and economic activity. But this Palestinian expertise and individual initiatives inside and outside [of Palestine] were never allowed to integrate within a public communal work.

Samed, he suggests, makes such common work possible and therefore can make it possible for Palestinians to create radically new possibilities.

The Samed experience, like so many other Palestinian experiments in living otherwise, did not come to full fruition. When the PLO left Lebanon its capacity to continue to support these ventures was extremely limited. After the signing of the Oslo Accords and the return of PLO leadership to the occupied territories, most of the organization's energy was directed there. When you visit the camps in Lebanon today people will often describe a past geography that included Samed installations, but these no longer exist. Although one cannot call this experiment a lasting success, the effort to create alternative worlds and possibilities within a broad landscape of humanitarian need illuminates a key aspect of refugee responses to paternalism. This effort to change the international conversation (from pity to solidarity) and Palestinians' conditions of life (from being individuals in need to being collectively self-sufficient) seeks to find an exit from paternalist relations by creating another framework for experience and discourse.

Conclusion

What, then, is the significance of the refusals I have considered here? None of them are able to undo the hierarchies of humanitarian intervention or remove paternalism from this enterprise. The course of such refusals, in fact, underscores that, whatever providers and recipients may desire, paternalism may be impossible to overcome. But they also confirm that it is possible to have an effect on the operations of humanitarianism, to introduce limits to its paternalism, to redirect certain practices. However limited in effect, though, these refusals are important in several ways. For one, they make it clear that refugees think that there is a problem with humanitarianism and that part of that problem is its paternalism. And this position deserves serious attention: from both practitioners and scholars.

Palestinian refugee refusals around humanitarianism reveal actually-existing paternalism to be a practice that produces and structures relations; that resonates with and implicates a range of hierarchies, both local and global; and that has significant political import. By defying the condition of being a refugee registration refusals are in part an attempt to reject the underlying conditions that make paternalism appear necessary. By challenging the structure of the humanitarian system, protests against procedures are in part an effort to change the relationships that are part of a paternalist dynamic. By seeking a way out of the conundrums of the aid relationship experiments with alternative lives and futures are in part an effort to render humanitarian paternalism irrelevant.

Both humanitarian providers concerned with the delivery of aid and scholars interested in analyzing the meaning and workings of paternalism would do well to, at least sometimes, begin their analysis and evaluation from the position of recipients. This is not just a matter of respect, but of understanding. Humanitarian dynamics and paternalism more generally look different when recipient experiences and opinions are put at the center of analysis. It matters, of course, what humanitarians do. And they have ethical and political obligations to reflect on the consequences of their choices and actions. But their choices are not the only ones with ethical and political import. That so much of the consideration of paternalism starts from the perspective of the (potential) paternalist indicates just how deeply the judgments about capacity which underlie paternalist policy and action permeate. Much of the analysis of paternalism is itself structured by its conditions. Putting the experiences, demands, and refusals of those on the receiving end of these interventions at the center of analysis does not end paternalism, but it can decenter it.

Conclusion: The World According to Paternalism

MICHAEL N. BARNETT

Paternalism can be broadly understood as the substitution of one actor's judgment for another's in order to improve the object's welfare, interests, and happiness. Whether such actions evoke feelings of admiration or condemnation often depends on the eye of the beholder and whether one is the giver or the receiver. The subjects of the chapters – including human rights activists, asylum case officers, gender specialists, protection officers, UN officials, relief workers, peacebuilders, and legal experts – all present themselves as motivated by a sense of compassion and duty. Enacting an ethic of care and responsibility, they were attempting to correct perceived injustices, defend vulnerable populations from harm, and provide new opportunities and choices to marginalized and oppressed peoples. As Swaine observes of aid workers, but probably is true of many others mentioned in this volume, they were acting on an "imperative," the heartfelt belief that something had to be done. However, as she and others acknowledge, this imperative can lead them to act first and ask questions later, if ever. Sometimes they apologize for their neglect. At other times, though, they offer reasons why their unilateral actions were unavoidable, understandable, and perhaps even in the best interests of the population in need.

Yet few actors, regardless of the imperatives or circumstances, want to be seen as a paternalist or accused of acting paternalistically. Care is one thing, but control and domination are quite another. Wanting to improve the circumstances of the marginalized is a noble calling, but substituting their judgment for another's is generally perceived to be beyond the bounds of acceptability. There is a thin, and often invisible, line between care and control. But not all offenses are equal. Arguably the paternalism of the nineteenth-century imperial powers described by John Hobson is more offensive than the paternalism that occurs in Palestinian refugee camps as described by Ilana Feldman. Stephen Hopgood's chapter on female genital mutilation/cutting describes how Western actors have adopted different kinds of tactics in their century-long effort to stamp it out; some forms, he intimates, are more disrespectful than others. David Chandler draws our attention to a "new paternalism" in which acts of care by the West are no longer solely directed to Third World peoples but also are extended to include the reform of the powerful and the global institutions that affect the circumstances of the powerless. Drawing from her experiences in Darfur and elsewhere, Aisling Swaine describes an ethics of care that can neglect the voices of the individuals they want to help. For some, including Henry Richardson, the paternalism identified by Chandler and Swaine might be so gentle that they might not even be "in the ballpark."

This chapter uses the variation in our response to different instances of paternalism to reflect on two features of global paternalism that deserve further consideration. The first is the empirical, namely the historical-institutional forms of paternalism. Our judgment that some kinds of paternalism are more offensive than others implies that paternalism is not a single thing but comes in different shapes and sizes. The paternalism of the nineteenth century differs considerably from the paternalism that prevails in contemporary global and humanitarian governance. How? To make sense of this diversity, I argue that practices of paternalism can vary along several dimensions, that there is a pattern to this variation suggesting movement from a strong to a weak form of paternalism – what I will call paternalism lite – and that this movement owes to forces of liberalism and rationalization.

The second half pushes our emotions into ethics. Our emotional response to different instances of paternalism suggests not only that certain kinds are more egregious than others, but also that some instances might be more justifiable than others. Simply put, are there times when practices of care require some measure of power? Whether and when power can be justified in the service of care is a matter of practical urgency for those on the frontlines – the experts, professionals, specialists, and activists whose vocation and avocation is to make the world a better place. Reflecting on their experiences and those of others in the field, Autesserre and Swaine emphasize how peacebuilders and aid workers struggle daily over these issues. Paternalism is also a matter of urgency for those on the sidelines, the community of scholars who pass judgment on the world of practitioners and who teach students aspiring to join professions of global care. Critique is not enough. Following the legal theorist Joel Feinberg, the challenge is to reconcile the "general repugnance for paternalism with the seeming reasonableness of some apparently paternalistic regulations."[1] There is no magical formula or moral guidebook, but the chapters do suggest a series of cautionary questions.

Fifty Shades of Paternalism

Global paternalism exhibits impressive diversity and dexterity. One way to sort out these variations is to identify the central elements on which they differ. There are lots of viable candidates, and this volume did not seek to generate an exhaustive or ranked list. Still, the chapters are suggestive of some promising suspects, namely the means, scope, purpose, duration, sources of confidence, and mechanisms of accountability. Moreover, the values of these variables appear to correlate historically. Specifically, there seems to have been a simultaneous change in the acceptable means (from force to information); the scope (from wide to narrow); the purpose (from emancipation to immediate harm); the duration (extended to temporary); the sources of confidence (from faith to evidence); and the forms of accountability (from internal to external). If this argument has some merit, then it supports three further intuitions: there are different kinds of paternalism; these kinds might trend historically; and they do so because of underlying structural forces.

The Elements of Paternalism

The chapters identify six central elements of paternalism. The first element concerns the tools of interference. As in all forms of power, the means can vary from outright physical violence, which leaves the object little or no choice, to the existence of formal and informal institutions, which limit (and might even preserve the illusion of) choice. There can be the threat and use of force. Hobson's review of the nineteenth century highlights how force was often on the table. UNHCR has collaborated with states to use force to keep stability in camps and to forcibly repatriate refugees on the grounds that it was in their best

---

[1] Joel Feinberg, *Harm to Self* (New York: Oxford University Press, 1986), 25, cited in Peter de Marneffe, "Avoiding Paternalism," *Philosophy & Public Affairs* 34, 1 (2006).

interests.[2] Much more often, though, the chapters identified the use of knowledge and information – discourses of expertise, institutions that frame information and options in ways that are intended to steer the beliefs and decisions of the target population, and so on. In general, while global institutions can, and do, possess coercive power, they are more likely to rely on knowledge and information to do their work.

Paternalism also can vary in terms of scope, from surgical interventions to wide-ranging supervision. What are the range of areas and activities that are subject to oversight? In Hobson's chapter, liberal empires felt entitled to intervene in all aspects of society, politics, economics, and culture; for prudential reasons, and in the most sensitive areas, they might not do so, but they nevertheless believed they had the authority to roam near and far. In the contemporary period, trusteeships, transitional administrations, and peacebuilding operations involve themselves in all areas of life. The "to-do list" for peacebuilding operations, Autesserre observes, is impressively long and ambitious. In many of the other chapters, however, including those by Hopgood, and Merry and Ramachadran, outsiders are not claiming broad jurisdictional authority but more limited authority and bounded interference based on their professional expertise or ethical convictions. These sorts of interventions, then, are limited. Yet, as Hopgood observes in the case of FGM/C, even interventions that are seemingly narrow might nevertheless contain a more transformational element; part of the campaign to ban FGM/C is premised not simply on ending a practice deemed barbaric but also to instantiate the principle that individuals should become autonomous sovereigns that have the right to choose.

Paternalism also can vary in purpose, from the goal of protecting individuals from harming others and self-harm, to aspiring to create actors that are capable of reason and rationality. The British imperial power frequently attempted to introduce regulations in their colonies that were intended to limit cultural practices deemed injurious to self and others. In China they tried to outlaw foot-binding, in the Sudan they attempted to stamp out female genital cutting/mutilation, and in

---

[2] Elizabeth Holzer, *The Concerned Women of Buduburam: Refugee Activists and Humanitarian Dilemmas* (Ithaca: Cornell University Press, 2015); Barbara Harrell-Bond, *Imposing Aid: Emergency Assistance to Refugees* (New York: Oxford University Press, 1986).

India they attempted to outlaw Sati, where recently widowed women are burned on a funeral pyre. The chapters on rights, for instance, document interference that is primarily interested in protection rather than resurrection or emancipation. Merry and Ramachadran, Fassin and Swaine observe how activists, states, and international aid workers, respectively, attempt to protect populations at risk by establishing prohibitions on particular kinds of actions and extending legal protections and security to categories of actors.

Yet paternalists also express the goal of helping individuals develop reason and rationality and to alter the underlying institutional, cultural, political, and economic conditions so that individuals can expand their autonomy and determine their own futures. The liberal John Stuart Mill defended British imperialism in India on the grounds that it would help the Indians develop the mental capacities and social institutions to become free-thinking, reasoning peoples who were capable of self-governance (which would benefit the British).[3] His sentiments were hardly radical, for many colonizing peoples genuinely believed that colonialism could and should benefit the colonized population. Indeed, accusations that colonial administrators and commercial elites were exploiting the colonial peoples could unleash a torrent of outrage by the British public on the grounds that Britain was failing its role of trustee.[4] The League of Nations' mandatory system was premised on the idea that the international community has a responsibility to help the backward populations develop the skills for self-governance and that different countries could be graded based on how close they were to sitting at the adult table. A standard refrain in contemporary post-conflict and post-disaster operations is that the international community must "build back better," which can only be done if outsiders are prepared to rewrite the country in a way that, in their judgment, will produce development, peace, and security. Sometimes, as is in the case of peacebuilding chronicled by Autesserre, such transformational intentions are quite transparent. Yet at other times these possibilities and objectives are hidden by the presentationally limited nature of the

[3] Thomas McCarthy, *Race, Empire, and the Idea of Human Development* (New York: Cambridge University Press, 2009), 175; Don Habibi, "The Moral Dimensions of J. S. Mill's Colonialism," *Journal of Social Philosophy* 30, 1 (1999).
[4] Nicholas B. Dirks, *The Scandal of Empire: India and the Creation of Imperial Britain* (Cambridge, MA: Harvard University Press, 2006).

interference. Hopgood argues that the desire to eradicate FGM/C is embedded in a larger desire to create liberal selves. In this respect, it is reminiscent of the "capabilities" framework that articulates a causal model where certain kinds of primary capabilities are essential for the enjoyment and fulfillment of other kinds of rights and possibilities.[5]

Paternalism also can fluctuate in terms of its projected length, which generally varies based on prior assessments of the target's existing and potential capacity for reason. There is likely to be a direct relationship between the perceived permanence and severity of the incapacity, on the one hand, and the permanence and intensity of the interference, on the other. Social relations guided by racism often generate enduring patterns of control of one race over another. Traditional patrimonial systems are often defined by a patriarch (and, on rare occasions, a matriarch) whose responsibility is to oversee the collective interests of his extended family, and those under his protection are expected to heed his advice. Nineteenth-century colonial projects might have accepted that they had a responsibility to help the backward peoples develop the rationality and maturity needed to be deserving of autonomy, but, as a matter of practice, they acted as if this was an unending commitment. Yet most relations of paternalism are not until "death do them part" but rather are much more temporary in nature, sometimes lasting no longer than the contract; such term limits are most likely due to the institutionalization of sovereignty, which I will discuss later in the chapter.

Another point of variation is the source of the paternalist's confidence. Confidence can be a matter of faith. Faith-based paternalism exists when confidence derives from preternatural commitments which leave little room for doubt, most obvious when claims to know better cannot be challenged by empirical evidence. These nearly foundational claims help orient the self in relationship to humankind and the cosmos. Religious theology has this characteristic. "Theological propositions are unverifiable because the existence they posit – God, immortal souls, and so forth – do not, even if they exist, intrude on human experience in such a way as to provide compelling evidence for their verification."[6] Some secular thought has these very qualities as

---

[5] Martha Nussbaum, *Creating Capabilities: The Human Development Approach* (Cambridge, MA: Harvard University Press, 2013).

[6] Robert Westbrook, "An Uncommon Faith: Pragmatism and Religious Experience," in *Pragmatism and Religion: Classical Sources and Original Essays*, ed. Stuart Rosenbaum (Urbana: University of Illinois Press, 2003), 194.

well. For instance, many statements on human rights are founded on natural law and non-verifiable commitments; they cannot be proven or disproven but rather are a matter of faith. In terms of its effects, then, belief in God is not that different from a belief in humanity.[7] Alternatively, confidence can be founded on claims to superior knowledge that are based on developed theories and empirical evidence. In other words, it rests on science in its broadest possible meaning: the systematic effort to organize, develop, and accumulate knowledge in the form of verifiable and testable explanations and predictions.

And last, but hardly least, is accountability. This is not the place to review the debate on the multiple meanings of accountability; for my purposes, what matters most is whether the affected populations have the ability to hold accountable those who claim to be acting in their interests.[8] It is worth noting, though, that one of the requirements for being a paternalist is the willingness to disregard the views of the recipients. In any event, interveners tend to be subject to one of two kinds of accountability mechanisms. Internal accountability mechanisms are typically sown by self-doubt and a crisis of confidence; in other words, they are dependent on the conscience of the paternalizer. External mechanisms, on the other hand, allow affected populations to register their opinions, punish the abuse of power, and sanction officials who are not listening to their recipients or are seeming to care more about their own welfare than the welfare of those for whom they are responsible. Swaine provides excellent examples of how both possibilities can be proximate to one another, as she describes her own crisis of conscience that was triggered by the refugee women's attempt to get the largely all-male peacekeeping operation to take seriously their insights into how to reduce sexual assaults and crimes in the camps. Feldman's chapter on "refusals" also suggests how such acts can be linked to an attempt to change the terms of humanitarian action in ways that do not feel so degrading or infantilizing to the recipients.

---

[7] Stephen Hopgood, "Moral Authority, Modernity and the Politics of the Sacred," *European Journal of International Relations* 15, 2 (2009); and Ilana Feldman and Miriam Ticktin, "Introduction: Government and Humanity," in *In the Name of Humanity: The Government of Threat and Care*, eds. Ilana Feldman and Miriam Ticktin (Durham, NC: Duke University Press, 2011).

[8] Alnoor Ebrahim and Edward Weisband, eds., *Global Accountabilities: Participation, Pluralism, and Public Ethics* (New York: Cambridge University Press, 2007).

Table C.1 *Strong and Weak Paternalism*

Elements	Strong	Weak
Tools	Force	Information
Scope	Wide	Narrow
Purpose	Emancipation	Immediate harm
Projected duration	Long term	Short term
Source of confidence	Faith	Evidence
Accountability	Internal	External

The Changing Practices of Global Paternalism

In addition to attempting to identify the different elements of paternalism, scholars also have proposed that paternalism comes in different kinds. There is old versus new, hard versus soft, pure versus
impure, and on and on.[9] The contributors to this volume also offered
their own distinctions. Richardson distinguishes between "true" and
"aggravated" paternalism, Fassin between soft and hard paternalism,
and Hopgood between pure and pragmatic paternalism. Chandler
discusses the rise of a "new paternalism." Similar to all exercises in
the construction and use of ideal-types, the goal is not to capture the
essence and complexity of any single instance of paternalism, but
rather to generate meaningful comparisons across different instances
for the purpose of empirical analysis. In Table C.1 I offer my nomina-
tion: strong and weak paternalism.

A strong paternalism exists when: force is legitimate, interference
is wide-ranging, the purpose is to promote human development, the
project length is extended, the paternalizer's confidence is metaphysical rather than epistemic, and the paternalizer's actions are immune to
redirection by the paternalized. A weak paternalism exists when: force
is severely proscribed, interference is relatively restricted, the purpose

[9] William Glod, "Against Two Modest Conceptions of Hard Paternalism," *Ethical
Theory and Moral Practice* 16 (2013): 409–22; William Talbott, *Human Rights
and Human Well-Being* (Oxford: Oxford University Press, 2010); Lawrence
Mead, "The Rise of Paternalism," in *The New Paternalism: Supervisory
Approaches to Poverty*, ed. Lawrence Mead (Washington, DC: Brookings
Institution, 1997), 1–38.

is more toward stopping harm than promoting human development, the projected length is temporary, the paternalizer's confidence
has epistemic roots, and the paternalized possesses mechanisms that
potentially allow them to make their views known and hold the paternalizer accountable.[10]

The chapters, individually and collectively, suggest an important
historical change in the global paternalism, from strong to weak. The
world, in short, has entered into a period of "paternalism-lite." The
argument is not that there has been a synchronized movement along
all dimensions from strong to weak. I am mindful of three important historical caveats. The break is not so clean, and contemporary
paternalism retains features of its nineteenth-century predecessor.
Lester and Dussart's rich analysis of humanitarian governance in the
nineteenth-century British Empire, for instance, suggests that missionaries and other preachers of human progress often used the same
techniques associated with contemporary human rights activists.[11]
Relatedly, focusing on actor-to-actor networks and undifferentiated
structures, which frequently occurs with analyses of paternalism, often
misses how practices of paternalism can vary not only temporally but
also spatially and relationally. Lastly, situating these networks within a
broader structural context might help us better understand how seemingly separate actions are nested within a larger whole. For instance,
the ability of the UNHCR to avoid using more coercive techniques,
and thus project an image of clean hands and a pure heart, might be
made possible by the presence of other actors, such as governments,
that are prepared to do the dirty work.[12] Still, my hunch is that there
has been a general movement from the strong to weak variety.

[10] The strong and weak distinctions largely revolve not around paternalism's
relative effects but rather its visibility. As should be clear by now, this volume
has not focused on the impact of the practices of paternalism but rather the
practices themselves. As students of power have emphasized, sometimes the
most effective and enduring kinds of power are those that are neither seen
nor heard.
[11] Alan Lester and Fae Dussart, *Colonialization and the Origins of Humanitarian
Governance: Protecting Aborigines across the Nineteenth-Century British
Empire* (New York: Cambridge University Press, 2014).
[12] Michel Agier, *Managing the Undesirables: Refugee Camps and Humanitarian
Government* (New York: Polity Press, 2012); Elizabeth Holzer, *The Concerned
Women of Buduburam: Refugee Activists and Humanitarian Dilemmas*
(Ithaca: Cornell University Press, 2015).

There has been a change in the acceptable means – from the legitimacy of coercion to the reliance on information, dosed out, in, and through institutions. During the nineteenth century, many liberal imperialists argued that while force was unfortunate, it might be justified. Even liberal anti-imperialists such as J.A. Hobson acknowledged the possibility. Much like John Stuart Mill before him, and many "enlightened" socialists and liberals of his day, Hobson insisted that imperialism could be justified in those instances in which imperial control is used for the benefit of the world and the "lower races"; there is a marked improvement of the welfare of the local population; and the intervening actor is not acting on its own but rather is the agent of a "civilized humanity."[13] Although Hobson did not advocate the use of force, he left it on the table. In the contemporary period, it is harder to justify the use of force except in instances of extreme threats to life, limb, and security.[14] Peacebuilding operations, the modern-day equivalent of civilizing missions, rarely use force; indeed, the controversy is not that force is used but that force is not used often enough for civilian protection. Moreover, when force is deployed, it requires all kinds of justificatory rhetoric, which often dovetails with anti-paternalist sentiments.[15]

Force is out, but in contemporary paternalism beyond borders, information and knowledge are in. Nearly all of the chapters have something to say on this feature. Hopgood observes an important historical shift in how Westerners attempted to stop FGM/C, from the heavy-handed tactics of the nineteenth century to the greater reliance on persuasion. Merry, in her work in this volume and elsewhere, has demonstrated that governance through global indicators can generate a form of paternalism. An important function of indicators is to condense complicated and contested concepts into

[13] David Long, "Paternalism and the Internationalization of Imperialism: J.A. Hobson on the International Government of the 'Lower Races'," in *Imperialism and Internationalism in the Discipline of International Relations*, eds. David Long and Brian C. Schmidt (Albany: State University of New York Press, 2005), 76–7.

[14] See Martha Finnemore, *The Purpose of Intervention* (Ithaca: Cornell University Press, 2004).

[15] For a recent discussion of the relationship between early and contemporary liberal thought on justifications for interference, see Michael Doyle, *The Question of Intervention: John Stuart Mill and the Responsibility to Protect* (New Haven: Yale University Press, 2015).

bite-sized morsels that can become objectified, recorded, stored, and tracked. For instance, the estimated total of individuals who are involved in the "global sex trade" often include both those who have been forcibly moved from one place to another and those who have consented. Indicators, though, tell us what exists "out there," what constitutes a "problem," what kinds of interventions are needed, and who (often international authorities) should be involved in the intervention.[16]

The scope arguably has narrowed as well, though the movement has not been as great as the kinds of means that are used. Again, the comparison between civilizing missions and contemporary humanitarian governance is illustrative. The backward populations needed help – plenty of it – in all areas of life to develop the intelligence and institutions they needed to gain their independence.[17] During this period there were very few restrictions on what colonial authorities could and could not do; indeed, if they were going to unleash civilization, then very few areas were off limits. Guided by a folk science and religious thought, the civilizing missions of the nineteenth century advocated wide-ranging interventions in religion, education, science, health and nutrition, household dynamics, politics, and economics.[18] When colonial rulers did create principles of non-interference, it was largely because of a pragmatic decision to avoid particularly sensitive areas, including religion, custom, and gender, that might trigger colonial protest. Not all humanitarians of the period exhibited such prudence in controversial areas of life. Missionaries, for instance, were not satisfied creating schools and health clinics but also aimed to convert the populations to Christianity, the key path to civilization and salvation (a habit that

---

[16] Sally Engle Merry, Kevin E. Davis, and Benedict Kingsbury, eds., *The Quiet Power of Indicators: Measuring Governance, Corruption, and Rule of Law* (Cambridge: Cambridge University Press, 2015).

[17] For three excellent intellectual histories of the leading thinkers on the subject of the relationship between liberalism and imperialism, see Sankar Muthu, *Enlightenment Against Empire* (Princeton: Princeton University Press, 2003); Jennifer Pitts, *A Turn to Empire: The Rise of Imperial Liberalism in Britain and France* (Princeton: Princeton University Press, 2005); and Uday Singh Mehta, *Liberalism and Empire: A Study in Nineteenth-Century British Liberal Thought* (Chicago: Chicago University Press, 1999).

[18] Paul Varg, "Motives in Protestant Missions, 1890–1917," *Church History* 23, 1 (1954): 75–8.

often unnerved colonial administrators, who preferred stability over everything else).[19]

Although the scope of humanitarian governance can appear to have narrowed, underneath the surface it remains, in many ways, as sweeping as ever. Contemporary humanitarian governance continues to show tremendous ambition in all areas of life, but because of its technocratic quality, can appear to be much more limited than it is. Many organizations involved in humanitarian governance often present themselves as "technical" or "service providers" because they specialize in a narrow professional field; for instance, there are experts on rights, health, development, sanitation, education, criminal justice, constitution writing, and on and on. Said otherwise, whereas once interference was located in a single authority called the colonial state (and some closely connected associates), today there are many different authorities with distinct specializations operating within more restricted confines. Yet, if these distinct activities are examined in the aggregate, the whole is greater than the sum of the parts, a point raised by students of governmentality.[20]

The reason why the scope of paternalism has not been altered is because its purpose, in many ways, has remained immodest. Civilizing missions no longer exist, but humanitarian governance appears to be a worthy heir, as the individual chapters attest. Three aspects of this transition deserve attention. The first is the general growth of humanitarian governance, if judged in terms of sheer numbers of missions, personnel, and resources. There are more and different kinds of actors involved in the goal of regulating and improving human life. Second, ideologies of developmentalism continue, including the notion that different communities and populations can be placed on some sort of developmental continuum, that the more advanced show the less advanced their future, and that the more advanced have a

---

[19] Brian Stanley, "Christianity and Civilization in English Evangelical Mission Thought, 1792–1857," in *Christian Missions and the Enlightenment*, ed. Brian Stanley (Grand Rapids: W.B. Eerdmans Pub., 2001).

[20] Michael Merlingen, "Governmentality: Towards a Foucauldian Framework for the Study of IGOs," *Cooperation and Conflict* 38, 4 (2003): 361–84; Ole Jacob Sending and Iver Neumann, "Governance to Governmentality: Analyzing NGOs, States, and Power," *International Studies Quarterly* 50, 3 (2006): 651–72; Stephen Campbell, "Construing Top-Down as Bottom-Up: The Governmental Co-option of Peacebuilding 'From Below'," *Explorations in Anthropology* 11, 11 (2011): 39–56.

responsibility to help hasten the backward population's evolution.[21] Although those involved in humanitarian governance no longer use the politically incorrect language of civilizing mission, they often see themselves as involved in transformational politics that are intended to turn less-developed societies into advanced ones. Peacebuilding operations, in this respect, might be seen as civilizing operations in all but name.[22]

Although the purpose of humanitarian governance and interference remains recognizable, the expected duration has shortened. Again, the contrast between the colonial and post-colonial era is illustrative. In the colonial era, and especially for those colonialists who believed that the uncivilized races were backward and likely to stay that way for the indefinite future, the underlying assumption was that the colonial powers would be responsible for their development for decades to come. As ideologies of racism and primitivism began to lose out to ideologies of equality and humanity, the ascendant assumption was that all peoples were deserving of autonomy and self-determination (unless proven otherwise). Beginning with the mandatory period and the League of Nations, the assumption was that the colonized states would, sooner rather than later, become sovereign. By mid-century, the presumption was that non-sovereign states would become sovereign, sooner if not immediately, a change that owed less to the fact that these states had crept higher on the measuring stick of moral development, and more to the delegitimization of the metric. In the post-conflict operations of the post-Cold War period, states that "forfeited" their sovereignty were presumed to be on the road to recovery nearly as soon as the operation was authorized.

The basis of confidence seems to have shifted from faith-based to evidence-based, though the shift does not seem to have been as abrupt as a secularization-guided worldview suggests. The West viewed its

---

[21] However, Marxist ideologies also contained their own strands of developmentalism.

[22] On liberal peacebuilding see Roland Paris, *At War's End: Building Peace after Civil Conflict* (Cambridge: Cambridge University Press, 2004); Richard Ponzio, "Transforming Political Authority: UN Democratic Peacebuilding in Afghanistan," *Global Governance* 13, 2 (2007): 255–75; David Chandler, *Empire in Denial: The Politics of State-Building* (Ann Arbor: Pluto, 2006) and Mark Duffield, *Global Governance and the New Wars: The Merging of Development and Security* (London: Zed Books, 2001).

own phenomenal development as evidence of its natural superiority over the backward peoples, giving them confidence that they knew best. The scientific and technological revolutions, according to them, were obvious indicators of their superiority, and such revolutions, they further assumed, owed in no small measure to the blessings showered upon them by the Almighty.[23] The bible and the steam engine combined to create paternalizers brimming with a sense of superiority and confidence, which, in turn, informed their belief that they could, and must, operate without the consent or input of the local populations. After all, they had neither God nor the steam engine.

It is no longer fashionable among card-carrying liberals to reference God in their demand for action, and over the recent decades, justification is frequently found in discourses of natural law, universalism, and cosmopolitanism. In contrast to positive law that presumes law exists when there is an agreement between two or more states that have the legal authority to enter into binding agreements, natural law presumes that states and non-state actors have certain kinds of rights, protections, privileges, and responsibilities that owe from the simple fact of our humanity. Universalism and the idea that there are (however thin) ethics enveloping all individuals makes territorial borders less fortified and encourages us to see each other as bound by a common morality. And cosmopolitanism demands that we judge our duties and obligations to others not on the basis of their passports, race, gender, or some other discriminating feature, but rather, once again, on our shared humanity. Principles of humanity not only provide a license, but also a moral obligation, to act. To not act when there are crimes and assaults against humanity is to indict our own humanity. Faith continues to provide a sense of confidence and demand for action.

Although faith-based paternalism continues to exist – present in religious and secular discourses of humanity – evidence-based paternalism has ascended.[24] Experts rule on the global scene. Missionaries and colonial administrators departed the colonies, replaced by a growing number of experts in international and non-governmental

[23] Michael Adas, *Machines as a Measure of Men: Science, Technology, and Ideologies of Western Dominance* (Ithaca: Cornell University Press, 1990).
[24] For a compatible observation, see McCarthy, *Race, Empire, and the Idea of Human Development*, 181; Jeanne Morefield, *Covenants without Swords: Idealist Liberalism and the Spirit of Empire* (Princeton: Princeton University Press, 2005).

organizations housed in the newly decolonized world.[25] The post-war paternalists are not superior because they are closer to God, come from the right Western country, or have the right skin color; instead, it is because they have the right kind of training, education, and knowledge. And, over time, hands-on experience began to matter less than advanced training and professional credentials. Perhaps the biggest change from the era of colonialism to the era of sovereign states is that paternalism became institutionalized and internationalized in large international and non-governmental organizations that operate in the name of humanity.[26] Even the relief sector, once defined by volunteerism and welcoming to all those with a good heart, has become increasingly dominated by those with advanced degrees and by possessors of esoteric knowledge.[27]

There has been a dramatic change in the character of accountability, arguably from being an afterthought (or given no thought) to being acknowledged and occasionally practiced. Prior to World War I, the prevailing assumption among the colonial powers was that because non-Western peoples were "children" who were unable to govern themselves, there was no more reason to ask them for consent than

[25] Keith David Watenpaugh, "The League of Nations' Rescue of Armenian Genocide Survivors and the Making of Modern Humanitarianism, 1920–1927," *American Historical Review* 115, 5 (2010); Timothy Mitchell, *Rule of Experts: Egypt, Techno-Politics, Modernity* (Berkeley: University of California Press, 2002); Michael N. Barnett and Martha Finnemore, *Rules for the World: International Organizations in Global Governance* (Ithaca: Cornell University Press, 2004).

[26] See Frederik Cooper, "Modernizing Bureaucrats, Backward Africans, and the Development Concept," in *International Development and the Social Sciences*, eds. Frederick Cooper and Randall Packard (Berkeley: University of California Press, 1998); Mark Duffield, *Development, Security, and Unending War: Governing the World of Peoples* (Cambridge: Polity Press, 2007); Michael N. Barnett, *Empire of Humanity: A History of Humanitarianism* (Ithaca: Cornell University Press, 2011); Warwick Anderson, *Colonial Pathologies: American Tropical Medicine, Race, and Hygiene in the Philippines* (Durham, NC: Duke University Press, 2006); Matthew Connelly, *Fatal Misconception: The Struggle to Control World Population* (Cambridge, MA: Harvard University Press, 2008); Mark Mazower, *No Enchanted Palace: The End of Empire and the Ideological Origins of the United Nations* (Princeton: Princeton University Press, 2008); Morefield, *Covenant Without Swords*, 108–12.

[27] Peter Walker, Karen Hein, Catherine Russ, Greg Bertleff, and Dan Caspersz, "A Blueprint for Professionalizing Humanitarian Assistance," *Health Affairs* 29, 12 (2010): 2223–30.

there was a child. If they did object initially, hopefully they would come to see the wisdom of colonial rule, much as children see the wisdom of parental rule later in life. This has changed across the board. Feldman's chapter observes that one way in which early relief efforts to the Palestinians differ from recent efforts is the expectation that refugees participate in their assistance. Merry and Ramachadran's chapter focuses on the issue of consent, which did not seem to be a source of concern for earlier campaigns to stop human trafficking. Although there is widespread agreement that principles of participation are often more cosmetic than real, their mere presence, and the very need of external interveners to refer to them, is symbolic of an important change in the practices of contemporary humanitarian governance.[28]

The simultaneous rise of technocracy and the normative demand for accountability introduces a tension familiar to all forms of governance: the rule of the experts versus the rule of the people. In democracy, the rule of the people, there is deference to the "general will," the "majority," and the "will of the people" on various grounds, including autonomy, liberty, and the belief that the people know best. In technocracy, the rule of experts, there is deference to those who have the knowledge. Experts, then, are not expected to always respect the preferences of the people but instead are supposed to use their presumably objective knowledge and judgment. As Larson aptly states, "because such crucial decisions are both assisted by expert advice and esoteric technologies, and increasingly involved with matters of great scientific and technological complexity, the average person is ... disenfranchised by his lack of expert knowledge."[29] Although it might be worrisome if others had such unchecked authority, it is because they are seen as using scientific knowledge for the public good that the rule by experts is often preferred to rule by the elites, markets, or even the

---

[28] David Mosse, *Adventures in Aidland: The Anthropology of Professionals in International Development* (New York: Berghahn Books, 2011), 4; Magnus Boström and Christina Garsten, eds., *Organizing Transnational Accountability* (Northampton, MA: Edward Elgar Publishing, 2008); Adam Branch, "Against Humanitarian Impunity: Rethinking Responsibility for Displacement and Disaster in Northern Uganda," *Journal of Intervention and Statebuilding* 2, 2 (2008).

[29] Magali Sarfatti Larson, "The Production of Expertise and the Constitution of Expert Power," in *The Authority of Experts: Studies in History and Theory*, ed. Thomas L. Haskell (Bloomington: Indiana University Press, 1984), 39.

people.[30] A similar development is occurring in global governance, with the important caveat that expertise appears to be outrunning democratic principles.

There has been a shift from strong to weak paternalism, though it bears repeating that some elements seem to have moved more than others. Nevertheless, in comparison to the nineteenth century, we appear to be in a period of "paternalism-lite." Why? At the top of the list of suspects are the internationalization of liberalism and rationalization. We might or might not live in a global liberal order, as some international relations scholars speculate, but there is little question that principles closely associated with liberalism have had a fundamental impact on the character and constitution of international relations.[31] Although liberalism is not a single thing and there are important variants of international liberalism, liberal values, such as equality, independence, sovereignty, national self-determination, consent, and rights, comfortably circulate in, and help to orient, world affairs. Although liberalism does not rule out interference, and, in fact, can be productive of its own brand of interference, it has erected legal, ethical, and political barriers to unwanted interference.

This change is largely narrated through the globalization of sovereignty. The institution of sovereignty, of course, pre-dates the emergence of political liberalism, but the rise of political liberalism contributed both to the demise of imperial rule and colonialism and to the internationalization of sovereignty. Sovereignty represents a set of claims, rights, and entitlements that grant the state considerable capacity in international affairs. It is the supreme legal authority in international relations. It enshrines the principle of non-interference. And, because of its legal standing and the principle of non-interference, its internal affairs are its own. Part of the justification for this sphere of

---

[30] See Cass R. Sunstein and Robert H. Thaler, "Libertarian Paternalism Is Not an Oxymoron," *The University of Chicago Law Review* 70, 4 (2003); Thomas L. Haskell, ed., *The Authority of Experts: Studies in History and Theory* (Bloomington: Indiana University Press, 1984), ix–xxxix. On professions and paternalism, see Dennis F. Thompson, *Political Ethics and Public Office* (Cambridge, MA: Harvard University Press, 1990), 161–4.

[31] Georg Sorenson, *A Liberal World Order in Crisis: Choosing between Imposition and Restraint* (Ithaca: Cornell University Press, 2011); James L. Richardson, *Contending Liberalisms in World Politics: Ideology and Power* (Boulder: Lynne Rienner, 2001); Martin Hall and John M. Hobson, "Liberal International Theory: Eurocentric but not Always Imperialist?" *International Theory* 2, 2 (2010): 210–45.

influence is that the state is representative of the "nation" that is contained within its territorial borders, and the nation should enjoy self-
determination. Because of the belief that nations should be allowed to
evolve as a result of their own internal rhythms, and not because of the
whims, beliefs, and interests of those outside its borders, the principle
of non-interference also includes the principle of consent.

The globalization of sovereignty has not necessarily translated into
a presumption that all states are deserving of the same degree of deference and respect. Sovereignty remains dependent on social recognition –
it is not a natural right – and there is continuing debate over when
such recognition should be conferred or withdrawn. A central point
of controversy concerns whether or not the state's domestic character,
constitution, and conduct should influence its eligibility for membership in the international society of states. Political liberalism has had
a lot to say on this subject, impacting international practice. Various
strands of political liberalism hold that state sovereignty is dependent not simply on living by the rules of international society but also
on having domestic legitimacy, which, in turn, is dependent on having
popular sovereignty and the consent of the people. If the state is seen
as at war with its population and not taking adequate responsibility
for its care, then it is not deserving of sovereignty.[32] Liberal states make
the grade; illiberal states, however, often do not. And once they are
deemed unworthy of sovereignty, then they can lose the rights associated with sovereignty, including the right to be a gatekeeper between
international and domestic society. This conclusion connects the old-
style liberalism of John Stuart Mill to the new-style liberalism of John
Rawls. For Mill, the principle of non-interference does not extend to
barbarian peoples. For Rawls, the law of peoples includes "the duty of
non-intervention" but only for "well-ordered states" that possess some
unidentified measure of legitimacy and representativeness. Principles of
non-interference, however, do not apply to "outlaw states," situations
of grave violations of human rights, and less well-ordered states.[33]

[32] Arthur Isak Applbaum, "Forcing a People to Be Free," *Philosophy & Public Affairs* 35, 4 (2007).
[33] John Rawls, *The Law of Peoples: With the Idea of Public Reason Revisited* (Cambridge, MA: Harvard University Press, 1999). Also see Applbaum, "Forcing a People to be Free"; Richard Shapcott, "From the Good International Citizen to the Cosmopolitan Political Community," *International Politics* 50, 1 (2013): 138–57.

If the state is no longer seen as being able to represent the interests of its people, then who is? The vacuum created by the disappearance of sovereignty is potentially filled by outsiders, such as non-governmental organizations and the "international community."[34] During the colonial period, well-meaning missionaries and liberal humanitarians frequently operated with the belief that they were an upgrade over the backward despots who exploited their own people. "Such power-backed paternalism, while admittedly despotic, was at the same time progressive and thus was superior to the indigenous forms of self-rule found in less developing societies, which, while no less despotic, were evidently less progressive."[35] Consequently, a standard refrain from European states was that colonial states had to earn their sovereignty by demonstrating their civilized nature.[36] Although the presumption that Third World states were guilty until proven innocent has now inverted to the assumption that they are innocent until proven guilty, the same moral reasoning remains in contemporary humanitarian governance. NGOs routinely present themselves as better representatives of local populations than their government officials. They do not claim that they are the ideal representative, but rather the second-best alternative given the situation. Simply put, if the state was operating as it should, then they would not be necessary.[37] These international rescuers are not only supposed to be the functional equivalent of the states – that is perform governance functions until the state can do its job – but are also supposed to help build up the state.[38]

[34] This is why many scholars of international relations oppose any weakening of sovereignty. See Robert H. Jackson, *The Global Covenant: Human Conduct in a World of States* (New York: Oxford University Press, 2000), 412; William Bain, *Between Anarchy and Society: Trusteeship and the Obligations of Power* (Oxford: Oxford University Press, 2003), 26, 173; William Bain, "The Political Theory of Trusteeship and the Twilight of International Equality," *International Relations* 17, 1 (2003): 59–77; and William Bain, "In Praise of Folly: International Administration and the Corruption of Humanity," *International Affairs* 82, 3 (2006): 525–38. However, see Lene Mosegaard Søbjerg, "Trusteeship and the Concept of Freedom," *Review of International Studies* 33, no. 3 (2007): 475–88.

[35] McCarthy, *Race, Empire, and the Idea of Human Development*, 171.

[36] Antony Anghie, *Imperialism, Sovereignty, and the Making of International Law* (New York: Cambridge University Press, 2007).

[37] Jennifer Rubenstein, *Between Samaritans and States* (New York: Oxford University Press, 2014).

[38] See, for instance, Stefano Recchia, "Just and Unjust War Reconstruction: Just How Much Interference Can be Justified?" *Ethics & International Affairs*

In addition to the internationalization and institutionalization of liberalism, rationalization has also left its mark on practices of global paternalism. Rationalization largely originates from the belief that the world can, in principle, be reduced to calculations, means–ends reasoning, and cost–benefit analysis. From this simple move has come a revolution in world affairs. Specifically, rationalization led to: the development of methodologies for calculating results, abstract rules to guide standardized responses, and procedures to improve efficiency and identify the best means to achieve specified ends; the creation of bureaucracies that contained specialized knowledge, spheres of competence, and rules to standardize responses and to drive means–ends calculations; and the emergence of professions that had specific knowledge, fixed doctrine, and vocational qualifications that derive from specialized training. These enduring qualities of rationalization, and the rational-legal authority that comes with them, are embedded around the world and in all kinds of organizations, including nongovernmental organizations, states, and international organizations.[39]

Rationalization has shaped global practices of paternalism in several ways. Paternalism operates according to an ethic of consequentialism, because the presumption is that the act of paternalism betters the situation of the paternalized relative to the target left to his own judgment. And, the ethic of consequentialism, in its modern-day formulation, is linked to utilitarianism and the possibility of comparing results in terms of their comparative advantages. John Stuart Mill argued for, and against, paternalism based on utilitarian calculations. Institutions have become the preferred means of interference, and part of the reason why institutions are given such a role is because they are presumed to operate according to rationality principles. Rationalization accounts for the general shift from faith-based to evidence-based paternalism, and experts, perhaps the quintessential effect of rationalization, are given the authority to intervene. The move from internal to external accountability also owes a debt to rationalization. One rationale for

---

23, 2 (2009): 105–87; Kristoff Lidén, "Can Self-Determination be Promoted Through Political Interference? The Principle of Representative Governance," unpublished manuscript (December 2011).

[39] Gili Drori, John Meyer, and Hokyo Hwang, eds., *Globalization and Organization: World Society and Organizational Change* (New York: Oxford University Press, 2006); John Boli and George Thomas, eds., *Constructing World Culture: International Nongovernmental Organizations Since 1875*

accountability is that unless those in power are held to account, they will not learn or have any incentives for improving their operations. Consequently, mechanisms of external accountability are absolutely critical for sharpening the efficiency of the chosen interventions.[40]

One final, but very important, point on the empirics of global paternalism: paternalism seems quite alive and well, and perhaps just as prevalent as ever. The speculation is that paternalism has trended from strong to weak because of global liberalism and rationalization – not that paternalism has receded. Indeed, the chapters speak not simply to the continued presence of paternalism, but also to its possible growth, at least in terms of frequency. There has been a splintering of authority. Whereas once authority was largely contained in the sovereign state, the expansion of the kinds of public and private authority distribute voice and agency to more actors than ever before. The number of international governmental and non-governmental organizations whose purpose is to protect and promote human life keeps growing. And where care goes, the possibility of control almost always follows. These institutions of global care, moreover, are both a cause and an effect of new moral imaginations and ethics of responsibility that permit and demand interference in the lives of others. And in this "age of humanity," we are obligated to help not just some people in need but all people in need. Principles of humanity and impartiality suggest that our responsibilities are boundless and determined by need, a claim most closely identified with Peter Singer.[41] However, as Merry and Ramachadran warn, the more people there are to protect, the more intervention there is to undertake.

Our responsibilities are not just moral but also causal, and our causal responsibilities seem to have grown in lockstep with our moral imagination and globalization. In this expanded ethic of responsibility, we are obligated to help those who have been hurt by our intended and unintended actions. In his contribution to this volume, David Chandler argues that this kind of ethic of responsibility has become more prominent, evident by the mobilization of care in the West on the basis that

(Stanford: Stanford University Press, 2009); and Barnett and Finnemore, *Rules for the World.*

[40] Mark Sheehan, "Reining in Patient and Individual Choice," *Journal of Medical Ethics* 40, 5 (2014): 291–2.

[41] Peter Singer, *The Life You Save: How to Do Your Part to End World Poverty* (New York: Random House, 2010).

their actions frequently have unintended and negative effects on those on the other side of the world. The ethics of such a move are encapsulated by Iris Marion Young's "social connection model."[42] Many of the consumer-based movements operate on this logic – our ability to buy consumer products at a low cost is dependent on the oppressive labor conditions in sweatshops in places like Vietnam. Because we are beneficiaries of someone else's hardship, we have a responsibility to alleviate their suffering and to promote their well-being. Even though an important addendum to this ethic of causal responsibility is that we are most responsible for those we have most impacted, this age of globalization and complexity has widened our responsibilities to the point that they become endless, perhaps to the point of oversaturation.

The Ethics of Paternalism

Paternalism is not just a concept of analysis; it also is a concept of evaluation. It can take different forms and it can give more or less offense – but no matter the form, it is still offensive. And yet, despite its many offenses, none of the contributors goes so far as to propose the banishment of paternalism (except the arrogance and high-minded attitudes it often entails). Instead most of the chapters make either explicit or implicit references to paternalism's occasional necessity and acceptability. Swaine accepts that when she was in the field, she probably engaged in acts of paternalism, some quite justifiable. Autesserre, who is quite hard on peacebuilders for their paternalism, nevertheless wants to retain a space for the use of power over the populations of concern. It would be best if assistance came in the form of a helping hand, but there are times when a push is needed. It would be preferable if assistance came in response to requested support or in solidarity, but there are times when those who help must be willing to tell people what they need. Our moral intuitions tell us that paternalism is wrong, but not always.

[42] Iris Marion Young, "Responsibility and Global Justice: A Social Connection Model," *Social Philosophy and Policy* 23, 1 (2006): 102–30. Also see Robert Goodin, *Protecting the Vulnerable* (Chicago: University of Chicago Press, 1986); Catriona Mackenzie, Wendy Rogers, and Susan Dodds, eds., *Vulnerability: New Essays in Ethics and Feminist Philosophy* (New York: Oxford University Press, 2013).

If our moral intuitions tell us that paternalism is generally wrong, but that power in the service of care might sometimes be defensible, the question becomes: When? As tempting as it might be try to write a manual for "how to be an ethical paternalist" or a "best practices" for global paternalists, this is neither the time nor place, and I am certainly not the person, to do so. In fact, a large part of the literature on paternalism, especially in the area of applied and medical ethics, has this ambition. Rather than summarize their findings, I want to use the chapters, and to harness our emotions, to try to track when paternalism has crossed the line from acceptable to unacceptable. When is it no longer acceptable to substitute one person's judgment for another? The challenge, it seems, is not just staying on the right side of the line but also staying away from a slippery slope. We applaud an ethic of care. We are prepared to accept that an ethic of care might require a dose of interference. We worry, though, that the patient might suffer the effects of an overdose. To keep the conversation focused and tightly bound to the contributions, I will focus on paternalism in humanitarian governance.

To begin, and as I mentioned earlier, the ethics of paternalism rest on an ethic of consequentialism.[43] Simply put, the general defense of paternalism is that the target will be better off than if he was allowed to make his own decisions. In other words, we are comparing two different outcomes: one in which we interfere and one in which we do not. The case for paternalism, then, rests on the prediction that the benefits will outweigh the costs. What are the benefits? They can be material, cognitive, or emotional. What are the costs? They also can be material, cognitive, and emotional. In this battle between the two different camps on the relative costs and benefits of paternalism, an often unstated evaluative measure is the sanctity of autonomy. For those who oppose paternalism, autonomy is not just any good, but rather a superior good. Consequently, many who oppose paternalism do so on the grounds that while it might generate short-term material benefits, the autonomy costs outweigh the material benefits. For those who are prepared to raise a defense of paternalism, the often unstated claim is that autonomy is overrated. How much, precisely, is autonomy worth? Can we measure a unit of dignity? How much is a unit of dignity

---

[43] Danny Scoccia, "In Defense of Hard Paternalism," *Law and Philosophy* 27, 4 (2008): 351–81.

worth in terms of future possibilities? The paternalist, of course, is the one who is making these calculations.

But not everyone who might benefit from paternalism is a candidate. Instead, the actor must demonstrate some sort of incapacity that interferes with her ability to know or act in her own interests. It is at this moment that critics of international paternalism become particularly agitated. What, precisely, counts as evidence that an actor is limited? Most of the conversations in humanitarian governance turn not on the individual but rather on the society as the unit of analysis. There is something about the societal context and immediate circumstances in which an individual finds herself that makes it impossible for her to know or act on her interests. But how do we know whether or not an individual or society knows its own interests?

The chapters suggest three moves that are related to the need to judge the possibility of intervention based on some broad measure of human and moral progress. The first is the explicit reference to a moral benchmark, and this moral benchmark tells us which kinds of populations need to be protected and what they need for the immediate and future welfare. And, as Didier Fassin suggests, the decision of who needs protecting is related to our own sense of identity. The second is the presence of an "absence." As David Spurr argued in relationship to colonialism, the West has come to know the rest not by what it possesses, but rather by what it lacks.[44] What were these societies missing? God, education, technology, democracy, political institutions that promote and defend human freedom, and so on. A similar logic exists today in various kinds of interventions for the promotion of human welfare, including the capabilities approach. The third metric is freedom, which often is assessed in terms of whether or not it is possible for individuals to give meaningful consent. "Unfree" societies are not just those in which individuals are not allowed to speak their minds, but also those in which individuals might be so oppressed that they do not even realize their preferences are helping to reproduce their own repression. As Lila Abu-Laghud astutely observed, representations of another's lack of freedom, which is often blamed on culture, often provide the spark for rescue

[44] David Spurr, *The Rhetoric of Empire: Colonial Discourse in Journalism, Travel Writing, and Imperial Administration* (Durham, NC: Duke University Press, 1983).

missions – even if those who are to be rescued do not know that they
are in need of saving.[45]

The use of moral benchmarks and implicit measures of "freedom"
and "consent" contain many dangers, some well known, including
moral imperialism, and others less so. One of the lesser known dangers
is that because it locates the limitations within culture and society, it
distracts from the possibility that the outsider, who feels a responsibility to help, might in fact be partially to blame for the impoverished
condition. This is a version of "blaming the victim." Paternalism tends
to locate the reasons for incapacity and the lack of judgment in the
characteristics and immediate circumstances of the person of interest.
For paternalists beyond borders, the reasons why individuals are in
need is because they have not yet developed the required rationality and/or because of existing and proximate cultural, political, and
economic constraints. But what of the possibility that individuals and
societies are in need because of causes that are introduced from afar?
What of the possibility that those who are the givers have created
a demand for their "generosity" because their prior actions are the
cause of the circumstances of the vulnerable? In this volume, Chandler
argues that there is an emerging ethic of responsibility that increasingly incorporates this possibility, and he cites the work of Thomas
Pogge as an example. Chandler points to an interesting development,
but is it more than a cry in the dark? Has it displaced other ethics of
responsibility that place the onus on the actor of interest? Swaine notes
how growing interest in participation by the recipients in the decisions
of the aid agencies owes not simply to democratic instincts but also to
the perception that the lack of participation might have been partially
responsible for previous failures. Swaine makes an excellent point, but
she also acknowledges the tremendous hypocrisy between what outsiders say and what they actually do – in short, talk of participation
and accountability is quite cheap. In general, the moral benchmarks
used to judge who needs help can reproduce the caregivers' continued
sense of superiority.

It is because of the danger that moral imperialism will become indis-
tinguishable from paternalism that defenders of humanitarian governance offer the following cautionary guidance. First, interveners should

---

[45] Lila Abu-Lughod, *Do Muslim Women Need Saving?* (Cambridge, MA: Harvard
University Press, 2013), 20.

lean toward basic threats to survival and away from broader eman-cipatory campaigns. In the lexicon of humanitarianism, aid agencies should address the symptoms of suffering and avoid any attempt to solve the causes.[46] I once had a conversation with a veteran of Doctors Without Borders about his experiences with paternalism. He con-fessed that one reason why he preferred being a physician, and being a physician with a medical relief agency, is because it focused the mind on immediate suffering and mitigated against the paternalism that often accompanies the move to address root causes. Second, interfer-ence should be central to well-being. But often the most trivial areas of life can be tied to human flourishing, opening the door to intru-sive and potentially wide-ranging interventions. Third, humanitarian governance should stick, as much as possible, to means rather than ends. As Dennis Thompson argues, "To justify paternalism, we must identify some impairment that can be described independently of the end or good an individual chooses ... We should look for impairments that arise from social structures or affect large numbers of people in similar ways."[47] In a similar spirit, Sigal Ben-Porath argues that institu-tions will foster meaningful choice if they help individuals develop an awareness of their options and the capacity to exercise them, enable rights, and foster what T.H. Marshall called social rights.[48]

The chapters also suggest the drift toward paternalism-lite is not only a matter of historical record but also should be viewed as a welcome development. By and large, paternalism done well is a paternalism that operates with a light footprint and a gentle hand, gets in and gets out, and is circumscribed. In other words, the mistake made by many pater-nalists is not that they have been paternalistic but rather that they have used a strong push when a gentle nudge would have been enough. That said, in her recent, highly spirited defense of paternalism, Conley raises the point that if we truly believe someone is making the wrong deci-sion, then we should be prepared to use as much force as is needed.[49] In

---

[46] Scoccia, "In Defense of Hard Paternalism."

[47] See Dennis F. Thompson, *Political Ethics and Public Office* (Cambridge, MA: Harvard University Press, 1990), 156.

[48] Sigal Ben-Porath, *Tough Choices: Structured Paternalism and the Landscape of Choice* (Princeton: Princeton University Press, 2010), 19.

[49] Sarah Conly, *Against Autonomy: Justifying Coercive Paternalism* (New York: Cambridge University Press, 2013).

general, what makes paternalism more or less defensible is not only the situation but also the chosen technologies of domination.

Then there is the question of who is the right actor to substitute his judgment for another's. In short, who is the right authority? As a general rule, our objections to paternalism seem to increase as we migrate from the interpersonal to the global, in part because we are more suspicious of authorities the more distant they are from the object of concerns.[50] We expect parents to have the last word regarding what their children can and cannot do, and we defend their authority to do so on the grounds that, because of their immediate bond, they will know what is in their children's best interests, will allow their decisions to be guided by what is in the best interests of the child, and have the immediate responsibility to protect their children from potential harm and to guide them from childhood to adulthood. Our willingness to grant the state the same authority in domestic affairs is more circumscribed, but there are conditions under which society accepts that the state restricts our autonomy because it is in our best interests and the best interests of society. Yet once paternalism crosses a border, our objections multiply and our outrage amplifies.

The chapters point to the sense of community.[51] As paternalism scales up from the intimate and continuous interaction to the itinerant and the imaginary, the sense of community declines. In order to highlight the degrees of difference, many international relations scholars have turned to Ferdinand Tönnies's classic distinction between *gemeinschaft* and *gesellschaft*.[52] *Gemeinschaft* is largely translated as a sense of genuine community, in which members feel a thick sense of belonging to each other, to the point that their identity derives from

---

[50] This is a subtle but significant undercurrent in the essays in a recent special issue on the "Good State" in *International Politics* 50, 1 (2013).

[51] This is neither the time nor place to devolve into a discussion regarding the concept of political community. For three contrasting views see Will Kymlicka, *Liberalism, Community, and Culture* (New York: Oxford University Press, 1991); Michael J. Sandel, *Public Philosophy: Essays on Morality In Politics* (Cambridge, MA: Harvard University Press, 2005); and Chandran Kukathas, *The Liberal Archipelago: A Theory of Diversity and Freedom* (Oxford: Oxford University Press, 2003). My reading of this literature, moreover, suggests that much of the battle is fought over the domestic terrain and the dominant view is that any deep sense of community does not exist in cross-boundary relations.

[52] Ferdinand Tönnies, *Community and Society* (Mineola: Dover Publications, 2011).

the collective, and they feel a deep sense of obligation for each other's welfare and fate. *Gesellschaft*, on the other hand, is understood as society, in which individuals are bound together not by identity but rather by interests, and group association is instrumental rather than intrinsic to the self. International relations scholars have been dubious of the claim that a genuine international community exists. For many, the "international community" must always be surrounded by scare quotes, not only because it is a fantasy, but also because its discourse permits all kinds of unwelcome and illegitimate interventions. Consequently, international relations scholars use the language of community advisedly and cautiously and almost always restrict it to those transnational spaces that are constituted by ongoing and layered networks of interactions.[53]

The variation in a sense of community is generally related to the perceived legitimacy of the community's institutions. Specifically, the more the sense of community is imprinted on, and guides, the institutions of governance, the more they are imbued with legitimacy. Briefly, legitimacy has two dimensions.[54] There is procedural legitimacy, in which decisions made by the state are seen as having followed the correct path. There is also substantive legitimacy, in which the state's decisions are seen as being consistent with society's values. To the extent that the state gets high marks for both procedural and substantive legitimacy, the public is more likely to see the state's decisions as reflecting their interests and more likely to comply with its decisions; to the extent that the state gets low marks, the public is more likely to feel removed from, threatened by, and resistant to the state's decisions. There is a clear analytical link between paternalism and procedural and substantive legitimacy. Paternalism is most easily justified and defended when there is a strong sense of community that shapes the decision-making process and outcomes. For instance, there are two typical responses to the claim that motorcycle helmet laws are paternalistic: they are paternalistic, and justifiable, because those who do not wear helmets

[53] For its adoption in international relations, see Emanuel Adler and Michael N. Barnett, *Security Communities* (New York: Cambridge University Press, 1998); Barry Buzan, *From International to World Society? English School Theory and the Social Structure of Globalisation* (New York: Cambridge University Press, 2004).

[54] Mark C. Suchman, "Managing Legitimacy: Strategic and Institutional Approaches," *The Academy of Management Review* 20, 3 (1995).

increase the welfare costs to society; they are not paternalistic because the laws were passed through a democratic process.

The conditions that make paternalism potentially defensible in domestic governance are absent in international governance, a possibility raised by Hobson. There is a relatively thin sense of community. There is the absence of genuinely representative institutions. The organization of the international system around the principle of sovereignty severely restricts the development of a sense of international community, the creation of genuinely representative institutions, and the manufacturing of legitimacy. Global institutions are thus engaged in a constant struggle to convince others of their legitimacy. The state is the unit of authority, unit of protection, and unit of identity. There is no legal authority superior to the state in international affairs, which, of course, underwrites the principle of non-interference. One of the state's chief roles is to provide security for its citizens from both internal and external threats. And the state is not just a legal and functional entity; it also is supposed to be reflective of the "nation" that is contained within its territorial borders, which provides an additional brace for the principle of non-interference. Accompanying the principle of non-interference is the notion of consent; comparable to the citizen in modern liberal polities, the state in international society has the exclusive right to give and deny consent to interventions by outsiders. It is because of the absence of representative institutions at the global level that accountability remains so urgent.

Global practices of care are an expanding element of modern international society. They are a fact of life. So, too, is paternalism. While practices of care need not be accompanied by power and domination, they often are. The challenge is not only to understand how paternalism operates in international affairs, but also to better understand the ethical challenge it represents. Paternalism might be unjustifiable on many occasions, but it might be equally unjustifiable to know that something could be done and to decide to do nothing. The world of care cannot live with paternalism, and it cannot live without it.

Index

Abu-Lughod, Lila 91–2
agency and guilt 139–40
aid, *see* humanitarian aid
Ali, Ayaan Hirsi 91
altruistic aims of imperialism 108–9
 analytical dimensions of paternalism
  16, 34–5
Anderson, Mary 178–9
Arendt, Hannah 26–7, 139–40
Arneson, Richard 59
'arrogant intervention' 72
asylum
 as case study 78–9
 contemporary paradigms of 79–80
 discrediting of asylum seekers 82
 and female genital mutilation 84–6,
  88, 90–1
 gender and 88–95
 historical origins of 79
 institutionalization of 89–90
 LGBT persons 86–8
 liberal paternalism 88–95
 recognition of claims for 80–2, 83–4
 social groups, recognition of 83–8
Atholl, Duchess of 268
Autesserre, Séverine 37–8, 72, 161
authority
 concept of 19–20
 consent and 19–20
 delegated authority 20–1,
  29–30, 32–3
 expert authority, *see* expert authority
 'in authority' or 'of authority' 20
 legal authority 20–1
 moral authority 20–1
 paternalism and 95
 rational authority 20–1
autonomy
 assumption of 137, 328–9
 conceding of 214

democracy and 331–2
denial of 194, 196, 259
deserving of 321, 328–9
importance of 14
interference with 12–13, 21, 67,
  69–70, 108, 110, 124–5, 127,
  132–3, 342
liberalism and 7, 231
liberty and 69–70
paternalism and 8–9
power and 260–1
promotion of 57–8, 77, 320
protection of 256, 260
respect for 21, 55, 222
and 'soft' paternalism 276
value of 338–9

Barnett, Michael 48, 105, 106, 107,
  109–10, 122
'benevolent sexism' 217–18
Bernstein, Elizabeth 94
Bindel, Julie 273
Boddy, Janice 90, 285–6
Brooks, David 49, 53
Butler, Judith 284

care
 control and 4–6, 9, 27
 duty of 132
 paternalism and 13–14
 power and 3–4, 5–6
 superiority, sense of 24
Chandler, David 37, 106, 110, 132
Cheng, Sealing 244, 248
civilization
 'civilizing' mission of
  imperialism 111–16
 Eurocentric standard of
  112–14, 116–18
 sovereignty and 112–14